Representing Women in Renaissance England

REPRESENTING

Women

in Renaissance England

EDITED BY CLAUDE J. SUMMERS
AND TED-LARRY PEBWORTH

University of Missouri Press • COLUMBIA AND LONDON

Copyright © 1997
The Curators of the University of Missouri
University of Missouri Press, Columbia, Missouri 65201
Printed and bound in the United States of America
All rights reserved
5   4   3   2   1   01   00   99   98   97

Library of Congress Cataloging-in-Publication Data

Representing women in Renaissance England / edited by Claude J.
    Summers and Ted-Larry Pebworth.
        p.   cm.
    The original, abbreviated versions of these essays were presented
at the eleventh biennial Renaissance conference at the University of
Michigan–Dearborn, held October 7–8, 1994.
    Includes index.
    ISBN 0-8262-1104-6 (alk. paper)
    1. English literature—Early modern, 1500–1700—History and
criticism.   2. Women and literature—England—History—16th century.
3. Women and literature—England—History—17th century.   4. Women
in literature.   5. Renaissance—England.   I. Summers, Claude J.
II. Pebworth, Ted-Larry.
    PR418.W65R48   1997
    820.9'352042'09031—dc21   97-10984
                                                                      CIP

∞™ This paper meets the requirements of the
American National Standard for Permanence of Paper
for Printed Library Materials, Z39.48, 1984.

Designer: Mindy Shouse
Typesetter: BOOKCOMP
Printer and binder: Thomson-Shore, Inc.
Typefaces: Minion, Shelley Volante

For EMILY *and* DONALD SPINELLI

Contents

ACKNOWLEDGMENTS

This book and the scholarly meeting from which it originated have profited from the great effort, wide learning, and scholarly generosity of the conference steering committee: Diana Treviño Benet, Achsah Guibbory, Robert B. Hinman, Judith Scherer Herz, John R. Roberts, and Michael C. Schoenfeldt helped referee the submissions to the conference and offered valuable suggestions for revision. Their contributions have been extensive, and we join the authors of the essays in expressing gratitude for their insights and devotion. It is also our pleasant duty to acknowledge the support of the Horace H. Rackham Graduate School of the University of Michigan, John D'Arms, dean; and of the following administrators at the University of Michigan–Dearborn: Emily L. Spinelli, chair, Department of Humanities; John W. Presley, dean, College of Arts, Sciences, and Letters; and Robert L. Simpson, provost and vice chancellor for Academic Affairs.

Representing Women in Renaissance England

Claude J. Summers and Ted-Larry Pebworth

INTRODUCTION

Representing Women in Renaissance England is conceived as a contribution both to literary studies of the English Renaissance and to early modern gender studies. It focuses on women as writers and as subjects and objects of Renaissance nondramatic literature. Central to our enterprise are the feminist insights that *gender* is a relational term encompassing both men and women and that reading and writing are processes in which masculinity and femininity may be meaningfully discerned. In exploring the representation of women in the literature of Renaissance England, these essays share the belief that hierarchically ordered male-female relations influence nearly all aspects of human social relations, including those that are apparently not gendered at all. Conscious as they are of the fact that masculinity and femininity are unstable categories, the contributors to this volume also attempt to resist rigidly essentialized notions of gender, even as they are also aware that the literary representation of women is not merely an arcane academic concern but one that is necessarily entangled in social and political realities. Some of the essays in the volume participate in the exciting process of recovering and evaluating women writers whose works are only now entering the canon of English literature, while others examine gender issues in male-authored canonical texts. The contributors to this volume also offer correctives to oversimplified views of representations of women in Renaissance literature, frequently questioning received ideas not only about the patriarchy but also about women's responses to their varied positions within a society whose hierarchies were configured according to multiple considerations. These essays demonstrate that attitudes toward gender and gender roles in early modern England were complex and multivalent and resistant to reductive generalizations.

The representation of women is a crucial aspect of Renaissance literary culture. In its breadth and scope, this volume illustrates (though by no means exhausts) the centrality of the topic to our current understanding of the period and its literature. Raising fascinating questions of women's self-representation, of the appropriation of women's voices and sexuality by male authors, of literary history and male reader response, of women's roles as readers and audience, as well as a host of political and social issues, the essays included here broach most of the concerns that animate literary study at the end of the twentieth century. Using literary figuration as a gauge of the status of women in early modern England, raising theoretical questions as to the relative significance of gender as an interpretive factor in approaching Renaissance literature, considering the affinity of particular genres for women writers, examining the ways representations of women serve political ends, mapping the gendered power relations in love poetry of the period, querying the level of acceptance of the woman writer by her established male peers: the contributors to this volume explore issues central to a full understanding of the shifting literary culture of Renaissance England.

The original, abbreviated versions of the essays included here were presented at the eleventh biennial Renaissance conference at the University of Michigan–Dearborn on October 7–8, 1994.[1] The final versions printed here have benefited from the stimulating exchanges and responses afforded by the conference, and they intersect, reinforce, and challenge each other in significant and interesting ways. But the essays were written independently and without consultation among the authors. No topics or approaches were suggested or assigned, and none were proscribed. All the essays are historically grounded and critically vital, but they vary widely in their historical perspectives and critical allegiances and in their scope and focus. The only criterion for selection has been that each

---

1. Selected papers from the first ten Dearborn conferences have been published: those from the 1974 conference as *"Trust to Good Verses": Herrick Tercentenary Essays,* ed. Roger B. Rollin and J. Max Patrick (Pittsburgh: University of Pittsburgh Press, 1978); those from the 1976 conference on seventeenth-century prose as a special issue of *Studies in the Literary Imagination* (10.2 [1977]), ed. William A. Sessions and James S. Tillman; those from the 1978 conference as *"Too Rich to Clothe the Sunne": Essays on George Herbert,* ed. Claude J. Summers and Ted-Larry Pebworth (Pittsburgh: University of Pittsburgh Press, 1980); those from the 1980 conference as *Classic and Cavalier: Essays on Jonson and the Sons of Ben,* ed. Claude J. Summers and Ted-Larry Pebworth (Pittsburgh: University of Pittsburgh Press, 1982); those from the 1982 conference as *The Eagle and the Dove: Reassessing John Donne,* ed. Claude J. Summers and Ted-Larry Pebworth (Columbia: University of Missouri Press, 1986); those from the 1984 conference as *"Bright Shootes of Everlastingnesse": The Seventeenth-Century Religious Lyric,* ed. Claude J. Summers and Ted-Larry Pebworth (Columbia: University of Missouri Press, 1987); those from the 1986 conference as *"The Muses Common-Weale": Poetry and Politics in the Seventeenth Century,* ed. Claude J. Summers and Ted-Larry Pebworth (Columbia: University of Missouri Press, 1988); those from the 1988 conference as *On the Celebrated and Neglected Poems of Andrew Marvell,* ed. Claude J. Summers and Ted-Larry Pebworth (Columbia: University of Missouri Press, 1992); those from the 1990 conference as *Renaissance Discourses of Desire,* ed. Claude J. Summers and Ted-Larry Pebworth (Columbia: University of Missouri Press, 1993); and those from the 1992 conference as *The Wit of Seventeenth-Century Poetry,* ed. Claude J. Summers and Ted-Larry Pebworth (Columbia: University of Missouri Press, 1995).

essay contribute significantly to the understanding and informed appreciation of the representation of women in English literature of the Renaissance.

Helen Wilcox's study of devotional writing by Renaissance women focuses on works that engage in intimate spiritual dialogue with God. Examining texts by such writers as Mary Sidney, An Collins, Elizabeth Major, Mary Carey, Elizabeth Delaval, Anne Bradstreet, and Jane Cheyne, Wilcox demonstrates that devotional dialogue permitted an outspoken representation of the female self at a time when women were generally enjoined to silence in the religious sphere. Aware of the strengths that could be created out of weakness, these authors frequently used gender stereotypes, as well as the gendered language of devotion, to their own advantage in constructing tropes of self-representation. Some also called particular attention to the specific sufferings of the female body and to such feminine roles as daughter, mother, wife, and lover. Wilcox discovers in women's devotional experience a remarkably creative space for female self-representation. "Out of the defiance, modesty, humor, and sorrow of these texts," she concludes, "we hear, with all its paradoxical implications, the expressive speech of the female 'soule in silence.' "

Janel Mueller's study of the complications of intertextuality is at once a fascinating investigation into the source of Katherine Parr's crucial metaphor of the book of the crucifix and a sustained meditation on the utility of gender as an interpretive anchor for literary and historical understanding of women in English Protestantism. The discovery that Parr's odd metaphor in *The Lamentation of a Sinner* has its source not in the writer's gendered life experience as a learned lady, as a king's consort, or as a fervent Protestant convert, but in a sermon by John Fisher, leads Mueller to examine the stunning differences between the way the metaphor is used by the two authors. To account for these differences she considers but rejects gender as a significant factor, ponders the possibility that the generational divide between Parr and Fisher is a crucial reason, but resolves finally that "a more primary determinant of the difference between Fisher's and Parr's metaphors is the . . . difference between a Catholic and a Protestant." Mueller concludes that the particular gender trouble that we face in analyzing and interpreting religious texts is likely to be alleviated only by making a case for religion as having the status of a primary anchor of human life in social forms, along with race or ethnicity, class, and gender.

Pamela Joseph Benson explores the ways in which Sir John Harington "Englished" the discourse about women in his translation of Ariosto's *Orlando Furioso*. While Harington's *Furioso* has frequently been considered antifeminist, Benson argues that in fact it is profeminist, though in a peculiarly English way. Harington undermines Ariosto's philosophical defense of women by reorienting the *Furioso* toward issues that had been prominent in native English defenses of womankind since the mid-sixteenth century. He replaces the Italian humanist ideal of women as equals of men in ethical capacity with the domestic ideal of women as good wives. Harington praises Elizabeth I, but in a typically English way of representing her as specially favored of God rather than as illustrative of the more general proposition that women are capable of political leadership. At times, Harington encourages women to compete on the international scene as writers and governors, but more commonly he directs them away from the quest for fame and independence, encouraging them to be ambitious only to be good wives.

Gareth Roberts explores the traffic in the language of magic and witchcraft in the erotic negotiations between male poets and their actual or potential mistresses in Renaissance love poetry. When the male love poet presents himself as a magician, women are either spirits to be controlled or erotic objects to be coerced into love. In other poems, women are allowed supernatural power and active roles, but only at the price of demonization as witch or devil. In Renaissance love poetry, Roberts observes, "the discourses of magic and demonology subjugate women but empower men." Against this background of gendered power relations in the use of magic, the third book of Spenser's *Faerie Queene* can be seen as a surprising critique of contemporaneous love poetry. In book 3, Roberts argues, Spenser deliberately resists the usual representations of women as devils or witches, of men coercing women through magic, and the fiction of the power of magic to compel desire. In so doing, he rejects the role of love poet as magician and its consequent subjugation of women.

In her essay "Women in the Lyric Dialogue of Courtship," Ilona Bell turns particular attention to the role of the private female audience in Renaissance love poetry and explores connections between a poetics of courtship and an erotics of secrecy. Bell juxtaposes Isabella Whitney's *Admonition to al yong Gentilwomen,* a work that urges young women to protect themselves from the deception and betrayal posed by clandestine courtship and enigmatic rhetoric, and Donne's "The Legacie," a poem that has frequently been seen as an acerbic attack on female inconstancy addressed to a male coterie. Whitney's poem provides an illuminating context in which it becomes possible to see Donne's poem as epitomizing the enigma of lyric courtship, capturing "the hermeneutical dilemma that both the male poet/lover and the female reader/listener face." Bell's essay not only complicates conventional readings of "The Legacie" but also insists on the crucial role of women as the primary and prototypical audience for Renaissance love poetry.

Donne is also the subject of Cecilia Infante's essay, which focuses on his heroical epistle "Sapho to Philaenis." Placing the poem within a literary tradition revitalized by the English reception of Ovid's *Heroides* and within the subgenre of the female complaint, Infante interprets Donne's representation of Sappho as not only his imaginative projection of the desiring lesbian subject but also his tropic figure of poetic failure. She reads the poem as less an erotic or lesbian idyll than a linguistic fantasy configured in erotic terms. She concludes that Donne may have assumed the lesbian persona of Sappho as a means of revitalizing stale or ineffective idioms or as a figure for literary rivalry and exchange, but that he also promotes a theory of the woman as unrepresentable or presymbolic. Infante's essay raises significant questions about male representation and appropriation of women's voices and sexuality.

In an essay sensitive to the way discursive formations serve political ends, Lawrence Normand explores some of the complex ways in which women were represented as witches in the Renaissance. The representations of women in three related but divergent texts—the anonymous *Newes from Scotland,* James VI of Scotland's *Daemonologie,* and Jonson's *Masque of Queens*—all helped fashion sustaining ideologies for the ruling class. Normand argues that these works depict gradually decreasing feminine power as they move from the historical to the literary. In the masque, however, Jonson fashions an image of legitimate female power that challenges as much as supports patriarchy. Normand concludes that the uncanny power of the queens in the masque derives in part from Jonson's return to a popular representation of female power as magic.

In "Aemilia Lanyer and the Pathos of Literary History," Judith Scherer Herz meditates on the paradoxical fact that even after all the scholarly and critical attention recently devoted to Lanyer, she remains outside literary history. "She has a prehistory; that is, she belongs to someone else's literary history, Chaucer's and Mary Sidney's, for example, but properly speaking she has no history of her own." Concentrating on "The Description of Cooke-ham," Herz explores authorial presence and displacement in the *Salve Deus* itself, as well as such issues as the poet's relationship to the Clifford family and her multiple dedications. She concludes that the *Salve Deus* is "discontinuous both with other texts and with Lanyer herself, and discontinuous also with the containing narratives of literary history whether they are stories of scandal or of sainthood . . . or, more mildly, of the emergent professional writer."

Barbara K. Lewalski also calls attention to the reception of women's texts in the Renaissance by examining the extensive annotations by a hostile male contemporary in a copy of Rachel Speght's daring protofeminist tract, *A Mouzell for Melastomus.* The annotations provide a fascinating window on the way in which many controversialists engaged with offending texts and, in particular, on the way in which a misogynistic male reader responded to Speght's arguments by using silencing techniques. While the unknown annotator's attacks on women are entirely unoriginal, they are deployed in ways that remove the exchange from the playfulness and rhetorical gamesmanship of the *querelle des femmes* literature. Moreover, as Lewalski observes, "The endurance of his attitudes and strategies over several centuries suggests that they were not untypical."

In a study of Mary Wroth's *Love's Victory,* the late Josephine Roberts confronts the question of why the pastoral mode held a particular appeal for women writers of the Renaissance. Offering a landscape in which the political and social relationships of women might be questioned, challenged, and refashioned, the pastoral mode, with its coded language and multiple disguisings, offered a protective haven for women writers in which they could safely convey through hints and plausible denials their own most intimate relationships. In *Love's Victory,* Wroth not only hints at parallels with her own transgressive romantic alliances but also represents a broad spectrum of women, expanding the social roles usually assigned to female characters, and places them in situations in which they use their power reasonably and compassionately. She subtly questions patriarchal marriage and creates the effect of a dense network of interlocking tales centered on the ways in which women can exercise the power of choice despite the constraints of society.

Robert Evans presents the "Memorandum" of Martha Moulsworth as both a complex work of art and a complex historical document that resists re-ductiveness and oversimplification. He finds that Moulsworth's poem often seems to provide support for conflicting and even contradictory assertions by recent historians and literary theorists about the status of early modern women. The poem complicates generalizations about the oppression of women in the seventeenth century, about feminine anger and bitterness, and about women's self-respect. On these and other issues, Moulsworth's poem equivocates, "not because of ineptness but precisely because of its artistic and ideological com-plexity."

Paul Parrish explores the influence of first the presence, then the absence of a remarkable woman on the life and work of Richard Crashaw. He gives a detailed account of the way in which the Little Gidding community was set up, focusing on the "decisive and transforming roles" occupied by the women of the group, especially that of Mary Collet, the young woman who became the "intellectual and spiritual 'mother'" of the community. Parrish explores the "far-reaching implications and consequences in [Crashaw's] *representation* of a living virgin woman as his 'mother'" and his profound sense of anguish when their relationship was severed; and he concludes, "In a very real and powerful sense, the separation and dislocation from the virgin Mary Collet, the very best of the women Crashaw knew during his life, lead him ultimately to devotion to the Virgin Mary, the 'gratious mother' from whom 'exclusion and compleat excomunicacion' will not be possible."

In "Robert Herrick's Housekeeper: Representing Ordinary Women in Re-naissance Poetry," Roger Rollin considers many of the forty-six poems in

Hesperides that represent twenty-nine historically identifiable women. The fact that twenty-two of these women are from the lower and middle classes makes Herrick's collection unique in the period and, as Rollin asserts, firmly grounds *Hesperides* in the social history of his age. These untitled women include Herrick's maid (Prudence Baldwin), various kinswomen, the elusive Dorothy Keneday, Susanna Southwell, Bridget Lowman, and several others, all of whom would now be unknown had Herrick not written poems to or about them. Unlike his poems to his numerous "supposed" mistresses, these poems to and about real women praise not their beauty and youth so much as their virtues, thereby according them a place as "saints" within Herrick's "Poetick Liturgie." Rollin asserts that "crowning" these humble women with immortality through art "is a cottage industry in Herrick's Hesperidean garden world," and he notes that the representation of these actual women brings the reader close to "the ordinary seventeenth-century world Herrick actually inhabited . . . a world of relatives and friends and everyday life that for Robert Herrick turns out to be not so separate from the world of his art after all."

In "An Collins and the Experience of Defeat," Sidney Gottlieb counters the view of Collins as a passive creature, racked by pain and suffering, by emphasizing the boldness of her poetry. He points out her repeated defenses of her writing, her insistence that knowledge is as important to women as to men, and the involvement of her poems in the theological and political controversies of the age. In illustration of these points, Gottlieb analyzes "A Song composed in time of the Civill War, when the wicked did much insult over the godly," a poem that concludes with an apocalyptic vision in which a holy remnant—among which Collins includes herself—will ultimately prevail, bringing about the overthrow of the ungodly and the ascendence of the Son of Peace. While noting that Collins's exact political and religious affiliations are largely indeterminable, given the paucity of biographical fact and the lack of specificity in her poetry, Gottlieb nevertheless finds in her work the attractive qualities of "resiliency, creative accommodation, and artistic and expressive as well as physical and emotional courage."

In the final essay in the volume, Stella Revard examines the way in which female poets of the mid- and late seventeenth century—including Katherine Philips and an otherwise anonymous "Young Woman," as well as Aphra Behn— were received by their male contemporaries. She finds that when they were praised by men, as in the case of Abraham Cowley's encomiums on Philips, they were invariably commended as women first, with emphasis on their beauty and virtue, and only afterward as poets, with a somewhat condescending notice of their wit. Such praise deified the woman writer and removed her from competition with her male rivals. This strategy had the effect of limiting women as writers, since it confers only apparent victory on them while reserving real power for men. Revard's discussion of Behn centers on the Pindaric written to Thomas Creech, a translator of Lucretius, in which the poet criticizes "a nation and an educational system that denies knowledge to those like her solely on the basis of sex," but does so with such subtle skill and indirection that the male establishment could and did read her poem as praise of one of their own. Like Philips, Behn received plaudits from her male contemporaries not as an equal but as a "wonder" of her "sex."

In their varied approaches and distinct conclusions, these essays contribute significantly to a fuller understanding of the representation of women—by both male and female writers—in the Renaissance. In so doing, they illuminate particular texts and specific writers and call attention to recurrent themes. Perhaps most fundamental, however, they reveal how basic gender issues are to an understanding of the period and its culture. Collectively, they illustrate the manifold ways in which hierarchically ordered male-female relations are at the very heart of Renaissance literature.

Helen Wilcox

"My soule in silence"?

Devotional Representations
of Renaissance Englishwomen

I

The focus of this collection of essays is Renaissance Englishwomen, but the key word of its title is *representing*, a term capable of almost infinite interpretation and nuance. In the context of the discussions in this volume, "to represent" has at least three meanings, with implications for both the present and the past. One of the tasks of present-day historical and literary criticism is to provide a showcase or platform for women from the English Renaissance, where they and their works may now be encountered afresh—a process of "re-presenting" to a modern readership women who have long been invisible and silenced. The term *representation* also leads us to ask a second, more historical question: how were women themselves "represented" in the Renaissance, in the sense of constructed, spoken about, and portrayed by others, from the pages of conduct books to the stages of London's theaters? Third, and perhaps most important, the project of this volume encourages us to examine the means by which women "represented" themselves, particularly through the spoken or written word, during the English Renaissance. These three possible uses of the idea of "representing" are, of course, interrelated; for example, the representation of a female self or voice by a Renaissance woman is necessarily shot through with the ideologies of gender current at the time, while a late twentieth-century account of early modern texts is a "representation" that in itself also reinterprets in contemporary terms. I take this complexity to be a sign of the richness of the representative strategies and critical debates furthered by this volume.

I intend to concentrate on the third of the meanings of "representing" outlined above—that is, women giving expression to their own identity—with particular reference to devotional writing. By this last term I mean texts that enter into an intimate spiritual dialogue with God, rather than those that might be more broadly referred to as religious writing. The devotional works I have chosen include prose such as women's private prayers or meditations, but most of the sources used in this paper are devotional poems, written by Renaissance Englishwomen such as Mary Sidney, An Collins, Elizabeth Major, Mary Carey, Elizabeth Delaval, Anne Bradstreet, Jane Cheyne, and the unknown author of *Eliza's Babes*. My question is how did these women writers represent themselves in spiritual conversation with their Maker? In an era of intense religious activity and faith, the most vital and fundamental self-representation was indeed that of the individual soul to God; an error or misrepresentation in this arena could well have eternal consequences.

Katherine Parr wrote in 1547, "Beholde lorde howe I come to the, a sinner, sycke, and grevously wounded. . . . Cast me not oute of thy sight, although I have deserved to be cast in to hell fier."[1] The spiritual context here allows for—even demands—a rare indulgence by the female speaker. Despite an element of self-loathing, she is shining an intense spotlight on her physical and spiritual being. God is invited to "beholde" specifically in what state the speaker approaches him: "a sinner, sycke, and grevously wounded." She is conscious of where she deserves to go—to the fires of hell—but the purpose of her devotional language is to persuade God to keep his gaze on her: "Cast me not oute of thy sight." Ironically, at the point when a woman might be expected to be most self-effacing, in a dialogue with the ultimate patriarchal figure, her discourse favors self-focus as a means to mercy. This extreme of humility that turns into an obsession with the sinful self is a familiar phenomenon in devotion, but the striking feature here is the capacity of a woman's words to create and present an identity before God as a way to claim redemption for her soul. At a time when a woman's speaking in public, and writing for readers other than her own children, were severe transgressions of the feminine norm, devotional dialogue licensed an often outspoken representation of the female self.[2]

Devotional conversations, however, were no easy matter, particularly for women enjoined to silence above all in the religious context. St. Paul's command that women should "keep silence in the churches" (1 Cor. 15:34) was increasingly invoked during the late sixteenth and early seventeenth centuries in England. As Mary Sidney, countess of Pembroke, wrote in her translation of Psalm 62, establishing the paradoxes of the speaking female soul:

1. Katherine Parr, *The lamentacion of a sinner* (London: E. Whitchurche, 1547), n.p. See *The Paradise of Women: Writings by Englishwomen of the Renaissance*, ed. Betty Travitsky (Westport: Greenwood Press, 1981), 39–41.

2. For further discussion of this issue, see, for example, *Silent but for the Word: Tudor Women as Patrons, Translators, and Writers of Religious Works*, ed. Margaret P. Hannay (Kent: Kent State University Press, 1985), and Suzanne Trill, "Religion and the Construction of Femininity," in *Women and Literature in Britain, 1500–1700*, ed. Helen Wilcox (Cambridge: Cambridge University Press, 1996), 30–55.

> Yet shall my soule in silence still
> On God, my help, attentive stay:
> Yet he my fort, my health, my hill,
> Remove I may not, move I may.[3]

The soul, traditionally female and here expressed in the male-authored psalm but in the chosen language of the female translator, waits upon God in attentive silence, dependent on him for life, strength, and hope. We might describe the soul's condition as a sacred parody of the relationship of human female to human male in the Renaissance, depicted in a vocabulary of silence and attentiveness similar to that of contemporary conduct books for women. However, this silent female soul remains attentive partly because her attentiveness may change matters; she cannot "remove" or live apart from her God, but she may indeed "move," a powerful choice of word implying the influence she may have over him, leading him to feel compassion or to act on her behalf. To "move" was precisely what a Renaissance poet sought to do with words. As Mary Sidney's own brother put it, the aim of a poet is to "delight and teach": "delight to move men to take that goodness in hand, which without delight they would fly as from a stranger, and teach, to make them know that goodness whereunto they are moved."[4] This rhetorical power is assumed by Mary Sidney in relation to God, who as her primary intended listener/reader is to be affected by her words. The capacity to move, as described by Philip Sidney, suggests metaphorically the poetic influence of the silent soul. However, Mary Sidney's "soule" is, of course, expressed here in words that are not silent but eloquent, words that are hers as a poet though they resonate with the lyrical divine authority of the psalm she is translating. These layers of irony—self-representation in self-denial, authorship by means of (and sometimes in spite of) an inheritance of given divine texts, the unusually assertive female poet giving direct expression to the soul, which is itself conventionally (but passively) female—all highlight the fascinating complexity of women's devotional representations in this period.

The authors themselves were aware of the strengths that could be created out of weakness, a strategy based both on gender stereotypes and on spiritual precedent. The semianonymous "Eliza," for example, defended the writing of

---

3. Mary Sidney, Countess of Pembroke, "Psalm 62," in *The Psalms of Sir Philip Sidney and the Countess of Pembroke,* ed. J. C. A. Rathmell (New York: Anchor Books, 1963), 142. For a consideration of the presence of female voices in the translation of the (male-authored) Psalms, see Margaret P. Hannay, " 'Wisdome the Wordes': Psalm Translation and Elizabethan Women's Spirituality," in *Religion and Literature* 23.3 (1991): 65–82.

4. Sir Philip Sidney, *An Apology for Poetry,* ed. Geoffrey Shepherd (Manchester: Manchester University Press, 1973), 103.

her collection of devotional poems, *Eliza's Babes,* on the grounds of her own
"contemptible" and "ignorant" femininity:

> And now I dare not say, I am an ignorant woman, and unfit to write, for if
> thou wilt declare thy goodness, and thy mercy by weak and contemptible
> means, who can resist thy will?[5]

Here the assumed condition of woman as "weak" and "ignorant" is transformed
from an obstacle into a source of praise for the God who will deign to use such
means for glory. "Eliza" manages to represent herself in writing as acceptably
feminine, being "unfit to write," but also records the overturning of that sense
of inadequacy. By reporting her own self-denying speech she establishes not
one but two voices for herself: the one that confesses "I am an ignorant woman"
and the other that tells herself off for saying so and thereby calling God's plans
into question. Behind this ingenuity, however, lies a persistent tension between
uncertainty and assertion, between the "silent" and the expressive soul. In her
eighth "Contemplation," Anne Bradstreet describes this oscillation in detail:

> Silent alone, where none or saw, or heard,
> In pathless paths I lead my wand'ring feet,
> My humble eyes to lofty skies I reared
> To sing some song, my mazed Muse thought meet.
> My great Creator I would magnify,
> That nature had thus decked liberally;
> But Ah, and Ah, again, my imbecility![6]

Her instinct is to "magnify" the Lord, recalling the model of the Virgin Mary
whose song offered the female devotional poets an important example through
which to justify their expression of worship in personal verse. Bradstreet's
"mazed Muse" seeks a means to praise the creator of the natural world, which
is "decked" so "liberally"; "alone" and "silent" as yet, she hopes to be inspired
to formulate her own Magnificat. But the poem is an account of longing, not
of achievement; its mood is summed up in "would," not "did." The inhibiting
factor is what she calls her "imbecility," but the tension is already present in
words such as *silent* and *wand'ring* (the latter with its overtones of error and
sin) and the unbridgeable contrast between her "humble eyes" and the "lofty
skies." Female humility may have afforded "Eliza" an opportunity to be used

---

5. *Eliza's Babes: Or the Virgins-Offering. Being Divine Poems, and Meditations. Written by a Lady, who onely desires to advance the glory of God, and not her own* (London: M.S. for Laurence Blaiklock, 1652), 75. References given subsequently in the main text of this essay are to page numbers.
6. *The Works of Anne Bradstreet,* ed. Jeannine Hensley (Cambridge, Mass.: Belknap Press, 1967), 206.

by God, but as Bradstreet's verse shows, it could also turn into a crippling sense of "imbecility."

Despite their crises of self-doubt, Bradstreet, "Eliza," and their female contemporaries did indeed manage to find a devotional voice. Even in the "Contemplation" that we have just read, Bradstreet managed to complete her usual seven-line stanza, and, as is so often the case, the focus is a dual one: her "great Creator" and her own self whose narrative we follow and whose vocation (as well as human folly) we are invited to contemplate. This duality is a perpetual irony in devotional writing—the voice of the apparently humble speaker is always potentially in rivalry with the God who is being exalted by that speaker, as in, for example, Herbert's "Jordan" (II)—but for the female poet this tension is increased by the conventional expectation of silence and modest self-effacement. However, the very first poem in *Eliza's Babes* is anything but modest in suggesting the author's own delight in the expression of her devotion:

> I Glory in the word of God,
>   To praise it I accord.
> With joy I will declare abroad,
>   The goodness of the Lord.
>   (1)

God is the subject, in the sense of the topic and center of the stanza, but the subject in grammatical terms is the poet, enjoying the active verbs: "I glory," "I accord," "I will declare." Taken out of their religious context, such verbs are, for this period, decidedly unfeminine and, in sequence here, declare an animated self.

The presentation of one's self to the Almighty was an absorbing and, in fact, continual affair. As Lady Elizabeth Delaval wrote in her *Meditations* in the 1660s, part of the acceptance of the Christian faith is the realization that there is no time or space in which to escape from "the sight of my Lord and my judge." She noted in youthful eagerness a plan to control her fiery temper:

> I will retier my selfe to hide my unruly passion from all the world, where once reflecting upon God's presence will certenly soon calme my spirit's and make me rather full of shame then anger, who durst presume (even before his eye who can behold no impurity) to be discomposs'd and disturb'd, cary'd and hary'd away so from my own reason. . . . [7]

This extract clearly acknowledges that, although she may "retier" from the "world" in order to hide her passionate temper, there is no hiding from

---

7. *The Meditations of Lady Elizabeth Delaval*, ed. Douglas G. Greene (Gateshead: Surtees Society, 1978), 47.

God. Delaval expects that "reflecting upon God's presence" will make her feel ashamed of her behavior, but as the passage goes on it is evident that mere reflection on God is an impossibility: she becomes conscious of being perpetually before his all-seeing and all-judging "eye." Her "discomposs'd and disturb'd" state cannot be hidden; indeed, she finds that although she is "cary'd and hary'd away" from her own reason, she is not so much beside herself as realizing a disconcertingly genuine self. In this sense we who read Delaval's *Meditations* are placed in a God-like position; what is hidden by Delaval's "retierment" from the world, perhaps her own true nature, is disclosed to us in her text. Devotion, like autobiography, is not only a representation—it is also a revelation of self.

The tropes of self-representation that we have seen so far in these women's texts operate for the most part within the already gendered language of devotion—that is, a feminized soul dependent on the power of grace. When these devotional conventions emerge in the work of women writers, I would suggest that we may observe two significant effects. On the one hand, there is an intensification of the speaker's vulnerability through the parallels between the inscribed feminized soul and the prescribed situation of woman—as in, for example, the case of the lines from Mary Sidney or Anne Bradstreet. On the other hand, as in the case of "Eliza" and Elizabeth Delaval, the soul's right to praise, to sue for grace, or to discover layers of selfhood offers a freedom to the speaker that is all the more notable when the voice is female.

II

But do the women's texts move beyond this relatively familiar, though particularly nuanced, dialogue of devotion to any more consciously feminine self-representation? One consistent element in devotional works by women is an intense awareness of their own female bodies. Although a sense of the sinful weakness of the flesh is a traditional part of Christian thinking, it is especially strong in women's spirituality through the long-established association of the feminine with body rather than mind, the defining of women by the reproductive function of their bodies, and the identification with original female desire and corruptibility in the person of Eve. Not surprisingly, therefore, a number of Renaissance Englishwomen turned to devotional writing, it seems, through their sense of the miseries of a woman's body. An Collins wrote her 1653 *Divine Songs and Meditations* because of "grief," "crosses," and "frailty," words whose mixture of metaphor and actuality suggests a combination of physical and mental suffering.[8] Lady Jane Grey described herself in prayer as

8. An Collins, "The Discourse," in *Divine Songs and Meditations* (London: R. Bishop, 1653), 2–7, cited from the modernized text in *Her Own Life: Autobiographical Writings by Seventeenth-Century Englishwomen*, ed. Elspeth Graham et al. (London: Routledge, 1989), 57–61.

a "pore and desolate woman," and her cumulative self-despising and self-pity ends with a reference to her "vile" body:

> defiled with sinne, encombered with affliction, unqueeted with troubles, wrapped in cares, overwhelmed with miseries, vexed with temptations, and grevousllye tormented with the long imprisonment of thys vile masse of clay my body and bloude.[9]

This prayer arose from a very specific "imprisonment" (after her nine days' reign as queen of England), but the roll call of extreme adjectives is not unusual. In the prayer of any less prominent woman, the "imprisonment" would simply have been not *of* but *in* the "vile masse of clay my body." Elizabeth Major was moved to compose her 1656 *Honey on the Rod* after the experience of a severe illness, which (echoing the prayer of Lady Jane Grey) she terms the "bondage" or "prison" of affliction. Major adds, "my sighs are many, and my heart is heavy. I, I am she that hath seen affliction."[10] This last statement is an almost direct quotation from Lamentations 3:1, in which Jeremiah pronounces, "I am the man that hath seen affliction." Although it was common for writers to adopt the biblical "he" in their own echoes, Major significantly feminizes the quotation and represents herself as the woman who has seen affliction.

Lady Jane Cheyne was stirred to address God in verse on account of her perception not of the sufferings of her own female body but those of her sister, who died in childbirth in 1663. The poem, though adopting some formal conventions of the elegy, is deeply troubled:

> O God thy Judgments unto sinfull eye
> Were greate, when I did see my Sister dye,
> Her last look was to heaven, from whence she came,
> And thither going, she was still the same,
> No Discomposure in her life or Death,
> She lived to pray, prayer was her last Breath:
> And when Deaths heavy hand had closed her eyes,
> Me thought the World gave up it's Ghost in Cryes.[11]

The tones of protest are clearly discernible in this woman's lament for the death of her sister in particularly (and all too familiarly) female circumstances.

9. Lady Jane Grey, "A certaine prayer made of the Lady Jane in the time of her trouble," in John Foxe, *Actes and Monuments of These Latter and Perillous Dayes* (London: John Daye, 1563), 919.

10. Elizabeth Major, *Honey on the Rod: Or a comfortable Contemplation for One in Affliction* (London: Thomas Maxey, 1656), A4^{v} and 2.

11. Lady Jane Cheyne, "On the death of my Deare Sister the Countesse of Bridgewater dying in Childbed, Delivered of a dead Infant a Son, the 14:th day of June 1663," Huntington Library Ellesmere MS 8353, in *Kissing the Rod: An Anthology of 17th Century Women's Verse*, ed. Germaine Greer et al. (London: Virago, 1988), 118.

The dead woman had lived a blameless and holy life, summed up in the quietly feminine ideal of perfection, "No Discomposure"; why, then, did God's "Judgments" fall on her, allowing her to die in giving birth to a stillborn son? The poem avoids blasphemy by the choice of the word *greate* to describe God's apparently awesome and mysterious ways in permitting this double loss. However, Cheyne's questioning of the rightness of God's actions is expressed in the phrase "unto sinfull eye," suggesting that the speaker is well aware that her perspective on the event is so doubting as to be "sinfull." The protest here is against the often cruel implications of a woman's calling to be maternal and to care:

> A greater Saint the Earth did never beare,
> She lived to love, and her last thought was care;
> Her new borne Child she asked for, which n'ere cryed,
> Fearing to know its end she Bowed, and Dyed:
> And her last Vale to Heaven appeared to all,
> How much she knew her Glory in the call.
>
> (118)

Ironically, the "call" to the earthly form of glory for a woman—that is, motherhood—leads instead to misery, which then in turn becomes for her the sure route to heavenly "Glory."

The path to glory was not always so strewn with affliction in the devotional writing of these Renaissance Englishwomen. Elizabeth Major, for example, used her poetry as a means not only to glorify God and come to terms with her illness but also to embody herself triumphantly in the words of the poetic text as an offering to God. "The Author's Prayer" is a fine example, being a poetic embellishment of the text of her prayer "O my bless'd Lord and Savior Jesus Christ, have mercy on thy poor handmaid, Elisabeth Maior":

O	Gracious God, inhabiting	*E ternity*
My	Blest redeemer, that hast	*L ovingly*
Bless'd	me with hope, a kingdom to	*I nherit,*
Lord	of thy mercy give an humble	*S pirit,*
And	grant I pray, I may my life	*A mend:*
Savior	tis thou that canst my soul	*B efriend.*
Jesus	with grace my guilty soul	*E ndue*
Christ	promis'd grace, & thou, O Lord, art	*T rue;*
Have	care of me, deal out with thine own	*H and*
Mercy	to my poor soul, thou canst com-	*M and*
On	me a shower of grace, sin to	*A void,*
Thy	praise to sing, my tongue shall be	*I mploy'd:*
Poor,	Lord I am, with fear and care	*O press'd,*
Handmaid	to thee I am, in thee I'le	*R est.*

(191)

This devotional acrostic is an intriguing combination of prayer and poem, dialogue and monologue, self-denial and self-presentation. While the narrative emphasis is on her need of "mercy" and "grace," Major finds a poetic structure and logic gracefully to enclose a song of praise within two self-standing texts that give her a distinct identity. She is no ordinary "handmaid," but "Elisabeth Maior": her name itself is embedded in the text and, as the last word is spoken, embodied in the letters that form the poem. This is the closest to visual representation that the women poets ever come, and it is expressive of complete self-offering—for a woman's good name represented the essence of her being.

III

These Renaissance women thus represented themselves to God in their devotional texts through silence as well as song and through the miseries of shame and suffering as well as the offering of name and self as a gift to the Lord. In all these methods, we are conscious of something increasingly feminine about this self-expression, whether through the parallel social and religious construction of women as silent and humble, the spiritual connotations of the soul as female, the specific sufferings and callings of the female body, or the currency of a woman's name as her reputation and identity. There are, however, even more overtly feminine elements at play in some women's devotional representations. The relationship with God, always a gendered affair, is often specifically invoked as such by the women as a source of feminine identity and reference. An Collins, for example, borrows the biblical idea of the *hortus conclusus* or enclosed garden, traditionally taken to refer to the virgin womb of Mary, and uses it in "Another Song: In the winter of my infancy" to describe the chastity of her mind:

> Yet as a garden is my mind enclosed fast
> Being to safety so confined from storm and blast
> Apt to produce a fruit most rare,
> That is not common with every woman
> That fruitful are.[12]

Collins's chastity is mental and spiritual, specified in biblical terms that consciously draw attention to her femininity as a devotional poet. In contrast to women whose wombs are "fruitful," she has a fruitful mind that produces poems, a "fruit most rare," as the offspring (like *Eliza's Babes*) of her own female experience.

12. *Her Own Life*, 68. The source for the "enclosed garden" is Song of Songs 4:12.

Other women represented themselves more straightforwardly in maternal terms. Mistress Bradford, for instance, mother of the sixteenth-century English martyr John Bradford, not surprisingly made her motherhood the central feature of her prayer, which was offered "a little before his martyrdome":

> Lord, I praie thee make him worthie to suffer . . . for thy truth, religion, and Gospell sake. As Hanna did applie, dedicate, and give hir first child and sonne Samuel to thee: even so doo I deere father; beseeching thee, for Christ's sake, to accept this gift. . . . [13]

The speaker's consciousness of her feminine role here, and reference to her predecessor in the Old Testament, gives the prayer a double function. Mistress Bradford is offering her son to God and asks for him to be accepted as a suitable "gift"; at the same time she is presenting her own self to God as another Hannah, the Old Testament model of the self-denying woman who dedicates her child to God. There is a second duality in the prayer, concerning the relationships established. Mistress Bradford speaks as John's mother but also as the daughter of God. The entire prayer opens with the words, "Ah good father," and it closes, as we have seen, with a plea to her "deere father" to accept her offering. The sense of the supplicant as a child of God is nothing new here, but the combination of the strong, mature voice of the mother with the humble tones of the daughter reminds us of the complexities of the devotional dialogue with its simultaneous play of persuasion and acceptance.

The Renaissance Englishwoman was rarely her own self, but always someone's daughter, someone's mother, or, of course, someone's wife. Mistress Bradford's prayer drew on two of these gendered roles, but not on the third. "Eliza," however, who was mother to her poems, the "Babes" of her title, was bold enough to envisage a more spouselike relationship with God in her poem "The Lover":

> Come let us now to each discover,
> Who is our friend, and who our Lover,
> What? art thou now asham'd of thine,
> I tell thee true, Ime not of mine.
>
> And you will say when you him see,
> That none but he, desir'd can bee,
> He is the onely pleasing wight,
> Whose presence can content my sight.

13. "The praier that maister Bradfords mother said and offered unto God in his behalfe, a little before his martyrdom," in Thomas Bentley, *Monument of Matrones* (London: H. Denham, 1582), 2:215.

For He's the purest red and white,
In whom my soule takes her delight:
He to the flowrs [t]heir beauty gives,
In him the Rose and Lilly lives.

His pleasant haire with seemly grace,
Hangs by his faire sweet lovely face,
And from his pleasing eyes do dart
Their arrows which do pierce my heart.

These beauties all are richly grac'st,
For on his head, a crown is plac'st,
Of glory, which doth shine so bright,
As mortall eye can see this light,

This lovely Lord's, the Prince of Peace,
In him, my joyes will still increase;
For he's the true, and constant friend,
Whose love begun, will never end.

From Heaven he came with me to dwell,
And sav'd my soul from direfull hell,
'Tis he alone my heart doth gaine,
That keeps me from eternall pain.

While here I live, here will he bee;
Death cannot separate him from me:
And when I dye, he will me place,
Where I shall ever see his face.

Into his glory, hee'l take mee,
This doe I know, this shall you see
And now you know my loved friend,
My loves begun, it will not end.

                              (24–25)

    While much of this poem is a portrait of Christ, the "Lover" of the title, this is
a clear case of the female speaker portraying herself as his beloved partner. She
is not ashamed—rather, she is proud—to boast of this relationship with her
"lovely Lord" who is not only her lover but also her best friend and redeemer,
the saviour of her soul from "direfull hell." There is a remarkable physicality and
domesticity in the poem's descriptions; the lover with his "pleasant haire" and
"pleasing eyes" has come to "dwell" with her, and "While here I live, here he will
bee." The mutuality of this line suggests strong parallels with the seventeenth-
century ideal of companionate marriage. However, unlike earthly marriage,

which is pledged until "death us do part," this speaker's relationship cannot be broken by death but will then move into a higher key of "glory" that, once begun, "will not end."

The envisaging of the worshiper as the loving partner of Christ has biblical and liturgical precedent in the metaphors of the Song of Songs and the image of the Church as the bride of Christ. However, when it is not simply the soul of the human speaker that is feminized, but the body, too, as in the case of "Eliza," then some complications can arise; it is clear that Eliza had a more than merely spiritual sense of herself as "affianced" to Christ (A2). When the time comes for her to be married to an earthly "lord," "Eliza" protests to her heavenly lord in the opening line of a poem called "The Gift": "My Lord, hast thou given me away?" (42). Having given her heart as a "gift" to Christ her lover, she now finds that it is being passed on in turn to another man. She argues that it will be acceptable to her for her earthly husband to receive her as a gift from God, provided that it is clear that Christ retains her heart while her husband "only hath my earthly part":

> But Lord my heart thou dost not give,
> Though here on earth, while I doe live
> My body here he may retain,
> My heart in heaven, with thee must reigne.
>
> (42)

This, though outspoken, is a statement of a fairly orthodox position, ensuring that heavenly values always predominate over earthly ones. The penultimate stanza, however, suggests that the strongly envisaged relationship of the woman to Christ as lover can imply a subversion of conventional domestic authority:

> It was my glory I was free,
> And subject here to none but thee,
> And still that glory I shall hold
> If thou my Spirit dost infold.
>
> (43)

The word *glory* often recurs in these texts, but here it refers not so much to a glory that is to be attained in heaven but one of which she has a liberating foretaste now within marriage.

It is also possible to discover devotional texts by Renaissance Englishwomen in which the sense of the speaker as a wife has a more down-to-earth connotation. Elizabeth Delaval, whom we encountered earlier attempting to control her unruly teenage temper, went on to marry and records toward the end of her *Meditations* a very wifely prayer:

O forgive, I beseech thee, my husbands sins as well as mine. Open his eyes
that he may desern the wonderous things of thy law, and take his delight
therein. Mercyfully pardon my haveing been the occation off any of his
offences against thee, and grant, I humbly pray thee, O Lord my God,
that our prayers may never more be hindered by unkind disputes but that
we may live together in kindnesse and in peace.

(211–12)

It becomes clear from the reference to "unkind disputes" that either Delaval was
unlucky in her husband or she did not enjoy very much success in her efforts
to keep her bad temper at bay. What is intriguing in this short prayer is that
Delaval presents herself at first to God as the mediator for her sinful husband
and only afterward as, rather more humbly, possibly the cause of his sins. Her
negotiation with God is thus primarily confident and allows her to represent,
in the legal meaning of the word, both her husband and herself. This is indeed
an emancipation of the wifely speaker before God.

Devotional representation can readily imply a process of speaking up on
behalf of the self, defending oneself, or striking a bargain with God. This is
particularly true of an elegy written by Mary Carey on the death of her son in
1650:

> My lord hath called for my sonne
>   my hart breth's forth; thy will be done:
>
> my all; that mercy hath made mine
>   frely's surendered to be thine:
>
> But if I give my all to the
>   lett me not pyne for poverty:
>
> Change wth me; doe, as I have done
>   give me thy all; Even thy deare sonne:
>
> Tis Jesus Christ; lord I would have;
>   he's thine, mine all; 'tis him I crave:
>
> Give him to me; and I'le reply
>   Enoughe my lord; now lett me dye.[14]

Here the devotional female as mother starts off as obedient and accepting ("thy
will be done") but subsequently becomes more than a supplicant; she calls on
the equivalent parenthood of God and suggests that her son in exchange for

---

14. Mary Carey, "On the death of my 4th, and only Child, Robert Payler," in *Kissing the Rod,* 156–57.

his would be a fair deal. The ability to hold her own with God is Mary Carey's outstanding quality: it is unusual to hear the words "doe, as I have done" spoken *to* God rather than *by* him. As she moves further in persuading God to give away his son, the voice of the mother who "craves" a child merges with that of a lover who longs for Christ to be "mine all" and then is content to die. At that point she rests her case.

The question with which I began—how did these women writers represent themselves in the dialogue with their Maker?—thus has many answers. From humility to assertion, as mothers, daughters, and lovers, and in a spectrum from self-hatred to self-offering, these Renaissance Englishwomen went about the business of conversation with God. We have looked at only a small number of isolated moments, but it is important to add that representation was always also re-presentation; devotion is by its very nature a constantly repeated experience. In one of her rare poems, Elizabeth Delaval contrasts her own spiritual sloth with the activity of the lark:

> The early lark wellcomes the breake of day,
> But I (alass) drouse many hour's away.
> She to my God praises dos dayly sing
> Reproaching thus my slothfull idle sin;
> Whilest I do still neglect to worshipe him
> Till all the golden houer's of morning light
> Past a recall are vanish'd out of sight.
>
> (44)

The contrast suggests the cyclical nature of devotion, which must be repeated each day like the lark's dawn song of praise, partly because each day also brings the renewal of sin. Delaval is acutely aware that she neglects her chance to "sing" at each "breake of day" and offers devotion only when the "golden houer's of morning light" have long faded. The metaphor has implications also for the progress of life as a whole, which will equally quickly vanish "out of sight" and disappear "past a recall." As the poem goes on to demonstrate in its following stanzas, devotion not only enables the rescue of lost "houer's" and the re-presentation of the hopeful soul, but it also leads in turn to the gift by God of a "new life." The re-presentation is thus not only perpetual but reciprocal, too.

From the materials of language, tradition, and their own lives, these women devotional writers mold and create selves that make possible a continual process of dialogue and spiritual renewal. There is a strong sense of the limits of what it is possible to represent, but also of the enormity of the scope given by devotional expression in this period. As "Eliza" puts it in her poem "The onely bound,"

> My boundlesse spirits, bounded be in thee,
> For bounded by no other can they be.
>
> (36)

Although the ecstatic Eliza rejects all earthly limitation of her own "boundlesse" spirits, a woman was indeed regularly "bounded" in the early modern period, by the bonds of social and linguistic restraint and by the limitations placed on women by religion itself. However, to be "bounded" in the God who himself is boundless, while being set free from all other limitations, suggests a stunning image of the creative space for female self-representation that devotional experience offered. Out of the defiance, modesty, humor, and sorrow of these texts, we hear, with all its paradoxical implications, the expressive speech of the female "soule in silence."

Janel Mueller

COMPLICATIONS OF INTERTEXTUALITY

John Fisher, Katherine Parr, and
"The Book of the Crucifix"

The level of current interest in interpreting texts as registers of cultural change in early modern England bespeaks an increasingly shared perspective in literary studies that again seeks to take history seriously. As we literary-historical types now go about our usual business of intertextuality—analyzing texts and putting them into relation with other texts—we avoid dealing solely in textual formulations of our concerns. Unless they are tethered to extralinguistic referents of context, relations among texts seemingly cannot be freed from the specter of an indefinite regress of signifiers in play. Many of us have accordingly turned to an almost hallowed triad—the factors of race (or ethnicity), class, and gender—as anchors for our work on historical texts in historical contexts. Taken over from our social-science colleagues in the current vogue of interdisciplinary method swapping, these factors look so promising because race, class, and gender are both powerfully material in their bases and even more potently ideological in their social encodings and decodings.

Thus, we routinely suppose that if we analyze texts for what we call their race, class, or gender "inscriptions" and interpret them accordingly, we will be able to surmount disjunctions between world and word, between material facts and ideas in literature, and manage to make our criticism and historical work be about something that can count as real. We further assume that race, class, and gender, as fundamental constituents of human lives in social relations, will unfailingly leave significant markings in a text—or, what amounts to nearly the same thing in practice, we assume that the markings of race, class, and gender will yield significance more basic, more primary, than that conveyed by way, say, of the verbal and cognitive effects of rhetoric or poetics. To this triad of race, class, and gender I want to join the additionally powerful factor of a writer's generation, his or her biological and social moment, for we now know from historical linguistics that generationally diffused variation is the chief motor of language change.[1] Why should the situation not be analogous with literary change, a problem that we have much current trouble accounting for?

The "we" locutions that I have been using are not disingenuous. These reflections do indicate lines that my own critical thinking has taken, and I am aware of a number of colleagues who have been moving in this same direction. Nevertheless, I have come to regard the material that I present in this essay as something of a test case or a limit instance of the capacity of gender—particularly as now theorized—to anchor the literary-historical work that I have been doing on women in English Protestantism. I begin by explaining my concrete difficulties in a specific case and the available interpretive options as I saw them. I will end with some reflections on what for me remains a conjoint dilemma of methodology and interpretation: how to decide which factor to treat as determinative when more than one option seems available, and what interpretive difference it makes to decide one way or the other.

The heart of my material is an odd metaphor, "the book of the crucifix," which is arguably even a catachresis (an outright violation of figurative language) by traditional rhetorical criteria. The oddity of this metaphor consists in its conflation of long-divergent, even long-opposed domains in Christian symbolics: on one hand, the book as the Bible, Holy Writ, the acme of verbal truth; on the other, the crucifix as the simulacrum of Christ's bloody, suffering body, the most sacred object, the acme of nonverbal truth. I first encountered the metaphor of "the book of the crucifix" in the sustained use that Katherine Parr makes of it in her religious prose work *The Lamentation of a Sinner,* published in November 1547.

Parr was Henry VIII's last queen and his widow—also, in earliest years, an intimate of Henry's daughter, Princess Mary. Thanks to arrangements made with Catherine of Aragon by Parr's mother, one of the queen's ladies, to enroll her daughter along with Princess Mary under the tutelage of Juan Luis Vives, Katherine Parr received the most advanced Christian humanist education then thought suitable for a Tudor royal female and the other children admitted to her nursery.[2] But, however well lettered and Latined, such a female education did not constitute a sufficient incentive to authorship (as opposed to translation or

1. Too little notice, in my view, has been given to Richard Helgerson's *Self-Crowned Laureates: Spenser, Jonson, Milton, and the Literary System* (Berkeley and London: University of California Press, 1983), with its cogent definition of "the literary system" in terms of generational patterns. Robert O. Evans has my thanks for calling my attention to the pioneering work of Anthony Esler, *The Aspiring Mind of the Elizabethan Younger Generation* (Durham: Duke University Press, 1966).

2. For these biographical particulars, see Anthony Martienssen, *Queen Katherine Parr* (London: Secker and Warburg, 1973), 18–28.

patronage) for any woman of the earlier Tudor—that is, the pre-Elizabethan—period. In that period the catalysts for female authorship were education to a point of secure literacy—not necessarily including Latin, as in Parr's case—and the sine qua non, a conversion to Protestantism, with its emphasis on the equality of all souls before God and its urgent imperative to share the soul-saving news of the Gospel in order to make other Christians aware of their own accountability to God for their spiritual state.[3]

If the categories of the compilation and the familiar letter are excluded, Katherine Parr is the first certain instance in English of a woman writer.[4] Her first work, *Prayers or Meditations,* minutely reworks excerpts from Book 3 of Thomas à Kempis's *Imitation of Christ* in Richard Whitford's English translation, which was published about 1530. The end result moves Parr beyond adaptative translation into original composition while still holding to enough common ground in Christian orthodoxy to satisfy her religiously conservative husband, Henry VIII.[5] The publication of Parr's *Prayers or Meditations* in June 1545 with the king's authorization thus predates by more than a year the clandestine publication of Anne Askew's *First Examination* and *Latter Examination,* published in 1546 and 1547, respectively. Askew, a member of Parr's circle of ladies, records her investigation and condemnation for Protestant heresies that brought her to death at the stake.[6] Understandably, Parr would withhold her account of her own conversion to an objectionably Lutheran strain of

---

3. See the treatment of the (uneven) gradation from translation to original authorship in Elaine Beilin, *Redeeming Eve: Women Writers of the English Renaissance* (Princeton: Princeton University Press, 1987), chaps. 1–3, and the essays on Margaret More Roper, Elizabeth Tudor, and Anne Askew in Margaret P. Hannay, ed., *Silent but for the Word: Tudor Women as Patrons, Translators, and Writers of Religious Works* (Kent: Kent State University Press, 1985).

4. Julian of Norwich's scholarly editors take the view that she dictated her *Showings of Divine Love* (ca. 1393), while the *Book of Margery Kempe* (ca. 1436–1438) was unquestionably dictated by its illiterate author. See Edmund Colledge and James Walsh, eds., *A Book of Showings to the Anchoress Julian of Norwich* (New York: Paulist Press, 1978), vol. 1: Introduction; and *The Book of Margery Kempe,* ed. Sanford B. Meech, with annotation by Hope Emily Allen, EETS orig. ser. 212 (London: Oxford University Press, 1940), 153, for an extended passage in which Margery's scribe asserts his presence and describes his misgivings about some of what she dictates to him. *The Book of St. Albans* (1486), attributed in its earliest printings to Dame Juliana Berners, traditionally identified as the prioress of the nunnery of Sopwell in Hertfordshire, contains treatises on hawking, hunting, and heraldry that have been analyzed as compilations by different hands. See *The Boke of Saint Albans by Dame Juliana Berners,* ed. William Blades (London: Elliot Stock, 1905), 6–14.

5. See my "Devotion as Difference: Intertextuality in Queen Katherine Parr's *Prayers or Meditations* (1545)," *Huntington Library Quarterly* 53 (1990): 171–97.

6. On the relation between Askew and Parr, see Martienssen, *Queen Katherine Parr,* 189–223, building on John Foxe, "The Trouble of Queene Katherine Parre," *Actes and Monuments* (London, 1570), 2:1422–25. On the historical significance of this case, see Paula McQuade, " 'Except that they had offended the Lawe': Gender and Jurisprudence in *The Examinations of Anne Askew,*" *Literature and History,* 3rd ser., 3.2 (1994): 1–14, and Elaine Beilin's edition of Askew's *Examinations,* forthcoming in the Oxford University Press series, Women Writers in English, 1350–1850.

Protestantism from the notice of a violent husband who was sure to disapprove, publishing *The Lamentation of a Sinner* at the safe interval of nine months after Henry VIII's death.[7]

The intense self-reckoning into which Parr plunges in her *Lamentation* makes clear that her own book owes its existence to another book, which she calls "the booke of the crucifixe." She declares: "This crucifix is the boke, wherin God hath included all thinges, and hath most compendiously written therein, all truth, profitable and necessary for our salvacion. Therfore let us indevour our selfes to studye thys booke, that we (beyng lightened with the spirite of god) may geve hym thankes for so great a benefite" (*L*, sig. Ciir-v). Parr elaborates the metaphoric relation between "book" and, as she proceeds, not so much "the crucifix" as "the crucifixion"—the significance of the action of Christ's love for human souls rather than the material image or icon of it. "Inwardlye to behold Christ crucified upon the crosse," says Parr, "is the best and godliest meditacion that can be" (*L*, sig. Bviiiv). "To learne to knowe truly our owne sinnes, is to study in the booke of the crucifixe, by continuall conversacion in fayth. . . . If we looke further in thys booke, we shall see Christes great victory upon the crosse" (*L*, sigs. Ciir-v). "We may see also in Christe crucified, the bewtie of the soule, better then in all the bookes of the worlde. For who that with lively fayth, seeth and feleth in spirite, that Christe the sonne of god, is dead for the satisfiying and the purifyng of the soule, shall se that his soule, is appoynted for the very tabernacle, and mansion of the . . . majestie and honour of god" (*L*, sigs. Bviiiv-Cir).

This odd metaphor of the book of the crucifix (or Crucifixion) becomes the vehicle for Parr's figuration of a true apprehension of Christian faith as a process of intently reading the one message that really matters for the relation between Christ and the soul. When I began to consider how to interpret this metaphor, I certainly recognized that I was working with a crucial stretch of text. As a first move, I took the feminist scholar's turn toward autobiography as the likeliest form that gender marking would assume in a woman author's text. I hypothesized a scenario in which the "book of the crucifixe" was a metaphor coalescing those definitive developments in Katherine Parr's experience that brought her to the authorship of her *Lamentation*. These developments would include her

---

7. Henry VIII died in January 1547. Parr's reference to him as an English Moses who has led God's people out of captivity to Pharaoh, the bishop of Rome, clearly indicates that the king is still alive (Katherine Parr, *The lamentacion of a sinner, made by the most vertuous Ladie, Quene Caterin, bewayling the ignoraunce of her blind life* [London, 1547], sigs. Dvv–Dvir). Further citations will be abbreviated *L* and incorporated parenthetically in my text. For discussion, see Janel Mueller, "A Tudor Queen Finds Voice: Katherine Parr's *Lamentation of a Sinner*," in Heather Dubrow and Richard Strier, ed., *The Historical Renaissance: New Essays on Tudor and Stuart Literature and Culture* (Chicago: University of Chicago Press, 1988): 15–47.

superb education, the authority that she as queen of England learned to exercise through writing (in particular, the letters and proclamations that she issued when Henry appointed her regent while he undertook the reconquest of lost English territories in France in the summer and autumn of 1544), and, finally, her conversion as a mature woman from the Catholicism of her girlhood to a Protestantism rendered unmistakable by her embrace of justification by faith (this last apparently a consequence of the daily consultations that Henry required her to have with Thomas Cranmer, archbishop of Canterbury and ranking member of the Privy Council, while she acted as regent).[8]

On further reflection I imagined that, while a gender factor might account for the bookish character of the metaphor, a generational factor might account for its oddity. The mixed modalities of Parr's "book of the crucifixe" might be read as a mark of the transitional mentality of a person born (as she was) about 1513, before the printing press had gathered much momentum as a cultural medium, but so placed as to witness firsthand its steadily expanding force and impact. Moreover, the components of the metaphor—half text, half image— might be interpreted as trace elements in the experience of an adult convert to Protestantism, that religion of the Book par excellence, who in growing up had been habituated to older modes of visuality and to the use of images in Catholic worship. However, for all of these imagined autobiographical resonances to hold, confirming the factors of gender and generation—Parr's historical specificity—as determinants of my proposed interpretation, there was a condition that the metaphor of "the book of the crucifixe" really had to fulfill. It had to be Parr's own creation. I wanted to believe that it was, of course, yet I suspected that it might not be.

While working on my 1988 article about *The Lamentation of a Sinner*, I hoped to resolve my uncertainty about the originality of Parr's metaphor. At that time my hopes were deceived because my best findings were merely negative. I found some weak support for my hunch that the book of the crucifix was a metaphorical oddity of early modern date because none of the indexes to writers of the Church in either the Latin or the Greek series of the Migne *Patrologia* included "book" among the profuse imagistic equivalences that they listed for Christ's cross.[9] Moreover, since *The Lamentation* begins with Parr's account of coming to awareness of her justification by faith in Christ, and thus offers

---

8. Martienssen, *Queen Katherine Parr*, 180, 205–6; for discussion, see Mueller, "A Tudor Queen Finds Voice," 28–33.

9. To illustrate the relative remoteness of any analogues: Christ is called a "book" (liber) by Rabanus Maurus (*PL*, vol. 112, col. 987) and by St. Bruno the Carthusian (*PL*, vol. 152, cols. 545, 805); he is called "a book written within and without" (liber scriptus intus et foris) by Adam Scotus, echoing Ezekiel 2:10 (*PL*, vol. 198, col. 774). Of the cross, Alcuin pronounces that it "is a sign, the sign of the living God" (signum Dei vivi, crucis est signum) (*PL*, vol. 100, col. 1129).

the first conversion narrative in English, I looked in Luther, in Tyndale, and in other early Tudor Protestants for adumbrations of her metaphor of the book of the crucifix. But there too I turned up nothing significantly similar.[10] The closest I came overall in that research was a passage in Erasmus's *Enchiridion Militis Christiani* (which was written in 1501 and published in 1503; the first enlarged edition appeared in 1518), a book that Parr is known to have owned. Erasmian piety, moreover, is the best publicized of Parr's prominent interests as queen.[11] In his seventeenth rule Erasmus advises

> that thou mayest with . . . profyte, in thy mynde recorde the mistery
> of the cross: It shalbe hovefull that every man prepare unto hym selfe
> a certayne way and godly crafte. . . . Suche may the crafte be, that in
> crucifyeng of every one of thyne affectyons, thou mayste applye that parte
> of the crosse whiche most specially therto agreeth. For there is not at
> all any maner eyther temptacion eyther adversyte, whiche hath not his
> proper remedy in the crosse.[12]

This passage focuses the extremities of inward spirituality and struggle on the figure of Christ crucified, as Parr does in the first-person soul-searching that opens her *Lamentation,* but Erasmus offers no intimation of a book of the crucifix. Could I conclude that the metaphor was Parr's own? Clearly not. I could conclude only that gender and generation had not been ruled out as its possible autobiographical determinants.

In due course I discovered the exact formulation—"the book of the crucifix" —in a sermon by John Fisher, bishop of Rochester, who together with Thomas More was beheaded as a traitor in 1535 for refusing to swear the Oath of Supremacy. The sermon containing this metaphor was preached on an unspecified Good Friday, for which no Fisher scholar has been able to fix a year. However, a passing reference to "the B. of R. Innocent" (if this phrasing can be trusted to be Fisher's own, and not a printer's interpolation) seems to me to provide reasonable grounds for dating the sermon to the period 1531–1534, a time when the nomenclature "bishop of Rome" would have been de rigueur for

10. Luther comes closest, yet not very close, in articles 20 and 21 of his *Heidelberg Disputation* (May 1518): "He deserves to be called a theologian . . . who comprehends the visible and manifest things of God seen through suffering and the cross. A theologian of glory calls evil good and good evil. A theologian of the cross calls the thing what it actually is" (*Luther's Works,* ed. Helmut T. Lehmann and Harold J. Grimm [Philadelphia: Fortress Press, 1957], 31:52–53).

11. F. Rose-Troup, "Two Book Bills of Catherine Parr," *The Library,* 3rd ser., 2 (1911): 40–48; James K. McConica, *English Humanists and Reformation Politics* (Oxford: Clarendon Press, 1965), chap. 7; John N. King, "Patronage and Piety: The Influence of Catherine Parr," in Hannay, ed., *Silent but for the Word,* 48.

12. Erasmus, *Enchiridion Militis Christiani: An English Version,* ed. Anne M. O'Donnell, S.N.D., Early English Text Society. o. s., no. 282 (Oxford: Clarendon Press, 1981), 178–79. In quoting I have modernized *s* and *u/v* and expanded printers' contractions.

any public reference in England to a pope and when Fisher himself was shifting from acquiescence to resistance regarding Henry VIII's claimed headship of the English church.[13] When and how Parr became acquainted with Fisher's Good Friday sermon is unknown; its transmission and eventual printing are as uncertain as the year that he preached it. If, conjecturally, she heard it between 1531 and 1534 as the wife of John Neville, Lord Latimer, a ranking peer in Parliament, she, a Catholic at that time, would just have turned twenty years of age. It is easy to see why this Good Friday sermon attracted her attention and stayed in her memory, for it is a conceptually ingenious and spiritually stirring composition.[14]

At no juncture in Fisher's long preaching career (from about 1501 until its abrupt suspension when he was arraigned for treason in 1534) was it permissible to own or read an English Bible without authorization from one's bishop; such was the perceived strength of the menace that Lollardy still posed to Catholic orthodoxy.[15] In keeping with these historically specific constraints, Fisher maintains that the crucifix will serve to arouse a right response as well as the Scripture for Good Friday will. He will infuse the physical object with signification drawn from two verses of the Old Testament reading assigned for that day in the liturgy. The words will literally be read onto the object of devotion, thus merging the biblical text into the ceremonial action of the rite for Good Friday—the veneration of the crucifix standardly mounted on the grille or screen separating the church nave from the choir and its altar. So Fisher opens by signaling his interpretive intervention that will make a book of a crucifix:

13. Convocation first acceded to the royal supremacy in February 1531 after Fisher managed to lodge his famous qualification "as far as Christ's law allows" and the formal submission of the clergy to the king's headship took place in May 1532, presumably with Fisher's mounting discomfiture. When the Act of Supremacy began to be enforced by oath in the spring of 1534, Fisher explicitly refused to take the oath and was confined to the Tower of London in April. He was executed on June 22, 1535, with More following him to the block on July 6. See John Guy, *Tudor England* (Oxford: Oxford University Press, 1988), 128, 131, and 135, and Richard Rex, *The Theology of John Fisher* (Cambridge: Cambridge University Press, 1991), 9.

14. The *Short-Title Catalogue* lists one edition only (STC 10899) of *A spirituall consolation, written by John Fyssher to hys sister Elizabeth,* to which *A Sermon verie fruitfull, godly, and learned, . . . Preached upon a good Friday, by the same John Fisher* is appended in continuous pagination. The hypothetical ascription of printer and date [W. Carter, 1578?] is derived from A. F. Allison and D. M. Rogers, *The Contemporary Printed Literature of the English Counter-Reformation between 1558 and 1640: An Annotated Catalogue,* vol. 2, *Literature in English* (Aldershot, Hants., Eng.: Scolar Press, 1994), no. 273. This Good Friday sermon has attracted much less critical attention than others by Fisher—his defiance of Luther, his memorial sermon on Henry VII, and his series on the Penitential Psalms, for example. Rex, *Theology of John Fisher,* 217, notes the cursory discussions by J. W. Blench and Edward Surtz, S.J., but offers only a brief synopsis of his own (46–49). Arthur Kinney's admiration for Fisher's sermon is such that he supposes (personal communication) that it was delivered more than once. If so, the occasions on which it might have been heard multiply accordingly.

15. For an authoritative account of Lollardy, see Anne Hudson, *The Premature Reformation* (Oxford: Clarendon Press, 1988).

"The Prophet Ezechyell telleth that hee sawe a booke spread before him, the which was written both within and without. . . . This booke to our purpose may bee taken unto us, the Crucifixe, the which doubtlesse is a merveylouse booke, as wee shall shewe heereafter."[16] Fisher offers an object of devotion— "the image of the Crucifixe"—as a substitute equivalent to Scripture in evoking Christ's consummate love for humankind. "Who that will exercise this lesson, he shall . . . come to a great knowledge both of Christ & of him selfe. A man may easily say & thinke with him selfe (beholding in his hart the Image of the Crucifixe), who arte thou, and who am I" (*S*, 388).

This question, says Fisher, was posed by Saint Francis of Assisi, in whose exemplary spirituality "meditation and imagination" were "so earnest, and so continuall, that the token of the five woundes of Christ, were imprinted and ingraved in thys holy Sancytes bodye" (*S*, 391). Thus promoting the Franciscan spirituality that figures prominently in English religion during Henry's reign, Fisher admits that the devotions of ordinary Christians cannot "attayne" such "hygh fruite" as the stigmata. Yet ordinary Christians can take the crucifix, as a book for their instruction, to their hearts: "Thus who that list with a meeke harte, and a true fayth, to muse and to marvayle of this most wonderfull booke (I say of the Crucifixe) hee shall come to more fruitefull knowledge, then many other which dayly studie upon their common bookes. This booke may suffice for the studie of a true christian man, all the dayes of his life. In this boke he may finde all things that be necessarie to the health of his soule" (*S*, 390). At length, when closing his sermon, Fisher steers away from any possible construal of his book of the crucifix as a call for popular Scripture reading, instead renewing his exhortation to imitate Saint Francis's devotion to the crucifix as physical object: "Thus . . . it is an easie thyng for any man or woman to make these two questions wyth them selfe. O my Lorde that wouldest dye for me upon a Cross, how noble and excelent art thou? & agayne, how wretched and myserable am I?" (*S*, 391–92).

After I found the book of the crucifix metaphor in Fisher, my feminist scholar's hypothesis about its uniquely autobiographical expressiveness for Katherine Parr lay pretty much in ruins. She had not created her key metaphor. Fisher ostensibly had; he seems to imply this when he introduces it: "This booke *to our purpose may bee taken unto us*, the Crucifixe, the which doubtlesse is a merveylouse booke, as wee shall shewe heereafter" (emphasis added). But I had another problem, and that was the utter paucity of other autoreferential

16. John Fisher, *A Sermon verie fruitfull, godly, and learned, upon thys sentence of the Prophet Ezechiell, Lamentationes, Carmen, et vae, very aptly applyed unto the passion of Christ: Preached upon a good Friday,* in *The English Works of John Fisher,* part 1, ed. John E. B. Mayor, Early English Text Society, e. s. no. 27 (London: N. Trübner, 1876), 388. Subsequent references will be abbreviated *S* and incorporated parenthetically in my text. In quoting I have modernized *s* and *u/v* and expanded printers' contractions.

markings in Parr's text. Even if I shifted my interpretive focus away from the book of the crucifix metaphor—the site, for me, of paramount intensity and expressiveness—there was only one certain self-identification of the first-person speaker in the entire *Lamentation*. This was Parr's passing reference to "king Henry the eight, my most sovraigne favourable lord and husband" in the course of hailing him as a Moses who had brought God's English people out of bondage to the papal "Pharao," "Bishop of Rome" (*L*, sig. Dvir).[17] Confronting the hard textual facts, I considered whether I could salvage autobiographical significance for Parr's *Lamentation* by pursuing a generational difference even if I had to give up a gendered one. Could the oddity of the metaphor in question be usefully tracked to an origin in an early, transitional phase of modern print culture?

Fisher was born about 1469, six years before William Caxton set up the first English printing press in Westminster, making him Parr's senior by two generations (forty-four years). Perhaps Fisher could be situated as an exponent of the late medieval manuscript culture in which he came to adulthood and in which the Lollards' fervor for judging all things by God's book continued to be rigorously suppressed. Would a corresponding generational placement of Katherine Parr throw significant light on what she did with Fisher's metaphor? Certainly, the circumstances prompting Fisher's coinage had radically altered by the time Parr used it to figure her justification by faith. Fisher himself had been discredited as a spokesman for Catholic orthodoxy to the extent of suffering a traitor's death. What is more, vernacular Scripture reading was so far from being illegal by 1538–1540 that Henry VIII was mandating that the so-called Great Bible, whose publication he had authorized, be made available for public reading in the parish churches of the realm.

To work toward an interpretation in terms of a generational divide, I realized, would make the differences between Fisher's text and Parr's the most salient features of both. She did not significantly follow his precedent in elaborating the metaphor. There is conspicuous evidence that Fisher envisaged his book of the crucifix as an artifact dating from before the era of print. He exhibits a truly metaphysical ingenuity as he details why he calls the crucifix a book. A book has "boardes" (still a current term for "hard covers" among bibliographers), leaves, lines, writings, and "letters booth small and great." The two planks of Christ's cross are the "boardes" of the book of the crucifix, on which its leaves, "the armes, the handes, legges, and feete, with the other members of his most precious and blessed body," are spread. No "Parchement skynne" was

---

17. See, further, my remarks on how Parr "screens topicality, polemic, and personality from her text" and the muteness of her gender identification (explicit only in her name on the title page until her late reference to her royal husband) in Mueller, "A Tudor Queen Finds Voice," 41–42.

ever so stretched and hung up to dry in order to make a writing surface as Christ's body was stretched and laid out upon the cross. And on its spread skin the lines to be read are the marks of the whiplashes, the red letters his blood, the blue letters his bruises, the five capital letters the great wounds in his two hands, his two feet, and his side, "for bycause no parte of thys booke shoulde bee unwritten" (*S*, 393, 394, 395, 396). Fisher develops his extended conceit of the crucifix as an illuminated manuscript. He then proceeds to read this manneristically drawn image, so evocative of figure groupings in early sixteenth-century Netherlandish and Rhineland paintings of Christ's Crucifixion and deposition from the cross, as a "wryting" of "lamentation" (*S*, 397).

Parr inflects their shared theme of lamentation and their shared metaphor of the book of the crucifix in a systematically different fashion. While *The Lamentation of a Sinner* engages as lavishly as the Good Friday sermon does in a rhetoric of emotion—apostrophe, rhetorical questions, serial parallelisms, stark antitheses—her treatment of the Crucifixion never becomes graphic and pictorial like his; instead, it remains consistently theological and phenomeno-logical. Parr opens with *lamentation,* the key word of her title, and unfolds her concomitant shame, her confusion, her misery, perversity, and presumption as she develops her self-accusation of being altogether insensible of Christ as her crucified savior—being, that is, without the faith that justifies. "I did as much as was in me, to obfuscate and darken the great benefite of Christes passion: . . . And therfore I count my selfe one of the moste wicked and myserable sinners, bycause I have ben so much contrary to Christ my saviour. . . . What cause nowe have I to lament, mourne, sigh and wepe for my life, and time so evil spent?" (*L*, sigs. Avr-v, Aviiv).

Parr's turn from phenomenology to theology proceeds through reiterations of Tyndale's key term for Scripture, the *promises,* to explain "what maketh me so bolde, and hardy, to presume to come to the lord . . . who is only the Advocat, and mediatour betwene god and man to helpe and relyve me, . . . beyng so greate a Sinner"—"trulye nothinge, but hys owne woorde," "the promise of Christ." "He promiseth, and bindeth him selfe by hys worde, . . . to all them that aske hym with true fayth: . . . For fayth is the foundacion, and grounde . . . : and therfore I wil saye, Lord encreace my fayth" (*L*, sigs. Biir-v, Biiiv).[18] She

18. Compare William Tyndale in *The Parable of the Wicked Mammon* (1529): "See therefore thou have God's promises in thine heart. . . . The promises, when they are believed, are they that justify; for they bring the Spirit, which looseth the heart, . . . and certifieth us of the good-will of God unto usward. . . . Christ is our Redeemer, Saviour, peace, atonement, and satisfaction; and hath made amends or satisfaction to Godward for all the sin which they that repent (consenting to the law and believing the promises) do, have done, or shall do. . . . For in the faith which we have in Christ and in God's promises find we mercy, life, favour, and peace" (*Doctrinal Treatises and Introductions to Various Portions of the*

shifts to merge theology with phenomenology in giving this account of the advent of her justifying faith: "I never had this unspeakeable and most high charitie, and abundant love of god, printed and fixed in my heart dulye, tyll it pleased god of hys mere grace, mercy, and pitie, to open myne eyes, makyng me to see, and beholde with the eye of lively fayth, Christ crucified to be myne only saviour and redemer. For then I beganne (and not before) to perceyve and . . . knowe Christ my Saviour and redemer" (*L*, sig. Bvv). "Therfore inwardlye to behold Christ crucified upon the crosse, is the best and godliest meditacion that can be," Parr affirms, and precisely at this point she introduces her metaphor. "Therfore to learne to knowe truly . . . is to study in the booke of the crucifixe, by continuall conversacion in fayth: . . . this crucifix is the boke, wherin God hath . . . most compendiously written . . . all truth profitable and necessary for our salvacion" (*L*, sigs. Bviiiv, Ciir).

Viewed along a generational divide, it is Fisher who returns the book of the crucifix to earlier roots in Franciscan devotion, there seeking to renew the mystical rapture of the saint with his divinely conferred stigmata as a talisman against the continuing danger of Bible-reading by the laity.[19] It is Parr who brings the book of the crucifix into Protestant print culture, promoting Bible-reading by the laity through her equation of this metaphor with the promises of the Gospel, apprehended in Tyndalian fashion as the felt truth of one's personal salvation. With these findings, however, I found myself confronting another question. Could I sustain the premium on difference that resulted from emphasizing the generational factor yet claim to have fairly interpreted what, intertextually considered, is a relation of verbal identity—the same words, "book of the crucifix"? I had yet taken no critical notice of the measure of likeness between Fisher's and Parr's texts, so I began to examine how far this extended. Beyond the verbal identity of the key metaphor, I found that other likenesses were generated by a further intertextual relation: their shared recourse to Erasmian motifs and themes. This material promotes perceptions of continuity in Fisher's and Parr's religious experience by documenting, for each, a pair of connections with the two best-known works of Erasmus in England, the *Enchiridion Militis Christiani* and the *Paraclesis*.

In the *Enchiridion*—a book that Fisher as well as Parr is recorded as owning—Erasmus variously calls the saving act of divine love that is Christ's death upon

---

Holy Scriptures, ed. Henry Walter, Parker Society vol. 25 [Cambridge: Cambridge University Press, 1848], 48, 52, 47).

19. Both Fisher's reference to beholding the image of the crucifix in one's heart and Erasmus's notion of recording the mystery of the cross "in thy mind" (cited above) have affinities with the important devotional trope of "the book of the heart," the subject of a book-in-progress by Eric Jager.

the cross "philosophia Christi" and "a Christian man's book."[20] Fisher's Good Friday sermon echoes the one formulation, referring to the Crucifixion as "another higher Philosophie which is above nature," "the very Philosophie of Christian people" (S, 389). Parr echoes the alternative Erasmian formulation because she refuses to refer to Christian faith as philosophy, in keeping with its Protestant categorization as "carnall and humane reasons" (L, sig. Aviv). After invoking Saint Paul, who called Christ "the wisedome of god," she can join with Erasmus in identifying personal, experiential knowledge of "Christ crucified" with what is learned from study in "a christian mans boke"—the titular metaphor of the *Enchiridion Militis Christiani*—and then turn directly to identify this with "the booke of the crucifixe" (L, sig. Civ-Ciir).

The second instance where Erasmus serves as intertext is the notable passage in *Paraclesis* that exhorts vernacular reading of Scripture upon all ranks of society, high and low, men and women, not even excluding the plowboy in the field. Fisher, steering clear of Bible-reading, urges devotion to the crucifix as the truest employment of all Christians: "every person both ryche and poore," "the poor laborer . . . when he is at plough earyng his grounde, and when hee goeth to hys pastures to see hys Cattayle," "the rich man . . . in his business. . . . And the poore women also . . . when they be spinning. . . . The ryche weomen also in everie lawfull occupation that they have to doe" (S, 391–92).[21] For her part, when Parr climaxes her *Lamentation* with a comprehensive vision of "all sortes of people" who "loke to theyr owne vocacion, and ordeyne the same according to Christes doctrine" (L, sig. Giir-v)—citing preachers, laymen, fathers, mothers, children, servants, matrons, and young women—she echoes the same passage in *Paraclesis*. And since "Christes doctrine," the Bible, is the book supremely emphasized by Erasmus and Parr, it is they who draw closest in this second intertextual tie. Thus, despite marked local differences in their respective appropriations, an intertextual approach to interpretation

---

20. On the importance of the *Enchiridion* as the best single source for Erasmus's conception of the Christian life, see Preserved Smith, *Erasmus: A Study of His Life, Ideals, and Place in History* (New York: Harper and Brothers, 1923), 55, 58; John Joseph Mangan, *Life, Character, and Influence of Desiderius Erasmus of Rotterdam* (New York: Macmillan, 1927), 1:174; and Johan Huizinga, *Erasmus and the Age of Reformation*, trans. F. Hopman (New York: Scribners, 1924; Reprint, New York: Harper, 1957), 54. Rex, *Theology of John Fisher*, 47, records that Fisher owned a copy of the *Enchiridion*. For Parr, see n. 11.

21. I am not implying that Fisher was disingenuous here, for current political circumstances sufficed to deter him from any overt endorsement of Erasmus's scripturalist brief in *Paraclesis*. As Rex pertinently remarks, "Fisher seems to have accorded a higher place to scripture and the vernacular in the Christian religion than we have been accustomed to expect of the late medieval English hierarchy" (*Theology of John Fisher*, 48; cf. 158–60).

leaves Fisher and Parr looking significantly alike in aspiring toward a Christian universalism that Erasmus had conceptualized for them both.[22]

So much for what might be done respectively to interpret Fisher's and Parr's books of the crucifix by emphasizing a generational factor on the one hand and intertextual relations—a key metaphor compounded with Erasmian affinities—on the other. Clearly there is a complex weave of differences and similarities here. Is the one to count as more significant than the other? And, if so, on what grounds should the judgment be staked—on intrinsic grounds of content or on extrinsic evaluation of the methodology employed? For example, since intertextual relations are classed with the history of ideas, now much discredited for failure to reckon with concrete social realities, we are likely to prefer a generational factor that deals more frontally with them.[23] But this very mention of dealing with one's objects of interpretation raises yet a further question for me. Can I really claim that a two-generation gap in age and experience in Henrician England accounts accurately and adequately for the characterization I have just given of Fisher's and Parr's metaphors? This is what I need to claim if I am to assign this factor the role of a primary determinant in my interpretation. As I began by saying, it is reassuring to think that our current approaches to texts by way of race, class, or gender (I added generation) are anchored by the combined weight of materiality and ideology and are thereby well grounded. But what if our interpretations by way of any or all of these factors come up short, as I think this one of mine manifestly does?

I would want to claim that a more primary determinant of the difference between Fisher's and Parr's metaphors is the emergent (and here clearly detectable) difference between a Catholic and a Protestant. The cutting edge is provided by Parr's central insistence on justification by faith—a tenet that the Council of Trent, which began meeting in 1548 to codify Roman Catholic orthodoxy, found unassimilable from first to last.[24] Then add that the two are historical contemporaries who deal in older and newer ways with the book of the crucifix and the authority of Erasmus—this gives us the generational factor, but not as primary. Then add that the two are a man and a woman—this gives us

22. Any adequate assessment of the Erasmian likenesses-within-difference that link Fisher's and Parr's texts would, however, also need to reckon with appropriations of *Paraclesis* by Tyndale in his English translation of the work and by Thomas Cromwell and Thomas Cranmer in citing it to defend their vernacular scripturalist program. Parr is not likely to have been ignorant of any of these at the time she wrote her *Lamentation*.

23. For a probing discussion of problems of methodology and subject matter, see Dominick La Capra, *Rethinking Intellectual History: Texts, Contexts, Language* (Ithaca: Cornell University Press, 1983), chap. 1.

24. On the importance of justification by faith as a confessional difference as early as the 1540s, see William P. Haugaard, "Katherine Parr: The Religious Convictions of a Renaissance Queen," *Renaissance Quarterly* 22 (1969): 346–59.

the factor of gender compounded with the further difference between Fisher's celibate state and Parr's married one, but still without a discernible effect on their divergent handlings of the book of the crucifix metaphor. Then add that the two are a bishop and a queen, a cleric and a layperson respectively—this gives us two more rank or status factors that crisscross gender by assigning different values to Parr and Fisher, but still without discernible impact on the textual difference, the metaphor in question. Yet what of the difference that seems to me so determinative here, the difference between a Catholic and a Protestant? It is obvious that religion presently has no theoretical standing comparable to that of race, class, or gender as a primary determinant of interpretation. If religion goes anywhere in current categories, it (like intertextuality) is lumped with the history of ideas.[25] So where does my interpretation leave me if I aspire to make it in newer methodological terms? At the close of this essay I will return to the question of constituting religion as a fourth primary determinant.

Here, however, I want to reflect on how troubling the recognized primary determinant of gender, in particular, has become for me in the interpretation of religious texts by women authors, particularly. In my earlier article I took the line that Parr's *Lamentation* challenges and baffles the prediction of feminist methodology that the fact of a woman author will eventuate in significant, gender-specific textual markings. In fact, apart from an arguably feminine-sounding disclaimer that "I have certeynly no curious learning to defende . . . but a simple zele, and earnest love to the truth, inspired of god, who promiseth to powre his spirite upon al flesshe: which I have by the grace of god (whom I moste humblie honour) felt in my selfe to be true" and the aforementioned brief reference to Henry VIII as "my most sovraigne favourable lord and husband" (*L*, sigs. Bviir-v, Dviir), Parr's "I" renders her gender all but undetectable. At best, gender in the two texts in question is a matter of inference from authorial positioning: Fisher's enactment of the male-only office of preacher as he publicly instructs the people with the words of the prophet Ezekiel, Parr's private self-accounting with no overtones of a public context or a judgment on others. It is the unsparing honesty and lack of individuation in that self-accounting, moreover, for which William Cecil's prefatory letter to *The Lamentation* most highly praises Parr as author, noting that she asks and makes no allowances for her gender or her royal rank.[26]

---

25. For a sharply reasoned, historically acute argument that religion was the principal category in which sixteenth- and seventeenth-century authors "thought through" a whole range of vital concerns, see Debora K. Shuger's *Habits of Thought in the English Renaissance* (Berkeley and Los Angeles: University of California Press, 1990).

26. In Cecil's words, "This good lady thought no shame to detect her sinne, to obteyne remission: no vilenes, to become nothing, to be a membre of him, which is al thinges i[n] all: no folye to forget the

Instead, Parr deploys her *I*'s and *me*'s to construct what I have termed a generic and genderless Christian responding to the message of salvation through faith in Christ crucified. "Truly I have taken no lytle small thing upon me, firste to set furth my whole stubbernes, and contempt in wordes, the which is incomprehensible in thought (as it is in the Psalme) who understandeth hys faultes?" she exclaims, assimilating the pronoun "his" to her case (*L*, sig. Aiv). Again, she laments in a similar gender elision, "And I most presumptuously thinking nothing of Christ crucified, went about to set furth mine owne righteousnes, saying with the proude Pharisey. Good lord I thanke the, I am not like other men" (*L*, sig. Avir). Thus, as I formerly read Parr's conversion narrative, its first-person author compiles the traits of an Everyman-Everywoman, a generic Christian soul: blind ignorance, cold and dead knowledge, a stone-hard heart softening into penitential lament, a dejected conscience suddenly overcome and joyed by the gift of divine love and forgiveness.[27] I tied these generic traits in with the other considerable evidence in *The Lamentation* of the universalism—the attempt to reclaim the etymology and the lowercase *c* for "catholicism"—and the personalism that energized early Protestants in their convictions that all souls are equal before God and that every soul is individually accountable to God. Parr conceives and casts herself as a subject for discourse on the shared grounds of humanity confronting divinity. Such (as mine is), she implies, are all souls. Such (as mine is) is the human soul.

Since recent theoretical developments have split social positionality (masculine and feminine roles) off from biology (sexed bodies) in defining gender as a determinant for interpretation, I am compelled to question from a number of angles my earlier claim that the "I" characterized and voiced in Parr's *Lamentation* is a genderless, generic Christian soul. In the first place, on the theoretical front where I began, if gender positionality is split off from sexed bodies, does gender as a primary determinant retain any measure of

---

wisdome of the worlde, to lerne the Simplicitie of the gospel: at the last, no displeasauntnes to submyt her selfe to the scole of the Crosse, the learning of the crucifixe, the booke of our redempcion, the very obsolute library of goddes mercye and wisdome" (*L*, 8–9). As a further example of the difficulty of locating gender in Parr's *Lamentation*, it might seem that not merely inference but a full-blown argument from silence was required to explain the lack of circumstantial specificity in Parr's conversion narrative as a feminine tactic employed to minimize the presumptive scandal of a queen of England in overt self-abasement in print. But, in turn, how would such an argument comport with Cecil's praise of Parr's outspokenness about her spiritual state?

27. Barbara Kiefer Lewalski, *Protestant Poetics and the Seventeenth Century Religious Lyric* (Princeton: Princeton University Press, 1979), provides a pathbreaking account of the composite features of this Protestant subjectivity, substantially revising that of Louis L. Martz in *The Poetry of Meditation: A Study in English Religious Literature of the Seventeenth Century*, rev. ed. (New Haven: Yale University Press, 1962).

its theoretically desirable materiality or only its ideological charge?[28] And if only the latter, what are the implications for gender as an alleged primary determinant of experience and the language used to talk about experience? Does splitting gender from anatomy plunge us back into the regresses of verbal indeterminacy from which we have sought and thought to free ourselves?

If gender is to figure now as a relational position, moreover, who can dispute the old dictum that all souls are feminine—or shall we say feminized?—when they register a personal relation to God? (I will specify: the Judeo-Christian God.) Some of the superabundant evidence for this dictum is familiar and scriptural: the erotic love between Christ and his bride, the soul, in the traditional allegorization of the Song of Solomon; the prophet Hosea's figuration of the idolatry of his fellow Jews in the lineaments of his own adulterous wife. Where, I want to know, does the splitting of gender from biological sex leave us in interpreting devotional and mystical texts written in the first person—texts in which religious affect predominates—no matter who their authors? Are such texts to be treated as gendered feminine? As generically feminine? As confounding gender difference because this determinant operates meaningfully only in human social relations, not in relations between humans and the divine? Caroline Bynum, who has done more than anyone to advance thinking on these questions, shows their extreme intractability by gesturing in opposite directions on the same page. On the one hand she signals "the feminist insight that all human beings are 'gendered'—that is, that there is no such thing as generic *homo religiosus*"; on the other she proclaims: "Gender-related symbols, in their full complexity, may refer to gender in ways that affirm or reverse it, support or question it; or they may, in their basic meaning, have little at all to do with male or female roles. Thus our analysis admits that gender-related symbols are sometimes 'about' values other than gender."[29]

In my view, the trouble that I have faced in seeking to analyze and interpret such sites of primary significance as the book of the crucifix metaphor is likely to be alleviated only by making a case for religion—understood, in the present case of Fisher and Parr, in terms of Catholicism and Protestantism—as exercising a potentially determinative force in human life and its linguistic and social forms, just as race or ethnicity, class, and gender (and generation?) are already taken to do. If religion is accorded such equal status, it will emerge as a primary determinant in certain contexts, just as the others do. At present these

---

28. See, especially, Judith P. Butler's *Gender Trouble: Feminism and the Subversion of Identity* (New York: Routledge, 1990) and *Bodies That Matter: On the Discursive Limits of "Sex"* (New York: Routledge, 1993).

29. Caroline Walker Bynum, "Introduction: The Complexity of Symbols," in *Gender and Religion: On the Complexity of Symbols,* ed. Caroline Walker Bynum, Stevan Harrell, and Paula Richman (Boston: Beacon Press, 1986), 2.

primaries appear an ill-sorted lot, showing how rough and unready the state of theorizing about them is. Nonetheless, it seems clearly desirable to me that materiality be predicated as a feature of all of them and be explicitly specified for all of them—religion too, if it is to be accorded the status of a primary determinant.[30] It seems equally clear to me that much more explicit allowance for historical and situational variation must be made regarding the material component of each recognized primary determinant in interpretation. If this is done, then it may prove possible, for any given determinant, to correlate a decline in its material manifestation and perceptibility with a reduction in its capacity for determination. In the late twentieth century, blue-jeaned "everybodies" apparently bear witness to the waning power of class distinctions, while developing surgical and endocrinological procedures for transsexuality may weaken the power of gender as a primary sociobiological determinant. As for religion in our own Western culture and era, two among many indications of its potential to figure as a primary determinant include the strongly materialized practices that mark conflicting stands on the issue of legalized abortion and the distinctive clothing worn by such diverse groups as orthodox Jews, the Amish, and members of the Nation of Islam and other Muslims.

If allowance for historical and situational variation is extended to Tudor England, we find class as a factor of primary difference being read as materially encoded in sumptuary laws and a network of protocols of deference and precedence, not in bodily features as such. This is why pretenders such as Perkin Warbeck could be genuinely dangerous, if the pretenses materialized in their dress and bearing were convincing. Similarly, gender as a factor of primary difference in Tudor England was read as materially encoded in female bodies viewed as male ones fallen short of fulfillment.[31] This is why the accession of Elizabeth I to the throne of England, for example, required interpretation as a special providence of God, with divine right as merely a secondary consideration.[32] Religion might be argued to read as a factor of primary

30. Admittedly, Louis Althusser has provided for the determining force of ideas in the cultural-materialist process by offering a fundamental revision of the Marxian binary of "base" and "superstructure." His influential work on "ideological state apparatuses," a category that easily accommodates the political mandates of Reformation and Counter Reformation Christianity, permits cultural potency to be claimed for religion without invoking considerations of materiality. However, it seems obvious to me that race or ethnicity, class, gender, and generation have attained the status of primary determinants because, in large measure, they register perceptually as physical facts about human beings. I want to pursue the possibility that religion can be put on the same footing.

31. See Thomas Laqueur, *Making Sex: Body and Gender from the Greeks to Freud* (Cambridge: Harvard University Press, 1990), chap. 2.

32. See Constance Jordan, *Renaissance Feminism: Literary Texts and Political Models* (Ithaca: Cornell University Press, 1990), 131, 202.

difference in sixteenth-century England on analogous material grounds: its sharply rival sets of objectifications of the holy.

Positing religion as such a materialized factor would immediately pick out as significant the contrasting object referents for Fisher's and Parr's books of the crucifix—both as exemplifications of the phenomenon and as sites where the determinative strength of the factor of religion thus materialized can be weighed interpretively. More broadly, positing religion as a materialized factor might help to make legible and intelligible certain currently underattended-to aspects of massively deployed social energies in sixteenth- and earlier seventeenth-century England. Although iconoclasm has drawn appreciable scholarly attention, the long-sustained contestations over sacramental dogma and its attendant modalities of worship (themselves encoded in and as bodily practices) have not yet done so.[33] I am thinking not only of the centrality of John Foxe's *Acts and Monuments* to Reformation English culture but also of the voluminous book wars fought over transubstantiation by generation after generation: Thomas More vs. John Frith; Stephen Gardiner vs. Nicholas Ridley and Thomas Cranmer; and Thomas Harding vs. John Jewel, for example.

By the same token turned to its obverse face, can we then proceed, as I suggested above, to theorize that race or class or gender or generation or religion lose force as primary determinants in specific historical and situational contexts when and if they diminish (or lose) their material component? Clearly, there is more hard work to be done at a fundamental level before we can feel sanguine about making our criticism and historical work be about something that counts as real. Toward what I am inclined to regard as not just the desideratum but the necessity of theoretically constituting religion on a par with the triad of race, class, and gender as a material determinant of human experience and expression, however, the way at present looks long and hard—given the sweeping negativism of Freudian and post-Freudian, Marxian, and modern secular predispositions regarding religion for starters. But I am prepared to make such a start nevertheless.

33. This literature notably includes Margaret Aston, *England's Iconoclasts* (New York: Oxford University Press, 1988), John R. Phillips, *The Reformation of Images* (Berkeley and Los Angeles: University of California Press, 1973), and Eamon Duffy, *The Stripping of the Altars: Traditional Religion in England, ca. 1400–ca. 1580* (New Haven: Yale University Press, 1992), as well as work on literary implications, especially in Milton studies: see Lana Cable, *Carnal Rhetoric: Milton's Iconoclasm and the Poetics of Desire* (Durham: Duke University Press, 1995), Ernest B. Gilman, *Down Went Dagon: Iconoclasm and Poetry in the English Reformation* (Chicago: University of Chicago Press, 1986), and David Loewenstein, *Milton and the Drama of History: Historical Vision, Iconoclasm, and the Literary Imagination* (New York: Cambridge University Press, 1990).

Pamela Joseph Benson

TRANSLATING ITALIAN THOUGHT ABOUT WOMEN IN ELIZABETHAN ENGLAND

Harington's *Orlando Furioso*

The publication of Harington's translation of Ariosto's *Orlando Furioso* in 1591 was a major event in the importation of Italian culture into England in the sixteenth century. While Spenser's nearly contemporary *Faerie Queene* is ostentatiously English despite its deep engagement with Italian literature— one need think only of *Brit*omart and *Art*egall—Harington's volume looks and sounds Italian; a reader encountering it might well feel that he or she was being exposed to something foreign and other. "The pictures and typography are modelled on Italian originals," as Simon Cauchi has shown, and the names of characters and references to many contemporary Italians retain their Italian spellings. Yet, this Italian veneer covers many rewritings of the text of the poem that distance it from Italian culture. As Daniel Javitch recently argued in *Proclaiming a Classic,* Sir John Harington's *Orlando Furioso in English Heroical Verse* is an expression of late sixteenth-century English literary and social culture. Harington Englished the discourse as well as the words.[1]

Outstanding among rewritten topics is the debate about the nature of womankind, a topic that has a very important place in the Italian *Furioso.* Statistical tables compiled by B. E. Burton in an unpublished Oxford B.Litt. thesis about Harington's revisions of the *Furioso* reveal that among the most consistently truncated, rewritten, and omitted topics were the praise and blame of womankind and the praise of Ariosto's patrons and their circle, especially his praise of contemporary women.[2] Harington's special interest in the topic of womankind is confirmed by the frequency with which the notes he added

1. Simon Cauchi, "The 'Setting Foorth' of Harington's Ariosto," *Studies in Bibliography* 36 (1983): 138. Daniel Javitch, *Proclaiming a Classic: The Canonization of "Orlando Furioso"* (Princeton: Princeton University Press, 1991), chap. 8.

2. B. E. Burton, "Sir John Harington's Translation of Ariosto's 'Orlando Furioso,'" B.Litt., deposited March 5, 1954, Bodley ms. B.Litt.,d.323. Burton does not discuss the changes in the topic of womankind or patrons in detail but makes the general assertions that "compression [is] conditioned by two things . . .

at the end of each book annotate passages about woman and women; most of these are original notes rather than adaptations of notes that had already appeared in Italian editions. These annotations are so important a part of the presentation of Harington's volume that, when I speak of Harington's *Furioso*, I mean the translated poem and the annotations.

Harington's *Furioso* has always had the reputation of being antifeminist. Modern critics assume it is so because they rely on the work of Townsend Rich, the only recent critic to assess Harington's handling of this topic, who pronounced it so, and Harington himself reports the critical contemporary response, which he, with his sense of being the class clown, may have encouraged. It seems that Harington first translated one of the more risqué stories in the poem and circulated it at court; the queen, "finding it necessary to affect indignation at some indelicate passages, . . . forbad our Author the Court, till he had translated the whole work, which he soon accomplished, and dedicated to herself. . . ."[3]

Evidently his complete translation did not exonerate him, because in "An Apology" for the *Metamorphosis of Ajax*, Harington reported that it had been asserted that his *Furioso* "had wronged not only Ladies of the Court, but all womens sex." In his self-defense, he argued that: one, he had been ordered to make the translation by the queen herself; two, the offensive passages were literally translated and thus Ariosto was antifeminist and not he; and, three, "as for the verses before alledged, they were so flat against my conscience, that I inserted somewhat, more then once, to qualifie the rigour of those hard speeches."[4]

This self-defense is reasonably accurate (except the assertion that Ariosto was antifeminist). Overall, by rewriting, eliminating, and introducing new material into the poem, Harington did not eradicate the original poem's favorable attitude toward women. Rather, he redefined it, usually by making the terms of praise of women more English and domestic but at some points by taking a more radical stand on woman's social and political equality than did his Italian original. Throughout this essay, I call the advocacy of a more masculine social and political role for women "protofeminist," because it anticipates

---

national and personal predilections and prejudices," (27) and that Harington "fills in with moral observations or with something that he thinks relevant, making a scene English rather than Italian, and the observations on a situation those of a conventional man" (28).

3. Townsend Rich, *Harington and Ariosto: A Study in Elizabethan Verse Translation* (New Haven: Yale University Press, 1940), 108. *Nugae Antiquae*, ed. Henry Harington, 3 vols. (London: for J. Dodsley and T. Shrimpton, 1779), 1:iii.

4. Sir John Harington, "An Apology," in *A New Discourse of a Stale Subject, Called the Metamorphosis of Ajax*, ed. Elizabeth Story Donno (New York: Columbia University Press; London: Routledge and Kegan Paul, 1962), 255, 256.

modern feminism, whereas I call the benign appreciation of women's abilities "profeminist." When Harington's *Furioso* praises wives for their capacities as managers, encourages women's writing, and asserts the natural ability of women to govern, it is protofeminist; when it praises wives for their capacities as chaste, comforting companions, it is profeminist.

Like Harington's *Furioso*, Ariosto's first edition of the poem (which was published in 1516) was accused of antifeminism, but according to Alberto Lavezuola, the author of "L'Osservationi sopra tutto l'Ariosto" in the lavish 1584 issue of the poem by Francesco de Franceschi—the primary edition on which Harington based his edition—the final version of the text (which appeared in 1532) solved the problem: "The poet redeems whatever credit he had lost with women for prior offenses." Lavezuola succinctly states the essence of the 1532 *Orlando Furioso*'s protofeminism. He says the poem shows that "virtue has always been exhibited by women as by men. They have a rational soul, speech, wit, intelligence."[5]

In Ariosto's poem the positive representation of womankind's potential to be as virtuous as men is achieved by the representation of individual female characters, the praise of women spoken by the narrator and others, and the notion of woman worked out in the events of the poem. For example, the topic of womankind's capacity for fidelity is developed in a three-episode series: the stories of Ariodante and Ginevra, of Rodomonte at the inn (including the inset novella about Giocondo and the heroic death of Isabella), and of Rinaldo and the Cispadano host (cantos 4 and 5, 27 through 29, and 42 and 43, respectively). In these episodes pro- and antifeminist characters debate with each other, female characters are heroically faithful and excusably unfaithful, and male characters are disgracefully unfaithful. Women's capacity to perform effectively in territories traditionally delineated as male, such as writing, government, and arms, is celebrated in two encomiums spoken by the narrator (one of which is extremely long) and is demonstrated by the deeds of the lady knights Bradamante and Marfisa, especially their disestablishment of the patriarchy of Marganorre and their replacement of it by a matriarchy. The result of this sustained attention to the topic of the nature of womankind is a philosophically grounded assertion of the moral, intellectual, and physical equality of women to men.

Given to empirical rather than abstract thought, Harington ignored the overarching theoretical framework that supports the individual moments of praise of women in Ariosto's poem and reconstructed speeches and scenes with regard only for the immediate effect. As a result, although some of the episodes in Harington's *Furioso* represent and advocate a social role for women that goes beyond the Italian original, the poem as a whole does not present

5. *Orlando Furioso di M. Lodovico Ariosto . . .* (Venice: Franceschi, 1584), 31v.

a philosophical foundation for its protofeminist assertions. This omission, I suggest, accounts for their having been ignored by readers.

Clear examples of Harington's undermining of Ariosto's philosophical framework by the interjection of English ideas about women occur in the episode from which the accusers against whom he defends himself in "An Apology" drew their evidence. This is the middle episode in Ariosto's series of three on the topic of fidelity; in the Italian poem it demonstrates the inaccuracy of assuming that all women are worse than men and that all women are alike. In it, two characters—the violent pagan knight Rodomonte and an opportunistic innkeeper—assert the antifeminist cliché that a faithful woman is as rare as the phoenix. The innkeeper tells a story in which a handsome young man named Giocondo and a king travel the world and cannot discover a single chaste woman, but an old man who hears the story eloquently defends womankind. Soon afterward the Lady Isabella chooses death rather than violation by Rodomonte, and her deed converts the pagan to a celebrator of women and evokes extreme praise from the poem's narrator. The calmly rational arguments made by the wise old man, the heroic actions of Isabella, and, to a lesser extent, the narrator's praise of her overturn the irrational, emotional, and negative evidence offered by the antifeminist characters. The arguments offer reasons to assume that women are as capable of the virtue of fidelity as men, if not more so, and Isabella's heroic death offers proof. The focus throughout this episode and the entire series is exclusively on woman's capacity for virtue. It provides evidence for women's equality with (or even superiority to) men.

The lines Harington's accusers cite as evidence against him, which he rejects as "flat against his conscience," come at the conclusion of Rodomonte's antifeminist tirade. He says, in Harington's English, "Ungratefull, false, and craftie y'are, and crewell, / Borne of our burning hell to be the fewell" (27.98). As this is the speech of a character consumed by antifeminist rage, to judge Harington to be antifeminist because he has increased the force of a character's tirade is unreasonable, as Harington says.[6]

The rest of Harington's self-defense makes sense too. Both of the examples of the way he qualified "the rigour of those hard speeches" spoken by Rodomonte move the poem in a distinctly English profeminist direction. He first refers to his omission of antifeminist material spoken by the narrator.

> . . . against railing Rodomont, I said thus,
> I tremble to set downe in my poore verse,

6. All quotations from Harington's *Furioso* are taken from *Ludovico Ariosto's "Orlando Furioso" Translated into English Heroical Verse by Sir John Harington*, ed. Robert McNulty (Oxford: Oxford University Press, 1972). Further citations will be made parenthetically in the text.

> The blasphemies that he to speake presumes;
> And writing this, I do know this that I
> Oft in my hart, do give my pen the lye.[7]

The four lines beginning "I tremble to set down" replace three stanzas in the Italian poem, in which the narrator equivocates on the subject of women's virtue. Immediately after Rodomonte's speech, Ariosto's narrator speaks in his own voice, asserting that Rodomonte was exaggerating; there must be one hundred good women for every bad one, even though his own personal experience has thus far confirmed Rodomonte's assertion. Should he one day encounter a woman who will be faithful to him, he will celebrate her in his writings. The narrator's reference to his own bleak experience of women confirms Rodomonte's claims even while it appears to be denying them. In strong contrast to his original, Harington unambiguously distances himself from the attack; as a translator he really can sound sincere when he employs the trope that his heart denies his pen.

The second way that Harington qualifies "the rigour of those hard speeches" is by adding a stanza in praise of wives just before the innkeeper tells the story of Giocondo's fruitless search for a faithful woman, a search provoked by his discovery of his own wife in bed with a servant.

> in another place, to free me from all suspition of pretended malice, & to shew a manifest evidence of intended love, where my autor very sparingly had praised some wives, I added of mine owne . . . so much as more I thinke was never said for them, which I will here set downe as *perpetuam rei memoriam,* and that all posteritie may know how good a husband I would be thought.
>
> > Loe here a verse in laud of loving wives,
> > Extolling still, our happie maried state,
> > I say they are, the comforts of our lives,
> > Drawing a happie yoke, without debate:
> > A play-fellow, that far off all griefe drives,
> > A Steward, early that provides and late;
> > Faithfull, and kind, sober, and sweet, & trusty,
> > Nurse to weake age, & pleasure to the lusty.[8]

---

7. "An Apology," 256.

8. Ibid., 256–57. This is the text of the stanza as he wrote it in "An Apology." The lines in his *Furioso* translation read,

> Straight all of them made answere they had wives,
> And, but mine host, all praised the happie state
> And said they were the comforts of their lives
> That draw a happie yole without debate,
> A playfellow that farre of all griefe drives,

Harington says he built this stanza on some sparing praise of wives in Ariosto's *Furioso,* but, in fact, Ariosto's narrator had merely reported that several men at the inn believed that their wives were faithful. Harington's encomiastic stanza is created out of whole cloth; its equivalent does not exist in Ariosto's text.

Indeed, this stanza's attitude about women and the nature of men's relationships with them is alien to Ariosto's poem. There, the debate about woman's capacity for fidelity is part of a comprehensive examination of woman's ethical capacity; the proof that she is at least as capable of constancy as man demonstrates that she is a participant in the same ethical system as man and should be judged and awarded privileges as man is; the final logical result of this proof is that woman is capable of virtuous public, political life. Although the context in which woman's fidelity is discussed in Ariosto's poem often is marriage, the practical qualities that make Harington's good wife—the ability to nurse her husband and to give him sexual pleasure—are beside the point. Harington, by speaking of why men should value their wives, violates the terms of the discourse that Ariosto established; he directs our attention away from the topic of the moral capacity of womankind. His inserted stanza effectively discredits some antifeminist claims, but it does not show that it is wrong on the particular issue that is the topic of debate—woman's capacity to be faithful and, thus, to adhere to the cardinal virtues.[9]

In shifting the focus of the discussion in the direction of the benefits of marriage, Harington reoriented the *Furioso* toward the issues that had been prominent in native English defenses of womankind since the mid-sixteenth century, texts such as *Mulierum Pean,* by Edward Gosynhill; *The Defence of Women,* by Edward More; *The Praise of Women,* by C. Pyrrye; and *Jane Anger Her Protection for Women,* which were published in 1542, 1560, 1569, and 1589, respectively. These works defended women against the charge that they were avaricious, shrewish, lascivious, and foolish and proposed instead that women were capable of being chaste, obedient, good wives; they offered sentimental images of women displaying traditional feminine virtues rather than offering a reasoned philosophical defense. For example, *Her Protection,* close in date to the English *Furioso,* praises women in terms similar to Harington's in order to remove the sting from the phrase *mulier est hominis confusio:*

> A steward early that provides and late,
> Both faithfull, chast and sober, mild and trustie,
> Nurse to weake age and pleasure to the lustie.
> (XXVII.108)

9. For a discussion of the representation of women in Ariosto's *Orlando Furioso* and of Italian and English texts in praise and defense of woman, see Pamela Joseph Benson, *The Invention of the Renaissance Woman* (University Park, Pa.: Pennsylvania State University Press, 1992).

We are the griefe of man, in that wee take all the griefe from man: we languish when they laugh; we lie sighing when they sit singing, and sit sobbing when they lie slugging and sleeping. *Mulier est hominis confusio,* because her kinde heart cannot so sharply reproove their franticke fits, as those madde frensies deserve.[10]

All these texts resemble Harington's in their offer of the good wife rather than the equal woman as the ideal figure opposed to the antifeminist model. The same ideal woman was extensively developed in English books containing marital advice. In *A Preparative to Marriage,* the locus classicus for the trope of chaste, silent, obedient, and patient wife published in the same year as Harington's *Furioso* (that is, 1591), Henry Smith, the Puritan divine, asks, "Who shall beare others burden if the Wife doo not beare her Husbands burden?" With the aim of instructing his listeners in how to achieve a happy marriage, Smith gives five rules for choosing a good wife and instructions on the wife's duties; both the rules and the instructions are based on assessing her ability to be good and to make a comfortable home.[11] Of course, it is not surprising to find this domestically formulated ideal in a sermon on marriage—a woman's capacity for generosity and kindness might indeed be crucial to the success of a marriage—but Harington's introduction of it into the *Furioso* disrupts the original poem's philosophical defense of womankind. The Italian humanist topic—the capacity of women for virtue—is replaced by a familiar English topic: the nature of a good wife.

Ariosto devoted the last of the three episodes in his series to the topic of marriage; this episode includes the story of the visit that Rinaldo pays to the Cispadano host, the story about his failed marriage that the host tells to Rinaldo, and the subsequent story of marital infidelities that his boatman tells. Even here, when the characters' conversation is about marriage, the practical virtues that make domestic life pleasing are not the topic, but, rather, faith and fidelity are, and the two-story sequence is part of the overall protofeminist case, even though it offers evidence that even the best woman can be tempted into adultery.

The protofeminist heart of this sequence lies in the moral character of the host's wife, which had been highly developed by her education. The host relates that her skill in traditional feminine domestic arts was matched by her scholarly knowledge; she had been given a humanist education by her father, and so, as Harington says, "in . . . scyences her skill was such / As was her fathers or almost as much" (43.18.7–8). Her great learning went hand in hand with a commitment to the traditional feminine virtue of chastity; she had firmly

---

10. *Jane Anger Her Protection for Women* (London: R. Jones and T. Orwin, 1589), sig. B3r.

11. Henry Smith, *A Preparative to Marriage* (Amsterdam and Norwood, N.J.: Walter J. Johnson, 1975), 35–43, 74–87.

rejected the advances of their attractive young neighbor. Not satisfied with this proof of her faith, the host explains, he used magic to disguise himself, successfully overcame her virtue by offering her magically enhanced jewels, and then revealed his identity. His outraged wife left him, and his success brought him nothing but misery. He now devotes himself to offering his male guests the opportunity to assess magically their own wives' infidelity, and every man who has accepted his offer has found his wife to be untrue. Although the conclusion "la donna è mobile" is inevitable, the test reveals as much about the fallibility of male nature as woman's. The husband is guilty of corrupting a woman as beautiful and perfect as the limits of human nature permit.

Harington translates most of this long episode closely, but he makes an omission that weakens the passage's humanist protofeminist side, and he adds a note that patronizingly excuses women by blaming men and that offers a sentimental solution to what is ultimately an insoluble problem of human nature in Ariosto's text. One of the main methods that the host's wife's father used to instill the proper values in her was to decorate their home with works of art depicting exemplary women, especially heroically chaste women. Harington reports that the father used educational artwork, but he omits the only detailed description Ariosto gives of one of these works, a huge octagonal fountain, and this omission removes evidence for the excellence of modern women from the poem because the fountain is a future-forecasting, protofeminist fountain. Each of its eight corners is supported by a pillar made up of two statues of men supporting a statue of a woman; although the episode takes place in the distant past, these men and women are Ariosto's contemporaries, and their presence predicts the virtue of women in his day and the appreciation they will find among male authors, like Ariosto, whose wife is included among the statues, anomalously supported by only one poet, Ariosto himself, of course.

Harington's omission of this description conforms to a plan he announced in his preface: he explained that he had omitted "either . . . matters impertinent to us or . . . some to tediouse flatteries of persons that we never heard of."[12] The description of the fountain fits both categories: it celebrates the nature of Italian womanhood of about three-quarters of a century before the publication of the English *Furioso* and so might be seen to be out of date and, in any case, "impertinent" to English people, and some of the women it praises were unknown to Harington's readership. Yet, by omitting these descriptions, Harington seriously unbalances the episode's representation of women because he omits thirteen stanzas of unmitigated praise of real women, praise for their virtue, beauty, and intelligence. In his version of the story, the lady stands alone as an inspiring example of the potential of womankind for virtue; her fall seems

12. *Furioso*, 15.

a definitive statement about the inevitability of women's failure, given the right circumstances, whereas in Ariosto's version, the modern-day women, all of whom are described as chaste, create the impression that most women with a good upbringing will be moral. Harington's omission of the statues removes the immediate, positive connection with the present; the counterbalance to the negative events is lost.

In the moral that he appends to this episode, Harington attributes a very antifeminist intention to the story and then suggests the wrongness of the story's conclusions about women, as though Ariosto's method of telling the story did not already offer a reading against the apparent grain. He makes Ariosto appear to be antifeminist and himself a defender of women. Harington calls it "simply the worst against women in all the booke, or rather indeed that ever was written,"

> if you marke the secret drift of it, shewing how a woman of so excellent
> education, so great learning, so rare beautie, so fine wit, so choise
> quallities, so sweete behaviour, so aboundant welth, so dearely beloved by
> her husband, could so easily be conquerd with the sight of three or foure
> jewels, and then for his comfort, how . . . all his married guests . . . spilt
> the drinke in their bosomes. This tale (admitting it to be true or probable)
> would argue women to be of exceeding covetousnes, but loe how easily
> all this is not onely to be excused for them but retorted upon men, for
> assuredly it is onely the covetousnes of men that maketh women (as we
> interpret it) to sell their chastities, for women indeed care for nothing
> but to be loved, and where they assure them selves they are loved, there of
> their kind and sweet dispositions they bestow love againe.[13]

Finally, Harington says, women yield to monetary persuasion because they know that men must really be serious when they offer things of value, since men hate to part with money. This moral does not assert women's ethical capacity and confirm the value of a humanist education for women, as the stanzas Harington omitted did. Like the earlier passage on wives, this one asserts that women's dispositions are naturally "kind and sweet." Once again, the abstract ethical problem of faith has been reduced to an immediate practical problem and the intellectual replaced by the emotional.

Harington's move away from Ariosto's theoretical defense of the ethical capacity of women is reinforced by many of the annotations that bring up Harington's sentimental view of marriage even when the passage being annotated has nothing to do with marriage. Such notes guide the English reader to thinking about the episodes to which they are appended in a way no Italian reader was guided. For example, the notes to book 11 use the occasion of

---

13. Ibid., 513–14.

Angelica's dressing in the clothes of a peasant woman (she is naked and must wear something) to praise "great Ladies" for wearing simple clothes and to quote a stanza from the "first Arcadia" left out of the printed book in which Sidney gives advice on how "to make a good and vertuous wife."[14] This stanza advises men to be faithful and to be evenhanded in their governance of their wives and in the distribution of goods to them. In sum, often where Ariosto's narrator speaks in the voice of an Italian humanist defender of women and says women are capable of the cardinal virtues, Harington's narrator speaks in the voice of an English defender of women and praises traditional female virtues—sober conduct and dress, fidelity, chastity, and good mothering skills—and his notes praise marriage. The Italian ideal is not obliterated, but it is made less distinct and forceful.

Despite his fogging of the philosophical notion of woman's capacity for the cardinal virtues that is contained in the parts of the poem having to do with fidelity, Harington's translation of the parts of the poem devoted to the deeds of lady knights and to praise of them is usually fairly faithful and gives a positive impression of women's military capacities just as the Italian poem does. For example, Bradamante's eloquent assertion that her spectacular performance as a knight gives her the right to be judged in competition with men despite her anatomy (at the Castle of Tristan [32.94–100]) is one of Ariosto's most protofeminist moments, and Harington's version of it is accurate. In one major case, however, canto 37 in its entirety, Harington's version of the text and his annotations to it remove ambiguities and qualifications present in the Italian poem. This particular passage, read in isolation from the rest of the poem, is more protofeminist than the Italian original.

Ariosto's canto 37 is the primary locus of his connection of women's intellectual capacity with a political role. It begins with a twenty-four-stanza proem in praise of women and then tells the story of the overthrow of Marganorre, an antifeminist tyrant, and the subsequent establishment of a matriarchy. Ariosto added this canto to the poem in the 1532 edition, and the proem was a major cause of Lavezuola's labeling of the new version of the poem as favorable toward women, although the representation of the matriarchy in the body of the canto does not put rule by women in a completely positive light. Harington retained Ariosto's praise of women's accomplishments in the proem but transformed Ariosto's ambiguous episode into an explicit defense of the natural ability of women to govern and the desirability of government by women.

Ariosto's encomiastic proem includes praise of women's heroic deeds and of the profeminism of male writers in the court circle in which the poet moved; Castiglione and Bembo are among those praised. Women's writing is praised,

14. Ibid., 130–31.

especially its ability to give fame to the authors themselves and to their subjects. Six of the stanzas are devoted to celebration of the poet Vittoria Colonna for making her husband immortal in her verse, and the narrator explicitly states that, nowadays, since there are such skilled writers of their own sex, women no longer need to rely on men (like Ariosto himself) to celebrate them but can immortalize women's virtues in their own verse, thus creating women's history written by women.

Harington kept the praise of women's deeds and the first reference to their ability to confer fame on others and themselves in their writing and eliminated the praise of specific male authors; he retained the praise of Vittoria Colonna but omitted the final reference to women's capacity to write themselves into history. His is nearly as forceful an encomium of modern women as Ariosto's, and his notes to the proem extend Ariosto's thought by providing examples of English women writers. If one is awarding praise for the writing of epitaphs for deceased spouses, Harington notes:

> that honorable Ladie (widow of the late Lord *John Russell*) deserveth no lesse commendation, having done as much for two husbands. And wheras my author maketh so great boast onely of one learned woman in Italie, I may compare (besides one above all comparison that I noted in the XX booke) three or foure in England out of one famelie, and namelie the sisters of that learned Ladie, as witnes the verse written by the meanest of the foure to the Ladie Burly, which I doubt if Cambridge or Oxford can mend.[15]

Harington's reference to the daughters of Sir Anthony Cooke in this note puts English culture into competition with Italian and stimulates English pride in the accomplishments of English women. Although Ariosto's original passage more frequently urges women to write about other women, Harington's translation reproduces Ariosto's essential points—women can and should write, and they can achieve fame for themselves and others by doing so—and his note suggests that there are English women capable of doing the job.

Harington's lines on this topic are more radical in their English context than Ariosto's were in their Italian one. Praise of women's writing of all kinds was a commonplace in Italian defenses of womankind from Boccaccio's *De Mulieribus claris* onward, whereas, much as women's learning was praised in Elizabethan England, their writing was a troubled topic, as both Margaret Hannay's *Silent but for the Word* and Elaine Beilin's *Redeeming Eve* show.[16]

---

15. Ibid., 434.

16. Margaret Patterson Hannay, *Silent but for the Word: Tudor Women as Patrons, Translators, and Writers of Religious Works* (Kent: Kent State University Press, 1985); Elaine V. Beilin, *Redeeming Eve: Women Writers of the English Renaissance* (Princeton: Princeton University Press, 1987).

Spurred on by a patriotic desire to show England's superiority to Italy, as he says, Harington ventured into the surprising new territory of encouraging English women to follow the model offered by their fellows, the Cooke sisters, and write themselves into history.

Harington's narration of the reform of the tyrant Marganorre's woman-hating patriarchy into a matriarchy is equally radical, indeed, even more radical because it goes beyond Ariosto's. According to both Ariosto's and Harington's versions, the victorious lady knight Marfisa forced all the men of the town to take an oath "That women should have rule, such powre, such graces / As men are wont to have in other places" (37.97.7–8). Ariosto's narration of the first acts of this new woman-governed state makes it seem that the new state will be as cruelly antimasculine as the previous state had been antifeminine. The tyrant is given over to the women for punishment, and their vengeance is represented as very nasty but also cruelly comic—an old woman drives the naked and handcuffed former tyrant with a cattle prod until he drips with blood, but she cannot continue hurting him because she is out of breath. Finally, the leader of the women, Ullania, who had suffered humiliation at Marganorre's hands, forces the tyrant to jump from a tower, "So that he could never get free and bother young women again . . . ; he had never jumped so far before in his life" (37.121.3–6; my translation). The cruel vengefulness of the women suggests the disadvantages of any government that gives one sex absolute authority over the other.

Harington's version of the conclusion of this episode is not comic; it repre-sents the establishment of a matriarchy as a positive achievement. Harington's main technique for turning the comic into the serious is to cut out the represen-tation of women's vengeful cruelty; he omits the old lady and her cattle prod. This omission also makes the matriarchy seem more rational and judicious, as does his attribution of the decision to force Marganorre to commit suicide to "judges" rather than to a single woman with a strong motive for revenge.

> [He] was at last by his sharpe judges driven
> To leape down headlong from a mightie towre
> Where all his bones and flesh were broke and riven.
> (37.102.4–6)

This is the description of an execution, an act of justice by a state, rather than the vengeance of women protecting their kind. As a result of Harington's rewriting, the scene now demonstrates the efficacy of female government.

Harington's note to the episode makes clear the seriousness with which he took the public aspect of the matriarchy and reveals the source of his radical ideas. He states that

> in the law made for women we may see that that sex is capable of rule and
> government and not to be excluded from the highest degree thereof (as a
> noble learned and learned noble man hath most amplie and excellentlie
> proved in a discourse of his which I happened by fortune to light upon
> though as yet, I thinke, imparted to few.)[17]

The implications of the assertion that women are "capable of rule" are
enormous because the statement justifies rule by any intelligent and skillful
woman who achieves power legitimately. This claim differentiates Harington's
position on rule by women from most of the politically motivated defenses of
Queen Elizabeth written throughout her reign; these followed the lead of John
Aylmer's 1559 *An Harborowe for faithfull and trewe Subjectes* and distinguished
her from other women by arguing that she had been raised to authority by
God and thus, legal as her government was and as excellent an example of
womanhood she was, she set no precedents for other women; Elizabeth I's
own Tilbury speech is in this tradition.[18] Spenser adopted this latter strategy of
praise in his *Faerie Queene;* it obviously flatters the queen doubly, by seeing the
hand of God in her accession and by praising her accomplishments, whereas
the strategy Harington adopts here praises the queen only as a realization of
virtues potentially available to all women.

A printed marginal gloss identifies "Lord Henrie Howard" as the noble
learned man who wrote this unusual discourse, and so the text referred to
must be *A dutiful defense of the lawful regiment of women* (published sometime
around 1571–1584), which Catholic Howard wrote at the request of Lord
Burghley but never published.[19] Howard bases his lengthy assertion of the
natural capacity and right of women to rule in part on extensive proof of
women's capacity for the cardinal virtues, as Ariosto did. From Howard's
arguments one could conclude that the inferior status of women in society
was wrong and that women could emulate Elizabeth and play a role in politics,
just as they could emulate the Cooke sisters and write. Harington's reference to
Howard's text shows that he understood its essential argument; he says quite
clearly that "that sex is capable of rule."

This single canto is a set piece in both the Italian and the English poems.
Because the encomiastic proem and the story of Marganorre were added as a
unit to the third edition of the original poem, the story is not interwoven with
others as most stories in the *Furioso* are, and, more than any other part of the

17. *Furioso*, 433.
18. George Whetstone in *The English Myrror* (1586) argues for women's natural capacity to rule,
but the text is not dedicated to the queen or one of her ministers.
19. Copies of Howard's Defense are in the collections of the Pepys Library, Magdalen College,
Cambridge: ms. Pepys 2191; the Bodleian Library, Oxford: ms. Bodl. 903; and the British Library,
London: ms. Add. 24,652.

poem, this canto has the capacity to stand on its own. By means of the changes that he made in the tone and content of the conclusion to the episode, this note asserting woman's natural capacity and right to rule, and the praise of women's writing and the note praising the Cooke sisters, Harington made this major part of the *Orlando Furioso* express a practical, political protofeminism that was entirely absent from the Italian poem and that was quite unusual in its English context.

It was also unusual in its Haringtonian *Furioso* context. Not only did Haring-ton dismantle the Italian philosophical framework that—by asserting women's equal capacity for fidelity and, thus, for the cardinal virtues—might have provided a foundation for this protofeminist assertion that they are naturally capable of public, political action, but in his version of the other major en-comium of women in the poem (20.1–3), he also weakened the link between great women of the past and the women of the present and in his notes praised the queen conventionally as an exception to her sex. Harington translated the account of ancient women's accomplishments with "sword" and "pen" faithfully, but he added a new line and a half in which he defines the virtues of women of his own day: "The young so sober, and the rest so sage / And all so chast . . ." (20.3.3–4). By using the vocabulary that he uses elsewhere in the poem to describe the ideal wife and that his contemporaries also used to define the ideal domestic woman, Harington suggests that modern women win praise by meeting the domestic ideal rather than by using their pens, let alone swords. Insofar as women contemporary with Harington are concerned, this English version of the encomium is profeminist in the tradition of English defenses of women. The expansive feeling of newly reopened opportunities for women that is present in Ariosto's encomium is absent from Harington's.

In his annotations, Harington praises one single modern woman for her use of sword and pen: Elizabeth I, of course. He amplifies the list of ancient examples and then adds:

> But for a perfite patterne of excellency in both kinds, both in governing
> the common welth most wisely, peaceably, and prosperously, and skill
> in all kind of learning and languages, Greeke, Latine, French, Italian,
> and Spanish, I may say it truely and without flatterie that our gracious
> soveraigne is to be preferred before any of them, yea before all of them,
> and therfore may justly be called the jewell or rather the wonder of all
> her sex.[20]

While calling Elizabeth "the wonder of all her sex" is such a cliché that Harington may not have thought about the connotations of the phrase, the implication

20. *Furioso*, 230.

that Elizabeth is unnaturally gifted and inimitable because she is essentially different from other women is present. Paired with the domestic praise given to modern women in the text, this note reinforces the impression of a double standard, one for ancient women and the queen, who are admirable for their accomplishments in traditionally male fields, and one for all other women, who are admirable for their accomplishments in traditionally female virtues.

Another example of Harington's treatment of Elizabeth as an exception occurs in the notes to the story of Giocondo, book 28, the story told by the innkeeper in an attempt to win the favor of the antifeminist pagan Rodomonte. This is the part of the *Furioso* that Harington first translated, the part that got him into trouble, and the note may be a response to the queen's complaints, as the story graphically describes a queen's commission of adultery with a dwarf and then goes on to prove that all women are naturally disposed to infidelity. As we have seen, Harington's stated strategy in this section of the poem was to qualify "the rigour of those hard speeches" against women by adding praise of women's nurturing virtues. Although this praise disrupts the consistency of Ariosto's philosophical proof of women's equal capacity for the cardinal virtues, it does create a positive impression of women.

Harington's note about the queen in this story undercuts his efforts to defend women because, like his praise of her in the note to the encomium in book 20, it praises her at the expense of other women. He says, "in the Queen of Lombardie that bestowed her love so basely we may see that no state nor degree is privileged from shame and slander except vertue and grace from above do keepe them from such enormous offences."[21] Although this episode does not seem to have immediate political relevance, the phrase "vertue and grace from above" is typical of the conventional political defense of the queen as specially privileged.[22] It represents her as favored by God and exempts her from the expectations one has of all other women. It in no way argues that Elizabeth's behavior provides a basis for rethinking our opinion of the social controls or the role established for ordinary women, and so it reinforces the story's representation of women as inclined to lasciviousness. The note accepts the antifeminist "truth" of the story despite the fact that in general Harington denies that the attitudes expressed by the antifeminist characters in this scene should be accepted. Defense of the queen takes precedence over defense of womankind and muddies Harington's position.

Finally, this lack of clarity is characteristic of the overall representation of womankind in Harington's *Orlando Furioso*. Unlike Ariosto's original, Harington's poem does not make a careful argument about women; the text is generally

21. Ibid., 324.
22. See John Aylmer, *An Harborowe for faithfull and trewe Subjectes* (Strasbourg [actually London: J. Day], 1559), sig. B3r, for example.

profeminist, but it is inconsistent in the variety of profeminism espoused. At times, it encourages women to compete on the international scene in learned writing and, even, in governing countries, but at others it directs them away from the quest for fame and self-reliance and encourages them to be ambitious only to be good wives. A reader of Harington's *Furioso* who was unacquainted with the original might be excused for not recognizing the poem as one of the major defenses of Italian humanist ideas about women because in this English version these ideas do not achieve dominance.

Indeed, as an accurate transmitter of Italian culture about women, Harington's *Furioso* is seriously flawed, but then, Harington never says that his goal is to transmit Italian culture in its pure state, if that ever might be possible. His title page suggests that he is more the author of the book in hand than Ariosto. It reads *"Orlando Furioso in English Heroical Verse* by John Harington," and his portrait along with the portrait of his dog dominate almost the entire lower third of the page, while Ariosto's portrait is given only the center of the top quarter. Harington's preface invites his reader, "being studious of the Italian," to compare the two texts but then asserts that because the poem is a fiction rather than a historical record, he is free from the obligation to translate literally: "I would not have any man except that I should observe his phrase so strictly as an interpreter nor the matter so carefully as if it had bene a storie in which to varie were as great a sinne as it were simplicitie in this to go word for word."[23] Harington's theory of translation enables him to create, even demands that he create, a version of the *Furioso* that translates Italian ideas into English ones as it translates the Italian words so that the poem may be understood by and pleasing to English readers. Judged by the standards he set, Harington's translation of the topic of the nature of womankind and her social role in the *Furioso* is a great success. The reader's inability to distinguish Italian humanist ideas does not indicate Harington's failure but rather his success.

But this success is due not only to the skill with which Harington renders Italian matter into English matter and Italian phrases into English ones. The success of *Orlando Furioso in English Heroical Verse* as an English text is attributable in large part to the notes to the text. As we have seen, Harington does not silently "translate" Italian culture into English culture; he calls attention to his infidelity to his original, to his changes and amplifications, in the notes. The reader is frequently invited to compare Harington's views with Ariosto's, English ideas and customs with Italian ones, and the result of this comparison is always favorable to England. Harington's frequent distancing of himself from the antifeminist sentiments expressed in the poem makes many of the bad things the poem says about women seem to be attributable to Ariosto and the Italians rather than to Harington and the English, who appreciate women as lovable

---

23. *Furioso,* 15.

companions. Thus, the reader of Harington's poem would be more likely to form the impression that Italian attitudes about women were more backward than English attitudes than to be impressed by the Italians' new thinking on the topic. Yet, at the same time he makes the poem's antifeminism seem to be Italian, Harington manages to evoke Italian women's reputation as advanced, put English women into competition with them, and make the English look still more advanced. Harington may not have set his goal as being to "overgo" the Italian *Furioso,* but thanks to his efforts at representing them, English culture overgoes Italian, English women overgo Italians, and Harington's *Furioso* is an important English profeminist, even protofeminist, document.

Gareth Roberts

Women and Magic in English Renaissance Love Poetry

That collection of essays "conceived in the turmoil of the early seventies" and edited by Renate Bridenthal and Claudia Koonz, *Becoming Visible: Women in European Society,* has a suggestive juxtaposition of two pieces. One is Joan Kelly's classic and still initiatory "Did Women Have a Renaissance?" which was preceded in the 1977 edition by the other, William Monter's "The Pedestal and the Stake: Courtly Love and Witchcraft." Kelly argues that the Renaissance regulated female sexuality and affectivity more than did the Middle Ages and that a manifestation (and also a means) of this regulation were Renaissance love codes that subordinated women, partly through the deployment by men and by male writers of ideals of female chastity. Monter's essay joins in its title two discourses in which women are antithetically stereotyped, although Monter is reluctant to connect these discourses; indeed, at one point he denies a connection.[1] But in some Renaissance fictions chaste and courtly ladies have alter egos who are witches. Spenser's witch Duessa masquerades in book 1 of the *Faerie Queene* as a noble, chaste romance heroine, and in Marston's play *Sophonisba* the witch Erichtho takes on the shape of the aristocratic Roman virgin Sophonisba to sleep with Syphax.[2] Clearly, both

---

1. *Becoming Visible: Women in European History,* ed. Renate Bridenthal and Claudia Koonz (Boston: Houghton Mifflin, 1977), 128. In this edition the two essays are 137–64 and 119–36. In the 2nd edition (1987) Kelly's essay remains (175–201), but Monter contributed the succeeding essay "Protestant Wives, Catholic Saints, and the Devil's Handmaid: Women in the Age of Reformations," 203–19. Monter was reacting against Jeffrey Burton Russell, *Witchcraft in the Middle Ages* (Ithaca and London: Cornell University Press, 1972), 279–84, especially 284, although he admits that "both courtly love and witchcraft were created by medieval European patriarchy" ("Pedestal," 135). For the continuing influence and stimulus of *Becoming Visible* see, for example, James Grantham Turner, ed., *Sexuality and Gender in Early Modern Europe: Institutions, Texts, Images* (Cambridge: Cambridge University Press, 1993), 1, and Jonathan Goldberg, ed., *Queering the Renaissance* (Durham and London: Duke University Press, 1994), 1.

2. For the beautiful woman with the alter ego of the hag see also Chaucer, "Wife of Bath's Tale," *The Works of Geoffrey Chaucer,* ed F. N. Robinson, 2nd ed. (London: Oxford University Press, 1966), 84–88.

witchcraft and courtly love are predominantly male constructions that imagine women in binary-opposite roles and social positions. The mistresses of courtly love codes have all the things that witches traditionally lack: the former are young, beautiful, aristocratic, chaste, and desirable; the latter are old, ugly, poor, sexually indiscriminate, and threatening. The early modern period was conscious of the stereotype of the old and ugly witch: "Whoever heard of a young witch before?" as one of the supposedly possessed Throckmorton children commented in surprise. Witches were expected to be "outwardly deformed, as these kind of creatures usually are." Reginald Scot's picture is the English locus classicus: "One sort of such as are said to bee witches, are women which be commonly old, lame, bleare-eied, pale, fowle, and full of wrinkles; poore, sullen, superstitious, and papists; or such as knowe no religion."[3] Shakespeare's arch patriarch, Prospero, constructs the two women who lived on his island in precisely these ways: the foul and uneducated witch Sycorax (old, ugly, dark, sexually contaminated, and unruly) and her binary opposite, his humanistically educated daughter, the Renaissance princess Miranda (young, beautiful, desirable, white, virginal, and generally obedient). The poet's lady and the witch mark extreme and opposite ends of a spectrum. Both witch and chaste mistress are figures constructed in discourses where male authors write, disfigure, and misrepresent women in their own interests: in pastoral manuals, demonological treatises, transcriptions of witchcraft interrogations and trials; and in love poetry, erotic persuasions, and courtesy books. And just as witches, at least in European juridical and demonological texts, are often represented as eroticized and highly sexual in their desires and practices, so, conversely, Renaissance love poets can manifest a wish to interrogate and regulate their desirable mistresses' sometimes alarmingly demonic behavior, actions, and effects. What, then, can be said about those moments in English Renaissance love poetry when the erotic negotiations between male poets and their potential or actual mistresses traffic in the language of magic and witchcraft?[4]

The connection is also made by John Gower who mentions in the section on wantonness in *Mirrour de l'Omme* the woman who in old age becomes love's sorceress and compels hearts to love by magic, since now she cannot do this any other way: John Gower, *The Complete Works*, ed. G. C. Macauly, 4 vols. (Oxford: Clarendon Press, 1899–1902), 1:110.9493–504.

3. *The most strange and admirable discoverie of the three Witches of Warboys* (London: J. Windet and others for T. Man and J. Winnington, 1593), reprinted in Barbara Rosen, *Witchcraft in England 1558–1618* (Amherst: University of Massachusetts Press, 1991), 287; see also *The French Intelligencer* April 6–13, 1652, cited in Robert Higgins, "Popular beliefs about witches: the evidence from East London, 1645–1660," *East London Record* 4 (1981): 36; Scot, *The Discoverie of witchcraft*, ed. Brinsley Nicholson, (London: Elliot Stock, 1886; reprinted, East Ardsley, Wakefield: E. P. Publishing, 1973), 1:ii, 5.

4. On love and magic generally, see Ioan P. Couliano, *Eros and Magic in the Renaissance*, trans. Margaret Cook (Chicago and London: University of Chicago Press, 1987); G. L. Kittredge, *Witchcraft in Old and New England* (Cambridge: Harvard University Press, 1929), 104–23; Keith Thomas, *Religion and*

First, a curious inequality becomes apparent. A Renaissance male poet in passion, despair, frustration, or disappointment may turn on his lady, pronouncing her effect on him, her behavior, or even her lack of responsiveness as the malevolent actions of a demon or the harmful *maleficia* of a witch. Yet, in the poet's own love persuasion, his attempt to "charm" a woman, he may explicitly figure himself as a magician whose love poem is a spell, a *carmen*, an amatory conjuration. Sidney knew of the "very vain and godless superstition" that spirits might be commanded by verses "whereupon this word charms, derived of *carmina*, cometh," and, in anticipation of Brabantio's fears, Egeus voices his anxieties about the bewitching power of *carmina*, the "rhymes" and "verses" of love poetry sung by male suitors:

> And, my gracious Duke,
> This hath bewitch'd the bosom of my child.
> Thou, thou, Lysander, thou hast given her rhymes,
> And interchang'd love-tokens with my child:
> Thou hast by moonlight at her window sung
> With faining voice verses of feigning love.[5]

Self-fashionings of love poets as magicians seem remarkably untroubled, given that orthodox opinion in the Renaissance saw all varieties of magic as suspicious or even diabolic, and the Henrican, Elizabethan, and Jacobean witchcraft statutes all enacted penalties against attempts "to provoke any person to unlawful love."[6]

In the first case, when the disappointed poet combines the erotics of love poetry with the discourses of magic and demonology, the mistress and her sins of commission or omission may be literally demonized by the combination. This may occur where love codes are most formal, in the sonnet sequences. In the *psychomachia* of Shakespeare's sonnet 144, the poet finds himself between

---

the Decline of Magic (London: Weidenfeld and Nicolson, 1971), 35, 226, 233–34, 245, 253–54, 442–43, 634–35, 660; John Winkler, *The Constraints of Desire* (New York and London: Routledge, 1990), 71–98. There is a growing amount of work on women and witchcraft. For a good summary and bibliography, see Merry E. Wiesner, *Women and Gender in Early Modern Europe* (Cambridge: Cambridge University Press, 1993), 218–38.

5. Sidney, *An Apology for Poetry*, ed. Geoffrey Shepherd (Manchester: Manchester University Press, 1973), 98; Shakespeare, *A Midsummer Night's Dream*, ed. Harold F. Brooks (London and New York: Methuen 1979), 1.1.26–31. The Latin *carmen* includes the senses of ritual utterance, spell, incantation, song, and poetry (especially lyric poetry) in a way no English word does. In his early work Ovid plays with the multiple meanings of *carmina*, see *Amores* 2.1.23–28. For Saint Augustine's use of *carmina* to designate "incantations," see Sister Mary Keenan, "The Terminology of Witchcraft in the Works of Augustine," *Classical Philology* 35 (1940): 296.

6. This formula is in all three statutes: 33 Hen VIII c. 8 (1542), 5 Eliz c. 16 (1563) and 1 Jas c. 12 (1604), which are all conveniently reproduced in C. L'Estrange Ewen, *Witch Hunting and Witch Trials* (London: Kegan Paul, 1929), 13–21.

the (temporarily) angelic youth and the tempting, corrupting "worser spirit," his mistress, whose vagina is hell-mouth. In the fifth song of Sidney's *Astrophil and Stella,* an enraged Astrophil calls Stella thief, murderess, tyrant, rebel, witch, and finally devil (73–84). As a witch Stella transforms and destroys the poet's body, passions, and mind; as devil she tempts and plagues. In Drayton's *Idea* sonnet 20 ("An evill spirit your beautie haunts Me still"), the poet is a demoniac possessed with the demon of the mistress's beauty, who manifests the classic symptoms recorded in the Gospels and in numerous cases of possession in the early modern period.[7]

One could diagnose these momentary revelations of the sonnet lady as a witch or a demon simply as a symptom of the sonneteer's conventional habit of Petrarchan paradox in attitude and expression: "You witch, you Divill, (alas) you still of me beloved" cries Astrophil (song 5, 87) and "this good wicked Spirit, sweet Angell Devil" are the concluding oxymora in the Drayton sonnet (*Idea,* 20.14). But this diagnosis is merely descriptive. These demonizations of the mistress are the inverse of attempts to idealize her as transcendentally pure, beautiful, and virtuous. Strenuous and only partially successful idealization pays the price of an equally violent demonization at those moments when the poet finds his idealization becomes unsustainable, and "the most extravagant praise of women, the most glowing idealization, must be understood in the context of . . . outbursts of fear and disgust."[8]

Early modern judicial accusations and visual representations of women as witches have been seen as related to attempts to regulate their sexuality, particularly when the accusations, the "confessions" of witches and representations of them, have a sexual content. The eruptions of the mistress as demonic in the economies of the sonnet sequences of Shakespeare, Sidney, and Drayton are

---

7. On the language of sonnet 144, see Shakespeare, *The Sonnets and A Lover's Complaint,* ed. John Kerrigan (Harmondsworth: Penguin, 1986), 59–60 and 375–76. The authors of the *Malleus Maleficarum* declare at the end of a catalog of the ills that are caused by women: "We conclude: all these things come from carnal desire which is insatiable in them [ie women]. Proverbs [30.15–16]: There are three insatiable things etc., and a fourth which never says 'Enough', that is, the mouth of the womb," Heinrich Kramer and Jakob Sprenger, *Malleus Maleficarum* (Frankfurt, 1580) *pars* 1 *quaestio* 6, 95. Both the translation of these verses in Proverbs and their use here in the *Malleus* are disputable. *Janua diaboli* was a patristic epithet for woman, Jeffrey Burton Russell, *Witchcraft in the Middle Ages,* 283. See also Page du Bois, " 'The Devil's Gateway': Women's Bodies and the Earthly Paradise," *Women's Studies* 7 (1980): 43–58. *Astrophil and Stella* in *The Poems of Sir Philip Sidney,* ed. W. A. Ringler Jr. (Oxford: Clarendon Press, 1962), 212–15; Compare Astrophil's experiences in lines 75–78 with Thomas Simpson's, who "had no power to leave her [Philippa Flower], and was, as he supposed, marvellously altered both in mind and body since her acquainted company," *The wonderful discoverie of the witchcrafts of Margaret and Phillipa Flower* (London: G. Eld for J. Barnes, 1619), reprinted in Rosen, *Witchcraft in England 1558–1618,* 371. *Idea* sonnet 20 in Michael Drayton, *The Works of Michael Drayton,* ed. J. William Hebel, Kathleen Tillotson, Bernard Newdigate, (Oxford: Shakespeare Head Press, 1931–1941), 2:320.

8. Du Bois, " 'The Devil's Gateway,' " 47.

both a symptom of and a renewed attempt at an unsuccessful strategy devoted entirely to regulating the mistress's sexuality, which is always problematic in these sequences. Representing women as desirable and chaste, and at other times as demonic, are related attempts to regulate them, and the first mode of representation is linked to its binary opposite in the second.[9] Certainly, such binary oppositions are discernible in the good-angel, bad-angel morality play of Shakespeare's sonnet 144; and *Idea* 20 may be balanced against *Idea* 35, "To Miracle," where again the lady works supernatural effects, but this time they are the miracles recounted in the Gospels, including the *casting out* of devils. This analysis would forge the link between idealized love codes and witchcraft that Monter refused to make. One might take the analogue between early modern judicial accusations and representations of women as witches and the place of these demonizations of women within the sonnet sequences' economy one step further. In *Astrophil and Stella* and in Shakespeare's sonnets, desire for the mistress, at its most problematic in these demonizations of her, conflicts with and is called into question by networks of male relationships and values: friendship, love, patronage, begetting of male children, duties of and to fathers, and service to the state.

However, when the male poet represents *himself* magically in love poetry, it is in the action of conjuring or charming women or indeed love itself and using the possibly more licit techniques of high magic. The theory and practices of high magic, intending the working of wonderful effects especially by compelling the assistance of spirits, can be seen in numerous early modern manuscript conjuring-books and the books of occult philosophy real and apocryphal of Agrippa of Nettesheim and Peter of Abano. These authors relied on knowledge, the authority of the operator, the power of words, and magically consecrated instruments. In the conjurations of high magic, as in the Roman Catholic ritual of exorcism with which they had affinities, spirits were adjured by names of God (often Latin, Greek, or Hebrew), the authority of the persons of the Trinity, and events in sacred history; "I conjure thee . . . by . . ." is the typical formula.

In the context of such magical practices one may find addresses to women that elide any secure distinction between "magic" and "poetry" in the form of *carmina* that aspire to cause love by the power of words and the magical efficacy of analogy. For example, in the British Library's Sloane ms. 3846, embedded

9. See Lyndal Roper, *Oedipus and the Devil: Witchcraft, Sexuality and Religion in Early Modern Europe* (London and New York: Routledge, 1994), passim; Charles Zika, "Fears of Flying: Representations of Witchcraft and Sexuality in Early Sixteenth-century Germany," *Australian Journal of Art* 7 (1989–1990): 19–40. For two quite different views of construction by related antitheses, see Sandra M. Gilbert and Susan Gubar, *The Madwoman in the Attic: The Woman Writer and the Nineteenth-century Imagination* (New Haven and London: Yale University Press, 1979), 3–44; and Stuart Clark's seminal "Inversion, Misrule and the Meaning of Witchcraft," *Past and Present* 87 (1980): 98–127.

in a context of magical practices, conjurations, instructions, and recipes, is a charm (written out as prose) that tries magically to bind the affections of a woman with the initials E. B.:

> Our lady loved her dearest soon,
> I love ye E———— B————.
> so well might shee love mee,
> as Jesus did that died on the tree.
> all such paines may shee smarte,
> that may dull her harte,
> joy may shee never have none,
> till all my will that shee have done,
> by the vertue of Jesus Christ,
> by his death and his uprise,
> neither eate nor drinke, nor sleepe
> nor to her selfe take any keepe,
> but burne in love for my sake
> & never other rest take,
> till shee incline & do my will.
> & thereto binde her heaven and hell.
>
> (f. 71)

Here is an instance where love magic has taken the form of rhymed verse, although it is in fact lineated as prose in the manuscript. Any attempt to declare this text "poetry" or "magic" would be redundant as it exists in an area where the overlap of certain sorts of magical, affective, and aesthetic effect might be registered by such ambivalent adjectives as "enchanting," "charming," even "bewitching." As magic these lines display many typical features of love conjuration, such as what we may find to be the indecorous invocation of instances of divine love, and indeed Christ's Passion, as magical analogues for an attempt to arouse desire. In one amatory conjuration, "For the accomplishment of the pleasure of the flesh," the spirits are adjured, among other religious allusions, "by the virginity and fruitfulnes of blessed Mary the mother of God" (B. L. Sloane ms. 3851, f. 58^v). It was a principle and practice of magical invocation to cite powerful religious analogy and therefore precedent for the accomplishment of the magician's operation. As (pseudo-)Cornelius Agrippa remarked on the rehearsal of scriptural or liturgical precedents in magic, "There is in the prayer a holiness *[sanctimonia]* not only in itself, but by the recalling of sacred things, such as holy scripture, history, works, miracles, effects, graces, promises, sacraments, sacramentals and the like." In the charm in B. L. Sloane ms. 3851, Mary's love for her son and her son's for mankind are enforcing magical precedent for E. B. to love the magician. But then many instances of medieval and Renaissance love poetry are similarly prone to confusions of sacred love and secular passion. The meter that identifies this passage as "poetry" is also often found in charms in early modern Britain.[10] As poetry this spell also incorporates clichéd symptoms of love from so many hundred years of Western European love poetry: pain, suffering, sleeplessness, burning in love, and loss of appetite. In just this way Herrick adjures Electra by a catalog of natural phenomena, silent nights, Hecate, time, and finally by Electra's own name, the best conjuration of all. A lute song by Robert Jones conjures the lady by her creator's piety, her mother, nurse, love, heavens, day, and night; and Drayton conjures Cupid by a catalog of classical allusions, to make Idea love him.[11]

Metaphorically, these poems reveal attempts to fashion and regulate their mistresses in paradoxical ways, for they simultaneously endow their mistresses with chastity *and* use their poetic magic to try and overcome it. There may well be analogous and paradoxical complicities between sexual desire and sacred purity in both love poetry and love magic: both ostensibly value purity, yet both rehearse it in their discourses to overcome the mistress's virtue, as can be seen in adjurations citing sacred precedents in attempts to compel love that are cited in this essay. High magic's insistence for successful operation on the purity of objects (virgin parchment, virgin wax, consecrated and suffumigated instruments) seems particularly strong in the practices of love magic, and there seems some evidence that the host, the most sacredly immaculate of Christian sacraments, was particularly employed in love charms.[12]

When the male love poet presents himself as a magician, women are either spirits to be controlled by him or women to be coerced into love by his magical operations. What is at stake in all the examples so far, of poetic combinations of love and magic, is power. When the male poet is magician, women may be represented fairly neutrally as the poetic *objects* (potential mistress or conjured spirit) of male amatory magic; in other poems women are allowed supernatural power and active roles only at the price of demonization as witch, devil, or possessing or obsessing demon. Women are troublesome and suspicious as

10. Pseudo-Agrippa, *Liber quartus* in *Henrici Cornelii Agrippae ab Nettesheym, De Occulta Philosophia Libri III. Quibus accesserunt Spurius Agrippae Liber de Ceremoniis Magicis. Heptameron Petri de Albano . . .* (Paris, 1567), 539. See Thomas Potts, *The Wonderfull Discoverie of Witches in the Countie of Lancaster* (London: W. Stansby for J. Barnes, 1613), sigs. K1ᵛ–K2, and the diagnostic prayers of Agnes Sampson, one of the North Berwick witches, Scottish Record Office JC 2/2 ff. 203–203ᵛ, 205.

11. Robert Herrick, "A Conjuration, to Electra," *The Poetical Works of Robert Herrick,* ed. L. C. Martin (Oxford: Clarendon Press, 1956), 257–58; Robert Jones, "To thee, deaf asp," in *The muses gardin for delights* (London: W. Stansby by the assignes of W. Barley, 1610), song xviii; "Cupid conjured," *Idea* 36, Drayton, *Works,* 2:328.

12. Thomas, *Religion and the Decline of Magic,* 35; Paulus Grillandus, *Tractatus Duo: Unus de Sortilegiis* (Frankfurt, 1592), *quaestio* 3, *numeri* 15–18, 26–30; Ruth Martin, *Witchcraft and the Inquisition in Venice 1550–1650* (Oxford: Basil Blackwell, 1989), 131–32, 162, 177–78.

either the agents *or* the objects of amatory magic. As a rider to this, to figure women as magical operators is a way of controlling women, but to figure men as magical operators is also a means of controlling women. In Renaissance love poetry generally, the discourses of magic and demonology subjugate women but empower men.

Further, one subspecies of the poem magically attempting to charm the mistress allows us to see, in its imitation of a classical model, a male poetic appropriation of a previously female magical voice and power and hence a disempowerment of the female. Some male *carmina* are modeled on the classical *pharmaceutria,* Theocritus, *Idylls* 2, and its Latin imitation, the latter part of Virgil, *Eclogues* 8. Two close imitations are Thomas Campion's lute song "Thrice Toss These Oaken Ashes" and a sestina by Barnabe Barnes, the last poem in *Parthenophil and Parthenophe.* In Campion's poem the mistress's silence is more powerful than the poet's song, and his "charmes" are broken by the art of the mistress's eyes. But Barnes's magical song achieves the sexual success never obtained in the classical models and rarely in English *carmina,* for the poem's last two lines are "For as she once with rage my bodie kindled, / So in hers am I buried this night." It is the kind of love conjuration to be found in Renaissance manuscripts that adjures spirits to bring the desired object physically to the magician: "yea, convay hir hether to me; truly cause hir to enter into this Chamber. . . ." In an eroticized demonological tableau, which is a striking "modern" addition to magical details culled from Theocritus and Virgil, Parthenophe is transported to the poet naked and on the back of a goat, just as witches traveled to the sabbat in continental accounts and engravings.[13]

In these two English imitations the poet has reversed the gender power relations of his classical models. A male poetic voice appropriates the female magical operations represented in the Greek and Latin originals. In Theocritus and Virgil the magical song is a woman's attempt to charm a man. This is clearly the case in Theocritus, and although Alphesiboeus's song is not gendered and he might be imagined as singing it in his own person, the imagined situation seems to be that he is singing a song in which a woman laments her love for Daphnis. Theocritus also originally and vividly imagined a particularly female subjectivity for the unhappy Simaetha, "a wretched woman, no wife but no longer a virgin" (2.41), constituted by her women friends, maid, and allusions to female enchantresses. In the English imitations, the male love poet has fashioned himself as magically and poetically powerful and authoritative

---

13. *The third and fourth booke of ayres,* III.xviii, in *The Works of Thomas Campion,* ed. Walter R. Davis (London: Faber and Faber, 1969), 154; Barnabe Barnes, *Parthenophil and Parthenophe,* ed. Victor A. Doyno (Carbondale and Edwardsville: Southern Illinois University Press, 1971), 127–30. B. L. Sloane ms. 3851, f. 58ᵛ; illustrations in Zika, "Fears of flying," 23, 26, 28, 33.

by appropriating the originally female voice of poems that in themselves are powerful authorities for the Renaissance because of their classical antiquity.[14] The English poetic voice becomes the imperative voice of the male practitioner of high magic, but the authority of that voice is constituted partly by the impressive panoply of magical techniques of the classical *pharmaceutria*, which were originally the property of women and deployed by them on men, but in Campion and Barnes are now turned on the mistress as a means of control.

It might be argued that these English poems, imitations of classical models now speaking with the voices of male magicians, simply mirror social reality in early modern England, as love magic and the making of love charms and aphrodisiacs were standard items in the repertoire of male and female cunning folk. Cases and accusations indicate that both men and women practiced amatory magic.[15] But the content and tone of these English poems is significantly gendered. They speak authoritatively because of the "science" (in its older senses) and magical technology they have acquired from their classical models, and they speak with a voice in the imperative mode typical of the early modern male conjuror and ceremonial magician. If this is so, are there ways in which we might actually think of the practices in love magic and these poems as gendered?

One feature characterizing the male practice of love magic, and perhaps all high magic, is the act of magical inscription to cause love in a woman, as Spenser so accurately notes when Britomart discovers Busirane, "Figuring straunge characters of his art, / With living blood he those characters wrate" (3.12.31.2–3). In instructions for love magic in manuscripts we find images of the magician and the desired object inscribed in the hour and day of Venus on virgin parchment in blood from the magician's left hand with the words "Sathan Lucifer Donskton" between them. We find magical words written on apples, a practice also in classical antiquity, in one case with bat's blood and given to the woman to eat, with an explicit acknowledgment of the magical typology of the temptation of Adam and Eve: "Lucifer, Sathanus, Rusal. And say. Conjuro to pomom [*sic*] per omnes damones qui tentaverint [*sic*] Adam et Evam in Paradiso ut quecunque mulier de te gustaverit in amore meo ardeat" ("I conjure you, apple, by all the demons who tempted Adam and Eve in Paradise,

<hr>

14. This is especially the case when the poet imitated is not only Dante's *altissimo poeta* but was also considered an expert in magic. Manuscript instructions for amatory magic claim to be "Taken out of virgill," B. L. Sloane ms. 3851, f. 59ᵛ. Abraham Fleming's translation of the *Eclogues* 8 implies that the knowledge of magic there is really that of the authoritative male poet Virgil and that he was pretending "as if himselfe had been utterly ignorant of such practises": *The Bucoliks of Publius Virgilius Maro* (London: T. Orwin for T. Woodcocke, 1589), 22.

15. Thomas, *Religion and the Decline of Magic*, 233–34; Kittredge, *Witchcraft in Old and New England*, 104–23.

so that whatever woman tastes you will burn with love for me" (f. 140ᵛ). A male magician is instructed to write magical letters and characters on his left hand with which he then touches the beloved on the breast before dawn.[16] The writing of love poems that aspire to cause an effect on the desired object reproduce acts of magical inscription in "real" magic.

There are also analogies between the operation of certain kinds of magic and the very activity of representing. To represent is potentially and sometimes actually, in the case of some magical operations using drawings or images, a magical act. To represent, one might say, can be to practice magic. In one male poet's famous definition of poetry ("Poesy therefore is an art of imitation, . . . that is to say, a representing, counterfeiting, or figuring forth— to speak metaphorically, a speaking picture"), among the many senses that both "figuring" and "picture" could have in the English Renaissance were magical ones. Britomart discovers Busirane "Figuring straunge characters of his art" (3.12.31.2), Donne in "The Bracelet" finds the coins in the bracelet now "Like many-angled figures in the booke / Of some greate Conjurer" (34–35), and in Donne's "Witchcraft by a Picture" the "picture" is a wax image used in magic.[17]

One way of thinking about magic is as a system of representations. Magical operation may be thought of as the application of the same system of likenesses that underlies metaphor: the significant substitution of one thing for another. This is most obvious in the techniques of image magic to cause harm—or love. The magical assumption about the representation in wax or on parchment and the person it represents, that they are the same although we know they are different, is the same as that underlying metaphor.[18]

But male representation and amatory magic do not go entirely uncontested by their female objects, who sometimes resist it or struggle against it. Campion's Virgilian charms are unsuccessful: "In vaine are all the charmes I can devise: / She hath an Arte to breake them with her eyes" (11–12). In a poem in *England's Helicon* (1600), "Hearbs, words and stones," the magical substances

16. B. L. Sloane ms. 3851, ff. 59–60; B. O. Foster, "Notes on the Symbolism of the Apple in Classical Antiquity," *Harvard Studies in Classical Philology* 10 (1899): 39–55; B. L. Sloane ms. 3851, ff. 140–141ᵛ. For magical writing to obtain love, on apples, bread, and the magician's hand, see B. L. Sloane ms. 3846, f. 15.

17. Spenser, *The Faerie Queene*, ed. Thomas P. Roche Jr. (Harmondsworth: Penguin, 1978); *John Donne: The Elegies and the Songs and Sonnets*, ed. Helen Gardner (Oxford: Clarendon Press, 1965). For Augustine *figurationes* were magically "significant drawings made according to the pattern of certain constellations": Keenan, "Terminology of Witchcraft," 296.

18. On magic and representations, see Marcel Mauss, *A General Theory of Magic*, trans. Robert Brain (London and Boston: Routledge and Kegan Paul, 1972), especially 60–90; and also the chapter on "Sympathetic Magic" in Sir James George Frazer, *The Golden Bough*, abridged ed. (London: Macmillan, 1957), 14–63. There are some suggestive ideas about magic and "making" in Mircea Eliade, *The Forge and the Crucible*, trans. Stephen Corrin, 2nd ed. (Chicago and London: University of Chicago Press 1978), 75, 88, 97–108, 170.

and techniques of the poem's title fail to move the lady's mind or win her maidenhead. With "a woman's reason" the lady argues against or mocks the magical attempts.

Donne's "Witchcraft by a Picture" is a complex and revealing depiction of a struggle for dominance between male and female amatory magic. In the light of my earlier discussion of some sonnets, it may be significant that this poem, with its new twist on a lover's bewitchment through the eyes, is in two stanzas that are each seven lines long, adding up to the fourteen lines of the sonnet. Donne's choice of magical procedures is interesting. Since female witches were often accused of attempting to harm or destroy through image magic, "witchcraft by a picture" might be thought of as a female art, as the first stanza implicitly assumes. However, magical operation by "images" was also a practice of high magic. Therefore, the struggle between the poet and the witch mistress in the Donne poem is initially enacted through the conceit of a kind of magic practiced by both female witches and male magicians. The poet has turned the "picture"[19]—the representation, usually made of wax—of the object of magic, especially of love magic, into two reflections of himself: one in the mistress's eye and the other in a tear on her cheek. He destroys these images, which might give the witch mistress power over him, by drinking the tear and leaving the room. The one image now left is in her heart where it is free from her malice. At the end of the poem the poet has triumphantly turned the tables in effecting a magical operation of his own that appropriates another kind of magic usually represented as female: fascination. "Fascination is a binding which having entered through the eyes of the fascinated from the spirit of the fascinator arrives at the heart." The poem too has enacted its magic for "amorous words have the power of bewitching," and in retrospect we realize that in the poem's very first line, "I fixe mine eye on thine," the poet himself effected a *fascinatio* whereby his image was impressed on the woman's eye and thence passed to her heart.[20] As in the imitations of Virgil and Theocritus, the male poet appropriates women's magic and uses it against women.

19. On images see Cornelius Agrippa, *De Occulta Philosophia* (Cologne, 1533), II xxxv–l, 178–94, especially "De imaginibus Veneris," II xlii, 185; Frances Yates, *Giordano Bruno and the Hermetic Tradition* (London: Routledge and Kegan Paul, 1964) and D. P. Walker, *Spiritual and Demonic Magic from Ficino to Campanella* (London: Warburg Institute, 1958), both passim. See "Picture" *OED sb.* 2d; compare with the "dyvers Images and pictures" of the Henrican witchcraft statute, Ewen, *Witch Hunting and Witch Trials*, 13.

20. Agrippa, *De Occulta Philosophia*, I l, 59. The nouns and pronouns in the seventeenth-century English translation reveal assumptions about gender roles in fascination: "Fascination is a binding, which comes from the spirit of the Witch, through the eyes of him that is bewitched, entering to his heart," *Three Books of Occult Philosophy* (London: R. W. for G. Moule, 1651), I l, 101. The *OED* records the earliest use of this word's primary meaning in 1605 in Bacon's *Advancement of Learning*: "Fascination is the power and act of Imagination intensive upon other bodies." On fascination and love, see Leonardo Vairo, *De Fascino Libri Tres* (Venice, 1589), especially 37–42 and his remark *"Verba amatoria fascini*

The power of the woman's eyes is, of course, a commonplace of Renaissance love poetry. Campion explicitly acknowledges its magic—"In vaine are all the charmes I can devise: / She hath an Arte to breake them with her eyes" (11–12)—and Donne does so implicitly, by appropriating it for himself. Its elision with *fascinatio* in some love poems and Donne's determined appropriation of it may reveal anxiety about this power that male love poets allow to women's eyes and cause us to reassess that uneasy but commonplace use of the verb *bewitch* (for the modern reader *only* a metaphor) when its subject is the mistress's eyes or her beauty.[21]

These contests make yet clearer a distinction between male and female magical power in relation to love. If the male poet magician operates through inscription, then the woman's power seems a mana innate, intrinsic to and operant through her body, par excellence through her eyes. It is a power different from the elite *art* of male magicians, their technology, science, learning, books, and powerful words. Further, male magical inscription is to operate on the mistress through her body: she is to eat the magically inscribed apples or bread; her breast is touched by the hand inscribed with magical characters; she will physically suffer the consequences of conjuration through pain, sleeplessness, and burning. Again Spenser's Busirane makes the point clear. In Busirane's tyrannical writing, the woman's body is painfully operated on magically as Amoret's body is turned into inscription, as the magician writes with blood from her exposed and pierced heart (3.12.30–31) and displays her aestheticized body and pain in the Masque of Cupid (3.12.19–21), in which she appears "dolefull Lady, like a dreary Spright, / Cald by strong charmes out of eternall night" (3.12.19.4–5).

This essay has, en route, been citing some Spenserian illustrations of the traffic between love and magic: the cruel and killing power of the mistress's eyes in *Amoretti* 49, a witch posing as a chaste mistress and a magician practicing his tyrannous magical art in books 1 and 3 of the *Faerie Queene*. And, of course, in the first two books of Spenser's chivalric romance, threats to male knightly virtue are most dangerously embodied in two seductive and destructive witches, Duessa and Acrasia.

---

vim habent," in a marginal note, 25. On fascinating women, see Scot, *Discoverie*, 12:xx, 226–28. On the physiology of love, the operation of the eyes and the imagination see Couliano, *Eros and Magic*, passim and particularly 29–30 for the "two related spiritual activities: the evil eye and love."

21. See, for example, Cleophila's song from *Arcadia*, book 3, Sidney, *Poems*, ed. Ringler, 82; Barnes, *Elegie* 8.29–30, *Parthenophil and Parthenophe*, ed. Doyno, 73; and poems using the conceit of the beloved's glance as that of a basilisk or cockatrice: Drayton, *Idea's Mirror* Amour 30, *Works* ed. Hebel, 1: 113; Chapman, *Ovid's Banquet of Sense* stanza 81, *The Poems of George Chapman*, ed. Phyllis Brooks Bartlett (New York: Russell and Russell, 1962), 73; Spenser, *Amoretti* 49, in Edmund Spenser, *Poetical Works*, ed. J. C. Smith and E. de Selincourt (London, Oxford and New York: Oxford University Press, 1970), 570.

Of the three books of the *Faerie Queene* printed in 1590, Spenser's legend of chastity is the most romantic with its polyphonic narratives depicting the diverse pageants played by love; its flights, separations, and woundings prompted by desire; and its lovers questing for union with each other. When the author introduced himself in the proem he announced two constituents of romance: chivalric adventure in his Ariostan promise in the first stanza to sing of "Knights and Ladies gentle deeds" (Proem 1.5) and love in his invocation of Cupid and Venus in the third. The marvelous, particularly the magical, may be said to be another constituent of romance and especially of the Italian *romanze*, the *Faerie Queene*'s immediate predecessors. It may already be a ghostly presence in the proem, as it always haunts a poet's invocation, however conventional. It is certainly a characteristic of book 3 of the *Faerie Queene*, which is also the most Ariostan of the three books printed in 1590. The author configures the desire of Britomart, Florimell, and Amoret in their various journeys, flights, and imprisonments; and in all their wanderings these female representations encounter magic in experiences that are often frightening or painful for them. When Busirane reads the reversal of his charms, even the valiant Britomart is horrified: he "measur'd many a sad verse, / That horror gan the virgins hart to perse, / And her faire lockes up stared stiffe on end" (3.12.36.4–6).

Book 3 represents relations of women and magic different from those in English love poetry as described in this essay and also different in some ways from those in the preceding two books of the *Faerie Queene*. Books 1 and 2 sometimes share the anxiety of some other Renaissance poems about the apparently beautiful mistress who is revealed to be foul within, and two of their ladies are really Circean seductresses who unman their knights. The "goodly Lady" Duessa is a "filthy foule old woman" and "divelish hag" (1.2.40.8 and 42.1) whose foulness is revealed when she is stripped at Una's request (1.8.45–50). Acrasia is that particularly dangerous paradox: a "faire Witch" (2.12.72.2) who has clearly fascinated Verdant (2.12.73.1–2 and 78.6–8).

But book 3 also continues with one feature of the first two books in that it allegorizes poetic representation as magical practice and offers an analogy between magician and author. In books 1 and 2 of the *Faerie Queene*, Spenser's readers encountered two parodies of the poet that both magically misfashion desire: Archimago and Acrasia. In book 3 they meet Merlin, who assures Britomart that her newly acquired love is in accord with heavenly destiny, and Merlin is, like the poet, both prophet and maker, whose looking glass is like the allegorical mirror, "Like to the worlde it selfe, and seem'd a world of glas" (3.2.19.9). The analogy between magician and author is observable in Archimago's manufacture of the False Una and is elaborated in the Bower of Bliss, where the relations of surface and substance, of delight and instruction and their deployment by authors, are problematized in the paradise garden of a witch.

When Spenser wrote of magical operators we can often see him self-reflexively contemplating his own poetic art. A good example is one moment in the night of bewildering, false representations that Redcrosse experiences in Archimago's hermitage, and it is the magician's making of the False Una:

> Who all this while with charmes and hidden artes
> Had made a Lady of that other Spright,
> And fram'd of liquid ayre her tender partes
> So lively, and so like in all mens sight,
> That weaker sence it could have ravisht quight:
> The maker selfe for all his wondrous witt,
> Was nigh beguiled with so goodly sight:
> Her all in white he clad, and over it
> Cast a black stole, most like to seeme for *Una* fit.
>
> (1.1.45)

Archimago's false "making" duplicates the activity of the poet of the *Faerie Queene* who fashions at its beginning a speaking picture of Truth in Una (1.1.4). This lady is a demon, a succubus who has assumed a body of compacted air, as in classic demonological theory. In both dream and waking the False Una is presented to Redcrosse through the medium of two modes of love poetry that Spenser himself would write and publish in 1594 in the *Amoretti* and *Epithalamion*. First, in his dream, she is brought to Redcrosse's bed attended by Venus and the Graces in a mock-epithalamic stanza (1.1.48). Then she confesses her love and throws herself on the knight's mercy in two and one-half stanzas of love complaint (1.1.51–53.4), which is full of clichéd rhetoric and declamation; their melodramatic tone is matched by vulgarly excessive assonance and alliteration:

> Yet thus perforce he bids me do, or die:
> Die is my dew: yet rew my wretched state . . .
>
> My weaker yeares
> Captiv'd to fortune and frayle worldly feares
> Fly to your faith for succour and sure ayde.
>
> (1.1.51.6–7 and 52.4–6)

Book 3 escapes from the simpler binaries that characterize the first two books of the *Faerie Queene* and are particularly visible in the antithetical patterns and structures of book 1, which is a vast and meticulously elaborated series of variations on the theme of the real opposition but apparent likeness of the false and true. Book 3 clearly provides a change of direction: in its exuberant narrative polyphony, its erotic quests, its female knight, and its refusal, even in the 1590 version, of closure. That change of direction is also observable in its representation of women, magic, and love.

This essay will make two relatively uncontroversial assumptions about the third book of Spenser's *Faerie Queene:* first, its narrative and allegory are largely constructed by relationships between women, and its significance is often figured in terms of female experience, images, and mythopoeia; second, it reflects not only on the diverse pageants of love but also on Renaissance love poetry. Against the background of this essay's argument so far about the relations of poetry, love, and magic, and of the women and men who traffic in them, Spenser's book of chastity becomes even more surprising as a critique of love poetry. Three magical incidents stand out: Britomart's falling in love with Arthegall's image in Merlin's mirror and Glauce's consequent magical attempts to *un*charm her (3.2.17–52); Florimell's experiences with the witch, her son, and the hyena (3.7.1–29) and the witch's subsequent magical manufacture of the False Florimell (3.8.1–10); and Busirane's magical attempts on Amoret and their defeat by Britomart (3.12). All three deliberately run counter to or are quite asymmetrical to the patterns in English Renaissance love poetry this essay has been recording: representations of women and magic in love poems that demonize, coerce, and subjugate them; representations of men whose magic empowers them and gives them authority, sometimes by taking it away from sources originally female. In addition, all three incidents reject the power of magic to affect love.

The House of Busirane (3.12) is often interpreted as an allegory of male poetic inscriptions of the female. Busirane's practices are those of love magic and love poetry. But in the final disturbance of roles in this incident there is a significant asymmetry to the usual gender positions this paper has been considering, for although the amatory magician is male, he is overpowered by a woman and forced to reverse his charms. In turn, the details of this moment when Busirane reverses his charms while Britomart brandishes her sword over him reveal him as a male Circe, usually the archetype for enchanting women,[22] and reveal Britomart as a steadfastly Ulyssean figure. This moment is a paradigm for Spenser's technique in book 3: allegorically to treat magic and love in moments of literary imitation but to give a surprising turn to the usual gender relations and hierarchies expected in and of those moments.

22. Compare with Ovid, *Metamorphoses,* 14:293–301; Gareth Roberts, "The Descendants of Circe: Witches and Renaissance Fictions," in Jonathan Barry, Marianne Hester, and Gareth Roberts, eds., *Witchcraft in Early Modern Europe* (Cambridge: Cambridge University Press, 1996), 183–206.

In Glauce's attempts to uncharm Britomart one woman operates on another, and the magic is not to cause love, as in the incident's classical sources,[23] but to take it away. *Faerie Queene* 3.2.30–51 closely imitates the pseudo-Virgilian *Ciris,* 220ff. And in Spenser's imitation of his classical source, the techniques of amatory magic pass from the hands of one woman into another's without male interference: from Virgil's nurse Carme to Spenser's Glauce.

When Florimell stays at the witch's house (3.7), the magical motifs are again not what one might have expected. The magical operator is rustic, homely, and "the most complete witch in the regular English tradition." Yet *she,* not a man, is the amatory practitioner who attempts to charm her son out of love with Florimell (3.7.21.1–4) and constructs the False Florimell as a substitute. The manufacture of the snowy lady (3.8.5–7) is clearly a parody of the blazon of a sonneteer's mistress and is manufactured from substances, such as virgin wax, that have significance in Petrarchan discourse and the practices of amatory magic. But its manufacturer is not the male sonneteer as magician and technician, but a witch: although the last time we saw a similar magical operation in the poem, a male magician (Archimago) made a simulacrum of a woman (1.1.45). In the making of the False Florimell, the very asymmetry to the usual patterns allows us to see more clearly the male manufacture of the female in sonnets and also the fears that lurk beneath that manufacture. Underneath the artificial and constructed appearance of the beautiful and snowily chaste lady lurks the demonic, for inside is "a Spright to rule the carkasse dead" (3.8.7.9). This spirit is male, and its expertise at female impersonation is that of the Elizabethan boy actor, for he needed no instruction

> Ne how to speake, ne how to use his gest,
> For he in counterfeisance did excell,
> And all the wyles of wemen's wits knew passing well.
> (3.8.8.7–9)[24]

---

23. The immediate source for the magical operations in the *Faerie Queene,* 3.2.49–52, is *Ciris,* 369–77, which in turn draws on Virgil, *Eclogues* 8, and Tibullus, thus stretching back the line of "female inheritance" of these techniques.

24. See K. M. Briggs, *Pale Hecate's Team* (London: Routledge and Kegan Paul, 1962), 75. With the virgin wax in 3.8.6.7, A. C. Hamilton compares some lines from a Sidney poem "What toong can her perfections tell" in his edition of Edmund Spenser, *The Faerie Queene* (London and New York: Longman, 1977), 376. For the use of virgin wax in amatory magic, see John Lyly (who got the information from Johann Wier, *De Praestigiis Daemonum,* IV ix), *Euphues and his England* in *The Complete Works of John Lyly,* ed. R. Warwick Bond, 3 vols. (Oxford: Clarendon Press, 1902), 2:119; Paulus Grillandus, *De Sortilegiis, quaestio* 3, *numerus* 15, 27; Scot, *Discoverie* 12:xvi, 209. B. L. Sloane ms. 3851, ff. 142–142ᵛ, describes the manufacture of an image of the beloved in virgin wax, its baptism, inscription with magical characters, piercing with needles, and final melting in a fire: "As the composition leapeth and swelleth so shall hir Heart." I owe the perception about the spirit as boy actor to one of my students, Jonathan Butler.

The allegorical treatment of love poetry in book 3 allows us a specularity that is not inevitably the point of view of Renaissance male authors, with their magical designs on women. Its refusal to replicate the usual gender roles and hierarchies in love and magic allows a clearer sight of what are, elsewhere in Renaissance love poetry, male poetic strategies that tend to naturalize and so conceal themselves.

The foregoing reading of some sections of book 3 of the *Faerie Queene* that contain magical incidents has much in common with some recent interpretations that have seen book 3 as offering possibilities of reading for, by, and as women and at the same time offering a critique of Petrarchan poetics.[25] These possibilities may even have something to do with Spenser's intense imitation in book 3 of Ariosto, whom Joan Kelly back in 1977 excepted as not assuming a relation of female dependency and male domination. But book 3 is more radical than simply offering possibilities for women readers as it also contemplates issues of gender and authorship. In moments such as Britomart's allegorization of her marine landscape (3.4.6–11) and in the sixth canto, with its almost exclusively feminine mythopoeia and etiologies, which also contains the generative core of the book in Venus's Garden of Adonis, we read examples of female authoring.

In book 3 Spenser has deliberately resisted the usual gender relations of women demonized by male writers, men coercing women through magic, and also the fiction of the power of magic to compel desire. By doing so he has exposed the usual magical tactics of Renaissance love poetry and has refused for himself the role of love poet as Renaissance magician and its consequent subjugation of women.

25. See, for example, Lauren Silberman, "Singing Unsung Heroines: Androgynous Discourse in Book 3 of *The Faerie Queene*," in *Rewriting the Renaissance: The Discourses of Sexual Difference in Early Modern Europe*, ed. Margaret W. Ferguson, Maureen Quilligan, and Nancy J. Vickers (Chicago and London: University of Chicago Press, 1987), 259–71; Maureen Quilligan, *Milton's Spenser: The Politics of Reading* (Ithaca: Cornell University Press, 1983); Dorothy Stephens, "Into Other Arms: Amoret's Evasion," in *Queering the Renaissance*, ed. Jonathan Goldberg, 190–217.

Ilona Bell

Women in the Lyric Dialogue of Courtship

Whitney's *Admonition to al yong Gentilwomen* and Donne's "The Legacie"

This volume celebrates the burgeoning interest in Renaissance women—as writers and subjects of Renaissance literature. This essay explores aspects of three distinct roles played by Renaissance women: those of poet, teacher, and audience. The first, the role of the woman poet, though rare at the time, is beginning to receive the critical attention it deserves. The second, the role of female teacher or moral authority, is rarely discussed for it directly controverts the dominant code of ethics that prescribes chaste, silent, and obedient Renaissance women.[1] The third, the role of private female lyric audience, though disregarded by modern scholarship, is widely acknowledged, and passionately debated, by Elizabethan social, moral, and literary critics.

Early modern women writers need to be read in their own right. Yet if we want to understand their full impact on English literary history, we also need to hear their voices in dialogue with male writers. Even though it is impossible to know what a particular Elizabethan woman might have been thinking or saying in response to a particular poem, by reading male poets/lovers such as John Donne alongside women writers such as Isabella Whitney, we can reconstruct the enigmatic, ambiguous conversation of Elizabethan courtship.

Recent studies of Elizabethan poetry and courtship focus on *courtiership*, on the advancement of careers at court. This essay begins with the premise, widely held by the Elizabethans but repeatedly denied by twentieth-century critics, that love poetry was conventionally written for courtship, in the sense of *wooing a woman with a view to sex or marriage.* The Elizabethans were accustomed

---

1. This essay is indebted to the rapidly growing bibliography of books on early modern Englishwomen and Renaissance literature that is too extensive to cite here. For an insightful study of the Elizabethan code of ethics, see "Nets and Bridles: Early Modern Conduct Books and Sixteenth-Century Women's Lyrics," in *The Ideology of Conduct: Essays in Literature and the History of Sexuality,* ed. Nancy Armstrong and Leonard Tennenhouse (New York: Methuen, 1987), 39–72.

to writing, reading, and hearing love poems "as if I were a mistress," to cite a crucial phrase from Sidney's *Defence of Poesie*.[2]

For T. S. Eliot, Northrop Frye, and the modernist poetics they helped construct, the lyric is by definition "the voice of the poet talking to himself—or to nobody"; a short poem "directly expressing the poet's own thoughts and sentiments"; "preeminently the utterance that is overheard." Because so much twentieth-century criticism defines the lyric as an expressive speech act, the illocutionary point of which is the "pure and direct expression of [the poet's] own intention," most critics of English Renaissance love poetry continue to stress the self-analysis, self-fashioning, self-advertising, or self-validation of the male poet.[3]

The assumption that English Renaissance poems were addressed either to the poet himself, or to nobody, or to a male coterie seems to be justified by the low rate of female literacy. Yet, as Margaret Spufford has demonstrated, reading literacy was much higher than writing literacy. Moreover, as Suzanne Hull has shown, a large number of printed books were written for and addressed to women in the middling and upper ranks of early modern English society.[4] To understand the full extent of women's involvement with and access to Elizabethan culture in general and English Renaissance lyrics in particular, we need to consider not only writing literacy and reading literacy but also listening literacy. For most Elizabethans, and especially women, listening was still the most important access to knowledge and culture.[5] In analyzing the theoretical and hermeneutical implications of the private, female lyric audience, it is important to remember that love poems were both read *by* and read or recited *to* Elizabethan women.

2. *Sir Philip Sidney's Defence of Poesy*, ed. Dorothy M. Macardie (London: Macmillan; New York: St. Martin's, 1964), 48.

3. Quoted respectively from T. S. Eliot, *On Poetry and Poets* (New York: Farrar, Straus, 1943, reprint 1979), 105; Northrop Frye, *The Anatomy of Criticism: Four Essays* (Princeton: Princeton University Press, 1957; New York: Atheneum, 1966), 249; and M. M. Bakhtin, *The Dialogic Imagination: Four Essays*, ed. Michael Holquist, trans. Caryl Emerson and Michael Holquist (Austin: University of Texas Press, 1981), 280.

4. Margaret Spufford, "First Steps in Literacy: The Reading and Writing Experiences of the Humblest Seventeenth-Century Spiritual Autobiographers," *Social History* 4 (1979): 407–35; Suzanne W. Hull, *Chaste, Silent & Obedient: English Books for Women 1475–1640* (San Marino, Calif.: Huntington Library, 1982).

5. In "From 'Listen, Lordings' to 'Dear Reader,'" *University of Toronto Quarterly* 46 (1976–1977), 113, William Nelson notes that "books of every conceivable kind, whether in prose or in verse, were commonly read aloud, sometimes by the author himself, sometimes by members of a household taking turns, sometimes by a professional reader. . . ." For information about the singing of lyrics, see John E. Stevens, *Music and Poetry in the Early Tudor Court* (Lincoln: University of Nebraska Press, 1961). For a study of oral tradition and Renaissance literature—though not the female lyric audience—see Walter J. Ong, *Rhetoric, Romance, and Technology: Studies in the Interaction of Expression and Culture* (Ithaca: Cornell University Press, 1971).

Elizabethan popular culture and high art are full of references to poetry's being used for courtship and seduction. Popular romances, such as Greene's *Neuer Too Late,* Lodge's *Rosalynd,* Grange's *The Golden Aphroditis,* or Gascoigne's *The Adventures passed by Master F. J.* recount clandestine courtships and seductions carried out by means of amatory epistles, epistolary love poems, and lyric dialogues. Shakespeare's comedies typically dramatize courtships conducted by means of love poems or poetic love language. To cite just two of numerous examples, at the beginning of *A Midsummer Night's Dream* Egeus accuses Lysander of secretly wooing Hermia with songs and sonnets:

> thou hast given her rhymes,
> And interchang'd love-tokens with my child;
> Thou hast by moonlight at her window sung
> With feigning voice verses of feigning love.

When Romeo and Juliet first meet, their lovers' dialogue constitutes a perfect Shakespearean sonnet and instantly spills over into a new quatrain.

The Autobiography of Thomas Whythorne consists almost entirely of a commentary on the songs and sonnets that Whythorne, a music master, sang and wrote to Renaissance women whom he was instructing and/or wooing and the responses he received from them. Whythorne even recalls one female student who wooed him with love lyrics: "she devised certain verses in English, writing them with her own hand; and did put them between the strings of [my] gittern." Gascoigne's *A Hundreth Sundrie Flowres,* one of the earlier published collections of Elizabethan poetry, provides headnotes explaining the private context. Women play a prominent role in the lyric dialogue. They are the lyric audience: "He wrote unto a Skotish Dame whom he chose for his Mistresse in the french Court, as followeth." They are lyric speakers: "A Lady being both wronged by false suspect, and also wounded by the durance of hir husband, doth thus bewray hir grief." Finally, they are authors: "With these verses you shall judge the quick capacity of the Lady: for she wrot therunder this short aunswer."[6]

Some of these poems are probably fictive fantasies written by Gascoigne and addressed or attributed to a woman. A few sound as if they were written by a woman in response to a poetic persuasion by Gascoigne. Other lyrics sound as if they may have been written by Gascoigne in the hopes of putting encouraging

---

6. *Midsummer Nights Dream* 1.1.27–31, *The Riverside Shakespeare,* ed. G. Blakemore Evans, et al. (Boston: Houghton Mifflin, 1974); *The Autobiography of Thomas Whythorne,* Modern Spelling Edition, ed. James M. Osborn (London: Oxford University Press, 1962), 21; *George Gascoigne's A Hundreth Sundrie Flowres,* ed. C. T. Prouty, *University of Missouri Studies* 17.2 (Columbia: University of Missouri, 1942), 111, 133, 115.

words into a mistress's mouth. A few may have been commissioned by Elizabethan women and written by Gascoigne, but even more were written by Gascoigne for Elizabethan men: "if ever I wrote lyne for my selfe in causes of love, I have written tenne for other men in layes of lust. . . . Even so (good Reader) I was a great while the man which dwelt at Billingsgate. For in wanton delightes I helped all men."[7] As the dedicatory epistle explains, Gascoigne had a thriving business, writing love lyrics for Elizabethan men to use in wooing women.

As *The Autobiography of Thomas Whythorne* and *A Hundreth Sundrie Flowres* both demonstrate, Elizabethan women play a central role in the lyric dialogue of courtship: as subjects, as authors, and, above all, as the primary and prototypical lyric audience. The presupposition of a female lyric audience has an important impact both on the evolution of the lyric genre and on the sex-gender system, for, as feminist criticism has shown, the *"hypothesis* of a female reader" inevitably "changes our apprehension of a given text, awakening us to the significance of its sexual codes."[8]

By reading the gaps and contradictions where a female oppositional discourse disturbs male poetic authority, we can recuperate the points of conflict and resistance—the sexual politics or gender unconscious—that make both poetry and courtship into discursive sites of social and sexual struggle. A sudden, inexplicable shift in tone, a fragmented, unstable metaphor, an amphibolous, antiphrastic conclusion, the marginal or oppositional voice of the female lyric audience is still audible—at the level of the subtext or the dialogic imagination where every utterance is "pregnant with responses and objections."[9]

This essay explores connections between a poetics of courtship and an erotics of secrecy. For the Elizabethans, poetry was the preferred language of courtship and seduction precisely because both poetry and seduction are, by their very nature, enigmatic and ambiguous. Whythorne and Gascoigne provide some of the most illuminating Elizabethan explanations of how and why enigmatic poetic rhetoric played such a crucial role in courtship and seduction. In the prefatory letter, Whythorne offers his private reader—"My good friend"—special access to the songs and sonnets that constitute even as they conceal the autobiography's inner, secret text:

> My good friend,—Recalling to mind my promise made unto you, I have
> here sent you the copies of such songs and sonnets as I have made from
> time to time until the writing hereof. And because that you did impart

7. *The Complete Works of George Gascoigne,* ed. John W. Cunliffe (Cambridge: Cambridge University Press, 1907), 1:16–17.

8. Elaine Showalter, "Towards a Feminist Poetics," in *Women Writing and Writing about Women,* ed. Mary Jacobus (London: Croom Helm; New York: Barnes, 1979), 25.

9. Bakhtin, *The Dialogic Imagination,* 281.

unto me at our last being together some of your private and secret affairs
past, and also some of the secret purposes and intents the which have lain
hid and been as it were entombed in your heart, I, to gratify your good
opinion had of me, do now lay open unto you the most part of all my
private affairs and secrets, accomplished from my childhood until the
day of the date hereof. The which as I do write unto you to gratify you
withal, so am I partly enforced thereunto, because I do think it needful
not only to show you the cause why I wrote them, but also to open my
secret meaning in divers of them, as well in words and sentences, as in
the whole of the same, lest you should think them to be made to smaller
purpose than I did mean.[10]

The phrase "a long discourse" (meaning both *a process or succession of time
or events* and *a narrative tale, a dissertation,* and *communication by speech* or
familiar intercourse) epitomizes the peculiarly mixed character of Elizabethan
writing that hovers uncertainly between private communication and written
text.[11] By drawing a parallel between "the secret purposes and intents" that
have "been as it were entombed" in his reader's heart and the "private affairs
and secrets" that "I . . . do now lay open unto you," Whythorne calls attention
to the intimacy of the original lyric situation and the privacy of the original
lyric audience. The autobiographical frame, written "to show you the cause
why I wrote them," strives to transform the reader from a critical outsider, free
to make potentially damaging or erroneous speculations, into a sympathetic
insider, privy to confidences and meanings the songs and sonnets originally
conveyed. Consider yourself, "My good friend," one of the initiated.

Whythorne apologizes in advance for any passages that "overslip" (or *let
slip by*) something "too broad" (too *erotic or indecent*)—though, as he knows
all too well, that possibility is precisely what makes private affairs and veiled,
secretive poetry alluring. The text enacts the enigmatic seduction it describes,
for at a deeper level it implies that the prose explanations illuminate only
the more "broad" or obvious aspects of the poems, and "overslip" (that is,
fail to mention) nuances still hidden within the text—the really juicy tidbits
that the reader has the pleasure of trying to discover. Whythorne's apology,
"a man cannot always speak in print," suggests, first, that private manuscript
poetry enjoys greater (though still incomplete) license than a printed text; and
second, that no one, not even an author, can ever fully elucidate the secrets
that literature contains because the text has its own mysterious vitality that
eludes transcription or containment. Even as Whythorne sets out to explain

10. Whythorne, *The Autobiography,* 1.
11. All definitions are taken from the *Compact Edition of the Oxford English Dictionary* (Oxford:
Oxford University Press, 1971).

the "secret meaning" hidden within the poems, he admits that additional secrets and meanings remain.

Like Whythorne's prose commentary, the headnotes to *A Hundreth Sundrie Flowres* identify the volume as a collection of coded, coterie verse, written to be used in particular situations of courtship or seduction. One headnote alerts us to the original private subtext—"Written to a gentlewoman who had refused him and chosen a husband (as he thought) much inferior to himself, both in knowledge byrth and parsonage. Wherin he bewrayeth both their names in cloudes." Another headnote warns us that the private lyric dialogue requires decoding: "The absent lover (in ciphers) disciphering his name, doth crave some spedie relief as followeth."[12] One fascinating minisequence describes G. G. and a witty gentlewoman wooing each other in riddles and cryptic verse that no one else in the party is capable of deciphering. One poem published anonymously in *A Hundreth Sundrie Flowres* is omitted from the later authorized collection, *The Posies,* because the veiled allusions to Gascoigne's affair with Elizabeth Bacon Breton and Edward Boyes are too easily recognizable.

Instructional manuals agree that enigmatic rhetoric is central to the poetics of courtship, though they vehemently disagree about whether such is the best use or the worst abuse of poetry. In *The Instruction of A Christen Woman,* Vives warns Renaissance women about the dangers of love poetry in general and secrecy in particular: "some men be so crafty in noughtynes, and can wrappe in darke sentence theyr myndes in suche wyse, that they may yet be vnderstanden of her what they meane, by that they speke vnto her: and yet shall the double sence cause, that they may deny that they ment so, and blame her for wronge takynge theeyr wordes, and vnderstandynge them in euyll sence, which they speak for no harme." Vives censures love poetry because it is ambiguous and secretive. Other writers recommend the ambiguity of poetic language, however, precisely because it enables a suitor to avoid embarrassment, should the woman scorn his advances. *The Courtier* counsels lovers to communicate "so warilye, that the woordes maye firste attempt the minde, and so doubtfullye touch her entent and will, that they maye leave her a waye and a certein issue to feine the understandinge that those woordes conteine love: to the entent if he finde anye daunger, he maye draw backe and make wise to have spoken or written it to an other ende." Ovid's *Art of Love,* which was well known in Elizabethan England, teaches male suitors to dissemble: "So woman's heart by eloquence is bowed. / But art must be disguised nor powers displayed."[13]

---

12. Gascoigne, *A Hundreth Sundrie Flowres,* 112, 142.

13. Juan Luis Vives, "*The Instruction of A Christen Woman:* A Critical Edition of the Tudor Translation," ed. Ruth L. M. Kuschmierz, Ph.D. diss., University of Pittsburgh, 1961, 84; Baldassarre Castiglione, *The Book of the Courtier From the Italian of Count Baldassare Castiglione: Done into English*

Letter-writing manuals, which first became popular during the Elizabethan period, advise suitors that love poems are especially useful in initiating and negotiating clandestine courtships and seductions. For example, Fulwood's *The Enimie of Idlenesse* contains two verse letters of seduction. One uses a mythic allegory: "A Secret Louer writes his will, / By storie of *Pigmalions* ill." Another declares an erotics of secrecy in its very title, "One writes in earnest, or in iest / As then shall like his Ladie best." The conventional catalog of female beauty becomes increasingly erotic as the blazon moves down her body to "Her tender thighes, her beding knees."[14] The pun on bedding/bending perfectly illustrates how an erotics of secrecy works. Should the woman fail to respond as the letter writer wishes, he can easily claim that *she* misread his meaning. Indeed, the more erotic the persuasion, the more useful a cover witty, enigmatic rhetoric provides.

Elizabethan manuals of rhetoric, such as Puttenham's *Arte of English Poesie* or Peacham's *Garden of Eloquence,* praise enigmatic rhetoric as the metamorphosis of secrecy into pleasure—or what we might call the free play of language. Puttenham not only explains the close connection between the poetry and practice of courtship but also reveals that the art of poetry, the art of politics, and the art of wooing a woman are alike deeply duplicitous.

Puttenham praises all "Figures and figurative speaches" for "drawing [the mind] from plainnesse and simplicitie to a certaine doublenesse," but he singles out "the Courtly figure *Allegoria,* which is when we speake one thing and thinke another, and that our wordes and our meanings meete not" as particularly appropriate for courtship, both amorous and political.[15] After describing the encoded language used by Queen Elizabeth and her courtiers, Puttenham quotes an epistolary exchange, written in couplets, by a pair of lovers eager to assure each other that their resolve has not been marred by a year's separation.

Though more worried about the abuses of rhetoric, Peacham also acknowledges that "Sometime notwithstanding darknesse of speech causeth delectation." For readers with "prompt wits and apt capacities, who are best able to find out the sense of a similitude," "darknesse of speech causeth" an intellectual thrill, reproducing on the symbolic level the erotic pleasure that the poet/lover and his beloved are simultaneously negotiating under "the darke vaile of Ænigmaticall speech."[16]

---

by Sir Thomas Hoby. Anno 1561 (London: David Nutt, 1900), 277; Ovid, *The Love Poems,* trans. A. D. Melville (Oxford: Oxford University Press, 1990), 99.

14. William Fulwood, *The Enimie of Idlenesse: Teaching a Perfect Platforme How to Indite Epistles and Letters of All Sortes* (London, 1582), 285–86.

15. George Puttenham, *The Arte of English Poesie* (1589, 1906; Kent: Kent State University Press, 1970), 196.

16. Henry Peacham, *The Garden of Eloquence* (1593; Gainesville: Scholars Facsimiles, 1954), 27, 29.

Given the close connection between a poetics of courtship and an erotics of secrecy, it seems noteworthy that perhaps the first original poem written and published by an Englishwoman is the 1567 *Copy of a letter, lately written in meeter, by a yonge Gentilwoman: to her vnconstant Louer. With an Admonitio[n] to al yong Gentilwomen, and to all other Mayds in general to beware of men'nes flattery By Is[abella] W[hitney]*.[17] The very title declares: first, the Elizabethans were using love poems to transact clandestine courtships; second, Elizabethan women were taking an active and critical role in negotiating their own courtships, using their critical powers to judge and criticize the veiled rhetoric of courtship; and third, women were claiming the power of speech and writing to protect themselves and each other from the deception and betrayal posed by clandestine courtship and enigmatic rhetoric.

The Copy of a letter is a fascinating document that deserves to be more widely read and analyzed for a number of reasons. As a literary text, "*written in meeter, by a yonge Gentilwoman*," it has an important place in the beginning of an English female lyric tradition. As a response to a male suitor, it offers an Elizabethan woman's adaptation and critique of the poetry of courtship. As a social document, *The Copy of a letter* offers an Elizabethan woman's assessment of clandestine courtships and privy contracts, or corner contracts.

Whitney claims that she first wrote *A letter* upon discovering that her unconstant lover betrayed their privy contract by making subsequent, secret plans to marry another woman. As ecclesiastical court records demonstrate, broken marriage contracts were a common social problem in early modern England.[18] Indeed, it is precisely the difficulty of determining which privy contract is the first privy contract that Donne plays upon at the beginning of "Womans constancy":

> Now thou hast lov'd me one whole day,
> To morrow when thou leav'st, what wilt thou say?
> Wilt thou then Antedate some new made vow?[19]

Whitney's *Copy of a letter* is all the more significant because it is published along with *An Admonitio[n] to al yong Gentilwomen, and to all other Mayds in general to beware of men'nes flattery*. Whitney's *An admonitio[n]* transforms

---

17. For two illuminating analyses of Whitney's poetry, see Betty Travitsky, "The 'Wyll and Testament' of Isabella Whitney," *English Literary Renaissance* 10 (1980): 76–94, and Ann Rosalind Jones, *The Currency of Eros: Women's Love Lyrics in Europe, 1540–1620* (Bloomington: Indiana University Press, 1990), 43–52.

18. See Martin Ingram, *Church Courts, Sex and Marriage in England, 1570–1640* (Past and Present Publications, Cambridge: Cambridge University Press, 1987).

19. All Donne's poems are quoted from *The Complete Poetry of John Donne*, ed. John T. Shawcross (Garden City, N.Y.: Anchor-Doubleday, 1967).

the personal experience of *A letter* into a social and political act, inviting "all" Elizabethan women—from *"al yong Gentilwomen"* to *"all other Mayds in general"*—to join together in facing and solving the challenges and difficulties of clandestine courtship.

Though cognizant of the magnitude and difficulty of her undertaking—"Oh, if I could good counsell g[iv]e, / my tongue should not be slacke"—Whitney remains undaunted:

> But such as I can g[iv]e, I wyll,
>   here in few wordes expresse
> Which if you do obserue, it will
>   some of your care redresse.

Drawing on her own experience of clandestine courtship, Whitney's *Admonitio[n]* offers advice to all Elizabethan women "whose hartes as yet w[th] raginge loue / most paynfully do boyle."[20] By immediately and openly declaring the force of female desire, Whitney rejects the moral code that equates female virtue with chastity, silence, and obedience.

To Whitney, courtship is at once a legal right that needs to be actively defended and a risky venture that needs to be carefully negotiated. Whitney specifically warns her female readers about books such as Ovid's "Arte of loue" that teach men "this same knacke," not only to please women with their "flattering tongues" and "their pleasant Songs" but also to deceive women with their feigned rhetoric:

> Some use the teares of Crocodiles,
>   contrary to their hart:
> And yf they cannot alwayes weep:
>   they wet their Cheekes by Art.
>   (A6r)

As Whitney claims to have learned from her own unconstant lover, some Elizabethan men "still / delude us in this wise."

Having discovered how important it is to play the role of a resisting reader, Whitney sets out to teach other women to distinguish playful, coded persuasion from deliberate, unscrupulous deception: "Sith it is so, we trust we shall, / take hede to fained lies." According to Whitney, the best way for women to distinguish the "fayre and painted talke" of "flattering tonges" (A6r) from proposals that are "constant, true, and just," is the test of time:

---

20. *The Copy of a letter, lately written in meeter, by Is[abella] W[hitney]* (London, 1567), sig. A5v. All further references to Whitney's poetry will be cited parenthetically.

Trust not a man at fyrst sight,
but trye him well before:
I wish al Maids within their brests
to kepe this thing in store.

(A6v)

At this moment when Whitney offers her most pointed piece of advice, she addresses "al Maids," urging them to exercise the power of courtship and to avoid the dangers of deceit.

Together Whitney's letter and admonition demonstrate that there is an important difference, not always easy to detect, between, on the one hand, puns, riddles, and enigmas used by lovers to signal sexual attraction and negotiate intimacy and, on the other hand, enigmatic or ambiguous language used by dishonest men to deceive and exploit trusting women. Whitney's warnings are echoed and confirmed by a variety of historical, prescriptive, and controversial texts, specifically written for and to women. For example, Christopher Hatton, when he was writing a letter of courtship to Alice Fanshaw in 1601, took great pains to distinguish his own "sincere" courtship from the "amorous gallants of our tyme yᵗ make a traffique of lovinge and a trade of dissemblinge, lovinge whom ere they see, and ownlie lovinge whilst they see."²¹

Roughly twenty years after the publication of Whitney's letter, the 1589 *Iane Anger her Protection for Women* cautions Elizabethan women, "When men protest secrecie most solemnly, beleeue them le[a]st, for then surely there is a tricke of knauery." Even casual poets/lovers could sometimes pose considerable danger to a woman's reputation, Anger warns: "It is a wonder to see how men can flatter themselues wth their own conceites: For let vs looke, they wil straight affirm that we loue, and if then Lust pricketh them, they will sweare that Loue urgeth vs: which imagination onely is sufficient to make them assay the scaling of halfe a dozen of vs in one night, when they will not stick to sweare that if they should be denied of their requestes, death must needes follow."²²

As Whitney and Anger teach their female readers (and us), any early modern woman who followed her own desires rather than her parents' carefully laid plans was painfully vulnerable to "deceit" that could threaten her honor and/or marital prospects. Inconstant suitors such as Whitney's erstwhile fiancé exchanged secret vows of love but continued to look about for a better match, undeterred by "promises [that should] be kept, / that you so firmly made" (A2v). Gay blades such as Gascoigne wrote private love poetry in pursuit of

---

21. *Correspondence of the Family of Hatton,* ed. Edward Maunde Thompson (London, 1878), 1:1.
22. *Iane Anger her Protection for Women. To defend them against* THE SCANDALOVS REPORTES *of a late Surfeiting Louer, and all other like Venerians that complaine so to bee ouercloyed with womens kindnesse* (London, 1589), sig. C3.

"inexprimable joyes, and therewith enjoyned both by dutie and discretion to kepe the same covert," but later published their poems in pursuit of fame and profit.[23] Fortune hunters such as Whythorne professed devotion and subjection with "flatterying tonges" but then recycled the poems, seeking patronage in place of the material rewards that courtship failed to attain.

Yet, at the same time, any man who strives to escape the frustrations of Petrarchism and invites the answering voice of female desire also makes himself painfully vulnerable. Like W. G., whose lover's complaint was published along with Isabella Whitney's, he could lose his heart to a "yonge Mayden, to whom he was betrothed. Who afterward being ouercome with flattery, she seemd utterly to swerue from her former promise without occasion, and so to forsake him" (B1r). Like Whythorne, he could woo a gentlewoman who offers encouragement but is finally either too dutiful or too pragmatic to marry against her parents' wishes. Or like John Donne, he could court a young woman who returns his love but prolongs his agonizing uncertainty because she has learned from the experiences of other Elizabethan women to "trust not a man at fyrst sight, / but trye him well before" (Whitney, A6v).

Early modern English courtship generally began as a private conversation between lovers, friends, and, if all went well, kinfolk. When it was successful, courtship led to the public acknowledgment of an earlier private relationship, either through a formal betrothal and a communal celebration or a clandestine marriage and the shock of the ensuing disclosure. The Elizabethan lyric, and especially the love lyric, also generally began as a private communication to family and friends. Yet, eventually, most lyrics moved beyond the original dialogue with a private lyric audience to a wider reading public. Successful lyric poetry often ended in publication of one sort or another, either wider, uncontrolled manuscript circulation or printed book, whether pirated, authorized, or posthumous. A poetics of courtship produced an erotics of secrecy when the private conversations of manuscript poetry and clandestine courtship steeled themselves against publicity and exposure.[24]

---

23. Gascoigne, *A Hundreth Sundrie Flowres*, 77.

24. On patronage and the circulation of poems in manuscript, see Kerrigan, Introduction to *The Sonnets;* Arthur Marotti, *John Donne, Coterie Poet* (Madison: University of Wisconsin Press, 1986); Margaret Maurer, "The Real Presence of Lucy Russell, Countess of Bedford, and the Terms of John Donne's 'Honour is So Sublime Perfection,'" *English Literary History* 47 (1980): 205–34; Ted-Larry Pebworth, "Manuscript Poems and Print Assumptions: Donne and his Modern Editors," *John Donne Journal* 3 (1984): 1–21; J. W. Saunders, "The Stigma of Print: A Note on the Social Bases of Tudor Poetry," *Essays in Criticism* 1 (1951): 139–64; Tennenhouse, "Sir Walter Ralegh and the Literature of Clientage"; Patricia Thomson, "The Literature of Patronage, 1580–1630," *Essays in Criticism* 2 (1952): 267–84.

Elizabethan poetry of courtship needed an erotics of secrecy not only to seduce unsuspecting maidens but also to protect private lovers' discourse from misprision by others. Many Elizabethan poems of courtship were specifically designed to mean one thing to a mistress and something quite different to a male coterie or the wider reading public. Indeed, that is why poems such as Donne's "The Legacie" pose such an interesting interpretive challenge.[25]

"The Legacie" begins as a witty jeu d'esprit addressed to the poet's mistress:

> When I dyed last, and, Deare, I dye
>   As often as from thee I goe,
>   Though it be but an houre agoe,
> And Lovers houres be full eternity,
> I remember yet, that I
>   Something did say, and something bestow . . .
>   (1–6)

This sounds like an amatory epistle, written and sent by the poet/lover to his mistress soon after his departure. Like the model love letters published in the letter-writing manuals, or the exchange of couplets quoted by Puttenham, or the verse epistle printed in *A Hundreth Sundrie Flowres* where "The absent lover (in ciphers) disciphering his name, doth crave some spedie relief as followeth," "The Legacie" seems designed to maintain communication.[26]

Yet, as in "The Curse," "The undertaking," "Womans constancy," or so many of those poems contained in Donne's *Songs and Sonets,* the initial tone of intimate teasing, or good-humored playfulness, becomes edgier by the end:

> Yet I found something like a heart,
>   But colours it, and corners had,
>   It was not good, it was not bad,
> It was intire to none, and few had part.
> As good as could be made by art
>   It seem'd, and therefore for our losses sad,
> I meant to send this heart in stead of mine,
> But oh, no man could hold it, for twas thine.
>   (17–24)

25. John Carey, *John Donne: Life, Mind and Art* (New York: Oxford University Press, 1981) comments: "This is an exasperating poem, of course. It takes ages to sort out the pronouns: and that's the point. We're made to share the speaker's disorientation" (189).

26. Gascoigne, *A Hundreth Sundrie Flowres,* 142.

This "probably mean[s] that it was a painted heart, i.e. a hypocritical one, not a 'true plain' one," Redpath explains.[27] Most modern critics agree that the conclusion is an acerbic attack on female inconstancy.[28]

Further, the final gesture toward generalization, "no man could hold it," suggests that this witty conclusion is intended not for a female lyric audience but for a male coterie of "prophane men" ("The undertaking"), eager to conclude, "No where / Lives a woman true, and fair" ("Song: Goe, and catche").[29] Most critics assume that the reference to "art"—"as good as could be made by art it seemed" (21)—alludes to female vanity, inconstancy, and duplicity, all of which are staples of Renaissance antifeminism.[30] Though calculated to sound delightfully cynical and cutting to a coterie of male wits, I think the line would sound very different to a pair of clandestine lovers.[31]

Corners, *secret or remote places,* suggest *actions done in a corner, privily or covertly.* Redpath notes, citing evidence from Donne's sermons, that " 'Corners' are often mentioned by Donne in association with untoward secrecy, suspiciousness, and lack of straightforwardness."[32] Yet, even if the Dean of St. Paul's thought corners unseemly between man and God, to clandestine lovers seeking marriage despite parental prohibition, "these corner contracts without consent of parents" are much sought after as a good. (The phrase comes from a 1585 sermon by Archbishop Sandys, but the term is idiomatic.)

"Colours" refer figuratively to *outward appearances, a show or semblance*

27. Theodore Redpath, ed., *The Songs and Sonnets of John Donne,* 2nd ed. (New York: St. Martin's Press, 1983), 116. John Shawcross explains the line thus: "The vital organ which has kept him alive is something like a heart, but it is changeable (fickle) like color and imperfect" (103). In *The Complete English Poems* (Harmondsworth: Penguin, 1971, reprint 1983), A. J. Smith offers a similar gloss: "it was not a real heart but an ingeniously simulated one, which, however, displayed emblematically its lack of the true characteristics of a heart, pure sincerity and straight dealing" (382).

28. Marotti attributes "The Legacie" to the Inns-of-Court period where Donne "addressed a male audience able to see through the equivocations of paradoxical reasoning," adopting a "strategy" that "merges successfully the spirited skepticism of the libertine verse and prose with the fashionable pose of the sophisticated amorist" (87). Marotti describes "The Legacie," as "another poem probably written in this period," in which "Donne connects the language of love, with its rhetorical colors, with the 'colours' (18) or deceptions and lies lovers practice on one another, as he converts a courtly Petrarchan lyric of compliment into a poem of satiric accusation" (314).

29. Redpath summarizes the poem thus: "The fantastic transition, through patent impossibilities, from the hyperbolically laudatory beginning, through the mock-search, to the deprecatory 'something like a heart', and finally exposure of the slipperiness of the woman, is conducted in masterly fashion" (115).

30. For a review of antifeminist stereotypes, see Katherine Usher Henderson and Barbara F. McManus, *Half Humankind: Contexts and Texts of the Controversy about Women in England, 1540–1640* (Urbana: University of Illinois Press, 1985), 47–63.

31. In *Doubting Conscience: Donne and the Poetry of Moral Argument* (Ann Arbor: University of Michigan Press, 1975), Dwight Cathcart cites "The Legacie" as an example of those Donne poems that ask the reader "to resupply the response of the 'you' " (32).

32. Redpath, *Songs and Sonnets,* 116.

that conceals the truth and, specifically in law, to *an apparent or prima facie right, sometimes in a bad sense.* These "colours" represent the false front that clandestine lovers adopt in order to conceal their courtship from family and friends. Together Donne's "colours" and "corners" make up a covert, private understanding between the male poet/lover and the female reader/listener— at once deliciously playful and desperately serious—about the ways in which "The Legacie" is itself *a show or semblance that conceals the truth* from parents and peers.

If we apply the legal meaning of colors—and there is reason to do so, not only because Donne was himself a lawyer but also because the dramatic situation of "executor and Legacie" (8) mimics a legal proceeding—the conclusion evokes English marriage law that granted any woman over the age of twelve the right to bestow her heart wherever she chose. In practice, of course, that lawful liberty was often obstructed by parents and denounced by the moral authorities.[33] If Donne's lyric courtship is to succeed, he must convince his female interlocutor that she is not her father's possession, that she has the *prima facie right* to confer her heart and honor upon whomever she wishes. Thus, "The Legacie" argues, her heart is "intire to none" (20): that is, it belongs entirely to no one, for she alone has complete possession. No man, neither her father nor any suitor chosen by him for her, can "hold" her, in the sense of *rule her, control her, own her as property, or restrain her from acting.* Yet, if her father cannot hold or rule her, how can John Donne?

Beneath its conventional "colours," beneath its superficial, stereotypical attack on female fickleness, the secret corners of "The Legacie" contain a serious exploration of the risks and responsibilities inherent in conducting a clandestine love affair. In the context of a clandestine courtship, the line—"as good as could be made by art / It seemed" (21–22)—refers not only to her artful attempt to balance his wooing against her family's resistance but also to his attempt to court her with his artful poetic persuasions. Yet, no matter how powerful his rhetoric, no matter how rigorous the argument that he should have all her love, no matter how tender his protestations or sincere his devotion, Donne does not, and cannot, control her heart: "But oh, no man could hold it, for twas thine" (24).

For me, "The Legacie" epitomizes the enigma of lyric courtship. Not only does "The Legacie" mean different things to different members of the private lyric audience but it also captures the hermeneutical dilemma that both the

---

33. According to Lawrence Stone, *The Family, Sex and Marriage in England 1500 to 1800* (New York: Harper Torchbooks, 1979), still the most influential history of early modern marriage, the predominance of arranged marriage essentially precludes courtship in the middling to upper ranks. More recent studies give more weight to romantic love, sexual attraction, and personal choice without, of course, denying the importance of social and material considerations.

male poet/lover and the female reader/listener face. As Isabella Whitney warns her female readers, lovers capable of artfully concealing their true feelings from the world are also capable of concealing their feelings from each other. Because early modern courtship was usually, at least in its initial stages, private, lovers could readily break off the courtship without embarrassing repercussions. Clandestine love affairs are by their very nature insecure, susceptible not only to fears of discovery from without but also to fears of betrayal from within. In some sense, the more successful the poetry and the more intimate the love affair, the more both the male poet/lover and the female listener/reader/lover have to fear. The more persuasively the poet addresses a particular woman, the more he risks being overheard and condemned by others. Yet, the more covertly and enigmatically he may write or speak to her, the more difficult it is for her to know how to interpret his meaning and purpose.

Surely, Donne's female interlocutor is no more artful than he is. What Donne finds at the center of "The Legacie" is "something like a heart." It is not actually a heart: it is the poet/lover's attempt to capture her heart in his words. The female reader and her heart remain outside the poem's margins, beyond the poet's control—the poem's lyric audience, not its construction. The poem can no more contain her heart than it can control her response. Finally, the heart, with all its colors and corners, might be either his or hers, since it is just as difficult for him to read her heart beneath her artful words as it is for her to read his heart beneath his artful words. As long as he does all the writing and talking, Donne can imagine but never really know how she will respond to his lyric persuasion. Seeking her approval and overcoming her resistance are the poem's motivation and purpose. By reminding his mistress that "no man could hold it, for twas thine," the conclusion urges her to exercise her "lawfull libertie" to think and act as she herself desires—the legal and ethical right claimed by the 1567 *A Letter sent by the Maydens of London, to the vertuous Matrones & Mistresses of the same, in the defense of their lawfull Libertie*.[34]

The female lyric audience's power to join the speaker in making it so by saying so is what distinguishes poetry of courtship from poetry of praise and blame. A Petrarchan poet can idolize and curse a sonnet lady to his heart's content, but poetry of courtship is a directive rather than a declarative or performative speech act. It requires an interlocutor. Its success or failure depends on her answering response. What will she say? What will she do?

---

34. The text, edited with an introduction by R. J. Fehrenbach, is printed in "A Letter Sent by the Maydens of London (1567)," *English Literary Renaissance* 14 (1984): 285–304. For a more detailed discussion, see Ilona Bell, "The Maydens of London: In Defense of their Lawful Liberty," *Women, Writing, and the Reproduction of Culture in Tudor and Stuart Britain*, ed. Mary Burke, Jane Donawerth, Linda Dove, and Karen Nelson (forthcoming).

These two simple questions are always present, preoccupying the poet/lover's imagination, influencing his choice of rhetorical strategies. Her response may either be anticipated by the poem, influenced by the poem, or incorporated into successive poems. At the same time, the poem may be validated by her approval, undone by her objections, or recomposed by quite different interpretations of his words.

To the satiric eyes of a male coterie—to those "prophane men" who "will no faith on this bestow, / Or, if they doe, deride" ("The undertaking," 23–24)—the conclusion of "The Legacie" sounds like yet another attack on female inconstancy. But to a private lyric audience—or to "some lover, such as wee" ("The Extasie," 73) who chooses to read the poem as "if I were a mistress"[35]—it becomes a poignantly veiled plea for reassurance, for a return letter containing her heart, the rough corners and disturbing colors smoothed over by her own assurances of loving constancy.

In *The Book of the City of Ladies*, Christine de Pizan urges women reading seemingly antifeminist poems such as "The Legacie" to "interpret them according to the grammatical figure of *antiphrasis*, which means, as you know, that if you call something bad, in fact, it is good, and also vice versa."[36] In "The Legacie," Donne perfects his skill at writing topsy-turvy, antiphrastic poetry that can be read in opposing ways: both as a consummate expression of antifeminist wit *and* as a pointed exposé of antifeminist prejudice.[37]

Most modern critics read "The Legacie" as an indictment of female fickleness, but Donne stipulates that "It was not good, it was not bad." Whenever Donne's "colours" seem, on the surface, most scornful of women, we should be most alert for "corners," for hidden verbal ambiguities that reexamine the gender stereotypes and question those male authorities who are all too ready to prescribe both what is "good" and what is "bad" *about* woman—as well as what is "good" and what is "bad" *for* woman.

Elizabethan poets, critics, and readers expect each other to read love poems as "if I were a mistress," as Sidney acknowledges in *A Defence of Poesie*. The result, according to Sidney, is an erotics of secrecy: "believe . . . with me, that there are many mysteries contained in poetry which of purpose were written darkly, lest by profane wits it should be abused."[38] Recognizing that erotic poetry is especially vulnerable to abuse by "prophane men . . . / Which will no

35. Sidney, *Defence*, 48.

36. Christine de Pizan, *The Book of the City of Ladies*, trans. Earl Jeffrey Richards (New York: Persea, 1982), 7.

37. For example, R. W. Hamilton, "John Donne's Petrarchist Poems," *Renaissance and Modern Studies* 23 (1979), argues that Donne uses "the Petrarchist heart imagery" as "a criticism of the lady, and to provide a humorous and doubly paradoxical climax to the poem" (51).

38. Sidney, *Defence*, 53.

faith on this bestow, / Or, if they doe, deride," Donne depicts the lyric act of concealment as a

> ... braver thing
> Then all the *Worthies* did.
> And a braver thence will spring
> Which is, to keepe that hid.
> ("The undertaking," 22–28)

By broadcasting the fact that poetry contains mysteries, the poet separates the initiated private audience from the uninitiated public audience, and to a certain extent that does keep those mysteries "hid." Yet, paradoxically, the more an author calls attention to veiled meanings "which of purpose were written darkly," the more he alerts his readers to secrets that remain to be uncovered. The real secret is that there is no end to secrets—or to possible interpretations. "But," as Sidney remarks in *A Defence of Poesie* right after invoking "a mistress" as the primary and prototypical lyric audience, "let this be a sufficient, though short note, that we miss the right use of the material point of poesy."[39]

---

39. Ibid., 48.

Cecilia Infante

Donne's Incarnate Muse and His Claim to Poetic Control in "Sapho to Philaenis"

When Donne composed his heroical epistle "Sapho to Philaenis" he was participating in a literary tradition revitalized by the English reception of Ovid's *Heroides,* a collection of semierotic letters fictively written by mythological women (with the one exception of historical Sappho) to the epic heroes who have abandoned them.[1] In the late sixteenth century, subjective female complaints were written by male authors who were attracted to the marginal position their female speakers occupied with respect to the dominant discourses of their time, primarily the traditional humanist, Neoplatonic, and Petrarchan rhetorics. A female speaker with a literary ancestry like Sappho[2] would also have provided her appropriator with an aesthetic means of self-consciously inscribing himself into a predominant, masculine poetic tradition, derived from the *Heroides,* which used the figure of the abandoned woman as a vehicle for exploring the margins of rhetorical tradition. In an almost Girardian network of literary relations, where the master designates the object to his imitators and rivals as desirable by desiring it himself, writers were drawn to representing notorious women like Sappho because other men had written about them, notably Ovid in Sappho's case. Within this tradition, the figure of Sappho functioned as a palimpsest where an author could carve his voice into

1. John Donne, *The Complete English Poems of John Donne,* ed. C. A. Patrides (London: J. M. Dent and Sons, 1985). All quotations from "Sapho to Philaenis" are from this edition. For a collection of female-voiced complaints written by male poets, see John Kerrigan, *Motives of Woe: Shakespeare and the "Female Complaint"* (Oxford: Clarendon Press, 1991). Lawrence Lipking also examines the abandoned female subject as a male literary construct in *Abandoned Women and Poetic Tradition* (Chicago: University of Chicago Press, 1988).

2. To avoid confusion, I distinguish the historical Sappho from Donne's representation of her by maintaining separate spellings of her name: the poet "Sappho" and Donne's "Sapho." For a selection of fictional Sapphos see the *Palatine Anthology: Greek Lyric II,* ed. and trans. David A. Campbell, 2nd ed., rev. G. P. Goold, Loeb Classical Library (Cambridge: Harvard University Press, 1982).

the layered record of the preceding styles and voices of those authors who had imaged her before.

In "Sapho to Philaenis," Donne took up the project he inherited from his classical predecessor in the fifteenth letter of the *Heroides* and grafted his modern claim for poetic authority onto the preexisting structure of Ovid's rivalry with Sappho. There are also echoes in Donne's poem of Sappho's own poetry, unmediated by the fictions produced by writers such as Ovid, that suggest he was familiar with her work as it was available in Renaissance editions. Independent of her Ovidian association, Sappho was significant to sixteenth-century readers as the emblem of female intellectual authority, featured routinely in the defense of women and in the female genealogies of the period. However, until Janel Mueller's and Stella Revard's comparative studies of Donne's poem with Sappho's extant poetry, criticism has focused largely on Donne's intertextual rivalry with his male poetic predecessor Ovid, accounting for Donne's use of Sappho as Ovidian imitation or Sapphic ventriloquism and rarely as a sign of Donne's doubled act of literary alliance with both a male and a female authority.[3] My primary questions of Donne's anti-elegiac epistle regard his decision to restore Sappho's lesbian identity—which Ovid had replaced with her longing for Phaon—and Donne's desire to represent his own voice in a synchronic conversation with the original authors in terms that ensured his recognition and his authority. I am also interested in the extent to which early women writers were constrained by a masculine literary tradition of voicing abandoned women that appears to invest male writers with the power to speak "for" and "as" women.

I agree with Janel Mueller's assertion that "Donne looked to the Sappho of 'Phainetai moi' (in some version) as a source of renewal for the well-worn

3. The current popular tradition of interpreting "Sapho to Philaenis" is still limited to a handful of readily accessible articles. Between the very short article on the poem's neoclassical rhetorical roots by Don Cameron Allen, "Donne's 'Sapho to Philaenis,' " *English Language Notes* 1 (1964): 188–91, and the most recent essay on the poem's homoerotic idiom by Paula Blank, "Comparing Sappho to Philaenis: John Donne's 'Homopoetics,' " *PMLA* 110 (1995): 358–68, appeared the readings that have shaped this poem's reception: Stella Revard, in "The Sapphic Voice in Donne's 'Sapho to Philaenis,' " in *Renaissance Discourses of Desire*, ed. Claude J. Summers and Ted-Larry Pebworth (Columbia: University of Missouri Press, 1993), 63–76, and Janel Mueller, in "Lesbian Erotics: The Utopian Trope of Donne's 'Sappho to Philaenis,' " in *Homosexuality in Renaissance and Enlightenment England: Literary Representations in Historical Context,* ed. Claude J. Summers (New York: Haworth Press, 1992), 103–33, both emphasize the roles played by the historical poet Sappho and her work in Donne's epistle. James Holstun and Elizabeth Harvey laid the foundation for criticism of Donne's poem. Although radically different in theoretical methods, Holstun and Harvey share the conclusion that Donne ultimately extinguishes Sappho's authority by following his male predecessor's example, even as he purports to recuperate the "real" Sappho by reversing Ovid's heterosexual representation of her in *Heroides* 15. See James Holstun, " 'Will You Rent Our Ancient Love Asunder?': Lesbian Elegy in Donne, Marvell, and Milton," *ELH* 54:4 (1987): 835–67; and Elizabeth Harvey, "Ventriloquizing Sappho: Ovid, Donne, and the Erotics of the Feminine Voice," *Criticism* 31:2 (1989): 115–38.

conventions of Renaissance love poetry." Stella Revard further persuades me of the intimate association between Donne's "Sapho to Philaenis" and Sappho's original poetry. Revard's comparative analysis of Donne's poem uncovers a network of allusions to Sappho's extant poems and fragments that details how Donne was imitating Ovid's poetry and participating in "the Renaissance rediscovery of Sappho as one of the leading lyric voices of erotic literature."[4] Certainly, Donne would have had access to "Phainetai moi"—Sappho's famous lyric on the ecstasy of beholding her lover (commonly called Fragment 31)—preserved and popularized in the Renaissance by the author referred to as Longinus, in his treatise *On the Sublime* (chapters 1, 2, and 10), by Plutarch in his dialogue *The Lover*, in several Latin and one exclusively Greek edition,[5] and by Henri and Robert Estienne in their appendix to the 1554 and 1556 Greek, Latin, and French editions of Sappho's contemporary fellow poet Anacreon. The availability of this poem and the appearance of Sappho's hallmark tropes in "Sapho to Philaenis" of the self-blazon, the comparison of the beloved to the gods, the translation of the speaker's body into language, the final blessing in imitation of Sappho's closing prayer in the "Ode to Aphrodite," and Donne's peculiar use of "discolores" (not a common word in Donne) as a possible substitution for Sappho's unique metaphor for erotic longing—"greener than grass"—persuade me that Donne was simultaneously invoking both Sappho and Ovid's parody of her poetics in *Heroides* 15.

One of the reasons a lesbian Sappho may have attracted Donne's interest as a candidate for a poem on poetic failure is that she could embody the lesbian conceit for poetic creation shared by his literary circle in their formal correspondence during the likely period of the poem's composition.[6] In his verse letters to his friends Donne characteristically conflates the sexual with the textual act in a poetic fantasy that renegotiates the terms of poetic production and control in favor of the poet. According to this trope, poetry is the offspring produced from the sexual union of the male poet and his "indifferent" muse. Although gendered female, the muse can only inspire poetry but not give it birth; that is the privilege of the male poet. In a verse letter to Rowland Woodward, Donne emphasized this generative, albeit dependent role of the

4. Mueller, "Lesbian Erotics," 113; Revard, "The Sapphic Voice," 69.

5. Fulvio Orsini's *Carmina novem illustrium feminarum* (1568), ed. Laurence Gambara (Antwerp: Christophor Plantin, 1568); for discussions of Sappho's Renaissance transmission see Joan Dejean, *Fictions of Sappho* (Chicago: University of Chicago Press, 1989); Mueller, "Lesbian Erotics"; and Revard, "The Sapphic Voice."

6. Although there is some disagreement as to the authority and dating of "Sapho to Philaenis," I accept Grierson's estimation that, based on internal evidence, the poem "must have been composed about the same time" as the elegies, around 1597 or 1598 (*The Poems of John Donne*, ed. Herbert J. C. Grierson, 2 vols. [Oxford: Clarendon, 1912], 2:91). I also follow recent convention in attributing the poem to Donne.

male poet in relation to his muse. Donne claims that his muse affects a "chast fallownesse," suggesting that the muse is fecund, even plowed, yet unsown, and so unyielding without the male poet's seed.[7] In a verse letter that Rowland's brother, Thomas Woodward, sent to Donne, he claims that Donne's wanton muse made love to him and his muse, and "Being a mayde still, got this song on mee"—a sort of virgin impregnation and male delivery.[8]

This configuration of lesbianism by Donne and by his fellows in their formal correspondence suggests why the lesbian was appropriate to their discourse on poetic creation and how their concept of the lesbian functioned metaphorically as a poetic figure (like the muse). When Donne invited Rowland Woodward to join his "Muse with myne, / For myne is barren thus devorc'd from thyne," the inference appears to be that a little lesbian frolicking will refresh the muses, who would then return to their poets with restored inspiration.[9] The masculine notion that lesbian love is only a prelude to sex with men was a stereotype promoted in the Renaissance with specific reference to Sappho in works such as Pierre de Brantôme's *Vie des dames galantes*.[10] Clearly alluding to, and assimilating, the grotesque figures of Martial's Bassa and Lucian's Philaenis, Brantôme testifies that not only did "Sappho, the supreme mistress of the art" of lesbian lovemaking finally return to a man (Phaon) for sexual satisfaction, but he has "heard many fair dames to avow, these sports can be no rival to men; & all their delights with other women serve for naught but to whet their appetite for a fine bout with men" (1:136). As a poetic metaphor, this masculine formulation of lesbianism emphasizes the unproductive nature of sexual and textual relations that exclude men; lesbian and muse alike, while autonomous in achieving sexual bliss, ultimately depend on the man to give their activity direction and purpose. This understanding of lesbianism also suggests that while the homosexual intercourse of the male poet's muse may stimulate poetic creation in her and in him, it is ultimately the male poet who conceives and delivers poetry. Donne's lesbian conceit thus guarantees his creative power as author by foregrounding the muse's dependence on the male poet for her fruition: poetry.

In his verse letter to Donne, Thomas Woodward refers to the behavior of their muses as "tribadree," which was understood as the act of simulating heterosexual sex either through rubbing—*tribein* means "to rub"[11]—or by using a dildo. A literary complement to this concept of lesbianism, which

---

7. "To Mr. *Rowland Woodward*" ("Like one who in her third widdowhood"), in *The Complete English Poems of John Donne,* ed. C. A. Patrides, 262. All citations of Donne's verse letters are taken from Patrides's edition.

8. "Thou sendst me prose and rimes," in *The Poems of John Donne,* ed. Grierson, 2:166–67.

9. "To Mr. R.W." ("Zealously my Muse"), 320.

10. Pierre de Brantôme, *Les Dames Galantes* (Paris?: Gallimard Folio, 1981).

11. T. Woodward, "Thou sendst me prose and rimes"; 2:166–67; Mueller, "Lesbian Erotics," 111.

could have influenced Donne's image of Sapho, is a pseudo-Lucianic dialogue on pederastic relations, in the *Amores,* that includes a brief digression on lesbian sex—one that links Philaenis to Sappho. One male speaker, apparently defending male heterosexual relations, exclaims to the other that if men should lie with men, then "let them [women] strap to themselves cunningly contrived instruments of lechery, those mysterious monstrosities devoid of seed, and let woman lie with woman as does a man. Let wanton Lesbianism—that word seldom heard, which I feel ashamed even to utter—freely parade itself, and let our women's chambers emulate Philaenis, disgracing themselves with Sapphic amours."[12] The emphasis here, construed from the male perspective, is on the unnatural and unproductive quality of lesbian relations, dependent as they are on the dildo, an impotent surrogate for the male member ("cunningly contrived instruments of lechery" and "mysterious monstrosities devoid of seed"). David Halperin recognizes this rare literary representation of male attitudes toward female homosexuality as "wholly negative in intent (if subversively potent in effect)."[13] Certainly, the implications of this literary archetype of lesbian sex are subversive when the sexual and textual association fuels an attack on the unnatural and unproductive act of female authorship. Ben Jonson appears to manipulate the tribade trope for literary creation (and its specifically masculine point of view) in the 1601 "Epigram on the Court Pucell" (in "Underwood") when he ridiculed Cecilia Bulstrode's poetry as the unnatural issue of homosexual rape (presumably with a dildo). According to Jonson, "What though with Tribade lust she force a Muse," Cecilia Bulstrode fails to produce legitimate poetry.[14] Within the terms of this tribade trope for poetic creation then, the muse (and the female writer according to Jonson's equation) cannot produce poetry; despite her tribadry, the lesbian muse depends upon her male poet's pen for her issue—the muse is "barran" or "fallow,"[15] to use Donne's terminology, independent of her male handmaiden; hence, Thomas

12. M. D. Macleod, trans. *Lucian VIII,* Loeb Classical Library (1967; Cambrige: Harvard University Press, 1979), 195. David M. Halperin drew my attention to this fiction of the tribade in the conference paper he delivered at "The Constructed Body," sponsored by The Institute of Humanities, University of Michigan, Ann Arbor, 1992. His critical reading of this passage appears in "Historicizing the Sexual Body: Sexual Preferences and Erotic Identities in the Pseudo-Lucianic Erôtes" in *Discourses of Sexuality: From Aristotle to AIDS,* ed. Domna Stanton (Ann Arbor: University of Michigan Press, 1992), 247; Harvey also offers an interpretation of this passage in "Ventriloquizing Sappho," 124; and Elaine Marks includes a discussion of literary representations of the tribade from Martial to Brantôme "as a wierd, comic object" in "Lesbian Intertextuality," *Homosexualites and French Literature,* ed. George Stambolian and Elaine Marks (Ithaca: Cornell University Press, 1979), 360–62. For discussions of Donne's literary sources for the name Philaenis, see Don Cameron Allen, "Donne's 'Sapho to Philaenis,' " 189–91; and Mueller, "Lesbian Erotics."
13. Halperin, "Historicizing the Sexual Body," 247.
14. Ben Jonson, *The Poems of Ben Jonson.* ed. Bernard Newdigate (Oxford: Basil Blackwell, 1936), 162. Mueller also comments on Jonson's lesbian configuration of poetic failure in "Lesbian Erotics," 111.
15. "To Mr. B. B.," 289; and "To Mr. *Rowland Woodward,*" 262.

Woodward can insist that his verse letter is the issue of a ménage à trois with his and Donne's maiden muse

> Which rub'd and tickled with thyne could not chuse
> But spend some of her pithe and yeild to bee
> One in that chaste and mistique tribadree.
>
> $(2-4)^{16}$

In much the same way as this figure of the promiscuous, yet fruitless tribade-muse was serving Donne and his poetic fraternity in their sequence of verse letters on male friendship and literary creation, the figure of Sappho, the female poet and lesbian, could incarnate the "fallownesse" of Donne's muse.[17] The iconography of Sappho clearly exploits the ambiguity inherent in aesthetic conventions of representing poetic inspiration.[18] Only a female poet—especially one laureated and holding a lyre—could symbolize, at the same time, both creative artist and divine muse. A poet interested in playing with the ambiguity of these gendered conventions could subscribe Sappho as his figure for poetic failure by emphasizing, even thematizing, her lesbian reputation and her subsequent "fruitless" legacy. Furthermore, the figure of Sappho probably appealed to Donne for a poem on poetic mastery because she had already been featured as the subject of two poems where the speaker's loss of linguistic control is primarily at issue in the text: "Phainetai moi" and Ovid's *Heroides* 15. Donne could therefore inscribe himself into literary history by rivaling both predecessors, Sappho and Ovid, in their own idioms.

Donne's most remarkable modifications on Ovid's fifteenth epistle are two: he condensed Sappho's complaint into the autoerotic action of a single dramatic frame;[19] and he restored Sappho's reputed lesbian eroticism (according to Donne's Sapho, lines 25–28, she abandoned Phaon when he developed masculine characteristics). Although Donne's speaker expresses her longing for a female object of desire, the dramatic action of her complaint insists on Sappho's

---

16. I interpret the representation of the lesbian muse—or "tribade," as Thomas Woodward refers to his and Donne's muses in this verse letter—as deprived of her uniquely female powers of reproduction for precisely the same reason that Paula Blank emphasizes the muses' "productive tribadism" (364). Building on Valerie Traub's work, Blank argues that "tribadism becomes the means by which (male) writers produce poetry" (364). For a discussion of Donne's verse letters and their primary subject— Donne's infatuation with Thomas Woodward—see George Klawitter, "Verse Letters to T. W. from John Donne: 'By You My Love Is Sent,' " in *Homosexuality in Renaissance and Enlightenment England: Literary Representations in Historical Context*, ed. Claude J. Summers (New York: Haworth Press, 1992), 85–102.

17. "To Mr. *Rowland Woodward*" ("Like one who in her third widdowhood"), 262.

18. For an extended study of this topic, see Judith Stein, "The Iconography of Sappho, 1775–1875," Ph.D. diss., University of Pennsylvania, 1983.

19. Ovid, "Sappho to Phaon," *Heroides and Amores*, ed. and trans. Grant Showerman, 2nd ed., rev. G. P. Goold (London: William Heinemann, 1977), ll. 123–34.

autoerotic, not homoerotic, desire ("restore / Me to mee"). There could not possibly be a more literal way of configuring the idea, one discussed in Donne's sermons and letters on writing, that the poet is reflected and reproduced in his poetry than to depict the poet Sappho rapt in erotic fantasy and masturbating before her own mirrored image.[20] No matter how concretely Sapho's poetic fantasy of Philaenis emerges in her imagination, ultimately only Sapho is reflected in her mirror ("Me, in my glasse, I call thee"). Given the figurative uses to which Donne and his fellows were putting the subject of the lesbian in their correspondence, it is possible to interpret Donne's fiction of Sappho not only as his imaginative representation of the desiring lesbian subject but also as his tropic figure for poetic failure and object of professional exchange.

In "Sapho to Philaenis," Donne dramatizes his intertextual rivalry for literary authority by inscribing himself into a text largely synthesized of Ovidian and Sapphic allusions. The derivative design of female-voiced poems such as Donne's suggests that the female complainant represents both an imaginative attempt to articulate female experience and a site of male literary innovation and professional alliance. Like his Ovidian pattern, Donne's Sapho is unable to materialize her lover using the power of poetic discourse. Quenched of her "holy fire" and abandoned by her "inchanting force," Sapho must overcome Philaenis's absence with an illusion of her presence, produced by the speaker's own reflection and rhetoric. Sexual desire burns hotter than poetic fire for Donne's Sapphic speaker, although each is constituted of the same element and quickly melts the impermanent image of her beloved, which is stamped in wax on Sapho's heart (l. 10). But Donne's Sapho locates her poetic failure to "drawe" her lover in the inadequacy of conventional verse forms:

> Where is that holy fire, which Verse is said
>   To have? is that inchanting force decai'd?
> *Verse* that drawes *Natures* workes, from *Natures* law,
>   Thee, her best worke, to her worke cannot drawe.
>   (1–4)

Sapho then searches for a rhetoric proper to the female subject, asking "For, if we justly call each silly *man* / A *litle world,* What shall we call thee than?" (ll. 19–

---

20. See Donne's well-known equation of himself with his poetry in his verse letter "To Mr. R. W." ("If as mine is"):

> As this my letter is like me, for it
>   Hath my name, words, hand, feet, heart, minde and wit;
> It is my deed of gift of mee to thee,
>   It is my Will, my selfe the Legacie.
>   (ll. 5–8, 290)

20). Discarding humanist philosophy as an inappropriate rhetoric for the *female* subject, Sapho endeavors to articulate the woman outside a system of language that privileges the male subject ("What shall we call thee than?"). She also rejects the language of Petrarchan aesthetics, stripping her female subject/object (really her own reflection in the mirror) of the alienating anatomy of the Petrarchan blazon: "Thou are not soft, and cleare, and strait, and faire, / As *Down,* as *Stars, Cedars,* and *Lillies* are" (ll. 21–22). Sapho then reclothes Philaenis in a rhetoric that anatomizes the female body: "But thy right hand, and cheek, and eye, only / Are like thy other hand, and cheek, and eye"; Philaenis's body is her rhetoric, as is Sapho's: "My two lips, eyes, thighs, differ from thy two, / But so, as thine from one another doe" (ll. 23–24 and 45–46). Sapho's struggle to retrieve the woman from the dominance of masculine discursive traditions and forge a language proper to the female erotic experience leads her to a poetics of idolatry. Like her desire, which Sapho admits is idolatrous in lines 27–28, Sappho's poetics are idolatrous because they reject metaphor and embrace a symbolic system in which the thing *is* what it represents, the sign is the signified. Transposing this theory of poetic signification onto the female body of her lover, Donne's fictional Sapho claims a mimesis that is necessarily a failed system of representation because it mistakes the "representation" for the "thing" represented. The question of the woman's body then becomes the question of the woman's body as language and what of that body can achieve symbolization. Like the prototext of Sappho's self-blazon in "Phainetai moi," where Sappho anatomizes how she "seems to herself" *("phainom' em' auta"),* Donne's Sapho also articulates herself in the language of the female body.

Sapho situates her female subject at a prelapsarian point of signification where the woman's body is itself the fertile source of rhetorical invention. She contrasts the perfection of immutable female sexuality with the fallen inconstancy of male carnality: Philaenis's "body is a naturall *Paradise,* / In whose selfe, unmanur'd, all pleasure lies, / Nor needs *perfection"* (ll. 35–36). Like the "chast fallowness" of Donne's verse letter-muse, Philaenis (really Sapho's reflection) is perfect in her "unmanur'd" immaculate virginity, for, as Sapho reasons, "Men leave behind them that which their sin showes" (presumably semen and children) "[a]nd are, as theeves trac'd, which rob when it snows. / But of our dallyance no more signes there are, / Then *fishes* leave in streames, or *Birds* in aire" (ll. 39–42). Unlike male sexuality and symbolic discourse, neither Sapho nor Philaenis can sin because they cannot sign. Like the muse, the lesbian is fruitless: both female figures are incapable of signification.

Although Sapho relegates the female subject to the undifferentiated realm of myth, her response to the poetic problem of representing the female subject can also succeed as a lesbian idyll. After all, Sapho does replace alienating traditions of amorous rhetoric with a woman-centered (feminocentric) perspective. For some readers, Sapho's autoerotic logic is the ironic virtue of the poem, at once tautological (as James Holstun argues) but also self-validating. Sapho's body-logic—where Philaenis's "right hand, and cheek, and eye, only / Are like thy other hand, and cheek, and eye," like Sapho's "two lips, eyes," and "thighs"—may be sophistic, but it also invests her with an autonomous subjectivity outside the dehumanizing idioms of poetic, philosophic, and religious discourse. Stella Revard argues that Donne's modification of Ovid's epistolary scenario enables female to speak to female, which ultimately "restores the poem to the female voice."[21] Janel Mueller also interprets Donne's representation of Sappho as a "Donnean trope that casts lesbian love as the supreme erotic fiction," concluding that "Through the personages of Sapho and Philaenis Donne, in my reading, really undertook to explore how utopian erotics might be gendered all-female."[22] Revard's and Mueller's readings are compelling, but they restrict their analysis to the subject of erotic fantasy, stopping just short of the linguistic fantasy embedded in these "utopian erotics." They also discount the pronounced autoeroticism of Sapho's idyll. Autoeroticism, like writing, precludes the presence of an Other: both imaginative activities are predicated on absence. To interpret this poem as Donne's representation of "lesbian erotics" reduces Donne's conception of lesbian sexuality to narcissism, as in Holstun's reading. To insist on reading anything feminine or lesbian in Donne's representation of Sapho is to confuse Sapho's autoeroticism with lesbianism, as Paula Blank recently noted of Holstun's reading.[23] Instead, I find it more interesting to pursue the tropic use of this autoerotic configuration as an erotic fiction presented to the reader as context for a larger aesthetic discourse (metadiscourse) on the boundaries of poetic signification. In my reading, Donne's "utopian trope" is less an erotic or lesbian idyll than it is a linguistic fantasy configured in erotic terms.[24]

   Although it is impossible to determine whether Donne, in the guise of Sapho, participates in or satirizes the conventional idealization of the female beloved, I suspect that any male poet who represented Sappho—the Renaissance emblem of female literary excellence—as the speaking subject of his poem about female poetic skill risked losing the claim to poetic authority that the poem was designed (in part) to effect. Readers uninterested in or unaware of the

   21. Revard, "The Sapphic Voice," 73.
   22. Mueller, "Lesbian Erotics," 108 and 118.
   23. Blank, "Comparing Sappho to Philaenis," 359.
   24. Blank argues that the physical "sameness" of homosexual identification functions as an appropriate idiom for Donne's "homopoetics"; and Blank is right, I think, to conclude that "Donne presents Sappho's version of homo-sexuality as humanly impossible to achieve, no matter who attempts to achieve it, as a figure of language that can never materialize in any other form" ("Comparing Sappho to Philaenis," 359).

intertextual project embedded in Donne's female complaint could allow the speaking female subject to emerge dramatically as the primary agent of Donne's poem and not as Donne's clever figure for aesthetic innovation. In most well-crafted female-voiced plaints, the tension between an author's desire to create a convincing fiction of a lamenting woman and his desire for professional recognition produced a situation wherein the "actual" writer was forced to draw attention to his (often masculine) authority and away from the sympathetic lure of his plaintful speaker.[25]

To control the problem of authority inherent in the female-voiced plaint, writers developed framing devices designed to draw the reader's attention to their literary art and authority. For example, in the series of complaints from Jane Shore (Edward IV's mistress) that developed into a literary fad in the final quarter of the sixteenth century, Michael Drayton's "Epistle of Mistres Shore, To King Edward the Fourth" illustrates how poets such as Donne used the faltering female subject as a vehicle both for redefining literary fashion and for challenging the authority and skill of their literary predecessors. Drayton contrasts Jane's opening configuration of her relationship to language as a "weak Child," a "poore Child" who doubtfully takes up an instrument under her master's command,[26] with his confident assertion of authorial power in his address "To the Reader" and in his annotations. Like Thomas Churchyard before him (who names himself in "Shore's Wife"),[27] Drayton positions himself within the male-authored tradition of Shore complaints by associating himself with his predecessors in the opening sentence of the epistle's annotation: first he justifies "why I entitle this Worke, ENGLANDS Heroicall Epistles [and] secondly, why I have annexed Notes to every Epistles end" (130). Drayton also appends "Arguments" to every epistle as a frame for his reader's interpretations of the text and as an opportunity to explain how his modifications improve upon his literary model, "OVID (whose Imitator I partly professe to be)" (130). Drayton then delineates the literary history of his female subject, explaining that "Two or three Poems written by sundry men, have magnified this womans beautie" (258): he even recognizes the founder of the tradition as "Sir Thomas Moore" (258). Although Drayton's fictional Jane goes on to deliver such a well-drawn critique of the dominant rhetorics misrepresenting women that it resembles the protofeminist attacks of writers such as Christine de Pizan—and could easily pass for the voice and argument of an actual writing woman if

25. See John Kerrigan, Introduction to *Motives of Woe*.

26. Michael Drayton, "Epistle from Mistres Shore, To King Edward the Fourth," *England's Heroical Epistles, written in imitation of the stile and manner of Ovid's epistles* in *The Works of Michael Drayton*, ed. J. William Hebel, 5 vols. (London: Oxford University Press, 1931–1941), ll. 1 and 7, 2:254.

27. Thomas Churchyard, "Shore's Wife" (1563), in *Mirror for Magistrates*, ed. Lily B. Campbell (Cambridge: Cambridge University Press, 1938), 371–86.

excerpted from its author's framed setting—Drayton's prefaces to the reader, arguments on the subject, notes, and annotated interpretations interrupt the reading experience latent in Ovid's psychologically intimate form (all formal controls absent in Donne's Ovidian poem). By controlling the power of the subject position and its "I" of enunciation, Drayton (unlike Donne) prevents the total imaginative fusion of reader and speaker; instead, it is the author and the literary ancestry of his subject that dominate the female-voiced epistle. Like Donne's Sapho, Drayton's female speaker clearly constitutes a stage on which the male poet performs a twin gesture of literary alliance: first, with the male literary establishment ("Two or three Poems written by sundry men") and second, with a male literary predecessor ("OVID [whose imitator I partly professe to be]").[28] However, unlike Drayton's fictional Jane, Donne's Sapho appears in an intertextual but unframed setting, which potentially invests her (if the reader is willing) with the authority and agency to emerge as the poem's principal speaker.

The female subject's struggle to claim a language of her own apparently appealed to male writers as an aesthetic strategy of exploring the limits of discursive signification or of reinventing their master discourses. Many writers in sixteenth-century England, especially those influenced by the reception of Ovid's *Heroides,* were attracted to the female subject position as a site for linguistic innovation: Sappho was one of several famous female figures, like Jane Shore, who became the focus of a "vogue of complaint poems about women in the 1590s," to borrow Hallett Smith's description of this literary trend in his article on Shakespeare's "A Lover's Complaint."[29] Within this popular tradition, Donne's compound fiction of Sappho (at once hers and Ovid's) would have presented Donne with not only a well-known historical and fictional woman but also a quintessential vehicle of alienated subjectivity—a female love poet and a reputed lesbian—for his act of literary rivalry with Ovid and his imitators and for Donne's poetic inquiry into the female subject's relation to poetic language.

In "Sapho to Philaenis," Donne's professional need for recognition and challenge to Ovid's poetics may help account for why Sapho's poetics of idolatry reinforce the notion that the female subject is not representable. Although Donne's speaker may satisfy her fantasy of discovering a rhetoric proper to the female experience, she nevertheless clearly overextends the limits of metaphor, ultimately assigning the female beloved to the strata of language where words

28. For an analysis of sixteenth-century Jane Shore complaints, see the third chapter, "A Rhetorical Pattern for English Female Heroes," of my doctoral dissertation, "Sappho and Jane Shore as Male Models of Female Speech and Subjectivity, England 1513–1624," University of Michigan, 1994.

29. Hallett Smith, "A Lover's Complaint" in *The Riverside Shakespeare,* ed. G. Blakemore Evans (Boston: Houghton Mifflin, 1974), 1781.

and things are not different: furthermore, Donne's principal goal is to actualize *his* creative authority, and not his female fiction's. Too believable a fiction would obscure the line between "actual" and "fictional" speaker. This idea is literalized in Donne's dramatic scene: before her mirror, Sapho anatomizes herself with reference to an *illusion* of another: ultimately, only Donne should emerge in the mind of his reader as the creative agent of the poem.

While the subgenre of the female complaint thus expanded the range of male authors, it potentially promoted male formulations of female sexuality and writing. The political danger of this literary practice for women writers ultimately depended on whether or not male-constructed female voices were accepted as *substitutes* for the participation of real women in literary discourse, precluding them from legitimately occupying the subject position themselves. Furthermore, one might well wonder if repeated male mimesis of female speech and female abandonment helped to shape women's apprehension of their own experience and their own language.

In the sixteenth century when the female complaint was in vogue, the political implications of this rhetorical tradition were not lost on the female writers of the day. Their primary concern regarded the use to which the female figure was put in antifeminist diatribes and Petrarchan love poetry. Jane Anger, in her 1589 "*Protection for Women* To defend them against the Scandalous Reports of a late Surfeiting Lover and all other Venerians that complain so to be overcloyed with women's kindness," specifically attacks those male writers who, having reached the limits of their artistic invention, turn to women for a renewal of their poetic powers. "The desire that every man hath to show his true vein in writing is unspeakable, and their minds are so carried away with the manner as no care at all is had of the matter. They run so into Rhetoric as often times they overrun the bounds of their own wits. . . . If they have stretched their invention so hard on a last as it is at a stand, there remains but one help, which is to write of us women."[30] More specifically, women writers such as Christine de Pizan, Margaret Tyler, Jane Anger, Constantia Munda, and Rachel Speght warned of the power of the dominant mimetic tradition, Petrarchism, to force "Woman" to symbolize her male creator's poetics and ideology, thereby reducing women to the dumb silence of an object (a written woman). Both rhetorical traditions represented and promoted images of women in terms largely foreign to their political, physical, and personal experience. In the *Book of the City of Ladies,* Christine de Pizan attacks the "testimony of so many notable men" (particularly Ovid) by admitting that "I could not see or realize

---

30. Jane Anger, "Her Protection for Women," in *Half Humankind: Contexts and Texts of the Controversy about Women in England, 1540–1640,* ed. Katherine Usher Henderson and Barbara F. McManus (Urbana: University of Illinois Press, 1985), 174.

how their claims could be true when compared to the natural behavior and character of women" (from the 1521 edition, translated by Brian Anslay).[31] In her 1617 "The Worming of a Mad Dogge," Constantia Munda also laments how the "idle muse" of male wit, "while it is at liberty, most impiously it throws dirt in the face of half humankind."[32] The Petrarchan idealization of the woman also drew protofeminist protest largely because it promoted an image of femininity as essentially incapable of symbolic import: women writers such as Jane Anger claimed that while these texts appear to represent a female subject, it is actually the discursive environment that she represents for her poet that is crucial to the poem and to its true subject, the male poet's subjective monologue—his "desire to show his true vein in writing."

Female complaints such as Donne's heroidean adaptation open up the question of how sexual difference operates linguistically in a text; after all, to be signed with a woman's name does not necessarily make a piece of writing feminine; likewise, a piece of writing signed with a man's name does not in itself exclude femininity. An important question embedded in this literature is whether or not a male writer is really capable of imitating women's amorous language or if his female impersonation is successful because it satisfies his audience's preconceptions of what women's erotic rhetoric should be. And given the body of conventions inherited from the *Heroides* and governing amorous expression, how then, to revoice Gabrielle Verdier's question of the *Portuguese Letters,* "does female expression of passion differ from male mimesis of it?"[33]

For a writer such as Donne, the purpose behind assuming the lesbian persona of Sappho might have been limited to linguistic experiments—a means of reinventing and revitalizing stale or ineffective idioms or as a figure for literary rivalry and exchange—but he nevertheless promotes a theory of female erotic desire as unrepresentable, reified like the Petrarchan beloved or the poetic muse. Sappho may proffer Donne a figurative site for poetic alliance; but for readers unconcerned or uninterested in the intertextual design of his poem, Sapho is less a trope than she is a woman speaking. Given Sappho's emblematic status in the Renaissance, it is possible that some early modern readers of "Sapho to Philaenis" wondered if the poem was intended to participate (if only imaginatively) in their struggle to generate utopian visions of female political and linguistic freedom. If read in the context of the rhetorical tradition that the male-constructed female complaint shared with early feminist protest, which

31. Christine De Pizan, *The Book of the City of Ladies,* trans. Earl Jeffrey Richards (New York: Persea Books, 1982), 4.

32. Constantia Munda, "Worming of a Mad Dogge" in *Half Humankind,* ed. Henderson et al., 250.

33. Gabrielle Verdier, "Gender and Rhetoric in Some Seventeenth-Century Love Letters," *L'esprit créateur* 23:2 (1983): 46.

promoted deliberative rhetoric as a specifically female idiom, the "feminist" tone of Donne's poem takes on credible dimensions.[34]

In 1980 Foucault contributed to a fundamental shift in traditional ways of reading, writing, and interpreting when he asked "What is an author?" and "What difference does it make who is speaking?"[35] These questions of authorship and authority form the base of poststructuralist and feminist criticism. Perhaps more than any other form of representing the female subject in the nondramatic literature of the English sixteenth century, female-voiced complaints modeled on Ovid's *Heroides* are ideal pedagogical material today because they resist most conventional interpretive schemes that depend upon clear distinctions between a male author, his female speaker, and that author's literary intentions. And if the male gaze is incorporated into the female speaker's confession, then the reader should be rightly suspicious of the female speaker's relationship to her male creator, especially when "she" emerges convincingly from her fiction of abandonment. The blurred distinction between "written women" and "writing women" in the literary tradition of the male-constructed female complaint appears to license men the liberty of speaking "for" and "as" women, which has implications for real women of ever occupying the position of writing subject themselves. For some readers, especially feminists, it is precisely because these female complaints involve the male writer with the fictional female subject that the difference between woman as aesthetic process and woman as sexual identity matters; so does the difference of who is speaking. Finally, students interested in the tradition of the female complaint, *l'écriture féminine* or, more simply, women's writing, should explore the impact that this subgenre of "women's writing" and its gendered rhetoric of abandonment—of which Donne's poem is one of many—had on the development of real women's writing and language, especially given the pedagogic role that the *Heroides* played in the education of both sexes through the eighteenth century. Because convincing female plainants in epistolary poems such as Donne's "Sapho to Philaenis" dramatize some of our most pressing political and aesthetic concerns—with women as speaking and writing subjects, the relationship of women to language, the ways sexual difference operates linguistically in a literary text—this disturbing body of literature presents teachers today with ideal works for encouraging students to scrutinize and criticize their inherited traditions of writing and reading.

---

34. For studies of the "decorum of the dispute," see Kerrigan, 52–63; and Betty Travitsky, "The Lady Doth Protest: Protest in the Popular Writings of Renaissance Englishwomen," *English Literary Renaissance* 14 (1984): 255–83.

35. Michel Foucault, "What Is an Author," *The Foucault Reader*, ed. Paul Rabinow (New York: Pantheon Books, 1984), 101 and 120.

Lawrence Normand

WITCHES, KING JAMES, AND *THE MASQUE OF QUEENS*

Since witches do not exist, the idea of a woman as a witch can only be a matter of representation. This is not to say, of course, that witches have not been thought to exist and to have real magical powers; or indeed that some women have not thought themselves to be witches; or that real, material effects have not flowed from the idea. It is merely to say that the relations in this case between representation and the real are especially complex and tenuous, though no less dangerous to the women involved in them. Some of the complex ways in which women may be represented as witches in the Renaissance emerge in three related texts written over eighteen years: the anonymous pamphlet *Newes from Scotland* (London, 1592?), James VI of Scotland's *Daemonologie* (Edinburgh, 1597; London, 1603), and Ben Jonson's *Masque of Queens* (performed at Whitehall on February 2, 1609). The first two concern the first major Scottish witch-hunt of 1590–1597, in which very many people, mostly women, were accused and some executed. *Newes from Scotland* reports the plot to sink the ships bringing James and his bride Anne home from Denmark after their marriage, and the witches' pact with the devil, who appeared to them in person. James's own *Daemonologie,* written while the witch-hunt was still going on, is an orthodox theorization of witchcraft, distinguished by the fact that its author was a king who participated in the witches' examinations and was the prime target of their supposed power. Jonson's masque, written long after these events, when James and Anne had assumed the English throne, presents witches as powerless and futile, a wholly negative image of women's exercising power. The texts provide representations of gradually decreasing feminine power; they move successively from the historical to the literary, from the pamphlet's writing of supposedly actual events to the masque's writing of imagery and symbol. In the masque,

My thanks to Stuart Clark, Gareth Roberts, Robert Mighall, and Derek Duncan for their help in the preparation of this essay.

however, a new formation of female power appears. In this series the possibility of reading the texts in such a way as to recover traces of the accused women's testimony, and hence their experience—to represent themselves, to give their own account of popular beliefs and practices, to oppose the meanings and fantasies imposed on them by their accusers—gradually diminishes from a point not high to start with. Women as witches become increasingly subject to a rewriting, indeed reinvention, which is in the interests of those who do the writing. Taken together these texts support Robert Muchembled's acculturation thesis that witchcraft is useful to political elites aiming to subject the common people to religious or moral reform. These representations of women help fashion sustaining ideologies for the royal and aristocratic ruling class.[1]

The anonymous author of *Newes from Scotland* uses language to turn real women into witches; his narrative supposedly reports the literal, historical truth. In *Newes from Scotland,* the witch-hunt starts from a woman and a social irregularity: the servant Geillis Duncane was absent from her master's house every other night. Her absences were unexplained. She was also a healer, known to take "in hand to help all such as were troubled or greeued with any kinde of sicknes or infirmitie" (8),[2] and it was her master noticing that she suddenly began to "perfourme manye matters most miraculous" (8) that made him suspect that "she did not those things by naturall and lawfull wayes, but rather . . . by some extraordinary and vnlawfull meanes" (9). The text's incoherence mirrors the very problem that Geillis Duncane presents: she is a woman whose actions men cannot comprehend, neither her master nor the writer. The narratives that follow in the pamphlet make sense only if the reader believes, like her interrogators, that Geillis Duncane is a witch. Her master wants

1. The authoritative account of Scottish witch-hunts is Christina Larner, *Enemies of God: The Witch-hunt in Scotland* (London: Chatto and Windus, 1981); see 68–69, 160, for the North Berwick witch-hunt. On *Daemonologie* see Rhodes Dunlap, "King James and Some Witches: The Date and Text of the *Daemonologie,*" *Philological Quarterly* 54 (winter 1975): 40–46. On acculturation see Robert Muchembled, "Witchcraft, Popular Culture, and Christianity in the Sixteenth Century with Emphasis upon Flanders and Artois," in *Ritual, Religion, and the Sacred,* ed. Robert Forster and Orest Ranum (Baltimore and London: Johns Hopkins University Press, 1982), 213–36; "Lay Judges and the Acculturation of the Masses (France and the Southern Low Countries, Sixteenth to Eighteenth Centuries)," in *Religion and Society in Early Modern Europe, 1500–1800,* ed. Kaspar van Greyerz (London: The German Historical Institute, and George Allen and Unwin, 1984), 56–65; and "Satanic Myths and Cultural Reality," in *Early Modern European Witchcraft: Centres and Peripheries,* ed. Bengt Ankarloo and Gustav Henningsen (Oxford: Clarendon Press, 1993), 139–60. For critiques of acculturation see Peter Burke, "A Question of Acculturation?" in *Scienze, Credenze Occulte, Livelli Di Cultura* (Florence: Leo S. Olschki, 1982), 197–204; and Jean Wirth, "Against the Acculturation Thesis," in *Religion and Society in Early Modern Europe, 1500–1800,* ed. Kaspar van Greyerz (London: The German Historical Institute, and George Allen and Unwin, 1984), 66–78.

2. All quotations from *Newes from Scotland* and *Daemonologie* are cited by page number from *Daemonologie and Newes from Scotland,* ed. G.B. Harrison (Edinburgh: Edinburgh University Press, 1966).

an explanation for her power to "perfourme matters of so great importance" (9), and so he "did with the helpe of others, torment her with the torture of the Pilliwinckes vpon her fingers, which is a greeuous torture . . . yet would she not confesse any thing" (9).

The impulsion to torture exceeds Geillis Duncane's transgressive nights out, or her healing powers, but her accusers justify it by finding the devil's mark on her throat that confirms a pact with the devil. She is redefined as evil, as having a body bearing a satanic sign, and tortured until she capitulates to the explanation of demonic conspiracy. As G. R. Quaife has noted, "in Scotland, the peasants often associated the healer with witchcraft and many Scots healers were tried as diabolic witches." The twentieth-century reader might see a servant girl's social or sexual freedom and a healing skill. Her master sees incomprehensible behavior in someone subordinated by gender and class, and he names her a witch. Geillis Duncane turns witch-accuser herself, in a typical example of what Lyndal Roper calls a fantasy "of revenge and of compensatory potency" in victims of witchcraft accusation. Duncane names other women who in turn reveal the plot to destroy the king, and the witch-hunt begins, involving "innumerable others in that partes, and dwelling in those bounds aforesaide" (11). The master wants to discover what the servant girl signifies, and he compels her to collaborate in producing a meaning for herself that he can understand. Roper has argued that witchcraft accusation and confession need not be thought of as having been simply one-sided, with an interrogator imposing his fantasies on a woman, but might have involved a transaction, with a woman collaborating with her accusers to produce fantasies within a witchcraft scenario that satisfied the ideological needs of both interrogators and woman. In those circumstances, a woman under interrogation as a witch was not merely "a conduit either of the traces of a vanished primitive religion, or of the witch beliefs of her interrogators"; rather, she should be understood as having created her confessions, in Roper's words, "out of the elements of fantasy available to her, from what her culture knew of the Devil and his ways, and [that] what she selected had a logic." *Newes from Scotland* struggles to turn the terror and violence of a witch-hunt into coherent textual logic. It shows women being forced by violence into becoming actors in a demonic narrative. As they are turned into witches they are subjected by discursive formations that serve political ends.[3]

---

3. G. R. Quaife, *Godly Zeal and Furious Rage: The Witch in Early Modern Europe* (London and Sydney: Croom Helm, 1987), 43. Lyndal Roper, *Oedipus and the Devil: Witchcraft, Sexuality and Religion in Early Modern Europe* (London and New York: Routledge, 1994), 244 n. 20, where the idea of compensatory potency is attributed to Norbert Schindler, "Die Entstehung der Unbarmherzigkeit. Zur Kultur und Lebensweise der Salzburger Bettler am Ende des 17. Jahrhunderts," in *Widerspenstige Leute. Studien zur Volkskultur in der frühen Neuzeit* (Frankfurt am Main: 1992), 301.

The most striking feature of *Newes from Scotland* is the account of something akin to the witches' sabbath, in which the devil instructs the witches to direct their arts against the newly wed James and Anne. Whatever fragments of real action may be embedded in this story, the author intends to show *women* attaching themselves to the devil for politically subversive ends. The men who are mentioned at the start disappear from the pamphlet. The sabbath in *Newes from Scotland* is almost exclusively female (except for the devil and a schoolmaster who acts as the devil's registrar) because the women's relationship with the devil is sexual: when they pledge allegiance to him "the Diuell dooth lick them with his tung in some priuy part of their bodie, before hee dooth receiue them to be his seruants" (12), and then "he would Carnallye vse them, albeit to their little pleasure, in respect of his colde nature" (18). It is specifically through female sexuality that the devil wins adherents to his strategy of evil. In the pamphlet there is no concept of sodomy that would include men's sexual attachment to the devil. The sabbath suggests the terror of women's collective actions; their independence or power is seen as profoundly antisocial and subversive. Two hundred women sail in sieves to the kirk of North Berwick "with Flaggons of wine making merrie and drinking by the waye" (13), and when they arrive the devil "did greatlye enueighe against the King of Scotland, [and] receiued their oathes for their good and true seruice towards him" (14). The women, now witches, supposedly raise storms and prepare potions to poison the king. The terrors that the pamphlet excites center on the idea of women acting together as a group, which seems so fearful that it has to appear as political crime: as insurgency and attempted regicide.

The pamphlet is designed to persuade readers of the reality of witches; and its rhetoric compels a reader to accept its point of view and exclude other points of view. In order to see the pamphlet's process of representation we need to resist its intention of turning women into witches. One mode of resistance might be insistently to rehistoricize by returning to the dittays, or statements of charges, against those accused, held in the Scottish Record Office.[4] But the pamphlet's author himself creates a spurious historicity in which authentic historical references, drawn from the dittays, are used to guarantee the reality of supernatural events by anchoring them to what is familiar. The devil's reality is supposedly guaranteed by his being historicized, and represented not as a spirit but as having a real physical existence, and entering history at real times and places and engaging with real women. The accused women, on the other

4. The dittays (indictments) against Agnes Sampson, Barbara Napier, Euphame McCalzeane, and John Cunningham (alias Fian) can be found in Scottish Record Office, JC 2/2, ff. 201–6ᵛ, ff. 213–14ᵛ, ff. 221–26ᵛ, ff. 195–96ᵛ. They are reprinted in Robert Pitcairn, *Ancient Criminal Trials in Scotland from A.D.1488–1596* (Edinburgh: The Bannatyne Club, 1833), 1:209–56.

hand, who actually existed, are dehistoricized by being absorbed into the fiction of the demonic pact. The pamphlet's political effect is to consolidate James's position as king, for what else did the devil's railing that the king was the greatest enemy he had in the world signify except that James was crucially implicated in the natural and supernatural cosmic scheme of things? No one could argue with the testimony of Satan himself, as told to actual women. The pamphlet ends with this very moral: "And trulie the whole scope of this treatise dooth so plainely laie open the wonderfull prouidence of the Almightie, that if he [James] had not bene defended by his omnipotencie and power, his Highnes had neuer returned aliue in his voiage from Denmarke" (29). This material is helping to fashion James's notion of his rights as king: that he has a unique relation with God that confers rights and powers upon him in relation to church and state. Satan's particular hostility suggests this as much as does God's supposed particular protection.

The fascination that the North Berwick witches had for James was such that he was present at many of the interrogations and questioned them himself. *Daemonologie* was written in response to the witch-hunt, and its anxieties too center on women. But the effects of its representations are more complex, for where the pamphlet shows particular women becoming witches, and through the demonic pact threatening the state, *Daemonologie* shows women generally as dangerous, as potential witches, and defines their power as frighteningly ambiguous but, ultimately, unreal. The book stands halfway between *Newes from Scotland,* in which there is a dissonance between the historical material and its theme of witchcraft conspiracy, and *The Masque of Queens,* which with its learned assurance turns witches into harmless creatures with little reality. *Daemonologie* attempts to produce something like the completeness of Jonson's ideological scheme, but it struggles to reconcile evidence from the witch inquisitions, popular customs and traditions, learned demonology, and political ideology. James wrote to subject the evidence of history to the claims of theory and a self-promoting ideology. If James ever felt terror at the supposed witches' plots against him in the early 1590s, then writing *Daemonologie* was surely a way of dispelling his fears, while at the same time exacerbating the fears of his readers. James wrote that witches are dangerously subversive to the whole commonwealth yet at the same time harmless creatures subjected by Satan's illusory powers, a contradiction that serves to enhance his own political position. In this double representation the witches' femininity is a crucial element.

For James the reason there are so many more women than men witches is that "that sexe is frailer then man is, so is it easier to be intrapped in these grosse snares of the Deuill, as was ouer well proued to be true, by the Serpents deceiuing of *Eua*" (43–44). Male magicians, on the other hand, are accorded a degree of respect because it is their ambitious search for knowledge that may entice them "to that black and vnlawfull science of *Magie*" (10). Certain traditional activities of women in popular culture are drawn into the demonological ambit, in particular medical remedies and love magic involving "the vertue of worde, herbe, & stone" (11) and "such kinde of Charmes as commonlie dafte wiues vses, . . . for preseruing them from euill eyes, . . . By curing the Worme, by stemming of blood, . . . Or else by staying married folkes, to haue naturallie adoe with other" (11–12). As these traditional activities of popular culture meet elite demonological theory, they are redefined in demonological terms as the "Deuilles rudimentes" (11), the first steps in satanic involvement to deceive women into believing that they have powers and thereby to satisfy their desire to "winne a reputation to themselues" (12), to "seeke to bee learned in that Arte" (12), or to run "directlie to the Deuill for ambition or desire of gaine" (12). It is peasant women's limited desires for power and reputation for themselves, gained in ways specific to women, that James seems to fear and locates as satanic. Traditional activities aroused suspicion and fear and left many women who practiced them vulnerable to witchcraft accusations.

In *Daemonologie,* women are also dangerous to the state because the devil can have easy sexual access to them. The devil can steal sperm from a dead body or borrow a dead body to appear in. The barrier assumed to exist between human and spirit worlds is all too easily breachable by women having sex with spirits, and in the sabbath the bond between the devil and a woman is ensured by sex. To the demonologist, the devil's mark signifies the forbidden mixing of human and demonic realms. A female body with the mark shows that the devil's attentions have transformed its nature from the human to the demonic. The mark denotes an imaginary elision of female sexuality and political subversion; a drama of a woman's seduction into a sexual attachment outside social and ontological boundaries, the ultimate significance of which (not necessarily known to the woman herself) is political: the overturning of the entire social order. To the modern interpreter of witchcraft, the search for the devil's mark may be a sign of intense sexual anxiety in men in authority when faced with women whose behavior they do not understand or wish to control, as the account of Geillis Duncane illustrates. In any case, women's representations have passed out of their own understanding and control and into the ideas of expert, elite demonologists.[5]

Surprisingly, though, *Daemonologie* does not present the sabbath with the same horror as *Newes from Scotland.* James indeed investigates the idea of

---

5. For a fuller discussion of the physical/spiritual theme in the context of German witchcraft, see Roper, *Oedipus and the Devil,* chap. 8, "Exorcism and the Theology of the Body." For an alternative account of *Newes from Scotland,* see Laura Levine, *Men in Women's Clothing: Antitheatricality and Effeminization 1579–1642* (Cambridge: Cambridge University Press, 1994), 120–33.

a woman's renouncing her baptism, pledging allegiance to the devil, and becoming an enemy of God as well as the king.[6] But while the text presents all women as potentially witches, it also makes that power uncertain, both real and unreal, actual yet illusory. According to James, these threatening women are ensnared in futile powerlessness because, the theory goes, the witches' effects are always done with God's permission, and, moreover, their power, which comes from Satan and seems real, is often illusory. The storms encountered by Anne and James were real but only because God permitted them. This has it both ways: witches have some real magical power, but it is all under God's control, though this is hardly reassuring if you are facing a real storm raised by witches. In the struggle between God and Satan, God has always already won, but Satan can have local victories. James notes that witches are dangerously subversive to the commonwealth *and* are harmless creatures subjected by Satan's illusory powers. This contradiction enhances his own political position.

Nothing should be clearer than the opposition between God and Satan, yet *Daemonologie* breaks down this absolute opposition. James generates fearful suspicion of women as Satan's agents working to destroy the state because the demonized women are impossible to identify as obviously different, as being outside society—they are inside as well and seem perfectly normal. His rhetoric produces uncertainty and fear. Naming the people to whom the devil is drawn, James in effect mentions everyone, men or women: either "the wicked," or "the best," or "the godlie" who have sinned or have weakness in their faith (47). Again, when he asks if someone should be considered guilty of witchcraft if they have *appeared* in some other accused person's possessed visions, he says that they should: "I think they are not a haire the lesse guiltie: For the Deuill durst neuer haue borrowed their shaddow or similitude to that turne, if their consent had not bene at it: And the consent in these turnes is death of the law" (79). In other words, anyone can be a witch; witchcraft is potentially everywhere; mere mental consent defines a witch.

This fear is pacified by James's political prescription, for the only exception to general susceptibility to demonic temptation is the king. As in a masque performance, his unique position gives access to the truth. In *Newes from Scotland* the reader is invited to wonder why "the Kings maiestie would . . . hazarde himselfe in the presence of such notorious witches" (29) and answers that the Almighty defends him. In *Daemonologie,* James develops this idea. If a private person catches a witch her powers will be undiminished; if a lawful magistrate catches her, her supernatural powers disappear, "For where God beginnes iustlie to strike by his lawfull Lieutennentes, it is not in the Deuilles power to defraude or bereaue him of the office, or effect of his powerfull and reuenging Scepter" (51). The reader is meant to see that witches have real power over everyone except divinely appointed kings. It is only the king and his magistrates who can offer defense against this fearful threat, only they who form the true outside of the society within which Satan operates freely. James is fashioning a notion of monarchy that possesses supernatural, divine power. This is magic, legitimated by its location in the royal person. James's supernatural spiritual power is greater than the witches', for he has confronted and defeated them without endangering himself. The claim for kingly spiritual power rests on historical events that become proof of divinely given power. Fear of women as witches, then, sustains patriarchal rulers in their places.

Daemonologie becomes a totalizing, absolutist discourse. It abolishes distinctions between white magic, wise women (as poor Geillis Duncane perhaps was), and traditional spirits like fairies and brownies. No legitimacy or power is accorded to traditional supernatural spirits and folk charms, such "as commonlie dafte wiues vses, for healing of forspoken goodes, for preseruing them from euill eyes" (11–12). No ambiguity or margin of tolerance is admitted in a totalizing scheme that could be, and indeed was, activated as a highly effective means of social control by central government. James banishes a popular understanding of spirits from his cosmos, citing "the Lawe of God, wherein are all *Magicians,* Diuines, Enchanters, Sorcerers, Witches, & whatsouer of that kinde that consultes with the Deuill, plainelie prohibited, and alike threatned against" (29). The extinguishing of popular spirits, and their relationships with human beings, works to Christianize (or rather Protestantize) the world by declaring as demonic all dealings with them. James's drive to exclude spirits has none of Milton's pathos when he wrote of that process occurring on the morning of Christ's nativity, for James's aims are political.[7]

Daemonologie leaves Scotland with a Protestant scheme of absolutes: God and Satan battling over the souls and bodies of the people, with the king as the sole legitimate source of power. The process of acculturation by which the populace is trained in the Protestantism of the elite requires that there be no neutral magical practices or spirits, and in the construction of this ideology ideas of women as witches play a central part. The real, historical women who were the unfortunate subjects of this ideological process have almost disappeared from the text of *Daemonologie,* though not completely, for faint traces of their voices can still be heard in such phrases as "they say themselues" (39) or "some of them sayeth" (39), even though the final interpretation of their words lies with James, who asserts his truth from the position of political authority. In his theorization of the North Berwick witches, the so-called events of the sabbath

---

7. For discussion of the social uses of witchcraft, see Larner, *Enemies of God,* 192–203.

(in fact, imaginary) provide the historical evidence for general rules about demonology.

In the witchcraft of *The Masque of Queens,* Jonson ignored history altogether in favor of learned discourse for his notion of women as witches: "I prescribed them their properties . . . out of the authority of ancient and late writers" (32–34).[8] The idea of the witch as a powerful, if perverted, woman who is a real historical presence disappears, to be replaced by images drawn from texts. Jonson's literary antiquarianism covers up the supposed political danger posed by witches, although James and Anne would surely recall fears of the Scottish witch-hunt of 1590–1592, when the devil was mustering witches against the throne, as the masque unfolded in Whitehall in February 1609. Despite the shared ambition of the witches of *Daemonologie* and of the masque to "overthrow the glory" (101) of royal power, the danger of state subversion posed by women convening with the devil vanishes from the masque, as do the women's sexual orgies and the Christian frame. Jonson locates female power and virtue exclusively in the figures of the queens, the "opposites" (16) of the witches. Jonson moreover seems intent on showing the unreality of witches as opposed to the reality of the queens. The clear opposition of witches and queens and the suppression and defeat of the witches' magic are necessary conditions for the formation of a new, legitimated magic that centers not on the fictional queens but on the real figure of Queen Anne. History is reintroduced into magic in the person of the queen.

The witches in the masque have no power at all, for they are products of texts that have already proved them to be powerless. Their charms do not work to call up the devil, and instead of his climactic appearance there is "a sound of loud music" (334) that dispels their magical efforts. Jonson psychologizes their desire for "Old shrunk-up Chaos . . . To strike the world and nature dead" (295–97). Their powers are moral rather than supernatural evil: ignorance, suspicion, credulity, slander, bitterness, rage, and so on. There is no terror in their futile magic and impotent rituals. What opposes Jonson's female witches is not male, elite power, as in *Newes from Scotland* and *Daemonologie,* but elite female power. Peasant powerlessness is contrasted with aristocratic strength and heroism. The antithesis to witches, however, is not men or unproblematical women (say, conventional and decorous aristocrats) but powerful, heroic queens—warrior women—and this structural asymmetry involves Jonson in complex, unstable negotiations between female and male power relations.

The real conflict in the masque is not between the harmless witches and the heroic queens, but, as Barbara Lewalski has suggested, between the heroic

8. All references to *The Masque of Queens* are to line numbers in *Ben Jonson: The Complete Masques,* ed. Stephen Orgel (New Haven and London: Yale University Press, 1969).

queens and the ideal king, for the queens challenge the king as sole possessor of royal power and virtue. This challenge emerges, however, from within a patriarchal frame. Jonson defers to patriarchal values in the text, in lines that note James as the ultimate source of the court's virtues. Female subordination is also indicated in the twelve queens' dependence on the male figures of their father, Heroic Virtue, who, in John Meagher's words, "descends to introduce them, making it clear that the brightness of the scene derives ultimately from him, as their fame is the result of their virtue." They also depend on King James, whom Heroic Virtue refers to as "that light from whence her [Bel-Anna's] truth of spirit / Confesseth all the luster of her merit" (406–7). According to Heroic Virtue, the king's court is a place "where every princely dame / Contends to be as bounteous of her fame / To others as her life was good to her" (416–18). Such power as Anne had to command from Jonson the theme of warrior queens and to direct its treatment and realization was constrained by the requirement of voicing the patriarchal priority and power claimed by her husband, and by the fact that her intentions for the masque had to be realized through the mind of a male poet who in turn drew inspiration from male-authored texts containing accounts of witches and queens. Reading the masque from a patriarchal point of view, fame for Anne and her ladies appears to be dependent on a male notion of virtue, which is obedience to the social values, including gender values, of the Stuart court.[9]

But this patriarchal framing is awkward and hardly accords with the impact of the queens themselves, which derives, as Lewalski points out, from splendid royal and military costumes, the triumphs, and the final songs that focus on them. What the masque shows are militaristic, powerful, women rulers, and it is the appearance in women of heroic virtue that is most emphatically emphasized. Yet the women's relation to their female opposites, the witches, is as complex as their relation to patriarchal power.

What Jonson might have offered is a contrast between disorderly women and conventionally orderly ones. Heroic Virtue's speech seems to depict the queens as just such orderly women subordinated to the patriarchal king. Yet the queens have a good deal in common with the witches, and some of their individual stories reveal women subjugating men and overthrowing patriarchal power. For example, Jonson wrote in his notes to the printed version of the masque that the witches' Dame is "Ate, or mischief," whom Homer describes as "swift to hurt mankind, strong, and sound of feet . . . walking upon men's heads;

---

9. Barbara Kiefer Lewalski, *Writing Women in Jacobean England* (Cambridge, Mass., and London: Harvard University Press, 1993), 36–39. John C. Meagher, *Method and Meaning in Jonson's Masques* (Notre Dame and London: University of Notre Dame Press, 1966), 123. For a patriarchal reading of the masque, see Jonathan Goldberg, *James I and the Politics of Literature: Jonson, Shakespeare, Donne, and Their Contemporaries* (Baltimore and London: Johns Hopkins University Press, 1983), 57–58, 87–88.

in both places using one and the same phrase to signify her power, 'harming men' " (530).[10] One of the queens has similarities to Ate: Valasca, a legendary queen of Bohemia, revolted against male tyranny by leading a group of women "to the slaughter of their barbarous husbands and lords" (546). According to Aeneas Sylvius, Valasca destroyed both the thumbs and the right eyes of the men she spared to prevent them from fighting again; and she won her victory by the aid of magic. In their commentary, Herford and Simpson wonder if Jonson would have included her among his heroines if he had known Silvius's history. Thomyris, another queen, exacted revenge on Cyrus for killing her son by defeating him in battle, killing two hundred thousand of his soldiers, and leaving "not a messenger surviving of his side to report the massacre" (543). Another queen, Camilla, who appears in Virgil's *Aeneid* book 7 as a virgin warrior, disturbingly has magical power: she "could lightly have skimmed over the topmost stalks of standing corn, never once hurting the tender ears in her passage; or upon the sea, suspended on the surging billows, could glide, never dipping her nimble feet in the liquid plain" (542–43). Heroic Virtue, in the figure of Perseus, is also involved with magic since Perseus acquired a magic helmet, shoes, and wallet from the female figures of the Graiai to help him slay Medusa (whose name means "the queen"). The categories of witch and queen, intended to be antithetical, threaten to infiltrate each other and lose their identity, because, in some cases, both use magic and both are motivated by rage and revenge. The question arises whether the queens, as Jonson represents them, are indeed absolutely different from the witches or are, rather, a true realization of the kind of power and autonomy that peasant women can only aspire to in magic? Is lower-class impotence contrasted with aristocratic power? Or do the queens, as Lewalski has suggested, "appropriate rather than destroy the power of the witches"? If that is so, then implicit in the representation of the queens is a threat to the monarch (and the coherence of the masque) like the threat posed by the Scottish witches: both challenge the established patriarchal order. Jonson's attempts to contain his images of heroic queens within a patriarchal frame are unstable as a result of their internal contradictions.[11]

Jonson's discursive formation of the queens, then, is constrained in two respects: he wishes to represent the queens as quite detached from the negative image of powerful women as witches; and he wants to maintain the

10. References to Jonson's dedication and notes for the masque are to page numbers in *Ben Jonson: The Complete Masques*, ed. Stephen Orgel.

11. Lewalski, *Writing Women in Jacobean England*, 37. Aeneas Sylvius, *Historia Bohemica* (1475) is mentioned in *Ben Jonson*, ed. C.H. Herford and Percy and Evelyn Simpson, (Oxford: Clarendon Press, 1950), 10:507. For the reference to Medusa and Perseus, see Marjorie Garber, "*Macbeth*: The Male Medusa," in *Shakespeare's Ghost Writers: Literature as Uncanny Causality* (New York and London: Methuen, 1987), 87–123, especially 97.

patriarchal frame that purports to accommodate, authorize, and inspire them and that they actually challenge. The problem of representing warrior queens as antithetical to the hags is primarily a textual one since Jonson had to use male-authored discourses about these female heroines, which attribute the queens' extraordinary, incomprehensible powers—exceeding the supposed natural limits of their sex—to magic. In a similar way, male-authored witchcraft discourses resort to supernatural explanations to account for low-born women with incomprehensible powers. Jonson's versions of the prodigious queens refashion the traditional accounts so as to rid them of magical explanation. The similarities between queens and witches might have led Jonson to present a different relation between antimasque and masque, in which, in Stephen Orgel's words, the "vital energy" of the antimasque is ordered and redirected into the world of the main masque.[12] This is what Jonson does in his next masque, *Oberon* (performed on January 1, 1611), as the satyrs are converted to Oberon's service. But Jonson chose instead to create a sharp distinction between queens and witches, despite their similarities in the sources. The queens' power is not independent of men, but neither is it compatible with male power; and the queens are not opposite to the witches (as the king was in *Daemonologie*) but in some respects are similar to them.

Jonson represents the heroic queens as free of the taint of magic, and has their power depend on the notion of virtue. Yet it is not the fictional queens finally who challenge the patriarchal king, but the real Queen Anne. Anne's double status as the fictional Bel-Anna and the real queen puts her on the border between real and fictional, and it is this positioning that allows Jonson to construct a notion of real magic that inheres in the person of the queen. Jonson provides Queen Anne with a legitimate, political kind of royal magic that can challenge the magic of the king. Banished in the figures of the witches, magic returns as a way of representing the powerful charisma of Queen Anne herself.

The queens are a conventional set of warrior women whose historical reality is vouched for by texts. Anne and the masquing noblewomen do not *represent* those historical figures, for it would be indecorous for noblewomen to impersonate someone else. Rather, they perform a ritual re-presentation of the figures of the queens. All of the accumulated powers and virtues of the eleven prodigious queens are concentrated in the figure of Bel-Anna, whose own virtues and powers are identical with the queens': "she alone / Possessed all virtues, for which one by one / They [the queens] were so famed" (392–94). The masquers' appearance, the triumphs, and the songs do not falsify Anne and her courtiers; rather, they make known, through codes of elite cultural knowledge,

12. *Ben Jonson: The Complete Masques*, ed. Stephen Orgel, 14.

the real qualities that Anne actually possesses: Bel-Anna "hath again brought forth / Their [the queens'] names to memory; and means this night / To make them once more visible to light" (403–5). The masque creates an image of Anne's true nature in the reappearance from the past of the heroically virtuous queens. Anne is the only queen present, the epitome of all the historical queens, and contains in her body all their powers and virtues, as the second song says: "How happier is that age, can give / A queen in whom all they do live!" (503–4).

In the masque's dedication to Prince Henry, Jonson alludes in sophisticated, even playful terms, to Neoplatonists who believe "every royal and heroic form to partake and draw much to it of the heavenly virtue" (478). Jonson describes a royal body as containing a divine soul from heaven and imagines three ways in which a divine soul might enter a body and thereby transform it to a royal body: "whether it be that a divine soul, being come into a body, first chooseth a palace fit for itself, or being come, doth make it so, or that nature be ambitious to have her work equal, I know not" (478). The result is a body materially transformed by its heavenly soul. In the popular imagination, if not in demonological theory, a witch has intrinsic power: a glance may harm, and a daughter may inherit her mother's power. For the demonologist such power must be illusory, although the devil's mark may signify the illusory power that flows from a pact with the devil. Geillis Duncane bore such a mark and was believed to have magical powers. There is an analogy between the popular understanding of witchcraft and the structure of thought that constructs Anne as a virtuous body. The reality of the witches' powers is confirmed by the devil's mark on their bodies; so the reality of Anne's power is guaranteed by her body in the masque. When, in the third song, the voice asks, "Who, Virtue, can thy power forget / That sees these live and triumph yet?" (516–17), there is a crucial overlapping of the legendary queens and the masquers. In a benign necromancy, the dead, legendary queens are brought back to life in the bodies of the Stuart aristocrats, for in the song "these" are both the masquers and the queens and they have a common identity. Jonson himself asks in the notes "why (which is more unnatural) . . . I join the living with the dead?" and answers that historical queens and aristocrats "all live, and together, in their fame, and so I present them" (547). Jonson's final gesture of printing the names of the masquers as "The queen's majesty," "Countess of Montgomery," "Countess of Arundel," and so on, which he calls "the celebration of who were the celebrators" (527–28), follows the same logic of identity between queens and masquers: the gesture of naming seeks to fix the queens' powers in the real persons of the masquers. The reality of the queens' gender-exceeding powers is attested by the real presence of, ultimately, Queen Anne. Jonson thus creates a spurious historicity, in that the body of Anne proves the reality of the heroic queens' powers, and vice versa. The logic is circular, as in the case of Geillis Duncane, whose body was made to bear a sign that confirmed an understanding of her that had already been formed by her accusers. In both cases, ideology precedes history and representation carries power.

In *The Masque of Queens* the enigmatic interrelationship of spectacle, words, and music requires the decipherment of aristocratic "inquiring eyes . . . [and] quick ears" (96–97). Sovereign powers are attributed to the queen in the masque that were denied in the politics of the seventeenth century. Heroic queens, of course, did not exist in 1609 any more than witches did. Expressed within the masque-world, the image of women's sovereignty represents a limited political challenge to the king as an image of what might be realizable for heroic women. In the masque the representation of women as witches changes, but it is still used in the service of political advantage.

In *Newes from Scotland* the incomprehensibility to men of peasant women's activities is dispelled by naming their activities as witchcraft and projecting that witchcraft as part of a demonic conspiracy intended, finally, to subvert the social order by destroying the king's power. The reality of witchcraft and its immediate historical threat are supposedly confirmed by the devil's appearances and the marks left by him on the women who become his adherents. Women as witches thus personify men's fears of the threats to patriarchal power by locating those fears in real, identifiable persons. Furthermore, the existence of such women demonstrates that the social order needs the king's unique royal power to protect it from witchcraft's challenge. *Daemonologie* places women as witches within a conventional intellectual frame, seeing them as victims of the devil's illusions and their powers as ultimately ineffectual and unreal. But the political import of the book—that only legitimate magistrates can overcome witches' power—is intensified by its paranoid vision of satanic power being ubiquitous and impossible to identify. The political absolutism that *Daemonologie* points to, including its subordination of women to men, has usually been seen in *The Masque of Queens.* But Jonson fashions an image of legitimate female power in the queens that challenges as much as supports patriarchy and draws on as much as rejects representations of peasant women as witches. Peasant women's witchcraft is represented as unhistorical, superstitious, and powerless. Aristocratic and royal women, on the other hand, share the same power as the historical queens. But behind the queens of the masque are their counterparts in Jonson's sources whose power is partly supernatural; and behind the prodigious person of Bel-Anna/Queen Anne is the popular, one might say fundamentalist, notion that a queen's, like a witch's, magical power is inherent in her body. The uncanny power of the queens seems to derive in part from Jonson's return to a popular representation of female power as magic that locates it beyond the reach of patriarchal discourse.

Judith Scherer Herz

Aemilia Lanyer and the
Pathos of Literary History

To feel how swift, how secretly,
The shadow of the night comes on.
          —Archibald MacLeish, "You, Andrew Marvell"

Where the story-teller is loyal, eternally and unswervingly loyal to
the story, there, in the end, silence will speak. . . . And where does
one read a deeper tale than upon the most perfectly printed page of
a most precious book? Upon the blank page.
          —Isak Dinesen, "The Blank Page"

The pathos of the MacLeish quotation, itself a revision of Marvell's figure of
time's chariot and the darkness of the grave, is both ground and effect of literary
history.[1] A name is called, a silence is broken, and one poet writes his way into
presence through the absence of another. But for this to happen there must be
a story already told, a narrative to disrupt, and a name to conjure with. What
we call literary history is that set of narratives that allow such confrontations
to occur. Of course, its stories are not neutral. They serve institutions and
ideologies. They are multiple, genealogical, and constituted after the fact to
account for the fact; they are teleological and pseudo-organic. But they are
the condition of utterance even though the result may be unpredictable and
not always happy. A. M. Klein, wrestling with the covering cherub in the
anguished reading/rewriting of "Lycidas" that is his "Portrait of the Poet as
Landscape," registered what he felt as his failure. "And some go mystical, and
some go mad" he wrote, and some years later in his house in Montreal, he
fell into permanent silence himself, not a word written, not a word spoken—

---

1. I am grateful to my friend and colleague, Bina Toledo-Freiwald, for suggesting that I look at the
Dinesen story. I probably have absorbed (neutralized?) it more than she would like.

to anyone.[2] But the silence we will is different from the silence that descends, especially if from the start there never was any sound other than silence. Where, to use Dinesen's words, is the storyteller, read literary historian, loyal to that story, capable of making that silence speak? Literary history knows how to read "the perfectly printed page of the most precious book," but the blank page? And why does that page tell a deeper tale? Is it because it is open to unforeseeable possibilities where nothing is foreclosed? Dinesen's parable is not in itself about literary history; it is about innocence and (dis)honor, but it is also about multiplicity in interpretation and it is as well a meditation on community, specifically female community, communities of writers (weavers, spinners, worshipers) and readers. It provides a wonderful provocation to our genealogies and classifications, our begats and becauses, suggesting as well that there may be other narratives than the ones we are used to, other ways of making the past speak.

Aemilia Lanyer offers a tantalizing instance of this parable. She exists both as a finely printed page (the presentation copy to Prince Henry is indeed a precious book)[3] and as a blank page, as both text and silence. So to pose the question—can she enter literary history?—is probably foolish. In an obvious sense she is already there. There is considerable evidence to attest to that: the two modern editions, the nine remaining copies of the original edition (not a terrible number—there are only thirteen known 1609 *Sonnets of Shakespeare* about, only two of the 1611 edition of Donne's *Anatomy of the World*), the many articles and essays, constituting a record of historical research that has opened important access to her text: all these would seem to speak to her presence in literary history. But what I want to argue is that despite such evidence Lanyer really has not and possibly cannot be written into that history, although she may be talked about from within its precincts. Her feminism, her theological imagination, her patronage relations may be described and assessed as recent scholarship has shown.[4] Her considerable generic and metrical competence may be scrutinized and explicated; even that familiar duo, the now neglected

---

2. A. M. Klein, "Portrait of the Poet as Landscape," *The Rocking Chair and Other Poems* (1948); Klein died in 1972.

3. Victoria and Albert Library, shelfmark 5675 8.L.20. See Susanne Woods, "Textual Introduction," *The Poems of Aemilia Lanyer: Salve Deus Rex Judaeorum* (New York: Oxford University Press, 1993), xxvii and xlviii, for a detailed description.

4. See Elaine Beilen, *Redeeming Eve: Women Writers of the English Renaissance* (Princeton: Princeton University Press, 1987), 177–207; Ann Baynes Coiro, "Writing in Service: Sexual Politics and Class Position in the Poetry of Aemilia Lanyer and Ben Jonson," *Criticism* 35 (1993): 357–76; Achsah Guibbory, "The Gospel According to Aemilia: Women and the Sacred in Aemilia Lanyer's *Salve Deus Rex Judaeorum*," in *Sacred and Profane: Secular and Devotional Interplay in Early Modern British Literature*, ed. Helen Wilcox, Richard Todd, and Alasdair MacDonald (Amsterdam: Amsterdam VU University Press, 1996), 105–26. Barbara K. Lewalski, *Writing Women in Elizabethan England* (Cambridge: Harvard University Press, 1993), 213–41; Janel Mueller, "The Feminist Poetics of Aemilia Lanyer's *Salve Deus*

sources and influences, may be identified, but Aemilia Lanyer still remains outside the literary history that is cataloging and processing her according to norms and conventions whose development she has not participated in. She has a prehistory; that is, she belongs to someone else's literary history, Chaucer's and Mary Sidney's, for example, but properly speaking she has no history of her own.

I am using the term *literary history* more as a marker of a relationship to and among texts than as a Library of Congress classification. Of course, it is also the latter, although even there it is not an entirely interchangeable term for historical scholarship (the title that the MLA uses in its volume, *Introduction to Scholarship,* for chapters by Barbara Lewalski in 1981 and Annabel Patterson in 1992), that is the cumulative textual, contextual, ideological histories of a sequence of artifacts called literature (and even some not so called) written (or spoken) in English since the time that Caedmon sang his hymn in the mead hall: its founding texts in English occurring in the last decades of the sixteenth century with EK's critical apparatus for *The Shepherd's Calendar* and Speght's edition of Chaucer. Such histories of literature are always in process, are always being rewritten, and are always rewritable as more documents are discovered or as new questions are posed to old texts. Yet despite often heroic attempts to make the past speak in the accents of the past, literary history has also depended since its inception as a genre (or set of genres—literary criticism, textual scholarship, literary biography) on a (relatively) conscious practice of anachronism, of reading backward. Thus, it reverses the truism: the present now becomes prologue to the past and in large measure creates the past. At the same time it attempts to function under the aegis of the admonition clearly articulated by Huizinga that the "need to understand the past as well as possible without any admixture of one's own is the only thing that can make a work history."[5]

Literary history occurs in the vexed space between these two conflicting imperatives (the verb *to recover* nicely inscribing that contradiction). But it involves something else as well, something we might describe as a condition of lost immediacy for both writer and reader; literary history is at once a textual condition and an intertextual space. As much as it is something we do to texts, it is something that texts do to us, or, more precisely, require of us. Literary history in this sense is an effect of a shift in the status of the literary itself. This shift occurs sometime in the late sixteenth or seventeenth

---

Rex Judaeorum," in *Feminist Measures: Soundings in Poetry and Theory,* ed. Lynn Keller and Christanne Miller (Ann Arbor: University of Michigan Press, 1994), 208–36; Susanne Woods, "Introduction."

5. J. Huizinga, "The Task of Cultural History," in *Men and Ideas,* trans. James Holmes and Hans van Marle (New York: Meridian Books, 1959), 49.

century, when the author, now a historicized subject, becomes the source of his own authority, when inspiration becomes imagination. In identifying this shift, Bill Readings, for example, focused on the reader, using Milton as the exemplary figure, insofar as Milton requires that the reader become a literary historian in order to read him, that is, become one whose understanding of literature is primarily historical. Literature, in this argument, is understood as an object to be recovered rather than an activity to be participated in. Literature as a concept is thus, in Readings's formulation, invented out of the death of literature as an activity. John Guillory, from a somewhat different perspective, understands the shift in terms of the shaping of an authorial consciousness, which he locates intertextually between Spenser and Milton.[6] The emphasis from this perspective falls on a process of self-begetting where origins (that which is not me) and originality (my power over origins) combine, either titanically as in the Bloomian epic model of struggle and overcoming/evading, or more commodiously, although not necessarily less anxiously. For Milton, the anxiety also arises from the fear of falling erroneous, of not being able to "express thee unblamed." In a formulation anticipating Readings's argument, Guillory claims that "what Milton writes about as a loss of vision becomes for subsequent poets the birth of imagination" (176). Still, although Milton points to that anxiety, unable, as Guillory suggests, to "sustain an absolute faith in his own inspiration" (172), he complicates Readings's theory even as he is its chief instance. By being the author who beyond any other is all presence, he resists the tug of history, of the secondary. We may, as his readers, have to become literary historians in order to read him, but his role remains priestly (and therein may lie the contradiction that continues to bedevil Milton criticism to this day).

One half-century earlier, Lanyer had expressed a version of that fear of falling in her Phaeton and Icarus allusions—"But my dear Muse, now whither wouldst thou flie, / Above the pich of thy appointed straine?"[7]—but her fear had far more devastating consequences. That the newly privileged imagination may be unable to sustain presence after the all too evanescent moment of utterance means in her case that there is neither a present moment for the reception of her book nor any space either social or literary, public or private, in which its utterance can have resonance. That anxiety is most audible in the dedicatory epistles intended to negotiate the public reception of Lanyer's text, but one hears it, as well, throughout the *Salve Deus,* and most powerfully in "The Description of Cooke-ham." Thus, what I am identifying as pathos is, for

---

6. Bill Readings, " 'An Age Too late': Milton and the Time of Literary History," *Exemplaria* 4 (1992): 455–68; John Guillory, *Poetic Authority: Spenser, Milton and Literary History* (New York: Columbia University Press, 1983).

7. Aemilia Lanyer, *Salve Deus Rex Judaeorum,* ed. Susanne Woods (New York: Oxford University Press, 1993), ll. 270–80. Subsequent references are cited parenthetically in the text.

Lanyer, a function of her thwarted relation to the literary history she inherited, insofar as it can yield neither literary currency (equivalent to spiritual value) nor social currency. But if presence cannot be sustained, if there is no echo, can there be literary history? What happens, as was the case for Lanyer, when text and author disappear not only from historical memory but also from and into the originating text itself? From such a perspective, Aemilia Lanyer is a literary historical subject outside of literary history. Constituted out of the desire for presence, for efficacy, she is without the agency to accomplish it and is ultimately separated from the text that might instantiate it.

For Lanyer the problem is compounded, indeed ironized, by the very way she first entered that literary history in which I am asserting her nonexistence. And that is, as the now familiar story tells it, through a very particular kind of literary history, the stories of great men, the great man in this instance being Shakespeare, whose name so far exceeds the author function as to stand not only for imagination but also for literary value itself. To be part of such literary history should ensure immortality, but that is certainly not the consequence of A. L. Rowse's relentless pursuit of the "real story" that the sonnets of Shakespeare are presumed to encode. For Aemilia Lanyer, the "She" in this story, is no Laura or even Stella: a scandal, rather; a dark lady (or so Rowse has it; Simon Forman, Rowse's source, never alludes to this) of Italian descent; the daughter of a musician, Bassano; the hastily married wife of another musician, Alfonso Lanyer; the quondam mistress of Henry Cary, the powerful Lord Hunsdon, Lord Chamberlain and cousin to the Queen (and patron, too, of Shakespeare's company), vexing our dramatist, knowing, too knowing, about matters sexual. Oh, that waste of spirit, that spending of shame.

Rowse found her in Simon Forman's diary wrapped in a euphemism, the odd word *halek* for the sexual act (possibly inspired by the Middle English, *halke*, as in *The Franklin's Tale's* "every halke and every herne," or nook, cranny, and corner; and Forman could well have come across the word there, for it occurs in the description of a clerk "lykerous" for hidden knowledge and natural magic, an interest Forman certainly shared). The desire of this astrologer of dark corners to halek is a recurring note in the diaries from 1582 onward, but it is particularly insistent in the Lanyer entries, 1597–1600, although he seems not to have gotten his way with her. He intersperses his account with comments that identify her family and her time with the Countess of Kent; he reports that she was "paramour to my old Lord Hunsdon," but "being with child she was for colour married to a minstrel" and that she is now concerned about her husband's preferment and her status.[8] Much of this Rowse checked

---

8. A. L. Rowse, *The Poems of Shakespeare's Dark Lady* (London: Jonathan Cape, 1978), 11; also see his *Simon Forman: Sex and Society in Shakespeare's Age* (London: Weidenfeld and Nicolson, 1974).

out in his lackadaisical scholarly fashion (he is amazingly dependent—or so his footnotes suggest—on the kindness of correspondents), and all of it he fed into his dark-lady, rival-poet scenario.

It is interesting that Rowse did choose to publish her poems. Possibly he felt they were the necessary evidence to demonstrate her existence, the date, too, feeding into the theory, since he assumes that the publication in 1610 or 1611 of the *Salve Deus* was prompted by and in response to the 1609 publication of Shakespeare's sonnets. But it is all evidence for the prosecution, including the presentation of Rowse's edition itself. Even the book title is not hers. Rather, it is called *The Poems of Shakespeare's Dark Lady*, with *Salve Deus Rex Judaeorum* taking second place as a subtitle. Nor is her name spelled as it occurs on her own title page, but as Forman spells it in his diary. To be sure this is the form it takes in most other historical evidence, but that is still not the way that her own book presents her. For Rowse, the *Salve Deus* unlocks the secrets of another and supremely privileged text but is allowed to carry no secrets of its own. For Rowse, she is all pretext. And not only does Lanyer give a name to the dark lady, she allows Rowse to clear Shakespeare of the imputation of homosexuality, since his narrative takes as self-evident the physical reality of the dark-lady affair; Forman is called as chief witness here. Hence, the erotic negotiations of the young man poems can be safely read as merely platonic courtesies in a discourse of class-structured deference.

Few now take the Rowse narrative very seriously, but everyone takes it. That is, nearly all writing on Lanyer positions itself in relation to it, even to discount it, although for all we know it may be true. Of course, true to what is the next question. The empty set that is Shakespeare biography? Possibly. To an understanding of or engagement with the sonnets? Not if we read them as Gregory Bredbeck does as taking "as their project the task of frustrating the ability to read erotic meaning." It is possible, of course, to use Rowse's "findings" rhetorically, as Lorna Hutson does, as a way of setting out an argument about interpretive power. Hutson argues that Shakespeare's *Sonnets* make visible a male discursive economy in which fair and dark, even if read as moral abstractions, are nonetheless abstractions that depend on the lady's darkness.[9] The *Salve Deus* thus becomes a countertext in which the so-called dark lady reverses the Shakespearean project by making women active agents of interpretation rather than the occasions of discourse among men. Rowse comes in handy here but only as a rhetorical occasion, one consequence of

9. Gregory Bredbeck, "Tradition and the Individual Sodomite: Barnfield, Shakespeare, and Subjective Desire," in *Homosexuality in Renaissance and Enlightenment England: Literary Representations in Historical Context*, ed. Claude J. Summers (New York: Haworth Press, 1992), 54; Lorna Hutson, "Why the Lady's Eyes are Nothing Like the Sun," in *Women, Texts and Histories 1575–1760*, ed. Clare Brant and Diane Purkiss (London and New York: Routledge, 1992), 21.

which is to turn Lanyer's text itself into a rhetorical occasion—that is, Hutson is less interested in the *Salve Deus* than in the problem of gendering interpretive power.

Lanyer's text provokes and can sustain considerable critical and theoretical investigation. It can offer evidence for a variety of projects: How were dedications read and received? What was their social and literary efficacy? How does one read literary religious discourse? In what sense can one talk of a feminist consciousness in theological terms? And what happens when one reads Lanyer along with Jonson or Donne or Herbert or Fletcher or Milton or Speght or Wroth?[10] There are any number of theoretical and critical moves that we can make in response to these questions, things we can do to the text, but I am here concerned with something quite different, and that is the prior claim the text makes on us, the way it demands a reading that responds to its inscription of its own impermanence. Traceable in the varied expressions of deference and self-abnegation and fully elaborated in the ongoing drama the poem enacts between the Countess and her client (staged even in the opening dedication to the Queen),[11] its culminating gesture of farewell is ultimately both a textual and a historical fact. Lanyer disappears from her book and into her book, the artifact itself that she so carefully constructed, in which she at once makes herself, represents that self, and effaces herself, only accidentally remaining, misnamed, misprized/mistaken.

That pathos is clearly audible at the close of the book itself in the last two texts that function as a double envoi, "The Description of Cooke-ham" and "To the Doubtful Reader." In the former, the mood is elegiac, the tone is shifting and uneasy. Its three characters—the Countess of Cumberland, her daughter, and the poet—can no longer walk, talk, and read in its walks and woods. In fact, the Countess and her family were themselves only temporary residents there, their own estate (in dispute for the next half-century) makes an entirely different story from this Penshurst/Virgilian Eclogue 1/lost-Eden pastoral, and it is only obliquely alluded to in the *Salve Deus* itself. The emphasis of this poem remains on the leave-taking, and it is most powerfully registered by the poet's displacement. In finishing her task, in making and presenting her little book, she removes herself forever from its world. So long as the text keeps speaking

10. Coiro, "Writing in Service," places Lanyer in interesting juxtaposition to Jonson; and Mueller reads her alongside Giles Fletcher's "Christ's Victorie and Triumph" as well as in the context of the Swetnam controversy, especially Speght's *Muzzle for Melastomus*, "Feminist Poetics," 217–18, 232–33. See Barbara Lewalski's essay in this volume for further reflections on the need to contextualize Lanyer's work.

11. Lanyer invokes the Countess in her dedication to the Queen, in part to validate her voice and the attention she is seeking from the Queen. The Countess's experience and her own are somewhat oddly aligned in these stanzas, slightly displacing the Queen from her own dedication ("To the Queenes Most Excellent Majestie," ll. 109–26).

(that is, Lanyer keeps writing), the awareness of the difference of degree between commoner and countess need not be felt:

> Unconstant Fortune, thou art most to blame,
> Who casts us downe unto so lowe a fame:
> Where our great friends we cannot dayly see.
>   (103–5)

Similarly, the difference of age between Lanyer and the Countess's daughter can be erased and the final gesture of farewell can be deferred. But the poem enacts that gesture as it ultimately silences its own echo: "Delightfull Eccho wonted to reply / To our last words, did now for sorrow die" (199–200).

At the center of this final poem there is a curious and tonally vexed scene that both enacts the moment of farewell and puts up a powerful resistance to it. Earlier, the stately oak, the setting for this scene, is introduced as a place of vision, the place from which the Countess surveys all the natural world and meditates on the spiritual. As her departure approaches, the tree concentrates the text's gathering dismay. It is recalled as a place of reading, of idyllic pleasure, now only to be experienced in memory, but a memory in which in an odd way the speaker can never really participate:

> But specially the love of that faire tree,
> That first and last you did vouchsafe to see:
> In which it pleas'd you oft to take the ayre,
> With noble Dorset, then a virgin faire:
> Where many a learned Booke was read and skand
> To this faire tree, taking me by the hand,
> You did repeat the pleasures which had past,
> Seeming to grieve they could no longer last.
> And with a chaste, yet loving kisse tooke leave,
> Of which sweet kisse I did it soone bereave:
> Scorning a sencelesse creature should possesse
> So rare a favour, so great happinesse.
> No other kisse it could receive from me,
> For feare to give backe what it tooke of thee:
> So I ingratefull Creature did deceive it,
> Of that which you vouchsaft in love to leave it.
> And though it oft had giv'n me much content,
> Yet this great wrong I never could repent:
> But of the happiest made it most forlorne.
>   (157–75)

The vicariousness of Lanyer's role in a world that she longingly evokes even as she registers its disappearance (figured in the somewhat ludicrous theft of the kiss) makes a more potent statement of her displacement than her earlier attempt to remain on the same plane of memory with the Countess and her daughter. Chiding herself then for thinking that her wit might be "too weake to conster of the great," she recalls the familiar gentilesse theme and claims "although we are but borne of earth, / We may behold the Heavens, despising death" (113–14). She had broached this theme earlier in the dedication addressed to Anne Clifford, the Countess's daughter (Clifford kept her father's name after her marriage to Dorset). There Dorset/Clifford is recalled as her playmate in a prefallen world:

> What difference was there when the world began,
> Was it not Virtue that distinguisht all?
> All sprang from one woman and one man,
> Then how doth gentry come to rise and fall?
>   (33–36)

It is a brave stance but belied by the text and its subsequent history, especially that history as it is inscribed in the *Salve Deus* itself.

There is, for example, no evidence that anyone ever read this little book (although it has moved about some libraries), despite the inscription of those noble readers at once nine worthies and nine muses in its multiple dedications, as well as all virtuous ladies in general, as well as a less specifically gendered virtuous reader, as well as even the doubtful readers incorporated into the text at its close. Indeed, there are not many texts with so large an assemblage of potential readers perched at the margins; *The Faerie Queene* is one, but in Lanyer's text the margins, crowded with noble readers, take up almost as much space as the text itself. The effect is thus entirely different from that created by the procession of seventeen sonnets, fourteen to noble lords and earls, two to great ladies, and one to all the ladies of the court, that accompanies *The Faerie Queene*. It is as if those lords and ladies had been assembled for the performance of a vast masque, each presented with a sonnet as a gracious favor. They in no sense encroach upon the subsequent text, and they are themselves preceded by a sequence of complimentary sonnets to the author. Furthermore, there is no evidence that the *Salve Deus* was read by the one reader most emphatically written into it, the Countess of Cumberland, who, the speaker claims, by "command[ing] praisefull lines of that delightful place" (meaning Cookham), created her as a writer, and by the example of her goodness, godliness, and grace redirected (quite literally, saved) the author's life.

The poem the Countess received was, in fact, a book of poems in which her "never dying fame" is inscribed in a narrative of the passion played out in her meditating heart so that "writing of thee" (the Countess) and setting "his glorie forth whom thou lov'st best" (Christ) become a single act. Even more than Donne's *First Anniversary*, published that same year, its conflation of compliment and religious speculation, epideixis and typology, radically rewrites (in a proto-Miltonic mode) Scripture itself.[12] Lanyer claims a divine illumination for this but does not hide the revisionism of her project:

> Yea in these Lines I may no further stray,
> Than his most holy Spirit shall give me light:
>   That blindest Weaknesse be not over-bold
>   The manner of his Passion to unfold,
>
> In other Phrases than may well agree
> With his pure Doctrine, and most holy Writ.
>   (301–6)

Something interesting happens over the stanza break: with "unfold" she safely and properly occupies the role of exegete; with "In other phrases," she becomes a Gospel writer herself.

This is a remarkable position to take (and remarkably carried out in the words of Pilate's wife, the portion of the Passion narrative identified on the title page as "Eve's Apology"). As many critics have pointed out, here and elsewhere in the poems Lanyer presents a passionate feminist manifesto *avant la lettre* on topics ranging from the nature of virtue to human responsibility to the structure and meaning of marriage. But it is difficult to align such passages with the poem's patronage negotiations. For all that the Countess is presented as a figure presumed to be sympathetic to the speaker's views, it is not at all certain that she was, the Countess's own insistent advocacy of her daughter's inheritance rights notwithstanding. It is even difficult to assess her interest in letters, despite the number of dedications offered to her. She, along with her sister, was certainly a learned lady (although she knew only English), but her taste seems to have been for philosophic writings. Her daughter, Anne Clifford, records in the margins of the 1619 diary: "I brought down with me my Ladies great Trunk of papers to pass away the time, which trunk was full of writings of Craven and Westmoreland [papers most certainly dealing with property rights and legal matters] and other affairs, with certain letters of her friends and many papers of philosophie."[13]

---

12. Guibbory, "The Gospel," argues that Lanyer's text should be read as a true gospel that is at once hermeneutically sophisticated in its reading of Scripture and daring in its rewriting.

13. *The Diary of Anne Clifford: A Critical Edition*, ed. Katherine Osler Acheson (New York: Garland, 1995). This is the only scholarly edition of the diary, based on the recently discovered Portland manuscript, as well as on the Knole manuscript that was the copy text for the two previous editions—Vita Sackville West's in 1923, and D. J. H. Clifford's (like Sackville West, also a descendant) in 1990.

There is interesting evidence concerning the Countess's tastes in the family triptych at Appleby castle, which Anne Clifford commissioned in 1646 or 1647 after she finally came into the estate that her mother had earlier fought unsuccessfully for. It shows the Countess in the central panel with only three books behind her (Scripture, Seneca, and a book of distillations and medicines), and one, the *Psalmes of David* (clearly not Mary Sidney's, since what is shown is a small book not a manuscript), in her hand. The flanking panels, by contrast, both of which depict her daughter (the left at age fifteen just after the time memorialized in Lanyer's "The Description of Cooke-ham," the right at age fifty-six, the time of the portrait), reveal forty-seven books, a veritable survey course of sixteenth- and seventeenth-century writers, including Spenser, Daniel, Donne—poetry as well as sermons, at least one of which was preached before her—Herbert, King, Greville, Wotton, Montaigne, Cervantes, with some Boethius, Epictetus, Augustine, Chaucer, and Ovid (among others) also clearly visible.[14] But there are no texts by women; no Aemilia Lanyer. Of course, except for the "Works" of Spenser, and of Daniel who had been Clifford's tutor, the books of the other clients of the Countess of Cumberland are not there either— the pathos of literary history extends to Henry Lok as well.

But the Countess occupies an entirely different position in Lanyer's text from that which she holds in the other poems dedicated to her. Not simply, as in Spenser's *Foure Hymnes,* is she "an excellent and rare ornament [along with her sister, Marie, Countess of Warwick] of true love and beautie."[15] Here she occupies the emotional center of the text itself. Like Donne's Elizabeth Drury, she mediates the logos, not as a typological abstraction but rather as the object of the poet's love. The considerable degree of erotic energy in the *Salve Deus* poems is mostly figured (as both Lynette McGrath and Wendy Wall have shown) through the feminized body of Christ.[16] Yet there is a surplus of such language and emotion that, even if it does not directly structure the poet/patron relationship, inhabits it. Just as the Countess and the object of her desiring worship blur, a theological and an erotic vocabulary also merge. Martyrdom, for example, in a passage that introduces the ecstatic sacrifices of

14. In her edition, Acheson provides a subtle reading of the portrait in terms of Anne Clifford's construction and dissemination of her image and that of her family. Also see Mary Ellen Lamb, "The Agency of the Split Subject: Lady Anne Clifford and the Uses of Reading," *English Literary Renaissance* 22 (1992): 347–68.

15. The dedication is "To The Right Honorable Ladies, the Ladie Margaret Countesse of Cumberland, and the Ladie Marie Countesse of Warwicke." *The Yale Edition of the Shorter Poems of Edmund Spenser,* ed. William Oram et al. (New Haven: Yale University Press, 1989), 690.

16. Lynette McGrath, "Metaphoric Subversions: Feasts and Mirrors in Amelia Lanier's *Salve Deus Rex Judaeorum,*" *LIT* 3 (1991): 101–13; also see her " 'Let Us Have Our Libertie Againe': Amelia Lanier's 17th Century Feminist Voice," *Women's Studies* 20 (1992): 331–48; Wendy Wall, *The Imprint of Gender: Authorship and Publication in the English Renaissance* (Ithaca: Cornell University Press, 1993), 319–30.

Stephen, Laurence, and Andrew, is described as the tasting of a "Sweetnesse that makes our flesh a burthen to us, / Knowing it serves but onely to undoe us" (1743–44).

The desire figured in the text (as well as its frustration) is, nevertheless, not reducible to an erotic narrative, either transparent or displaced. There is, to be sure, a stolen kiss, but the awkwardness and absurdity of the action diffuse the erotic. (Ann Coiro describes it as "gaspingly funny."[17] I find it more painful than funny, but it does epitomize, by its very incongruity, the incompatible social and literary systems observable in Lanyer's text.) There is certainly no libertine playfulness here, further marking the gap between writer and patron. The problem is, there is no available courtship language for Lanyer to appropriate (as Donne has ready in hand to court Lucy, Countess of Bedford, or his other great ladies, for example). For her, to write and to love is to live in the world that she has written but from which she is excluded at the very instant her writing ceases. This sense of potential disappearance from her own text (figuring her disappearance from literary history itself) gives an urgency to the theological daring of much of the Passion scene at the same time as it is complicated by the poet's "desiring," however (dis)embodied, however fictive that desire may be. Using the Countess as a staging space for this text—it is all imagined as happening within her mind, heart, and breast—allows Lanyer to claim for it an authority that she is uncertain she can sustain. But that too is challenged, if not undone, by distance, time, class, by the incompatibility of their narratives.

Thus, in lines that could serve as an epigraph for the "Time Passes" section of Virginia Woolf's *To the Lighthouse*, Cookham and the "little booke," the *Salve Deus* itself, fade from view:

> The house cast off each garment that might grace it,
> Putting on Dust and Cobwebs to deface it.
> All desolation then did there appeare,
> When you were going whom they held so deare.
>   (201–4)

The connection to Woolf's novel that I am suggesting here is by no means entirely arbitrary. For these lines do, in fact, link Lanyer as a ghostly presence to literary history, although it is not her own. In this history Lanyer's longing for Clifford's Cookham is Vita Sackville West's longing for Knole, a Clifford property (from Dorset), from which Vita was disinherited in a twentieth-century replay of the seventeenth-century disinheritance. Sackville West's 1923 edition of the Clifford diaries, transcribed from the Knole manuscript, is

---

17. Coiro, "Writing," 372.

certainly involved in the literary history of Woolf's *Orlando* (published in 1928, the year of the death of Vita's father and her consequent loss of Knole) and, more obliquely, in that of *To the Lighthouse* itself. Anne Clifford figures in this literary history, but Lanyer remains a ghostly echo, audible to us (but not to Woolf) through the voice of Lily Briscoe. " 'I'm in love with you?' No, that was not true. 'I'm in love with this all,' " Lily Briscoe could imagine herself saying to Mrs. Ramsay, "waving her hand at the hedge, at the house, at the children," had she not resisted the impulse to fling herself at Mrs. Ramsay's knee.[18] The *Salve Deus,* however, is just such a declaration. "I have had my vision" (310), they could both have said, poet/painter/client/friend, artificers of a vanished world.

In the final envoi, "To the Doubtful Reader," the entire text—dedicatory epistles, Passion poem, legend of good women, love letter, eclogue—is returned to its own beginning in an account of the dream from which the book title had sprung (in the dedication to Mary Sidney, itself in the form of a Chaucerian dream vision, the entire book is figured as a dream). Returning the text to its beginning sets up a resistance to its ending, thus keeping the textual moment present. So long as that is sustained, the "rich chaines that tie" client to patron hold. But only so long. Thus, the text in its final moment writes in a resistance to literary history that was all too rapidly confirmed in its unfolding. The *Salve Deus,* I am suggesting, is discontinuous both with other texts and with Lanyer herself, and discontinuous also with the containing narratives of literary history, whether they are stories of scandal or of sainthood (the Forman/Rowse dubious lady or Elaine Beilen's "millenarian advocating the establishment on earth of God's will")[19] or, more mildly, of the emergent professional writer.

But, says the critic, why must it be discontinuous? Is there not a woman's history, only now properly reconstructable, where Lanyer can find a place, a history, moreover, constructed out of those very gaps and displacements? To the degree that literary history is our own construct, the answer is most likely yes, but problems remain. Chief among these is the nature of that construct. As Margaret Ezell has shown, the evolutionary model that developed out of Woolf's Judith Shakespeare (silenced and/or driven mad by patriarchal society) has structured our notion of a tradition of women's writing.[20] In Ezell's critique, this model, particularly as Gilbert and Gubar have elaborated it (and in their anthology institutionalized it), is at once romantic and totalizing. It describes a process of organic growth; it is developmental and teleological, valuing texts in

18. Virginia Woolf, *To the Lighthouse* (New York: Harcourt Brace, 1927), 32.

19. Beilen, *Redeeming,* 181.

20. Margaret Ezell, *Writing Women's Literary History* (Baltimore: Johns Hopkins University Press, 1993), 39–65.

proportion as they reflect ourselves. It valorizes a single tradition, which is seen to derive from an internalization of patriarchal values in the earliest period, moving then to expressions of protest, culminating finally in self-discovery. Lanyer has little place in this story.

Recently both Janel Mueller and Ann Baynes Coiro have emphatically written Lanyer into their accounts of other seventeenth-century texts (Fletcher's "Christ's Victorie and Triumph" and Jonson's "To Penshurst"). Coiro, following Ezell, reads Lanyer as an "anti-Shakespeare's sister" figure. Chiefly interested in the class dislocations in Lanyer's text (and in Jonson's), Coiro resists reading Lanyer as a woman poet, emphasizing rather her "complicated and subverting anger against gender roles and class roles," her "anger and fear of the power of women." The emphasis is on Lanyer's originality, the degree to which she must henceforth complicate our narratives of literary history, but not a specifically women's literary history. In contrast, the utopian inflection of Mueller's study— Lanyer is "our contemporary"; she is able "to articulate the transformative power of gender relations"—takes her "feminism" less problematically. But by identifying "the conditions that empowered female authorship" and by placing Lanyer's text in relation to the *querelle des femmes,* Mueller allows for a historicization of Lanyer's writing that is the precondition of the plural and less ideologically foreclosed literary history that Ezell calls for.[21]

What is at issue here is the difference between literary history as a set of not always compatible narratives and literary history as the condition of writing itself. Lanyer is now part of the twentieth century's view of the past, but her entrance is always already theorized; she is a character in someone else's script. In arguing that she is discontinuous with her own text, I am saying that she has no place in her own script, that she cannot will efficacy, however much she evokes both the literary and the social structures that ought to enable it. Historical scholarship will continue to try to reclaim her, but as David Perkins argues in the provocatively titled *Is Literary History Possible?* "any conceptual scheme highlights only those texts that fit its concepts . . . and inevitably falls short of the multiplicity, diversity, and ambiguity of the past."[22]

A final caveat: to underline the pathos in our inability to secure Lanyer's identity, in our inability to make her name serve the author function (for her name proliferates rather than limits meaning) all efforts of an informed, determined, feminist historical scholarship notwithstanding, may seem even more paradoxical at a critical juncture when the notion of the stable subject itself has been rendered problematic for even the most canonical of writers. For example, in an argument that suggests the impossibility—indeed futility—of

21. Coiro, "Writing," 369, 373; Mueller, "Feminist Poetics," 211.

22. David Perkins, *Is Literary History Possible?* (Baltimore: Johns Hopkins University Press, 1992), 51.

trying to date Milton's Sonnet 19 ("When I consider how my light is spent"), Jonathan Goldberg points to the sonnet's "lack of empirical unity, its refusal to situate itself in a moment that submits to the concept of self-sameness."[23] Once you unsettle the idea of the autonomous subject, canonicity offers no protection (nor need it, the Dinesen parable whispers). My syncretic sensibility would have it both ways—historical scholarship is important, dates do matter, life narratives are nontrivial, composed as they are on the flesh and the bone. Yet the moment of utterance is always displaced from, and can never be recovered in, its textual inscription. Once self-identity becomes a contested notion, what I am calling pathos, a writing large of the loss of presence, may simply be the necessary condition of all literary history—whether it is read out of the richly printed books in the Borgesian library of infinite possibility or (and maybe it is the same thing) divined in the ambiguous and undecipherable whiteness of the blank page.

23. Jonathan Goldberg, "Dating Milton" in *Soliciting Interpretation: Literary Theory and Seventeenth-Century English Poetry,* ed. Elizabeth D. Harvey and Katharine Eisaman Maus (Chicago: University of Chicago Press, 1990), 200.

Barbara K. Lewalski

FEMALE TEXT, MALE READER RESPONSE

Contemporary Marginalia in Rachel Speght's *A Mouzell for Melastomus*

The Beinecke Library at Yale has a copy of Rachel Speght's tract defending women—the first piece of polemic certainly written by an Englishwoman—that has some eighty-seven marginal annotations penned by a male contemporary.[1] They have been noted and briefly discussed by Cis van Heertum,[2] but the interplay of text and marginal commentary in this copy (Ih Sp 33 617m) deserves extended analysis, as it affords insight of a rare and remarkable kind into ways of reading, cultural attitudes, and gender issues in early modern England. Scholars are now giving increased attention to such topics as the audiences for early modern books, textual and other evidence as to how particular texts were read, and the cultural ramifications of some ways of reading.[3] But very little attention has been given to the reception of women's texts in this period—in large part because the evidence of reader response to the few women's texts we have is so hard to come by.

The great interest of the marginalia in Speght's *Mouzell for Melastomus* is precisely that the plethora of comments lets us see contemporary reader-

1. The Marginalia are also included in my edition of *Rachel Speght's Polemics and Poems* (Oxford: Oxford University Press, 1996), in the series "Women Writers in English, 1350–1850," ed. Susanne Woods and Elizabeth Hageman. I am grateful to the Oxford University Press and the Beinecke Rare Book and Manuscript Library, Yale, for permission to reprint this material.

2. Cis van Heertum, "A Hostile Annotation of Rachel Speght's *A Mouzell for Melastomus* (1617)," *English Studies* 6 (December 1987): 490–96.

3. See, for example, Evelyn Tribble, *Margins and Marginality: The Printed Page in Early Modern England* (Charlottesville: University of Virginia Press, 1993); H. S. Bennett, *English Books and Readers* (Cambridge: Cambridge University Press, 1970); Anthony Grafton, *New Worlds, Ancient Texts: The Power of Tradition and the Shock of Discovery* (Cambridge: Harvard University Press, 1992); Lisa Jardine and Anthony Grafton, "How Gabriel Harvey read his Livy," *Past and Present* 129 (November 1990): 30–49; Barbara A. Johnson, *Reading "Piers Plowman" and "The Pilgrim's Progess": Reception and the Protestant Reader* (Carbondale: Southern Illinois University Press, 1992); William Sherman, *John Dee: The Politics of Reading and Writing in the English Renaissance* (Amherst: University of Massachusetts Press, 1995).

response in action, directed toward a daring protofeminist woman's text. From this single case, of course, we cannot draw general conclusions as to how this work, or other challenging works by Aemilia Lanyer or Elizabeth Cary or Mary Wroth, were received by a male or mixed readership.[4] Nonetheless, the kinds of comments Speght's text elicited from this male reader point up what he found intolerable in her authorial claims and her protofeminist arguments as well as his strategies for dealing with both. The endurance of his attitudes and strategies over several centuries suggests that they were not untypical. I have reproduced the marginal comments in an appendix alongside the passage in Speght to which they refer; they are referred to below by the # sign and the appropriate number.

Rachel Speght, a well-educated young woman of the London middle class, has the distinction of being the first Englishwoman to identify herself, by name, as a polemicist and critic of contemporary gender ideology.[5] Her 1617 tract, *A Mouzell for Melastomus* (A Muzzle for the Black-Mouth) is the first of three responses to an anonymous tract, *The Araignment of Lewde, idle, froward, and unconstant women,* which, published two years previously, opened the rancorous Jacobean skirmish in the centuries-old *Querelle des Femmes,* or debate over the nature and worth of womankind.[6] Speght claims the honor of unmasking the author as Joseph Swetnam, a fencing master.[7]

Swetnam's tract is a rambling, boisterous, tonally confused but lively jumble of proverb lore, rowdy jokes, invective, authorities, anecdotes, and exempla about women's lechery, vanity, shrewishness, and worthlessness, cobbled together from the entire tradition of misogynist writing. Much of the time it reads like a commonplace book collection of extracts and quotations on women and marriage. Both Swetnam's tract and Speght's were published for the same bookseller, Thomas Archer, strongly suggesting that Archer sought out these

4. See, for example, Aemilia Lanyer, *Salve Deus Rex Judaeorum* (London, 1611); Elizabeth Cary, *The Tragedy of Mariam* (London, 1613); Mary Wroth, *The Countesse of Mountgomeries Urania* (London, 1621). For discussion of their oppositional themes and strategies, see Barbara K. Lewalski, *Writing Women in Jacobean England* (Cambridge: Harvard University Press, 1993).

5. See Lewalski, *Writing Women,* 153–75. This essay draws upon some material in that chapter. We cannot be sure on present evidence whether a woman wrote the earlier tract entitled *Jane Anger her Protection for Women* (London, 1589), or if so, who she is.

6. Rachel Speght, *A Mouzell for Melastomus, The Cynical Bayter of, and foul mouthed Barker against EVAHS SEX. Or an Apologeticall Answere to that Irreligious and Illiterate Pamphlet made by Jo. Sw. and by him Intituled, The Arraignment of Women* (London: Nicholas Oakes for Thomas Archer, 1617). I cite the *Mouzell* by signature and page number in this essay. For an account of the English Renaissance phase of the *Querelle,* see Linda Woodbridge, *Women of the English Renaissance: Literature and the Nature of Womankind, 1540–1640* (Chicago: University of Chicago Press, 1984).

7. Thomas Tel-troth [Joseph Swetnam], *The Araignment of Lewde, idle, froward, and unconstant women: Or the vanitie of them, choose you whether* (London, E. Allde for T. Archer, 1615). In later editions, his cover blown, Swetnam signed his epistle with his full name. Swetnam's only other known book deals with fencing, *The Schoole of the Noble and Worthy Science of Defence* (London, 1617).

tracts to promote a popular controversy. Swetnam's prefatory epistles seem deliberately calculated to provoke responses from women or their defenders: like most contributions to the *Querelle,* it is in the spirit of a rhetorical game.[8] He says he expects to be "bitten" by women, who will go about to "reprove" his book, but warns them not to answer lest they reveal their galled backs to the world; and he threatens women with a yet fiercer "second booke, which is almost ready." Swetnam needed no second book: this one proved popular enough to go through ten editions by 1634.

Two later responses to Swetnam (also dated 1617) carry allegorical authors' names: Ester Sowernam (punning on Swetnam) and Constantia Munda.[9] These tracts may or may not be by women. It is likely, as both Linda Woodbridge and Simon Shepherd have argued, that booksellers commissioned the Sowernam and Munda tracts to get in on the lucrative controversy and keep it going.[10] Subsequent works extending the controversy—a play and a series of tracts prompted by a fad of female cross-dressing in London in 1615–1620—were also anonymous and most likely by male authors.[11]

8. As Linda Woodbridge shows, throughout the English Renaissance the formal polemic controversy over women owed more to rhetorical convention than to ideological conviction or emotional involvement. In substance, these tracts (pro and con) recycled hoary arguments from the past; in form they relied heavily on the judicial oration and the outrageous paradox. Most of the writers were participants in an on-going game of wit played by men for their own and (they seem to have supposed) women's amusement. Swetnam draws heavily upon, indeed virtually plagiarizes from, John Lyly's "Cooling Carde for Phalautus and all Fond Lovers," appended to *Euphues* (London, 1578).

9. *Ester hath hang'd Haman: or, An Answere to a lewd Pamphlet, entituled The Arraignment of Women. With the arraignment of lewd, idle froward, and unconstant men, and Husbands . . . written by Ester Sowernam, neither maide, Wife nor Widdowe, yet really all and therefore experienced to defend all* (London: Nicholas Bourne, 1617). Constantia Munda, *The Worming of a mad Dogge: Or, a Soppe for Cerberus the Jaylor of Hell. No Confutation but a sharpe Redargution of the bayter of Women* (London: Laurence Hayes, 1617). For an account of these tracts see Woodbridge, *Women in the English Renaisance;* Ann Rosalind Jones, "Counterattacks on 'the Bayter of Women': Three Pamphleteers of the Early Seventeenth Century," in *The Renaissance Englishwoman in Print: Counterbalancing the Canon,* ed. Anne M. Haselkorn and Betty S. Travitsky (Amherst: University of Massachusetts Press, 1990), 45–62; and Simon Shepherd, ed., *The Women's Sharp Revenge* (London: Fourth Estate, 1985).

10. Though "Anonymous" and "Pseudonymous" may be female more often than we can know, the use of a female allegorical persona is not enough to indicate female authorship. The booksellers may have commissioned male writers to represent themselves as women rushing to improve on Speght's answer to Swetnam; or they may have sought out, or been presented with, tracts which in fact were written by women.

11. [Thomas Heywood?], *Swetnam the Woman-hater, Arraigned by Women. A new Comedie, Acted at the Red Bull by the late Queenes Servants* (London, 1620). This play stages the entire controversy as a legal trial and a street battle. Compare with *Swetnam the Woman Hater: The Controversy and the Play,* ed. Coryl Crandall (Lafayette: Purdue University Press, 1969). The cross-dressing tracts, all published in 1620, are *Hic-Mulier: Or, the Man-Woman: Being a Medicine to cure the coltish disease of the Staggers in the Masculine-Feminine of our Times. Exprest in a breif Declamation* (London: J. T., 1620); *Haec-Vir; Or, the Womanish-Man: Being an Answere to a late Booke intituled Hic-Mulier. Exprest in a brief Dialogue between Haec Vir the Womanish-Man and Hic-Mulier the Man-Woman* (London: J. T., 1620); and *Muld Sacke: Or the Apologie of Hic Mulier: to the late Declamation against her* (London: R. Meighen, 1620). For an account of the cross-dressing controversy, see Woodbridge, *Women and*

Speght resorted neither to allegory nor anonymity. Born, it would seem, in 1597, her family connections are with the clerical and medical professions in London. Her father, James Speght, was a rigorous Calvinist and rector of two London churches, St. Mary Magdalene, Milk Street (1592–1637), and St. Clement Eastcheap (1611–1637).[12] In her 1617 tract answering Swetnam, Speght describes herself as a serious, intelligent, religious young woman, not yet twenty, unmarried, with a sound education in those usually male subjects of grammar, rhetoric, logic, and Latin. If her father did not himself supervise her classical education, he must have arranged for it, and apparently he also allowed her to write for publication under his roof. Her husband, William Procter, was also a minister, and her godmother, Mary Moundford, was the wife of a famous city and court physician, Sir Thomas Moundford. Thomas Speght, the editor of Chaucer (1598, 1602), may have been a kinsman.

We can only speculate about what led Speght to answer Swetnam two years after his tract appeared. She may have decided herself to undertake the task. If not, either she was well-enough known, at the tender age of nineteen, to be approached by Swetnam's bookseller; or else, more likely, she was recommended to him by family or friends. Whatever the initial stimulus to write, Speght insists on her authorial identity. Her title page carries her full name; and in 1621 she published a second book, *Mortalities Memorandum*, in part, she declared, to reassert her authorship of the *Mouzell*, which had been attributed by some to her father.[13] That later work contains a poetic meditation prompted by her mother's death and also a fascinating dream-vision poem allegorizing her own rapturous encounter with learning and vigorously

---

the *English Renaissance*, and Jean Howard, "Cross-dressing, the Theatre, and Gender Struggle in Early Modern England," *Shakespeare Quarterly* 39 (1988): 418–40.

12. His tract, *A Briefe demonstration, who have, and of the certainty of their salvation, that have the spirit of Jesus Christ* (London, 1613), argues the Calvinist positions on justifying faith and the final perseverance of the Elect, using the classic proof-texts from Romans 8; its dedication alludes to his incorporation in the Goldsmith's guild. On January 6, 1611, he preached before the Lord Mayor and Aldermen of London an Epiphany sermon, *The Day-Spring of Comfort*, printed in 1613 and again in 1616 under the title *The Christian's Comfort*.

13. Rachel Speght, *Mortalities Memorandum with a Dream Prefixed, imaginarie in manner, reall in matter* (London: Jacob Bloome, 1621). The preface reads in part:

> Having bin toucht with the censures of [critical readers] . . . by occasion of my *mouzeling Melas-tomus*, I am now, as by a strong motive induced (for my rights sake) to produce and divulge this of-spring of my indevour, to prove them further futurely who have formerly deprived me of my due, imposing my abortive upon the father of me, but not of it. Their variety of verdicts have verified the adagie *quot hominem tot sententiae* [there are as many opinions as there are men] and made my experience confirme that apothegme which doth affirme Censure to be inevitable to a publique act. (sig. A2v)

defending women's education.[14] Clearly, this London daughter did not share the general view of the nobility and gentry that publishing is déclassé. As for gender constraints, in both books she disposes of them on unimpeachable religious grounds—the biblical command to use and not hide a God-given talent.

Speght's *Mouzell* breaks the mold of the *Querelle*'s rhetorical game. If Speght's language and argument are in some ways less daring than those of Sowernam or Munda, her undertaking is more serious: to make the authoritative Protestant discourse of biblical exegesis yield a more expansive and equitable concept of gender. To that end, she eschews many of the tired formulaic gestures of the *Querelle* defenses and devises a structure that allows her to attack Swetnam on particular points (as the genre required) but also to develop her own argument. Some attention to that structure and to her chief arguments and polemical strategies will illuminate the intertextual dialogue of the extracts and marginalia.

Throughout, Speght offers an effective rejoinder to Swetnam in the rhetorical category of ethical proof: the creation of a suitable persona. As the living refutation of Swetnam's charges against women, she presents herself as religious, learned, eminently rational, engagingly modest, unassuming, justifiably angry yet self-controlled, truthful, courageous in defending wronged women and their Creator. She modestly admits her youthful and female insufficiencies in learning, but counters that by displaying her capacity for logical argument, her lucid style, her knowledge of rhetoric, her ease with Latin quotations and wordplay (it may be "small Latin," but she seems in tolerably good control of it), her ability to manage a syllogism that proves Swetnam damnable, and her range of reference (beyond the Bible) to the Fathers and classical moral philosophers: Lactantius, Seneca, Aristotle, Zoilus, Livy, Pliny, Cicero, Saint Augustine, Plutarch. Against this persona she poses her character of Swetnam from the evidence of his tract: "the very embleme of a monster" (sig. A4), a blustering, scandal-mongering, indeed blasphemous bully who is

14. Speght's later life is a virtual blank. Seven months after *Mortalities Memorandum* was entered in the Stationers' Register, there is a record of marriage between "Procter, William, gent, bachelor, 29, and Rachel Speight, spinster, 24, daughter of Mr. James Speight, clerk, parson of St. Mary Magdalen, Milk Street, London, who consents" at St. Mary Woolchurch Haw, London, August 6, 1621 (Joseph Foster, ed., *London Marriage Licenses, 1521–1869* [London: Bernard Quaritch, 1887], 1098). Rachel's husband was probably the "Procter, William of Somerset (plebs)" who matriculated at Oriel College in October, 1609, at age sixteen (*Athenae Oxoniensis*, ed. Joseph Foster [Oxford, 1891], 3:1215). Baptismal records of two children, Rachel (February 26, 1627) and William (December 15, 1630) at St. Giles, Cripplegate, specify that William Procter is a minister. In 1625 the Procters were probably living at Upminster in Essex, just outside London, from which place one William Procter dated a published sermon, *The Watchman Warning*, first preached at Paul's Cross, September 26, 1624. He died in 1653 and was buried at All Hallows, Lombard Street; I found no record of Rachel Speght's death and burial.

"irreligious and illiterate," whose grammatical faults and stylistic errors reveal his abysmal ignorance, and whose disjointed and contradictory arguments reveal his intellectual, moral, and spiritual chaos. Her governing metaphor for her encounter with him is unequal combat, a David battling Goliath, or a Saint George with the Dragon. She is "yong and the unworthiest of thousands" doing battle with a "furious enemy to our sexe"; she ventures to "fling this stone at vaunting *Goliah*" (sigs. A3r-v); she is fearless because "armed with the truth" and the "Word of Gods Spirit" (sig. A4).

She begins with an "Epistle Dedicatorie" addressed to her primary audience, virtuous ladies "Honourable or Worshipfull" (aristocrats or wives of city officials), in which she claims that her youth and the danger of her enterprise require her to seek patronage and protection "from some of power." But she also reaches out to all virtuous and God-fearing women of every rank and class, "rich and poore, learned and unlearned," inviting them to see themselves as the common target of the malevolent Swetnam. Here and elsewhere she comes close to recognizing the common plight of all "Hevahs sex" as an oppressed gender in a misogynist, patriarchal society. But then she typically draws back, offering herself as the defender not of all women but of all good women. She hopes to bring them the comforting knowledge of Christ's esteem for them (sig. A3v), and to disabuse the "vulgar ignorant" from believing Swetnam's lies.

Her preface to Swetnam is in the satiric mode, a double-pronged attack on him as both illiterate and irreligious, using a railing style that is sometimes witty, sometimes heavy-handed. By his own bearbaiting metaphor he labels himself a dog (and thereby a cynic in Latin). He uses "such irregularities touching concordance" and "so disordered a methode" that a mere grammar-school student could correct him (sigs. Bv-B2). His failures in logic match those in grammar as he draws absurd conclusions and often contradicts himself. More important, he has put himself beyond the pale of Christianity: he blasphemes God by wresting and perverting Scripture; he dishonors God by disparaging woman "that excellent worke of Gods hands"; and he looks to "heathenish" authorities for his misogynist ideas (sig. B2v). His tongue-in-cheek claim that he wrote with his hand and not his heart simply proves him "an hypocrite in Print" (sig. B3).

Then come three commendatory poems under the names "Philalethes," "Favour B," and "Philomathes"—all of them probably by Speght herself.[15] They reinforce her youthful achievement and the David/Saint George analogues. These poems are followed by a witty acrostic poem on Swetnam's name (signed by Speght) as a further display of her talents.

15. Sig. B4r-v. "Philomathes" uses one of Speght's favorite terms, "obtrectation," and the verse in all three poems is very similar to Speght's in *Mortalities Memorandum*.

In the *Mouzell* proper she virtually ignores Swetnam in order to mount a serious, coherent, liberalizing critique of gender ideology couched in terms of the dominant discourse—Protestant biblical exegesis. Swetnam began his tract with a few misogynist jokes grounded upon Scripture, but he did not develop any serious argument or extended exegesis from his biblical texts, inviting Speght's condemnation of him for thus dallying with "the two-edged Sword of the Eternall" (sig. F2). By her extended examination of the Creation-Fall story from Genesis and other biblical texts (supported by many cross-references in the margins in the approved manner of Protestant theological argument), Speght looks past Swetnam to engage worthier antagonists—all those ministers or other commentators who find in Scripture some basis to devalue and wholly subjugate women.

Though many of Speght's points are commonplaces of liberal Protestant marriage doctrine and earlier defenses of women, her argument has considerable subversive potential precisely because it presses the dominant biblical/Christian discourse so far toward the affirmation of gender equality. She insists that that discourse affirms the moral and spiritual equality of women (thereby removing any essential ground for their subordination to men). And while she admits (as she has to) biblical texts proclaiming woman the weaker vessel (1 Pet. 3:7) and the man the "head" of the wife in marriage (1 Cor. 11:3), she interprets those texts in such a way as to deny any real basis for these assertions in female nature itself, as created or as redeemed. Gender hierarchy is made to seem simply a somewhat anomalous social institution.

Her central proposition regarding woman's excellence she bases on Proverbs 18:22, "He that findeth a wife, findeth a good thing, and receiveth favour of the Lord," and on the Genesis story of woman as God's best gift to man, analyzing that excellence in terms of Aristotle's four causes. The efficient cause of woman's creation is God himself, and so "the work cannot chuse but be good, yea very good" (9). The material cause, Adam's rib, is more refined matter than the dust from which Adam himself was made. The formal cause shapes both man and woman after the image of God—and there is no mention of woman's supposedly cold humors or imperfect bodies. Woman's final cause or end is to glorify God and give good counsel to her husband. Speght concludes that "God . . . makes their authority equall, and all creatures to be in subjection unto them both" (10). She also empties problematic biblical texts of damaging significance for women. The Fall story reveals Eve's good intentions in giving the fruit to Adam, and his greater guilt. Paul's statement (1 Cor. 7:1) that "it is good for a man not to touch a woman" refers only to the times and conditions of persecution—an impressive and potentially radical claim that culture and historical circumstances are determinants even of sacred texts. Similarly, Solomon's statement (Eccles. 7:30) that he had not found an upright woman among a thousand refers only to his own guilty association with his thousand concubines, not to women generally.

Her most radical claims are grounded upon Galatians 3:28, that under the New Testament, "male and female are all one in Christ Jesus" (7). She reads the parable of the talents as requiring that "no power externall or internall ought woman to keep idle, but to imploy it in some service of God" (12); and she demonstrates by writing this tract that some talents ask employment beyond the domestic sphere. Challenging the usual formula in treatises on marital duties (and in Swetnam) that defines separate spheres for men and women,[16] she cites examples from nature—pigeons, cocks, and hens—to argue that husband and wife should share all the offices and duties of life. She celebrates marriage as an estate far more excellent than the single life, invoking the familar pun, "merri-age."

Her epilogue concludes with a stern warning. Men who speak and write against women are guilty of that most odious vice, ingratitude toward God. They invite God's certain revenge for they revile his best gift and handiwork, "women I meane, whom God hath made equall with themselves in dignity, both temporally and eternally."

Appended to the *Mouzell* is another small tract with a separate title page, *Certaine Quaeres to the Bayter of Women*. The epistle to this tract, addressed to the "gentle," "well-affected," and "judicious" reader, presumably includes men of this sort as well as women (sig. Fr-v). Here Speght admits the limitations of her knowledge and experience due to her youth and the restrictions imposed upon her sex, but that stance carries a quite subversive subtext: if her "vacant hours" of study have made her so much more learned than Swetnam with his masculine advantages,[17] then her example makes the case for women's equal intelligence and equal capacity for education. In this epistle she takes up her satiric rapier again, explaining that the logical chaos of Swetnam's tract has prevented her from engaging with his arguments point by point. Her short preface throws down the gauntlet to Swetnam, pointing him to the specific queries posed in the following tract, "that if he please, hee may answer for himselfe" (28).

16. See, for example, Robert Cleaver, *A Godlie Forme of Household Government* (London, 1598), 170; William Whately, *A Bride-Blush: Or, A Direction for Married Persons* (London, 1616), 84; Swetnam, *Araignment*, 56.

17. Interestingly enough, in his fencing manual Swetnam insists on his limited formal education: "I was never at *Oxford* but while I baited my horse; nor at *Cambridge* but while one *Sturbridge* faire lasted" (sig. A 4); "I am no Scholler, for I do protest I never went to Schoole six moneths in all my life" (p. 195). This may be an effort to deflect Speght's taunts about his grammar, but as Swetnam's manual is not listed in the Stationers' Register and both works bear the publication date 1617 we cannot be certain that Swetnam's postdates Speght's. That is however likely, since Speght's *Mouzell* was listed in the Stationers' Register on November 14, 1616.

In *Certaine Quaeres* she instances a few specific examples of Swetnam's grammatical errors and illogic, spicing them with invective and puns. He counts women's changes of mood "wonderful," but she thinks him "far more *wonder-foole*" for his failures in grammatical concordance—for example, joining " 'women' plural and 'she' singular" (31). She also puns regularly on "as/ass," pointing to Swetnam: "And where-asse you say" (29); "such a monster in nature *Asse* your selfe"; "*Asse* you . . . have done" (29–30).[18] She also faults him for failing to recognize the biblical counterexamples to his generalizations about women's ingratitude or the cruelty of fair women.[19]

Who has annotated the margins of this text with such profusion? Perhaps Swetnam himself, rising to Speght's challenge and making notes of the rejoinders he might use in penning an answer to her tract. Supporting that assumption is the fact that the annotator knows Swetnam's text very well and readily undertakes to clarify Swetnam's positions or intentions or meaning in several passages. An example is the assertion (which Speght challenges) that women will not *"give thankes for a good turne"* (#67): "The authors meaning is, of those weomen [that] now live in these our days. Likewise when he speaketh of weomen hee doth not meane all weomen for that weare too absurde; butt [woe]men for the most part, are soe."[20] The strongest evidence for Swetnam as annotator is his knowledgeable explanation that one of the grammatical gaffes Rachel derided (#75) was in fact a printer's error: "Now the foole rides you, for that was the printers fault in puttinge in Woman for Woemen." Also, on at least one occasion (#78), the annotator undertakes to speak for Swetnam: "Let his Dixit stand for his Dico. for he hath spoken them. yett for charities sake beelieve him, if hee sayes hee loves you not."

Alternatively, the annotator may be another polemicist who made notes in Speght's text preparatory to writing a tract answering her and defending Swetnam. In support of this hypothesis is the writer's "third-party" stance as of one dealing (though hardly evenhandedly) between the two parties: "God have mercy on yea both; and make yea his servants; for sure neither booke hathe better owner" (#12). Or again, "Kisse & bee freinds" (#13). Perhaps more telling is one witty riposte that seems to reinforce rather than rescue Swetnam from Speght's puns designating him an ass (#72). Also, there are no verbal echoes, as might perhaps be expected, between Swetnam's published tract and these marginalia. Moreover, though the point cannot be demonstrated in brief compass, the annotator seems more irate and indignant toward women and

---

18. Speght's or the printer's italics point to the puns.

19. In addition, she catches him up on his occasional, inexplicable repetition of statements from the defenses of women and marriage that contradict the thrust of his argument.

20. See also #2, #76, #83, #85.

more zealous in his denigration of them than Swetnam does in his *Araignment,* which is in the spirit of the rhetorical game. But of course Swetnam might well marshal harsher and more derogatory arguments when defending his own book against the ridicule of a particular woman.

It is possible, though I think unlikely, that the annotator is some casual reader moved to rage by Speght's tract. The sheer number of annotations argues against it, as does, more forcefully, the writer's intimate knowledge both of Swetnam's work and of Speght's circumstances. He knows that she is a "priest daughter" (#73)—something she does not reveal in her own tract. He also knows her reputation as a sensible and discerning woman—before she published this book in the marketplace: "You your selfe weare one of the Juditious: but now by reason of your publique booke, not soe good as common" (#7). Another indicator may be the complete obliteration of two long notes (#3, #4), hardly necessary in a purely private document. If these marginalia are, as I think, notes toward an answer to Speght, that answer, if written, was likely never published. Speght would almost certainly have mentioned any such direct, full-scale attack in her preface to *Mortalities Memorandum,* where she refers to Sowernam and Munda by name and comments in general terms on the variety of opinions and censures her tract elicited.

But if the annotator's identity cannot be firmly established, his strategies for dealing with the first Englishwoman who dared to publish a serious defense of women are only too familiar. Some of his rejoinders condescend to Speght's youth and female ignorance, especially when she herself admits, as in #5, that her "Minority" imposes constraints on her: "She cannot chuse but maybe doe what she can." Or again, quarreling with Speght's exposition of the advice of Job's wife to "Curse God and Die" as irony or *sarcasmus* (#74), he declares, "If you conster this aright, then have I binne taught amisse: butt I had rather beeleeve a sound devine, then a shallow woeman." Or yet again (#76), he claims she has foolishly misunderstood Swetnam: "And therefore you frame that Indication, of your own misunderstandinge. O weake and ignorant woman."

Many more rejoinders are explicit sexual put-downs: puns on female genitalia, rude references to body parts or to sexual intercourse, slurs on Speght's chastity. Several of these respond to the commendatory poems, ostensibly by her admirers whom the annotator constructs as male:

> #16.   To the comparison of Speght to David slaying Goliath he retorts, "What? throwinge stones? Give mee her arse."
>
> #17.   To the expressions of admiration for her book, he mocks, "Shee is to bee admired at for her muzzell. why what manner of mouth hath shee, for that's her muzzell."

#20.   To the comment that she is like a patriot fighting for his country, he jeers, "Doth shee fight for her Cunt-rie. for a puddinge as soone."

#22.   To the reference to her as "A Virgin young" he gibes, "You dare not sweare for hir virginitie unlesse you bee her servant: and then you dare doe anie thinge."

#26.   To the comment that she is to be praised for her magnanimity in encountering such a foe, he puns that her encounter is with a "Philistine foe" who "carries his fire in his tayle."

#27.   To the declaration that in the combat she "beares the triumph," he retorts, "Thy mistress beares the prick & prizz away."

Other such ripostes and double entendres are scattered throughout the tracts. To Speght's charge that Swetnam usurps God's right in offering to judge women's thoughts (#70), the annotator observes, "Her thoughts manie times looke out att her Eyes, & come fourth in her wordes. Besides you may if you please, enter into her minde by hir bodyes gate; and have them all, sutch as they are." He also responds with ponderous wit to Rachel's challenge to Swetnam to incorporate bachelors into his proverb about wives as horses carrying married men to the devil:

#82.   Then you aske the quaestion how Batchelours travayle; why surely theie ride too, for companies sake, uppon sutch coltes as you are. Whoe neither amble nor trott perfectly, butt ride a good fayr gallop to the devill, and there wee have you.

       If married men ride, how travayle Batchelours: Why surely say you theie must goe on foot bycause theie want wives: butt I have prooved the contrarie, and have found them naggs to ride. Then thus I say: if married men bee theire wives Heads, then what head have Maides. why surely none, bycause they want Husbands.[21]

Another kind of sexual put-down interprets Speght's biblically grounded praises of marriage as evidence that she, like all maids, desperately wants and needs a husband: "Oh, for a husbande" (#47); "You pleade well for a husbande; & it is a great pittie, that you have not had a good one long since" (#48). To her *"merri-age"* pun (#49), he scoffs, "See how shee is carried away in a golden distraction: you must goe to Man, or all will bee spoyled."[22] Also, he takes her reference to Solomon's praise of woman as the crown of her husband (#54) as evidence that she intends to rule her husband-to-be: "The man is the head, and you would faine bee the crown[e] on the topp of his heade; you suckt that ambition from your first parent."[23]

21. See also #15, #21, #24, #46, #66, and #70.
22. See also #50, #52, #57.
23. See also #55, #58.

At times the annotator picks up a word or phrase of Speght's to aim a cheap shot at stereotypical female evils and weaknesses: women are vain, much marred, the cause of mens' pains, cares, and utter destruction (#10, #18, #31, #53).[24] He counters Speght's portrait of Swetnam as a blasphemer by construing her attacks on Swetnam as evidence that she lacks Christian charity. And he meets her assertion that she defends good, not bad, women (#64) by posing a question designed to trap her (as a good Calvinist) into self-condemnation: "In which of these sorts doe you include your selfe: if amongst the good; then do you justifie your selfe. if amongst those which are evill; then need wee noe farther wittnes. There is noe Medium."[25]

Several annotations respond to Speght's biblical exegeses arguing women's excellence. Some deny the relevance of her biblical examples (Miriam, Deborah, Hannah): "You commende those where never anie discommende. butt sett mee forthe sutch a woeman as one of these now livinge" (#44).[26] Others respond to her biblically grounded argument that woman is a good work of God by elaborating upon how women have marred the Creator's work by sin and cosmetic artifice:

> #39.   That worke can not chuse butt bee badd, yea verie b[add] which
>   woeman hath wrought her selfe: for since he framd her, she hath
>   p[ut] new colours of white and red uppon hir face; sett in new
>   teethe, either weares not hir own naturall haire, or if it bee, itt
>   is soe powd[red] and perfumed, that as, shee thinkes, shee hath
>   much mended hir creatours werke. Had theie [con]tinued as theie
>   weare at the first created, they had binn excellent: butt the manie
>   are soe chaunged in face, that you shall scarse knowe them from a
>   Pa[?].[27]

Some notes simply cite or allude to scriptural denunciations of women: "A Man may with scripture reproove weomen for in Manie places therin they are sett forth in theire colours" (#65).[28]

But the annotator seldom engages Speght's reinterpretations of Scripture, and when he does, he simply reiterates conventional misogynistic readings: Eve is "much more cunninge to deceive, then the devill" (#31).[29] If Solomon with all his wisdom could not find a good woman how can any man "hope for a good

24. He also reinterprets proverbs she reread from Swetnam—notably, the "sowre" woman as a kicking horse (#8)—and offers a few new ones (#38, #51).
25. See also #9, #64, #80, #87.
26. See also #67 and #68.
27. See also #29, #43.
28. See also #30, #62.
29. See also #32, #33.

woeman in these our latter dayes" (#37). Speght's historical contextualization of Paul's advice to men to live single and chaste is a "false exposition" (#36). And her reading of the parable of the talents (#45) he dismisses with a reference to Seneca's advice to teach by example not by precept—an obvious effort to reinscribe female silence.

If these marginalia are indeed notes toward an intended response to Speght by Swetnam or another writer, they provide a fascinating window on the way in which many controversialists engaged with offending texts and prepared to answer them in the time-honored manner—page by page, detail by detail. They hold a special interest for what they reveal about the writer's attitudes toward women, and about his sense of the polemical strategies likely to prove effective with his anticipated readership. His stereotypical attacks on women are entirely unoriginal—the matter of antifeminist polemic from antiquity on. And the verbal ripostes, personal insults, and sexual double entendres are common enough in polemic of all kinds in the period, as any reader of the Marprelate tracts, the *Querelle des Femmes* literature, or Milton's antiprelatical tracts can testify.

Yet these weapons are deployed in ways that take the exchange out of the province of rhetorical gamesmanship in this case, where the highly unusual target is a woman's text by a known female author. For one thing, the annotator makes Speght a particular example of the stereotypical follies of the entire sex—ignorance, weakness, voracious sexual appetite, desire to dominate men, vanity, unseemly speech, shrewishness, propensity to sin. Early modern male authors do not of course attack their male opponents with gender put-downs targeting the entire sex, because they themselves would be implicated in any such charge. For another, the sexual innuendos and blatant foul language take on special force when directed against a known, young, unmarried woman, highly vulnerable to insinuations of unchastity and indecorum. For yet another, the annotator largely ignores Speght's reasoned argument: he simply refuses to take her seriously.

Would these silencing techniques have worked if the annotator had in fact written and published his answer? Or would Speght, as I suspect, have included a spirited defense in the preface to her 1621 poems, where she so vehemently insists on her authorship of the *Mouzell*? We cannot know about that, or know why the writer decided not to publish: possibly he himself realized that such an attack on a well-connected young woman of good reputation might backfire. But we can recognize in these annotations some revealing early versions of what have proved to be quite durable tactics for trying to keep subversive women in their place.

APPENDIX

Yale University *Mouzell for Melastomus* (Ih Sp 33 617m)

The annotations are reproduced below, along with enough of Speght's text (left column) to clarify the intertextual dialogue. I use square brackets to note the few occasions when the marginal note is crossed out or illegible, and to record my guesses when a letter or word is blurred or was cropped when the text was rebound. Words which the annotator underlined in Speght's text are underlined here: often they are the precise target of the response.

Speght's Text	Marginalia
TITLE PAGE EPIGRAPH, PROV. 26.5	
1. *Answer a foole according to his foolishnesse, lest he bee wise in his owne conceit.*	Shee that calleth her booke foole is worthy to bee punished with Hell fire.
THE EPISTLE DEDICATORIE To all vertuous Ladies Honourable or Worshipfull, and to all other of Hevahs sex fearing God, and loving their just reputation, grace and peace through Christ, to eternall glory.	
2. seeing the *Bayter of Women* opened his mouth against noble as well as ignoble, against the rich as well as the poore.	hath But not against good woemen of which there are a few.
THE PREFACE Not unto the veriest Ideot that ever set Pen to Paper, but to the Cynicall Bayter of Women, or metamorphosed Misogunes, Joseph Swetnam.	
3. From standing water, which soon putrifies, can no good fish be expected	[Note crossed out and illegible]
4. Semblably, no better streame can we looke, should issue from your idle corrupt braine, then that whereto the ruffe of your fury (to use your owne words) hath moved you to open the sluce.	[Note crossed out and illegible]
5. Your dealing wants so much discretion, that I doubt whether to bestow so good a name as the Dunce upon you: but Minority bids me keepe within my bounds; and therefore I onlie say unto you, that your corrupt Heart and railing Tongue, hath made you a fit scribe for the Divell.	he cannot chuse butt maybe doe what she can.

6. Good had it beene for you to have put on that <u>Muzzell</u>, which Saint *James* would have all Christians to weare; *Speake not evill one of another.*

Likewise it is sayd, revile not those that revile: which muzzell would verie well have fitted your mouth in manie places of this booke.

7. by this your hodge-podge of heathenish Sentences, Similes, and Examples, you have set forth your selfe in your right colours, unto the view of the world: and I doubt not but the <u>Judicious</u> will account of you according to your demerit: As for the <u>Vulgar</u> sort, which have no more learning then you have shewed in your Booke, it is likely they will applaud you for your paines.

You your selfe weare one of the Juditious: but now by reason of your publique booke, not soe good as common.

8. As for your *Bugge-beare* or advice unto Women, that whatsoever they doe thinke of your Worke, they should conceale it, lest in finding fault, they bewray their galled backes to the world; in which you allude to that Proverbe, *Rubbe a galled horse, and he will kicke:* Unto it I answere by way of Apologie, that though every galled horse, being touched, doth kicke; yet every one that kickes, is not galled: so that you might as well have said, that because burnt folks dread the fire, therfore none feare fire but those that are burnt.

Kickinge is a verie ill quallitie in anie horse: which you can not cleare your feete of: for youre sowre wordes moove it against you. But a sound & good horse, and soe consequently a good woeman will neither kicke nor wince.

9. Further, if your owne words be true, that you wrote with your hand, but not with your heart, then are you <u>an hypocrite in Print</u>: but it is rather to be thought that your Pen was the bewrayer of the abundance of your minde,

You should rather have absolved him then to have given this harde sentence against him: for hee deal[s] with weemen, as weomen doe with theire children, to make them good. Yet are they loath to beate them, and manie times theire hands wilbee against theire hearts.

10. and that this was but a little morter to dawbe up agayne the wall, which you intended to breake downe.

[crossed out line] woemen be a wall, the wall is full of cracks, and needes much morter to mend it.

11.

Butt sure you are a Devile incarnate, if your heart went with your hande: and your tongue avouch it.

12. The revenge of your rayling Worke wee leave to Him, who hath appropriated vengeance unto himselfe, whose Pen-man hath included Raylers in the Catalogue of

God have mercy on yea both; and make yea his servants; for sure neither booke hathe better owner

them, that shall not inherite Gods Kingdome,
and your selfe unto the mercie of that just
Judge, who is able to save and to destroy.

13. *Your undeserved friend,*   Rachel Speght Kisse & bee freinds

DEDICATORY POEMS
In praise of the Author and her Worke
[First poem]
14. If little *David* that for *Israels* sake,   Neaver to little if olde enough.
   esteemed neyther life nor limbe too deare,
In that he did adventure without dread,
   to cast at him, whom all the hoste did feare,
A stone, which brought *Goliah* to the ground,
Obtain'd applause with Songs and Timbrels sound.

15. Then let another young encombatant   Neaver to younge if bigg enough
   receive applause, and thankes, as well as hee:
For with an enemie to Women kinde,
   she hath encountred, as each wight may see:

16. And with the fruit of her industrious toyle,   What? throwinge stones?
To this *Goliah* she hath given the foyle.   Give mee her arse.

17. Admire her much I may, both for her age,   Shee is to bee admired at for her muzzell.
   and this her Mouzell for a blacke-mouth'd wight, why what manner of mouth hath shee,
But praise her, and her worke, to that desert,   for that's her muzzell.
   which unto them belongs of equall right
I cannot; only this I say, and end,

18. Shee is unto her Sex a faithfull friend.   Shee is? She is a desperate vanity
                                    I'le warrant her, goe toe.

19. [signed] Philalethes   [Changed to] Philogunes

[Second Poem]
20. If he that for his Countrie doth expose   Doth shee fight for her Cunt-rie.
   himselfe unto the furie of his foe,   for a puddinge as soone.
Doth merite praise and due respect of those,
   for whom he did that perill undergoe:
Then let the Author of this Mouzell true
Receive the like, of right it is her due.

21. For she to shield her Sex from Slaunders Dart, Shee must have a large sheilde to
   and from invective obtrectation,   receive all the darts that are shott
Hath ventured by force of Learnings Art,   at her whole sexe.
   (in which she hath had education)

To combate with him, which doth shame his Sex,
By offring feeble women to perplex.

[Third Poem]
22. <u>A Virgin young</u>, and of such tender age,
As for encounter may be deemd too weake,

You dare not sweare for hir
virginitie unlesse you bee her servant:
and then you dare doe anie thinge.

23. Shee having not as yet seene twenty yeares,

I have knowen those that have
encounterd as valiant men as this at raw
fifteene and have made them yeilde their
weapon.

24. Though in <u>her carriage</u> older she appeares.

It seemes shee is of a good Carri-age.

25. <u>Her wit and learning</u> in this present Worke,
   More praise doth merit, then my quill can write:

By my troath, noe.

26. Her <u>magnanimitie</u> deserves applaud,
In ventring with a <u>fierie</u> foe to fight:

Neither, unlesse hee bee a Philistine
foe & carries his fire in his tayle.

27. And now in fine, what shall I further say?
But that she beares the triumph quite away.

Thy mistress beares the prick & prizz
away

A MOUZELL FOR MELASTOMUS
28. [Epigraph from Proverbs 18:22]
He that findeth a wife, findeth a good thing,
and receiveth favour of the Lord.

He that findeth a good wife. ["good"
inserted above the line].

29. The worke of Creation being finished, this
approbation thereof was given by God himselfe,
That *All was very good:*

It was verie good: but since the creation:
woeman hath mismade, & misform'd her
sisters thats not verie good

30. If All, then *Woman,* who, excepting man,
is the most excellent creature under the
Canopie of heaven.

Here the femall sexe is at variance
about man: for Jacob sayth, that woeman
is the worst creature under ye Sunn; Man
only excepted. Rachel sayes that man is
the most <u>excellent</u>: Oh excellent

31. To the first of these objections I answere;
that Sathan first assailed the woman, because
where the hedge is lowest, most easie it is to
get over, and she being the weaker vessell
was with more facility to be seduced.

The devill said, trust in himselfe
too bee to weake, & tender. Sett the
woeman to deceive the man, shee is
much more cunninge to deceive, then
the devill.

32. And if *Adam* had not approoved of that
deed which *Eve* had done, and beene willing to
treade the steps which she had gone, hee being

her Head would have reproved her, and have
made the commandement a bit to restraine him
from breaking his Makers Injunction: For if a
man burne his hand in the fire, the bellows
that blowed the fire are not to be blamed, but
himselfe rather, for not being carefull to avoyde
the danger: Yet if the bellowes had not blowed,
the fire had not burnt;

Eve first threw herselfe into the fire, and
pulled Adam after her.

33. no more is woman simply to bee
condemned for mans transgression: for by
the free will, which before his fall hee enjoyed,
hee might have avoyded, and beene free from
beeing burnt, or singed with that fire which was
kindled by Sathan, and blowne by *Eve.*

You may see by this how strong to
deceive, weomen are, against whose
engins, a mans will, is noe sure defence

34. 3 *Objection answered* [marginal note].

[adds "not" to read] 3 *Objection* not *answered.*

35. For the third objection, *It is good for a
man not touch a woman:* The Apostle makes it
not a positive prohibition, but speakes it onelie
because of the *Corinths* present necessitie, who
were then persecuted by the enemies of the
Church, for which cause, and no other, he saith,

[adds "to" to read] not to touch
that is, sinfully or incontinently

36. *Art thou loosed from a wife? seeke not a
wife:* meaning whilst the time of these
perturbations should continue in their heate;
*but if thou art bound, seeke not to be loosed:
if thou marriest, thou sinnest not,* only increasest
thy care: *for the married careth for the things
of this world, And I wish that you were without
care, that yee might cleave fast unto the Lord
without separation: For the time remaineth,
that they which have wives be as though they
had none:* for the persecutors shall deprive you
of them, eyther by imprisonment, banishment,
or death: so that manifest it is, that the Apostle
doth not heereby forbid marriage, but onely
adviseth the *Corinths* to forbeare a while, till
God in mercie should curbe the fury of their
adversaries.

This piece of scripture, like a two
edged sworde, hath cutt you into the
Graine, which makes you give this false
exposition: for the Apostle speaketh this,
to admonish us to live chastly for what
meomets [moments] bee when hee sayeth:
I would that all men weare even as I my
selfe am: That is, not only single man,
but also chast[e], which was a proper
gift of God given unto him:

37. The fourth and last objection, is that of
*Salomon, I have found one man among a
thousand, but a woman among them all have I
not found:* for answere of which, if we looke

If the wisest man that ever lived, in
[choosinge] of seven hundred wives &
three hundred concubines, could not
choose one that was upright: what

into the storie of his life, wee shall finde therein a Commentary upon this enigmaticall Sentence included: for it is there said, that *Salomon* had seven hundred wives, and three hundred concubines, which number connexed make one thousand. These women turning his heart away from being perfect with the Lord his God, sufficient cause had hee to say, that among the said thousand women found he not one upright. Hee saith not, that among a thousand women never any man found one worthy of commendation, but speakes in the first person singularly, *I have not found,* meaning in his owne experience: for this assertion is to be holden a part of the confession of his former follies, and no otherwise, his repentance being the intended drift of *Ecclesiastes.*

s[h]ould wee silly men hope for a good woeman in these our latter dayes.

38. I will proceede toward the period of my intended taske, which is, to decipher the excellency of women:

Proprio Laus, Sordet in ore.

39. The efficient cause of womans creation, was *Jehovah* the *Eternall.* . . . That worke then can not chuse but be good, yea very good, which is wrought by so excellent a workeman as the Lord: for he being a glorious Creator, must needes effect a worthie creature.

That worke can not choose butt bee badd, yea verie b[add] which woeman hath wrought her selfe: for since he framd her, she hath p[ut] new colours of white and red uppon hir face; sett in new teethe, either weares not hir own naturall haire, or if it bee, itt is soe powd[red] and soe perfumed, that as, shee thinkes, shee hath much mended hir creatours werke. Had theie [con]tinued as theie weare at the first created, they had binn excellent: butt the manie are soe chaunged in face, that you shall scarse knowe them from a Pa[?]

40. Secondly, the materiall cause, or matter whereof woman was made, was of a refined mould, if I may so speake: for man was created of the dust of the earth, but woman was made of a part of man. . . . This being rightly considered, doth teach men to make such account of their wives, as *Adam* did of *Eve, This is bone of my bone, and and flesh of my flesh:* As also, that they neyther doe or wish any more hurt unto them, then unto their owne bodies: for men ought to love their wives

Likewise hee that loves himselfe; loves his wife; and therefore, how comes it to passe, that manie men care not for their wifes, doe notwithstanding love themselves in the highest degree. allsoe that woemen complaine [of] want of love in their [hu]sbandes towardes them.

as themselves, because hee <u>that loves his wife,</u>
<u>loves himselfe:</u> And never man hated his owne
flesh (which the woman is) unlesse a monster
in nature.

41. Thirdly, the formall cause, fashion, and
proportion of woman was excellent: . . . For
as God gave man a lofty countenance, that
hee might looke up toward Heaven, so did
he likewise give unto woman. And as the
temperature of mans body is excellent, so is
womans. For whereas other Creatures, <u>by</u>
<u>reason of their grosse humours,</u> have
excrements for their habite, as foules, their
feathers, beasts, their haire, fishes, their scales,
man and woman onely, have their skinne cleare
and smoothe.

they wanted Reason, which should teach
them to provide for themselves; and
therefore god and Nature provided for
them.

42. And (that more is) in the Image of God
were they both created; yea and to be briefe,
<u>all the parts of their bodies</u>, both externall and
internall, were correspondent and meete each
for other.

[comment crossed out]

43. Fourthly and lastly, the finall cause, or
end, for which woman was made, was to
glorifie God, and to be a collaterall companion
for man to glorifie God, in using her bodie, and
all the parts, powers, and faculties thereof, as
instruments for his honour: As with her voice
to sound foorth his prayses, like *Miriam,* and
the rest of her company;

Sutch theie should bee, & not sutch
as theie are.

44. with her tongue not to utter words
of strife, but to give good councell unto her
husband, the which hee must not despise.

You commende those where never anie
discommende. butt sett mee
forthe sutch a woeman as one of these
now livinge.

45. Finally, no power externall or
internall <u>ought</u> woman to keep idle, but to
imploy it in some service of GOD, to the glorie
of her Creator, and comfort of her owne soule.

It was the sayenge of Seneca, Longum
est iter per praecepta; breve et efficex
per exempla; Shewe them, by your
example, and lett your deedes speake
unto them: Plus sonas (valde metuo)
quam vales.

46. The <u>other end</u> for which woman was made,
was to be a Companion, and *helper* for man;

A woeman was made for both endes.

47. Wherefore *Salomon* saith, <u>Woe to him that</u> <u>is alone</u>; for when thoughts of discomfort, troubles of this world, and feare of dangers do possesse him, he wants a companion to lift him up from the pit of perplexitie, into which hee is fallen:

Oh, for a husbande.

48. for a good wife, saith *Plautus,* is the wealth of the minde, and the welfare of the heart; and therefore a meete <u>associate for her husband</u>; And *Woman,* saith *Paul, is the glorie of the man.*

You pleade well for a husbande; & it is a great pittie, that you have not had a good one long since.

49. <u>Marriage is a merri-age</u>, and this worlds Paradise, where there is mutuall love. Our blessed Saviour vouchsafed to honour a marriage with the first miracle that he wrought, unto which miracle matrimoniall estate may not unfitly bee resembled:

See how shee is carried away in a golden distraction: you must goe to Man, or all will bee spoyled.

50. For as Christ turned water into wine, a farre more excellent liquor; which, as the Psalmist saith, <u>Makes glad the heart of man</u>;

Oh, for a husbande.

51. So the single man is by marriage changed from a <u>Batchelour to a Husband</u>, a farre more excellent title:

This is just as our old proverbe is; out of the fryinge pan into the fire.

52. from a solitarie life unto a joyfull union and conjunction, with such a creature as God hath made <u>meete for man</u>, for whom none was meete till shee was made.

Maydenhead for a husband.

53. *A vertuous woman,* saith *Salomon, is the* <u>*Crowne* of her husband</u>; By which metaphor hee sheweth both the excellencie of such a wife, and what account her husband is to make of her:

Shee is the crowne of her husbande: for as manie, & as great cares doe attende uppon a married man, as doe uppon the crowne of a kinge.

54. For a King doth not trample his <u>Crowne</u> under his feete, but highly esteemes of it, gently handles it, and carefully laies it up, as the evidence of his Kingdome;

The man is the head, and you would faine bee the crown[e] on the topp of his heade; you suckt that ambition from your first parent.

55. So <u>husbands should not</u> account their wives as their vassals, but as those that are heires together of the grace of life,

You make your way, against you gett a husbande.

56. and with all lenitie and mild perswasions set their feete in the right way, if they happen to tread awry, bearing with their infirmities, as *Elkanah* did with his wives barrennesse.

Theye tread theire shar[e?] awry oftentimes.

57. The Kingdome of God is compared unto the marriage of a Kings sonne:

This booke will bespea[ke] you a husband.

58. Thus if men would remember the duties they are to performe in being heads, some would not stand a tip-toe as they doe, thinking themselves Lords & Rulers,

Surely now I must thinke that either you are married, or fayrely promised for now you comend the[se]. and I wishe that your husbande, will learne this good lesson.

59. But least I should seeme too partiall in praysing women so much as I have (though no more then warrant from Scripture doth allow) I adde to the premises, that I say not, all women are vertuous, for then they should be more excellent then men, sith of *Adams* sonnes there was *Cain* as well as *Abel,*

For sayenge soe your tongue should Lye still.

60. so that of men as of women, there are two sorts, namely, good and bad.

of a bad man and a bad woeman, which is the best.

61. And if women were not sinfull, then should they not need a Saviour: but the Virgin *Mary* a patterne of piety, *rejoyced in God her Saviour: Ergo,* she was a sinner.

This argument is needelesse, for whoe ever yett denyed but weomen weare sinfull.

62. In the *Revelation* the Church is called the Spouse of Christ; and in *Zachariah,* wickednesse is called a woman, to shew that of women there are both godly and ungodly:

Qoate mee a place of scripture wheare man is called by sutch a name

63. But farre be it from any one, to condemne the righteous with the wicked, or good women with the bad (as the Bayter of women doth:)

There is noe one that either is, or doth good; noe, not one

64. Of the good sort is it that I have in this booke spoken, and so would I that all that reade it should so understand me: for if otherwise I had done, I should have incurred that woe, which by the Prophet *Isaiah* is pronounced against them that *speake well of evill,* and should have *justified the wicked, which thing is abhominable to the Lord.*

In which of these sorts doe you include your selfe: if amongst the good; then do you justifie your selfe. if amongst those which are evill; then need wee noe farther witnes. There is no Medium.

THE EPILOGUE

65. Great was the unthankefulnesse of *Pharaohs* Butler unto *Joseph* . . . But farre greater is the ingratitude of those men toward God, that dare presume to speake and exclaime against *Woman*, whom God did create for mans comfort. What greater discredit can redound to a workeman, then to have the man, for whom hee hath made it, say, it is naught?

A Man may with scripture reproove weomen. for in Manie places therin they are sett forth in theire colours.

CERTAINE QUARES TO THE BAYTER OF WOMEN
TO THE READER

66. Although (curteous Reader) I am young in yeares, and more defective in knowledge, that little smattering in Learning which I have obtained, being only the fruit of such vacant houres, as I could spare from affaires befitting my Sex.

Virgo pudicitiam notat aetatemq[ue] puella. You speak like a mayd, not like a Virgin. I am young sir and scorne affection; 'um, 'um, 'um.

QUAERES

67. If it bee true, asse you affirme, Pag.2. line 26. That *women will not give thankes for a good turne.*

   I demand whether *Deborah* and *Hannah* were not women, who both of them sang hymnes of thankesgiving unto the Lord;

Two amongst tenne thousande: the authors meaning is, of those weomen [that] now live in these our days. Likewise when he speaketh of weomen hee doth not meane all weomen for that weare too absurde; butt [woe]men for the most part, are soe.

68. And where-asse you say; Pag. 4. line 22. *that a woman that hath a faire face, it is ever matched with a cruel heart, and her heavenly lookes with hellish thoughts:* you therein shew your selfe a contradictor of Scriptures presidents: For *Abigail* was a beautifull woman, and tenderhearted; *Rebekah* was both faire of face and pittiful.

Still you bringe in examples of the dayes of olde. butt it is not sayde that theye then weare soe; butt that most part of those which now live, are soe.

69. As for your audacitie in judging of womens thoughts,

[comment crossed out, illegible]

70. you thereby shew your selfe an usurper against the King of heaven, the true knowledge of cogitations being appropriate unto him alone.

Her thoughts manie times looke out att her Eyes, & come fourth in her wordes. Besides you may if you please, enter into her minde by hir bodyes gate; and have them all, sutch as they are.

71. If your assertion, That *a woman is better lost then found, better forsaken then taken*

There is a singular worde pointinge at a singular ill-conditioned woeman.

(Page 5. line 4.) be to be credited, me thinkes, great pitty it is, that afore you were borne, there was none so wise as to counsell your father not to meddle with a woman, that hee might have escaped those troubles, which you affirme, that all married men are cumbred with, Page 2. line 20.

72. As also that hee might not have begotten such a monster in nature *Asse* your selfe,

> Asses have four leggs
> and hee hath but two:
> Crisse-crosse Kisse his Asse
> and make not sutch a Doe.

73. (like the <u>Priest which</u> forgot he was Parish Clearke) defame and exclaime against women, as though your selfe had never had a mother, or you never beene a child.

> You have forgott that you are a priest daughter, for instead of preachinge you rayle right downe.

74. In saying (Page 10.line. 25.) that *Jobs wife counselled her husband to curse God,* you misconster the Text; for the true construction thereof will shew it to bee a *Sarcasmus* or *Ironicall* speech, and not an instigation to blasphemy.

> If you conster this aright, then have I binne taught amisse: butt I had rather beeleeve a sound devine, then a shallow woeman.

75. Page 11. line 8. you count it *Wonderfull to see the mad feates of women, for shee will now bee merry, then sad:* but me thinkes it is farre more *wonder-foole* to have one, that adventures to make his Writing as publique as an In-keepers Signe, which hangs to the view of all passengers, to want Grammaticall Concordance in his said Writing, and joyne together *Women* plurall, and *shee* singular, *Asse* you not onely in this place, but also in others have done.

> Now the foole rides you, for that was the printers fault in puttinge in Woman for Woemen.

76. have you not feared blasphemously to say, *that women sprung from the divell,* Page 15. line 26. But being, as it seemes, defective in that whereof you have much need (for *mendacem oportet esse memorem)* you suddainely after say, That *women were created by God, and formed by nature, and therefore by policie and wisedome to be avoyded,* Page 16. line 12. An impious conclusion to inferre, that because God created, therefore to be avoyded: Oh intollerable absurdity!

> To be avoyded, is as much as to say avoydable: [that] is, that men are able to avoyd them by polycy and wisdome. And therefore you frame that Indication, of your owne misunderstandinge. O weake and ignorant woman.

77. *Men I say may live without women, but*
women cannot live without men, Page 14,
line 18. If any Religious Author had thus
affirmed, I should have wondred, that unto
Satans suggestions he had so much subjected
himself, as to crosse the Almighties providence
and care for mans good, who positively said,
It is not good for man to bee alone;

That you may see dayly, that men may
live without weomen: Wheather that
sayenge did only concerne Adam, whoe
then was alone, I will not argue: Butt
surely I thinke It was not ment of all men:
for manie have both lived and dyed single men,
and without question it was good for them,
soe to bee alone.

78. But being that the sole testimony heereof
is your owne *dico,* I marvell no whit at
the errour, but heartily wish, that unto all the
untruths you have uttered in your infamous
booke, you had subscribed your *Dico.* that
none of them might bee adjudged truths: For
mendacis praemium est verbis eius non adhiberi
fidem.

Let his Dixit stand for his Dico. for
he hath spoken them. yett for charities
sake beelieve him, if hee sayes hee loves
you not.

79. *Therefore stay not alone in the company of a*
woman, trusting to thy owne chastity,except thou
bee more strong then Sampson, *more wise then*
Salomon, *or more holy then* David, *for these,*
and many more have beene overcome by the
sweete intisements of women, Page 22.
I may as well say *Barrabas* was a murtherer,
Joab killed *Abner* and *Amasa* . . . ; therefore
stay not alone in the companie of a man,
trusting to thy owne strength, except thou bee
stronger then *Josiah,* and more valiant then
Abner and *Amasa,* for these and many more
have beene murthered by men. The forme of
argumentation is your owne, the which if you
dislike, blame your selfe for proposing such a
patterne, and blush at your owne folly.

You have wisely prooved that you have
played the foole for companie: and I see
that you will rather[.] and indeede I thinke
you are better able to follow a foole, then
to leade him.

80. Page 31. line 15. *If God had not made*
women onely to bee a plague to man, hee would
never have called them necessarie evils. Albeit I
have not read *Seaton* or *Ramus,* nor so much as
seene (though heard of) *Aristotles Arganox*
[errata corrects to *Organon*], yet by that I have
seene and reade in compasse of my
apprehension, I will adventure to frame an
argument or two, to shew what danger, for this
your blasphemy your [*sic*] are in.
    To fasten a lie upon God is blasphemy: But
the *Bayter of women* fastens a lie upon God:
ergo, the *Bayter* is a blasphemer.

It is not good for man to bee alone
Gene: 2:28. Therefor[e] theie are
necessarie. That the[ie] are evill, I neede
bringe no proofe. Therefore to fasten a
lye upon a man is a sure token of a
wicked [dis]position.

81. *If thou marryest a still and a quiet woman, that will seeme to thee that thou ridest but an ambling horse to hell, but if with one that is froward and unquiet, then thou wert as good ride a trotting horse to the divell.* Page 35. line 13.
If this your affirmation be true, then seemes it, that hell is the period of all married mens travailes, and the center of their circumference. A man can but have either a good wife or a bad; and if he have the former, you say he doth but seeme to amble to hell; if the latter, he were as good trot to the divell:

Hell is not the period of married mens travayles, but a place the which, in his way to Heaven, hee must of necessitie, passe thourough. For that is the neerest and reddiest way to Heaven: Butt wheather theire wives amble or trott with them, theie themselves know best.

82. But if married men ride, how travaile Batchelours? surely, by your rule they must go on foote, because they want wives; which (inclusively) you say are like horses to carry their husbands to hell. Wherefore in my minde, it was not without mature consideration that you married in time, because it would be too irkesome for you to travaile so tedious a journey on foote.

Then you aske the quaestion how Batchelours travayle; why surely theie ride too, for companies sake, upon sutch coltes as you are. Whoe neither amble nor trott perfectly, butt ride a good fayr gallop to the devill, and there wee have you.

If married men ride, how travayle Batchelours: Why surely say you theie must goe on foot bycause theie want wives: butt I have prooved the contrarie, and have found them naggs to ride. Then thus I say: if married men bee theire wives Heads, then what head have Maides. why surely none, bycause they want Husbands.

83. *Shee will make thee weare an Oxe feather in thy Cappe.* Page 44. line 4.
   If Oxen have feathers, their haires more fitly may be so termed then their hornes.

You interprett the Hornes to be feathers, & not the author himselfe. This is the virtue of a guiltie conscience. Heu quam difficile est crimen non prodere verbis.

84. *Page 51. line 16. Many are the joyes and sweete pleasures in Marriage, as in our children,&c.*
   Page 34. line 5. There are many troubles comes gallopping at the heeles of a woman. If thou wert a Servant, or in bondage afore, yet when thou marriest, thy toyle is never the nearer ended, but even then, and not before, thou changest thy golden life, which thou didst leade before (in respect of the married) for a

[A line in the margin beside these several contradictory quotes from Sweetnam presumably indicates that his comment #85 pertains to them all].

droppe of hony, which quickely turnes to be as
bitter as wormewood.
   Page 53. line 19. The husband ought (in
signe of love) to impart his secrets and counsell
unto his wife, for many have found much comfort
and profite by taking their wives counsell; and
if thou impart any ill happe to thy wife, shee
lighteneth thy griefe, either by comforting thee
lovingly, or else, in bearing a part thereof
patiently.

85. *Page 41. line 12. If thou unfouldest any*   Ironia Dicta
thing of secret to a woman, the more thou
chargest her to keepe it close, the more shee
will seeme, as it were, with childe, till shee
have revealed it.

86. It was the saying of a judicious Writer,   Theie are butt soe manie pills
that whoso makes the fruit of his cogitations   overspreade with hony which you
extant to the view of all men, should have his   havinge soe greedilie gaped after; and
worke to be as a well tuned Instrument, in all   now swallowed, have given you this
places according and agreeing, the which I am   gentle vomitt, & made your tongue voyde
sure yours doth not: For how reconcile you   of evill wordes. [the rest crossed out and
those dissonant places above cited?   illegible]

87. wishing unto every such *Misogunes,* a   How can shee in the first place wishe
Tiburne Tiffenie for curation of his swolne   a halter on him, and then afterward bid
necke, which onely through a Cynicall   him farewell. Unlesse shee speake that
inclination will not indure the yoke of lawfull   inhumane proverbe, Farewell & bee
Matrimony, I bid farewell.   hang'd.

Josephine A. Roberts

Deciphering Women's Pastoral

Coded Language in Wroth's *Love's Victory*

For the women writers of early modern England, the pastoral mode held undeniable appeal. As Louis Montrose has shown, Queen Elizabeth I eagerly joined in the creation of a pastoral persona through calculated references to herself as a milkmaid with a pail on her arm in her speeches to Parliament in 1576 and 1586. Her courtier poets, including Mary Sidney, countess of Pembroke, quickly responded with their own pastorals, which on the surface might seem encomiastic, but often masked subtle strategies, whereby (according to *The Arte of English Poesie*) they might "insinuate and glaunce at greater matters." That pastoral was regarded as the humblest of literary forms actually served as an advantage to women, who were largely excluded from composing in the more public genres of heroic poetry, but the pastoral was also paradoxically viewed as an elite and refined discourse, in which (in the words of Drayton) "the most High, and Noble Matters of the World may be shaddowed . . . and for certaine sometimes are."[1]

The death of Queen Elizabeth did not put an end to women's pastoral; if anything, the seventeenth century witnessed an even greater outpouring of pastoral writing by such figures as Aemilia Lanyer, Mary Wroth, Elizabeth Brackley, Jane Cavendish, An Collins, Margaret Cavendish, Katherine Philips, Elizabeth Wilmot, and Aphra Behn. Nor was women's fascination with the pastoral limited to England alone, for as Ann Rosalind Jones has demonstrated,

---

1. Louis Montrose, " 'Eliza, Queene of shepheardes,' and the Pastoral of Power," *English Literary Renaissance* 10 (1980): 153–82. For Elizabeth's references to herself as milkmaid in her speeches to Parliament, see J. E. Neale, *Elizabeth I and Her Parliaments 1559–1581* (London: Jonathan Cape, 1953), 366; *Elizabeth I and Her Parliaments 1584–1601* (London: Jonathan Cape, 1957), 117. *The Arte of English Poesie*, ed. Gladys D. Willcock and Alice Walker (Cambridge: Cambridge University Press, 1936), 38. Willcock and Walker make a convincing case for ascribing this work to George Puttenham. "To the Reader of His Pastorals" (1619) in *The Works of Michael Drayton*, ed. William Hebel et al., (Oxford: Shakespeare Head, 1961), 2:517.

many Italian female poets, including Tullia d'Aragona and Gaspara Stampa, enthusiastically adopted the pastoral mode.[2] Moreover, they shared with the English writers an interest in pastoral as a means of redefining the social and political relationships between men and women. Their redefinitions ranged widely from Lanyer's radical pastoral vision in "The Description of Cooke-ham" of an all female society to the more conservative household described by Elizabeth Brackley and Jane Cavendish in the entertainment written for their father, in which they appear to affirm existing social structures but conclude by incorporating the bold and openly satirical shepherdess, named Jearer, into their community. Indeed, the pastoral mode supplied these poets with the freedom to represent women in a variety of social stations and social roles—as rulers, mothers, daughters, sisters, friends. Unlike male-authored pastoral, where the female characters largely function to affirm inherited patriarchal values, pastorals written by women reveal a greater willingness to experiment with the social system by expanding the authority and significance of women characters and by enhancing their power and agency.[3]

Yet one element common to pastorals written by both men and women is the use of highly coded language. Montrose, in fact, defines pastoral as the "coded performances [of] a community of speakers and auditors, writers and readers." One of the most important early examples of Elizabethan pastoral, Spenser's 1579 *Shepheardes Calender,* came equipped with its own set of glosses attributed to E. K., who interpreted the feigned titles according to what he believed was the "common custome of counterfeicting the names of secret Personages." The pastorals themselves often referred to the necessity of decoding the figurative language of the texts. In a performance before Elizabeth I at Sudeley during the progress of 1591, Daphne is rescued from Apollo by the power of the queen's presence. As she kneels to make an offering to the monarch, Daphne declares, "These tables, to set downe your prayses, long since, *Sibillas* prophesies, I humbly present to your Majesty, not thinking, that your vertues can be deciphered in so slight a volume, but noted."[4] Pastorals by women

2. *The Currency of Eros: Women's Love Lyric in Europe, 1540–1620* (Bloomington: Indiana University Press, 1990), 123–25.

3. For excerpts from the pastoral entertainment by Brackley and Cavendish, see *Kissing the Rod: An Anthology of Seventeenth-Century Women's Verse,* ed. Germaine Greer, Susan Hastings, Jeslyn Medoff, and Melinda Sansone (New York: Farrar Straus Giroux, 1988), 106–18. For discussion of the limited roles assigned to women in male-composed pastorals, see Harry Berger Jr., "Orpheus, Pan and the Poetics of Misogyny: Spenser's Critique of Pastoral Love and Art," *ELH* 50 (1983): 27–60, and Renato Poggioli, "The Pastoral of the Self," *Daedalus* 88 (1959): 686–99.

4. Montrose, "Of Gentlemen and Shepherds: The Politics of Elizabethan Pastoral Form," *ELH* 50 (1983): 448. E. K.'s gloss to "Januarie," *The Shepheardes Calender,* in *Spenser's Minor Poems,* ed. Ernest de Sélincourt (1910; reprint, Oxford: Clarendon, 1970), 18. *Speeches Delivered to Her Majestie this Last Progresse* (Oxford, 1592); reprinted in *The Complete Works of John Lyly,* ed. R. Warwick Bond, 3 vols. (Oxford: Oxford University Press, 1902), 1:480.

rarely make explicit the codes by which their works may be understood, but one exception is Mary Wroth's play, *Love's Victory*, which was written in close proximity to her pastoral romance, *The Countess of Montgomery's Urania*, of which the first part was printed in 1621.

Wroth's play survives in two manuscripts: an incomplete version at the Huntington Library (lacking the opening dialogue between Venus and Cupid, their appearance at the end of the third act, and most of the fifth act) and a complete version in the library at Penshurst. When Michael Brennan edited the Penshurst manuscript for the Roxburghe Club, he noticed that the dark-red leather cover was embossed in gold with two symbols: the "s fermé" (a diagonally crossed *s* that Wroth used in her correspondence to represent her identity as a member of the Sidney family) and a curious monogram consisting of a number of letters intertwined and superimposed over each other. Although he was able to distinguish a number of the letters, he regarded the monogram as "a clue not so far deciphered."[5]

Within the text of the *Urania*, Wroth describes this type of monogram as a device in which all the letters of a name are "delicately composed within the compasse of one."[6] If we look closely at the symbol (see Figure 1), all of the letters are inscribed within the letter *A*, and the complete name is that of *Amphilanthvs*, the leading male character of the *Urania*. The symbol appears repeated five times on the front cover of the manuscript and five times on the back. Interestingly, the cipher can also be read as inscribing the name of *Pamphilia*, Amphilanthus's beloved. But *why* place this curious device on the cover of a work that does not include either Amphilanthus or Pamphilia as characters? What does the presence of this symbol contribute to our interpretation of the drama? One possibility is that the cipher was to designate Amphilanthus (William Herbert) as the recipient of a presentation copy of *Love's Victory*, but this theory is challenged by the provenance of the manuscript, which according to Brennan has remained in the Penshurst Library since the seventeenth century.[7]

Within the prose fiction Amphilanthus assumes a number of disguises: he appears successively as the Knight of Love with a bleeding heart on his shield

5. *Lady Mary Wroth's Love's Victory: The Penshurst Manuscript*, ed. Michael G. Brennan (London: Roxburghe Club, 1988), 16. All subsequent quotations refer by act and line number to Brennan's excellent edition.

6. *The First Part of the Countess of Montgomery's "Urania,"* ed. Josephine A. Roberts (Binghamton: Medieval and Renaissance Texts and Studies, 1995), 339.

7. I am grateful to Viscount De L'Isle, M.B.E., for permission to reproduce the cover of the Penshurst manuscript of *Love's Victory*. I also wish to thank Kathleen Topping, head of Heritage Services, Centre for Kentish Studies, Maidstone, for assistance in obtaining the photograph of the cover, which does not appear in Brennan's volume.

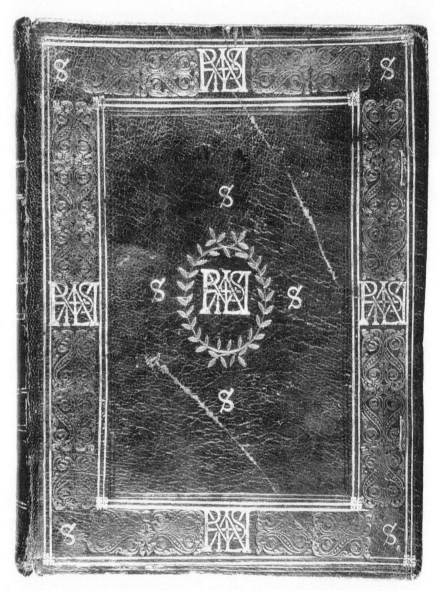

Cover of the Penshurst manuscript of Wroth's *Love Poetry*.

(100), the Shepherd-knight (167), and the Lost Man (376), but one of his most intriguing disguises is that of the Knight of the Cipher (339), who carries the monogram of his beloved Pamphilia on his shield. Wroth uses the term *cipher* on several occasions to refer to the interweaving of the initials of a beloved's name. Pamphilia actually carves a cipher into the bark of an oak (325), and when much later Perissus visits the same garden he sees the cipher but discreetly pretends not to know it, thereby preserving her secrecy (490). The term *cipher* could refer more generally to other forms of coded writing, as Bacon uses the term in his *Advancement of Learning.*[8] And it might also stand for the number zero, or for one of little worth, a disguise fully in keeping with the ever repentant Amphilanthus.

Early in the *Urania,* Amphilanthus journeys with Pamphilia to Cyprus, where they arrive at Venus's Temple, the Throne of Love. A priest explains that because Venus believes herself "not so much, or much lesse honour'd then in ages past" (48), she has created a "triall of false or faithfull Lovers." Although Pamphilia and Amphilanthus succeed in rescuing the other lovers who are locked within the Throne (as prisoners of Jealousy, Despair, Fear, Hope, and Longing), their adventure demonstrates the tyranny of love over every aspect of their lives. Wroth uses the episode of the Throne of Love as a point of reference in part 1 of the *Urania,* as well as the unpublished Newberry manuscript of part 2, when years later the lovers return to Cyprus to reflect upon the enchantment (2: fol. 58^v). Within her play Wroth creates a close parallel to this key episode in *Urania* by having her major pair of lovers, Philisses and Musella, journey to Venus's Temple as witness of "the truest, and most constant love" (5.111).[9] The introductory dialogue between Venus and Cupid establishes the same motivating force as in the *Urania,* that the Queen of Love believes that her people have grown forgetful of her power and that they must now be brought into submission in order for her to regain her "auncient glory" (1.34). Cupid

8. Two of Elizabeth I's manuscripts, written for her stepmother Katherine Parr, bear the cipher of the letters HENRY KATHERIN, embroidered possibly by the princess herself on the covers: see Margaret H. Swain, "A New Year's Gift from the Princess Elizabeth," *The Connoisseur* 183 (August 1973): 358–67. Another example of a cipher is that of the seventeenth-century poet Constance Fowler, who inscribed the initials of her brother in a device reproduced by Jenijoy La Belle, "A True Love's Knot: The Letters of Constance Fowler and the Poems of Herbert Aston," *Journal of English and Germanic Philology* 79 (1980): 20–21. Bacon, *The Advancement of Learning and New Atlantis,* introduction by Thomas Case (London: Oxford University Press, 1951), 2.6, 160–61. Bacon argues that there are three advantages of ciphers or secret writing: "that they be not laborious to write and read; that they be impossible to decipher; and, in some cases, that they be without suspicion" (160).

9. Margaret McLaren (291) observes a contrast between the external barriers that separate Philisses and Musella and the more internal forces that separate Amphilanthus from Pamphilia: "An Unknown Continent: Lady Mary Wroth's Forgotten Pastoral Drama, 'Loves Victorie,'" *The Renaissance English-woman in Print: Counterbalancing the Canon,* ed. Anne M. Haselkorn and Betty S. Travitsky (Amherst: University of Massachusetts Press, 1990), 276–94.

readily agrees to punish all those who scoff at love, but he does not promise to bring happiness to everyone; he declares categorically, "Some shall love much, yett shall noe love injoye" (1.29).

The motif of Cupid's vengeance is a familiar one to readers of the *Urania*. The characters of the prose fiction frequently blame Cupid for their misery, as does Steriamus when he unwittingly laments to his rival Amphilanthus that Cupid has tyrannized "upon my slaughtered heart" (66). Wroth presents the tale of Celina as a case of Cupid's vengeance: "insolent thou wert to love; scornfully, peevishly reviling him, and now but deservedly thou art pained, and he justly revenged" (643). Further examples include the shepherdess Lemnia (651) and a headstrong nymph, whose words echo the play's title: "now doe I see that Cupid can use his slights and conquering hand on Princes as well as on us . . . and wraps himself in the trophies of his soe mighty victories" (2: fol. 50ᵛ). In one of her key speeches early in the *Urania*, Pamphilia herself argues that the power of Cupid can be known only "by his severall usage of his subjects" (94). Wroth's narrator frequently observes that even kings and queens fall under love's command, as Pamphilia herself is painfully aware. The power of love to subjugate all is a source of fascination to Wroth, for she observes again and again how figures of authority are reduced in status to the level of their own servants, or as Lindamira notes, "in Loves Court all are fellow-subjects" (500).

Within the play Wroth similarly points to the disturbing consequences of having Venus and Cupid as supreme rulers. While the queen seems to hold authority over her son, she readily admits that Cupid "did . . . mee once harme" (1.15), probably an allusion to her affair with Adonis. Wroth subtly reveals the baser side of Venus at the end of act 1, when she leans out of the clouds and like a fishwife bellows to her son, "Fy, this is nothing, what? Is this your care? . . . I wowld have all to waile, and all to weepe" (1.385–87). Although never as broadly comic as her counterpart in Shakespeare's *Venus and Adonis,* Wroth's Queen of Love takes a genuine interest in seeing mortals suffer, and in the dialogue added at the end of act 3 (not found in the Huntington manuscript), Venus specifically insists that Lissius has not endured enough pain (3.355). Wroth thus hints that the process of securing supremacy comes only at a human price. While she found ample precedent for the use of Venus and Cupid as mythological commentators, she goes far beyond her sources in presenting these figures in the process of asserting absolute power.[10] At the end of act 4, Venus's Priests actually sing triumphantly, "Rebels now thy subjects bee" (4.467).

Wroth's veiling of political issues beneath her presentation of these gods has some precedent in seventeenth-century visual arts and masques. During his stay

---

10. For Wroth's possible sources, see Josephine A. Roberts, "The Huntington Manuscript of Lady Mary Wroth's Play, *Loves Victorie,*" *Huntington Library Quarterly* 46 (1983): 169–70.

in England from mid-October 1620 to mid-February 1621, the Flemish painter Anthony van Dyck completed a daring portrait, discovered only recently, of Sir George Villiers, duke of Buckingham, and his wife, Lady Katherine Manners, in the guise of Adonis and Venus.[11] Described by art historians as a *portrait historié,* the work hints at the social supremacy of Buckingham and his wife; it may have been designed strictly for the couple's private chambers, but the portrait would give pause to courtiers familiar with Buckingham's reputation as one of James's favorites. In a daring and provocative scene, Buckingham (covered only in a short drape) embraces his wife, who as Venus is naked from the waist up. Van Dyck's "Adonis and Venus" thus richly reflects the world of courtly disguise that is part of the cultural context of *Love's Victory.*

The disguising found in Wroth's pastoral is similarly enigmatic and puzzling. The central pair of lovers, Philisses and Musella, bear an outward similarity to Sir Philip Sidney and Lady Penelope Rich, as Carolyn Ruth Swift has shown. Indeed, Wroth reveals a fascination with her uncle's supposed love affair in the *Urania,* where Pamphilia listens to the life story of Sildurino, beginning with the downfall and execution of his grandfather (John Dudley, earl of Warwick and duke of Northumberland) and his star-crossed romance with Mirasilva (489–92).[12] Her uncle's purported romance may well have provided Wroth with precedent for her own liaison with William Herbert, and Lady Rich furnished her a powerful example of an independent woman who defied social convention by later bearing Lord Montjoy five children out of wedlock. Through the medium of pastoral, Wroth could present what on the surface appears to be a fictionalized version of her uncle's affair, while at the same time hinting at the parallels between her uncle's romance and her own.

Wroth included in the Newberry manuscript of the *Urania* a number of characters who also appear in *Love's Victory.* In her prose romance she presents a band of eight courtiers disguised as shepherds, led by Belario ("a new Orpheus") and his sister Clorina (2: fol. 3), who may allude to Sir Philip Sidney and his sister, Mary Sidney, countess of Pembroke. Wroth also includes the characters Arcas, Rustic, and Magdaline (Dalina) in both works. Because Wroth composed the Newberry manuscript in the 1620s at the same time as her pastoral play, it is impossible to determine which work came first.

---

11. For a reproduction of Van Dyck's painting of Buckingham and his wife, see *Anthony van Dyck,* ed. Arthur K. Wheelock Jr. et al. (Washington: National Gallery of Art, 1990), 125. For an account of the discovery of the portrait, see Michael Jaffé, "Van Dyck's 'Venus and Adonis,'" *Burlington Magazine* 132 (1990): 696–703. Van Dyck later painted Buckingham's daughter, Lady Mary Villiers, with her cousin Lord Arran dressed as Cupid: see *Anthony van Dyck,* 297.

12. Swift, "Feminine Self-Definition in Lady Mary Wroth's *Love's Victorie* (c.1621)," *English Literary Renaissance* 19 (1989): 171–88. The name Mirasilva (wonderful wood) recalls Sidney's Mira in the *Old Arcadia,* where Philisides describes her as his beloved (*OA* 73, *AS* Song 5, and *Other Poems* 5).

Yet at several points in the play there are dislocations in the multiple disguising of Philisses and Musella. In act 5 the character named "The Mother" constrains her eldest daughter to fulfill the terms of her dead father's will by marrying a wealthy lord. Historical records show, however, that after her father's death, Penelope Devereux lived with the earl and countess of Huntingdon as her guardians, and they were responsible for arranging her marriage with Lord Rich.[13] Penelope had only limited contact with her biological mother, Lettice, who had remarried and no longer had any control over her daughter's future. The character of "The Mother" in *Love's Victory* thus seems more of a reflection of Wroth's own ambivalence concerning the role her mother played in arranging her marriage to Robert Wroth.[14] Within the play Wroth depicts The Mother as strongly influenced by the slander of Arcas, who spreads false rumors concerning Musella's wanton behavior (5.389). This detail, too, is more in keeping with some of the autobiographical material found in the tale of Bellamira (176) in the *Urania*.

In presenting the miraculous triumph of the lovers in act 5, Wroth borrowed heavily from the conventions of pastoral tragicomedy, where the characters triumph over the forces of death.[15] Equally important in helping her shape the conclusion was Shakespeare's *Romeo and Juliet*, which she echoes repeatedly throughout the fifth act. Wroth's reshaping of the tragic ending is significant, for as she imagines an alternative to the enforced marriages to Rich and Wroth, she also defines her power as an author to restructure the lovers' fates. Instead of a fearful, bumbling friar, Wroth supplies the courageous female figure of Silvesta, who risks her own life to offer a potion to the lovers. Although once in love with Philisses herself, she places the happiness of the couple above her own, even though she will be threatened with burning at the stake. While the shepherds run to the Temple for the arranged marriage, Rustic stumbles on the path (5.272), which he superstitiously interprets as a sign of greater mishap—here a variation on Friar Lawrence's warning, "They stumble that run fast" (2.3.94). Indeed, Rustic is too late, for the lovers have already exchanged their vows. Wroth completes the rewriting of Shakespeare's

13. Sylvia Freedman, *Poor Penelope: Lady Penelope Rich, An Elizabethan Woman* (London: Kensal Press, 1983), 45–46. Freedman notes that despite her resistance to the marriage, Penelope does not seem to have blamed her mother and actually named her first child in her honor.

14. The Sidney correspondence reveals that Wroth's mother participated in arranging the marriage. In his letter of July 14, 1604, Robert Sidney wrote to his wife that Robert Wroth would soon be arriving at Penshurst: "How all matters stand between his father and me he will tell you" (*Historical Manuscripts Commission*, De L'Isle, 3:127). The marriage took place at Penshurst on September 27, 1604.

15. See Barbara K. Lewalski, "Mary Wroth's *Loves Victory* and Pastoral Tragicomedy," in *Reading Mary Wroth: Representing Alternatives in Early Modern England*, ed. Naomi J. Miller and Gary Waller (Knoxville: University of Tennessee Press, 1991), 88–108, and *Writing Women in Jacobean England* (Cambridge: Harvard University Press, 1993), 296–307.

tragedy by having The Mother ask pardon of her living daughter and offer her blessing.[16]

Wroth also creates an alternative to the representation of marriage as the goal of a woman's life by showing Silvesta's decision in act 5 to "make a cleane shift to live without a man" (5.187). When the Forester offers to sacrifice himself to save her from death, the audience may expect that Venus will intervene to bring the couple together. In the *Urania,* Wroth includes several female characters who, following disappointment in love, dedicate their lives to serving chaste Diana. For example, Alarina disguises herself as the shepherdess Silviana and chooses to live alone. Not unexpectedly, she soon gives up what she calls her "descipherd life" (223) and returns to her former identity as Alarina (482). While the audience of *Love's Victory* may anticipate the same reversal, Wroth defies pastoral convention by having Silvesta determine her own destiny as a single woman, regardless of the consequence that the Forester will die. Gary Waller rightly calls attention to Silvesta's rejection of "benevolent patriarchal marriage," but even more important is her assertion of the value of the single life.[17] Silvesta's decision to live alone may have held special significance for Wroth, who remained a widow for more than forty years.

Silvesta's choice is all the more interesting because Venus insists nevertheless that she is her "instrument ordain'd" (5.491) and subject to her power. Venus warns that if mortals dare write against love, "you will but frame / Words against your selves" (2.324–25). Yet Wroth uses the power of pastoral to incorporate a critique under the guise of praise. She shows the regal Queen of Love dropping her mask to scream down orders to Cupid and exposes her sadistic delight in prolonging human agony. Even her supremacy is cast in doubt by Silvesta's final allegiance to Diana. In her veiled criticism of Venus, Wroth had the example of her aunt's pastoral dialogue in honor of Astrea, where one of Mary Sidney's shepherds, Thenot, appeared to sing the praises of Queen Elizabeth, while the other shepherd, Piers, questioned whether all panegyric might be lies. Wroth also had the precedent of her own ambivalent treatment of Venus and Cupid in her sonnet sequence, *Pamphilia to Amphilanthus,* with its depiction of the struggle for dominance between mother and child. Venus is variously portrayed as "the Goddess of desire" (P58.5) and "the Queene of lust" (P95.13), who vainly strives to control the cruelty of her son.[18]

---

16. Wroth twice uses a version of the phrase, "wed you to your grave": in *Love's Victory* (5.75; 245) and in *Urania* (249). Juliet uses a similar expression, "my grave is like to be my wedding-bed (1.5.135), and Capulet insists, "I would the fool were married to her grave!" (3.5.140).

17. *The Sidney Family Romance: Mary Wroth, William Herbert, and the Early Modern Construction of Gender* (Detroit: Wayne State University Press, 1993), 241.

18. Mary Sidney's "Dialogue between two shepheards" may have been written in anticipation of Queen Elizabeth's visit to Wilton, as the printed title in Francis Davison's *Poeticall Rhapsody* (1602)

Interestingly, the two matriarchs in Wroth's play—Venus and Musella's unnamed "The Mother"—resemble each other in their harsh and autocratic use of power. Wroth exploits the contradictions between Venus's own past career of transgressive desire and her present determination to arrange the lives of her mortal subjects. Although Musella's mother knows that her daughter despises Rustic and is unwilling to wed solely for financial gain, she insists on the marriage after hearing rumors spread by the male shepherd Arcas that Musella is wantonly pursuing Philisses (5.391–92). The Mother sees her role as that of a guardian of patriarchal values, and by trusting in Arcas rather than Musella, she genuinely becomes her daughter's foe (5.335). But Wroth averts a tragic ending by showing how Silvesta mediates the mother-daughter conflict by defending Musella's right to choose her own husband, even at great personal risk: "I / Will rescue her, or for her sake will dy" (5.176–77). Although Venus remains confident that she is still in complete control of the mortals at the end of the play, Wroth's character Silvesta has symbolically outmaneuvered both mothers in bringing about the union of the lovers, while serving as a vocal critic of their use of power to hold others in subservience.

One of the most startling representations of women in *Love's Victory* is the minor character Dalina, whose name is a shortened version of Magdaline (traditionally a prostitute). Dalina occupies the comic role of the earthy lover often found in pastoral drama, such as Audrey in *As You Like It*. Yet Wroth redefines her role so that she becomes a genuine critic of the traditional rites of courtship. She is boldly outspoken, often disagreeing with the decisions of the male characters. She aggressively assumes the role of leader of the pastoral games and insists on the rights of women to pursue their own desires. In violation of the code of secrecy, she openly describes her past affairs with a shepherd, a farmer, and two "jolly youths" whom she loved at the same time. When they insisted that she choose one or the other in monogamous marriage, she flatly refused.[19] Although mocked by the male characters in *Love's Victory*, Dalina becomes a genuine ally of the other women, especially Musella, and offers advice on how to surmount society's restrictions. "I know the world" (3.267), Dalina confidently proclaims, and she proves this by detecting Arcas's treachery before anyone else begins to suspect his involvement in slandering Musella (5.150). Wroth also shows Dalina's self-determination at the very end

suggests, but there is no record of the Queen's visit, and it is unlikely that the pastoral was presented in person: see Margaret P. Hannay, *Philip's Phoenix: Mary Sidney, Countess of Pembroke* (New York: Oxford University Press, 1990), 165–66. Citations are to Wroth's sequence in *The Poems of Lady Mary Wroth*, ed. Josephine A. Roberts (Baton Rouge: Louisiana State University Press, 1992).

19. Dalina closely resembles the "Lady of the oddest passion," who obstinately refuses to choose between two lovers in the *Urania* (453).

of the play when she freely chooses a husband for herself. Unlike Musella, who refuses to marry for money, Dalina shrewdly makes "a good exchange" (5.551) in selecting Rustic as her partner. There is never any question as to who will be in charge.

Wroth's play thus represents a broad spectrum of women—from goddesses to prostitutes. A distinctive feature of the drama is the community of women who unite in support of the freedom to determine their own destinies. They challenge the authority of the two powerful mothers who try to enforce rigid and inflexible control over others. Silvesta occupies the most extreme position by choosing to remain single, but she aids and counsels Musella in her decision to marry Philisses. Silvesta even shows her how it is possible through clever strategy to circumvent the social impropriety of a woman's active pursuit of a man (3.79). By including the comically promiscuous Dalina in the community of women, Wroth also indicates the extent to which she envisions a range of choices.

The appearance of the cipher on the cover of *Love's Victory* alerts readers of the manuscript to the presence of what Musella calls "the secretts of the mind" (1.305). The multiple disguises found in the pastoral allow Wroth to present several narratives simultaneously, even if the romance associated with the names of "Pamphilia" and "Amphilanthus" would probably be evident only to her inner circle of readers and listeners. Whereas the cipher can be read as inscribing the names of Wroth's fictional lovers from the *Urania* and her sonnet sequence, it may also incorporate the names of the two major protagonists of *Love's Victory:* Philisses and Musella. Just as the cipher superimposes letters on top of letters, the multiple disguises found in *Love's Victory* create the effect of a dense network of interlocking tales through which Wroth explores how women can exercise the power of choice despite the constraints of society.

Wroth's drama clearly shows some of the reasons that the pastoral mode held special appeal to seventeenth-century women writers. As the example of *Love's Victory* suggests, the pastoral offered a landscape in which the political and social relationships of women might be questioned, challenged, and refashioned. As much as Venus asserts her autocratic supremacy over humankind, Wroth subtly undercuts it, suggesting that there are many forms of chaste love, apart from patriarchal marriage. Within the play, Wroth expands the social roles assigned to the other female characters and places them in situations in which they use their power reasonably and compassionately. Finally, the coded language of pastoral enabled Wroth to convey the most intimate representation of her personal life, under the guise of the Sidney-Rich romance, by means of multiple disguising that permits her to hint at and deny the identification. Wroth's use of the veil of pastoral suggests how the mode offered a protective haven for early women writers as they emerged in the politically turbulent seventeenth century. Through the coded language of her pastoral Wroth anticipates what Lois Potter calls the "secret rites and secret writing" of the royalist writers of the Interregnum.[20]

---

20. *Secret Rites and Secret Writing: Royalist Literature, 1641–1660* (Cambridge: Cambridge University Press, 1989), 38–71. See also Annabel Patterson's analysis of the coded language in royalist romances: *Censorship and Interpretation: The Conditions of Writing and Reading in Early Modern England* (Madison: University of Wisconsin Press, 1984), 159–202.

Robert C. Evans

DEFERENCE AND DEFIANCE

The "Memorandum" of Martha Moulsworth

One risk of interpreting the writings of early modern authors involves simplifying both the writers and their works. In fact, simplification is almost inevitable, since we know so little about the writers themselves and since, in many cases, it is so difficult to reconstruct relevant contexts, even when the primary "literary" texts themselves survive. Such problems are particularly acute in the case of women writers, because we often know so little about their general and specific circumstances and because their "literary" works are rarely plentiful or abundant. Few women writers of the English Renaissance produced a large body of work—an oeuvre—of the sort that makes it possible to speak with the same confidence one can muster in dealing with such male authors as Spenser, Jonson, Donne, Milton, or Shakespeare (let alone Greene, Middleton, Nashe, Daniel, Drayton, Wither, or even John Taylor, the astoundingly prodigious "water poet"). The works of such men consume feet of shelves in any decent library, whereas the surviving works of women authors can usually be tucked neatly into slim single volumes.

Yet even when these women writers are read together and in bulk (that is, precisely *as* women), dangers arise. Because we are so interested just now in women's writing, and because our interest is greatly motivated by our own contemporary social and political concerns, we inevitably run additional risks of simplification. We risk, for instance, interpreting these authors so that they speak chiefly to our own preoccupations; we risk using their works to confirm our particular views of social and literary history or to demonstrate the validity of recent theoretical or critical approaches. Moreover, we risk treating their texts primarily as historical or ideological documents and thus failing to appreciate them precisely as works of *art*—as sophisticated demonstrations of linguistic skill, thematic complexity, and structural craft. Of course, male authors run the same risks, but the sheer bulk of their surviving works commonly makes them less easy to pin down or pigeonhole. And, because male authors have usually been treated first as writers and only secondarily (if at all) as men, the artistry of their works is far less likely to be neglected. Even in death, then, male authors often enjoy the luxury of being taken as more fully rounded, more fully complex, more fully human than their female contemporaries, whose writings are so relatively scarce, whose lives are so little known, and whose works are perhaps less likely to be appreciated as complicated works of art.

All these factors make the recently discovered "Memorandum" of Martha Moulsworth a particularly intriguing poem.[1] For one thing, the poem itself tells us a good deal about Moulsworth's life and attitudes; for another, plenty of other biographical evidence about its author survives. Most significant, however, is that Moulsworth's poem resists simple readings of any sort. The poem simultaneously proves accessible to beginning students, provocative to seasoned readers, and intriguing as evidence of both a large historical moment and a single human life. It helpfully defies simplification, either as a document or as a poem. It therefore raises historical and interpretive questions relevant to many writings by numerous other early modern women.

Who was Martha Moulsworth? She was the daughter of Robert Dorsett, a friend and tutor of Sir Philip Sidney. She was the godmother of William Prynne, the famous Puritan who lost his ears for defying king and bishops. In her will, Moulsworth left Prynne five pounds, yet she was also the mother-in-law of a royalist hero who had recently died for his cause. She was the wife, successively, of three successful men, and she was herself a feisty advocate of vigorous preaching who twice defended her position in law courts and twice triumphed there. She read widely and took copious notes, and eventually she became a writer herself.[2] In fact, Moulsworth's recently discovered "Memorandum" is fascinating in several respects—as a complex historical document, as one of the first contributions to a new literary genre, as a manifesto for radical social change, and (I will argue) as a poem worth studying in its own right.

---

1. For the first printing of the poem, plus commentary, see *"My Name Was Martha": A Renaissance Woman's Autobiographical Poem,* ed. Robert C. Evans and Barbara Wiedemann (West Cornwall, Conn.: Locust Hill Press, 1993). For old- and modern-spelling texts and facsimiles, plus many interpretive essays, see *"The Muses Females Are": Martha Moulsworth and Other Women Writers of the English Renaissance* (West Cornwall, Conn.: Locust Hill Press, 1995). All quotations of the poem in the present article are from *"The Muses Females Are."* Finally, for a diverse collection of student responses to the poem, see *"The Birthday of My Self": Martha Moulsworth, Renaissance Poet,* ed. Ann Depas-Orange and Robert C. Evans (Princeton: Critical Matrix: The Princeton Journal of Women, Gender, and Culture, 1996).

2. Biographical essays on Moulsworth—based on surviving wills, a funeral sermon, and numerous other documents—appear in *"The Muses Females Are,"* which also prints full texts of the surviving documents. For a briefer discussion, see Robert C. Evans, "A Silent Woman Speaks: The 'Memorandum of Martha Moulsworth, Widdowe,'" *Yale Library Gazette* 69 (1995): 149–62.

After lying virtually unnoticed and unread for more than 350 years, "Memorandum" has now begun to attract significant critical attention. Writing in 1632, Moulsworth penned an autobiographical poem that, in fifty-five artfully constructed couplets, thoughtfully reviews her own fifty-five years of life and imagines her continued existence in heaven. Moulsworth describes the whole range of her life, moving from birth to anticipated death and sketching her relations with her father, her three husbands, her children, and her God. She expresses many of the opinions and values we might expect from a woman of her class and creed, but she also writes in ways that still have power to startle.

She seems, for instance, to have been one of the first persons in England to call for establishing a women's university, and her confidence in women's potential to rival and even exceed men seems more characteristic of the late twentieth century than of the early seventeenth. Yet her apparently immense capacity for spiritual, emotional, and physical affection contributes to her complex tone, making her seem anything but strident. Complexity, indeed, seems the keynote of her poem and persona: the more we examine both, the more nuanced they both appear. Her poem challenges many of our standard preconceptions about her period and about the roles and traits of its women. All in all, she seems to have been an intriguing woman, writing at an intriguing historical moment, and capable of writing in intriguing ways.

Scholars and critics who have now examined the poem have found it variously engaging. Here I can give only a taste of their views, simply to indicate the poem's interest both as a piece of history and as a piece of writing.[3] Esther Cope, for instance, calls the poem one of the "few available descriptions of early modern widowhood written by a widow," while Frances Teague stresses Moulsworth's significance as a nonaristocratic woman author who also helped develop an alternate view of the link between women and the muses—a view emphasizing "mutuality, . . . models for accomplishment and support for education." John T. Shawcross, however, argues that although Moulsworth's emphasis on feminine accomplishments is "a big step in the right direction," her poem is nonetheless "channeled through a sexually divided marital world, a class-stratified world, and a world in which gendering of activities of the mind prevails." As these reactions suggest, the poem lends itself to diverse readings, partly because its complexity reflects a complex era.

---

3. The essays from which I am about to quote are published in "*The Muses Females Are.*" In the interests of conserving space, I will not note them individually by title. Recent reviews of the first edition have agreed that the poem possesses real artistic merit. Thus, David Norbrook comments that the poem "has a degree of formal interest well beyond the documentary" (*Notes and Queries* 239:4 [December 1994]: 566), while Nancy Gutierrez calls the work "both a fascinating historical text and pleasingly complex work of art" (*Sixteenth Century Journal* 25:4 [1994]: 936).

I wish to maintain, however, that "Memorandum" is also complex artistically. Thus, I find useful Josephine Roberts's argument that the poem combines elements from "three of the dominant modes of autobiographical writing of women of the early seventeenth century"—the dream vision, the mother's legacy, and the classical epitaph. Similarly helpful is Curtis Perry's emphasis on the poem as depersonalized *ritual* (an emphasis with obvious implications for concepts of authorship). Meanwhile, Germaine Greer sees the poem as a self-conscious "literary construct . . . in which radical re-invention strategies are in operation." Differently suggestive is Isobel Grundy's emphasis on the poem's complicated numerology. "Through number," Grundy contends, "as well as through her verbal skills, her Christian faith, her appreciation of her husbands and her solidarity with her sex, Martha Moulsworth redeems her single, separate identity." In fact, Anne Lake Prescott argues that "Memorandum" provides unusually explicit evidence for numerical approaches to Renaissance verse, yet Prescott also makes a convincing case for Moulsworth's general cleverness and ironic wit. "What makes Moulsworth's jests so attractive," she contends, "is the impression they give of an irrepressible humor that itself derives from a sense of distance from the self, from the divided perspective that wordplay at least momentarily requires." Finally, Anthony Low stresses Moulsworth's innovative place in the traditions of English elegy and love poetry as well as the artistry of her rhetoric. He concludes, in fact, that her poem "embodies its innovations in a rhetorical language of admirable power and skill."

Because Moulsworth's artistry is the subject of lengthy discussions elsewhere, there seems little need to repeat those arguments here. Previous commentators have emphasized, for instance, how the whole poem uses techniques of *balance* to harmonize competing tones, thus lending the work a satisfying equilibrium. Practically every detail exemplifies this balance, often quite subtly. Moulsworth expresses a wide variety of emotions, including deference and defiance, weariness and strength, frustration and joy, pride and humility, stubbornness and submission, ambition and contentment, sexual pleasure and deep religious faith. Here, however, I want to look simply at one crucial passage, not only to suggest how "Memorandum" works as a work of art but also to prepare for a later discussion of the complex way the poem intervenes in our contemporary critical debates.

Perhaps the most fascinating passage for modern readers is the one in which Moulsworth ascribes the beginning of her education to the direction of her learned father and then describes her loss of learning and her consignment to the marriage market:

> By him I was brought vpp in godlie pietie
> In modest chearefullnes, & sad sobrietie

> Nor onlie so, Beyond my sex & kind
> he did wth learninge Lattin decke [my] minde
> And whie nott so? the muses ffemalls are
> and therfore of Vs ffemales take some care
> Two Vniuersities we haue of men
> o thatt we had but one of women then
> O then thatt would in witt, and tongs surpasse
> All art of men thatt is, or euer was
> Butt I of Lattin haue no cause to boast
> ffor want of vse, I longe agoe itt lost
> > > Lattin is nott the most
> > > marketable mariadge
> > > mettall
> Had I no other portion to my dowre
> I might haue stood a virgin to this houre
> But though the virgin Muses I loue well
> I haue longe since Bid virgin life ffarewell.
> > > > (ll. 27–42)

This, apparently, is one of the earliest moments (if not *the* earliest) at which an English woman calls for a woman's university. Simply as a piece of history, then, this passage would seem significant. Yet this passage, like the entire work, also seems poetically complex. One might mention, for instance, how at the beginning Moulsworth makes religious values precede more narrowly personal ones; or her poise in pairing both adjectives and nouns and adjective-noun phrases; or her effective use of abrupt shifts and ironic juxtapositions; or how she uses humor to defuse anger; or how her bitterness gives her humor a poignant edge; or how she balances reason and emotion, anger and anguish, modesty and self-assertion, an imagined future with an actual present; or the way she simultaneously expresses wit, resentment, satisfaction, frustration, pleasure, and pain. All these aspects of the passage have been discussed elsewhere, yet much more remains to be said.

In the first line, for example, Moulsworth syntactically emphasizes the priority of her father while also linking him, her, and God, expressing piety to both her human and divine parents while also metrically stressing the key word *vpp* (l. 27). That word suggests elevation of every sort, as Moulsworth soberly, modestly, and apparently cheerfully gives her two fathers the credit for any virtues she displays—a tactic that complicates her later shift to apparent anger and self-assertion. Similarly, lines 27–28 play nicely with short *o* sounds to emphasize a sudden shift to long *o*'s in "onlie so." Just when we might be tempted to see Moulsworth as merely pious, modest, and sober, she abruptly desires more; yet just when she might seem to be rejecting her early training, she asserts that it was her father who nurtured her educational ambition.[4] In this poem, males are not merely oppressive, and in fact here as elsewhere "Memorandum" is too complex to be reduced to simple either/or polarities. Even in challenging "patriarchal" restrictions, Moulsworth honors her particular patriarch.

Typical of the poem's skill is Moulsworth's choice of individual words. The verb *decke,* for instance, might at first seem inexact—until we remember that it connotes attiring or adorning in rich array. It thereby implies the stereotypical female concern with superficial beauty, but what is being decked here is the "mind." Finally, the choice of this word also exemplifies Moulsworth's tendency to play with sounds, since "decke" picks up from "sex" in line 29, just as "learninge Lattin" typifies her general interest in (but not obsession with) alliteration. Yet these techniques of continuity help underline the equally prevalent twists of tone and subject that lend the poem energy, as in the brief, simple, emphatic outburst "And whie nott so?"—whose force is reinforced by its plain Anglo-Saxon monosyllables.

Other examples of the poem's linguistic complexity could be cited. Thus, the fact that the muses are called "ffemales" concedes that they are not real, living *women.* This implicit concession gives some poignancy to line 32, but that line can also be read as a veiled warning. The mythical muses, after all, cannot really "take . . . care" of women, but men might still be wise to "take care" (to be on guard) nonetheless. In a highly personal poem, Moulsworth speaks for a larger group (for "Vs"), yet even as she speaks on behalf of women, she also seems to address the larger English nation ("we"). This "we," however, does not fully include women; its two universities are universities "of" men—not only filled with men but also designed specifically for them. Moulsworth metrically emphasizes the specific word for each sex, just as she also skillfully uses meter to stress such crucial words as *I* and *virgin.* That last word, moreover, shifts its meaning slightly at each appearance, referring first to social role, then to fantasy and myth, and finally to a frankly sexual significance. We have come a long way from the passage's opening stress on piety, modesty, and sobriety, for in line 42 Moulsworth is preparing us for the next major section of her work, which will imply the physical pleasures of wedded love.

The complexity of Moulsworth's "Memorandum," however, goes beyond the examples just mentioned; it includes, as well, the complicated ways the poem engages the historical contexts in which it is inevitably enmeshed. Moreover, the poem also bears a complicated relation to modern scholarly debates *about*

---

4. To make matters even more complex, biographical evidence suggests that Moulsworth's father was dead by the time she was three years old. The claims that she was "brought vpp" by him (l. 27) and that he taught her Latin therefore seem exaggerated. Any number of reasons for such exaggeration can be imagined; many of these are discussed by Anne C. Little in *"The Muses Females Are."* In any case, Moulsworth's (deliberate? inadvertent?) inaccuracy makes her poem even more intriguing.

those contexts. In fact, often "Memorandum" seems to provide support for conflicting or even contradictory assertions by recent historians and literary theorists, and so the poem continually reminds us how difficult it is to make broad or simple generalizations about any person or text, especially ones from the distant past. Moulsworth's "Memorandum" will inevitably frustrate anyone intent on depicting that past in too simplistic or doctrinaire a fashion.

One of the best and most convenient overviews of the status of early modern women, as well as one of the best guides and contributions to recent scholarly debate about that topic, is *The Patriarch's Wife*, by Margaret J. M. Ezell. This book not only surveys much relevant data but also offers a distinctive approach by challenging the common assumption that the early modern family was narrowly or tyrannically "patriarchal."[5] In a fine summary passage, Ezell concludes that "So many gaps existed between the rigid theory and the actual enforcement that its degrading and restrictive nature was not immediately felt. . . . The patriarch's wife, both in the family and in society, wielded considerable power, whether acknowledged in theory or not, but that power was to a large extent displayed on a private level, not through the public institutions" (*PW,* 163).

Moulsworth's "Memorandum" certainly offers ample support for such assertions; her voice seems neither weak nor overwhelmed, and her poem can be seen as part of the very process of challenging and undermining patriarchal authority posited by Ezell. Moulsworth's poem often seems to buttress Ezell's argument that early modern women were less oppressed, both in their imaginations and in their daily lives, than we have sometimes assumed.[6]

Yet the poem also offers support for historians and critics who emphasize the oppression that Renaissance women did indeed suffer (in every sense of that word). Thus, although Moulsworth's willingness to articulate her frustration shows that she was not completely oppressed, the frustration itself suggests that for her, at least, the "degrading and restrictive nature" of patriarchal authority was in fact "immediately felt" (*PW,* 163). It seems to have been an aspect of life that this thoughtful, sensitive woman could not and did not ignore.[7] Here as so often elsewhere, her poem resists being pinned down or pigeonholed: when carefully interrogated, it almost always reveals more than we may be

---

5. Quotations, hereafter cited parenthetically, are from Margaret J. M. Ezell, *The Patriarch's Wife: Literary Evidence and the History of the Family* (Chapel Hill: University of North Carolina Press, 1987). To conserve space, and to distinguish this book from a more recent one by Ezell cited below, I will use the abbreviation "*PW*."

6. As an example of a critic with whom she disagrees, Ezell herself cites Peter Malekin, *Liberty and Love: English Literature and Society 1640–88* (London: Hutchinson, 1981), 140. Ezell considers the key source for this view to be Lawrence Stone's *The Family, Sex and Marriage in England, 1500–1800* (London: Weidenfeld and Nicolson, 1977); see *PW,* 4.

7. For a recent and valuable survey of the topics discussed in this paragraph, see Margaret L. King, *Women of the Renaissance* (Chicago: University of Chicago Press, 1991), 157–239.

seeking. Thus, if we look in this poem for evidence of oppression, we will find it, but we will find much else besides. And if we seek evidence here of feminine self-respect, we will find that too—but not only that.

Moulsworth provides plenty of support for Ezell's contention that early modern women were more independent in thought and deed than some recent feminists have sometimes contended. Yet Moulsworth also provides evidence to support the stereotypical view of a defining, even confining, patriarchy. However, because Moulsworth *does* provide evidence for both views, she provides evidence for neither view in any simple, unequivocal fashion. Her poem is the kind of work that both confirms and challenges the assumptions with which we approach it, and in this respect it seems highly relevant to our reading of other texts by other early modern women.

Typical of the poem's complexity, for instance, is its bearing on the whole issue of the likely results of greater education for women. Ezell, for example, argues that the standard modern view, which stresses patriarchy's oppressiveness, "assumes that education leads to the overthrow or subversion of authority which ignorance unwittingly tends to sustain" (*PW,* 6). "Based on this logic," Ezell later continues, "one explanation offered for the relative quiescence of seventeenth-century women in the face of the supposed increase in patriarchal authority over their lives is the decline in support for education of girls . . ." (*PW,* 10). Ezell contends, in contrast, that women in the early seventeenth century could boast more educational opportunities and achievements than we often suppose (*PW,* 12, 16), and because many educationalists during this period "strongly questioned the role of the classics in male education, urging the inclusion of vernacular and modern languages in the curriculum," Ezell suggests that "one cannot even point to the prominence of modern romance languages in female education of this period as a definite sign of discrimination" (*PW,* 16).[8]

Moulsworth's "Memorandum" bears on this debate in complex and intriguing ways. On the one hand, it reveals an intelligent, well read, and articulate woman who nonetheless clearly felt cheated (by the accident of her sex) of access to even greater education. She openly chafes against the prejudice that denies women the right to learn Latin in a formal scholastic setting (ll. 29–32), and she considers access to classical languages crucial to full development. Thus, she seems to indict sexism as vigorously as any feminist, yet she also depicts

8. As proponents of the views with which she disagrees, Ezell mentions, for instance, the following (*PW,* 10, 228): Antonia Fraser, *The Weaker Vessel: Women's Lot in Seventeenth-century England* (London: Weidenfeld and Nicolson, 1984); Felicity Nussbaum, *The Brink of All We Hate: English Satire on Women, 1660–1750* (Lexington: University Press of Kentucky, 1984); J. R. Brink, *Female Scholars: A Tradition of Learned Women before 1800* (Montreal: Eden Press, 1980); and Jan de Bruyn, "The Ideal Lady and the Rise of Feminism in Seventeenth-Century England," *Mosaic* 17 (winter 1984): 19–28.

a male (her father) as the one figure actively interested in making her truly educated. Furthermore, although she uses the education she *has* attained to challenge "patriarchal" stereotypes and although she even proposes a practical and frankly radical social innovation to combat oppression, she also honors many males (especially God), and her religious and social vision seems largely traditional and conservative. "Memorandum" thus again seems to buttress arguments that stress oppression, even while also supporting the view that women were less oppressed than we sometimes assume.

Similarly complex is the relation between this poem and the stereotype of the so-called Good Wife. Ezell argues that the "popularity of the character of the Good Wife . . . suggests that women did not move [male] seventeenth-century essayists and poets only to misogynistic venom" (*PW*, 37).[9] Indeed, men frequently celebrated the Good Wife, emphasizing the significance of her "labor in the family," extolling her labor's dignity, praising her capacity to "govern her household," and lauding her as a loving companion and as "the partner and the reflection of her husband" (*PW*, 38, 39, 40). She was supposed to exhibit devotion to him and his interests, but she was not supposed to be "feeble, incapable, or servile" (*PW*, 41). Ezell convincingly maintains that this much-celebrated ideal shows that patriarchy was never as monolithic, oppressive, or unquestioned as is sometimes assumed.

Part of the special interest of Moulsworth's "Memorandum" is that it offers us an "inside view" of the Good Wife stereotype—a view as seen by a good wife herself. Whereas most writings praising good wives came from men, Moulsworth seems to have both fit and accepted the stereotype. She seems, for instance, to embrace the ideal of marriage as a partnership of loving companions, and she also seems to have valued the autonomy and respect she enjoyed with her third husband:

> wth him I led an easie darlings life.
> I had my will in house, in purse[,] in Store
> whatt would a women old or yong haue more?
>   (ll. 66–68)

In short, Moulsworth offers valuable evidence, from a woman herself, of the genuine appeal of the Good Wife role. Typically, however, things are not quite so simple, for "Memorandum" also suggests the frustrations of being limited

---

9. As examples of the critics with whom she disagrees Ezell cites, for instance, the following (*PW*, 36–37, 230): Suzanne W. Hull, *Chaste, Silent, and Obedient: English Books for Women 1475–1640* (San Marino, Calif.: Huntington Library, 1982), and Hilda Smith, "Feminism and the Methodology of Women's History," in Berenice A. Carroll, ed., *Liberating Women's History* (Urbana: University of Illinois Press, 1976), 368–84, especially 377.

merely to that role. These frustrations seem especially striking since they are expressed by a woman who seems to have been generally (and genuinely) content with her marriages and her existence. The fact that even such a good wife as Moulsworth was not entirely satisfied suggests again the complexities of both her cultural situation and her poem.

Moulsworth's "Memorandum" is culturally intriguing in other ways as well. It offers, for instance, an implicit defense of women written *by* a woman—a significant fact, since most defenses were actually written by men (*PW*, 49). In addition, it helps define the ideal of a Good Husband, again from a specifically feminine point of view. Moulsworth's husbands (especially the third) clearly seem as stereotypical as any Good Wife: husband number three was neither (to use Ezell's words) "a playboy spendthrift" nor "an impotent miser" (*PW*, 102). He was neither selfish nor immoderate, and he seems to have regarded marriage as a fellowship and to have been "both a friend and a lover" (*PW*, 103, 104, 105). Indeed, more than many women of her time, Moulsworth seems to stress the physical as well as the spiritual pleasures of marriage (*PW*, 105), as she does in lines 42, 45, 47, and 58. Yet there are also touches of that "wry sophistication and detachment" that Ezell sees as typifying women's attacks on marriage (*PW*, 108). Here as elsewhere, then, Moulsworth is never simple. She seems to share, for instance, the widespread Renaissance assumption "that marriage is the natural condition of adult life" (*PW*, 128), but she seems also capable of imagining how life might differ if a women's university existed.

However, the interest of Moulsworth's "Memorandum" is enhanced all the more when we look at it from the perspective of another recent and highly helpful book by Ezell, *Writing Women's Literary History*. This theoretical and wideranging study provides even further means of appreciating the significance of Moulsworth's poem.[10] Here Ezell once again challenges modern preconceptions, and once again Moulsworth's poem, intriguingly, seems simultaneously to support both Ezell and the scholars she criticizes. Ezell argues, for instance, that modern feminists tend to emphasize anger as a defining trait of much feminine writing. Early women writers who fail to fit this pattern tend to be treated as uninteresting anomalies because they fail to match preconceptions derived from "a nineteenth century male image of authorship" (*WW*, 26).[11]

10. See Margaret J. M. Ezell, *Writing Women's Literary History* (Baltimore: Johns Hopkins University Press, 1993). To save space and to distinguish this book from *The Patriarch's Wife* (earlier abbreviated *PW*), I will hereafter abbreviate the later title as "*WW*" when citing the book parenthetically.

11. As examples of critics from whom she dissents, Ezell cites, for instance, the following (*WW*, 25–26, 169): Ellen Moers, *Literary Women: The Great Writers* (Garden City, N.Y.: Doubleday, 1976); Sandra M. Gilbert and Susan Gubar, *The Madwoman in the Attic: The Woman Writer and the Nineteenth Century Literary Imagination* (New Haven: Yale University Press, 1979); Sandra M. Gilbert, "Patriarchal Poetics and the Woman Reader: Reflections on Milton's Bogey," *PMLA* 93 (1978): 368–82; Catherine R.

Clearly Moulsworth's poem, with its emphasis on contentment and love, fails to fit this pattern neatly. Yet, just as clearly, Moulsworth does express feminine anger, bitterness, and irony—although those traits are themselves balanced by joy and self-respect. Once more her poem equivocates, not because of ineptness but precisely because of its artistic and ideological complexity. Here as elsewhere, then, it is meaningfully ambiguous and significantly ambivalent. It speaks to modern concerns yet seems rooted in its own Renaissance world, and perhaps it suggests that both, ultimately, have much in common.

The significance of Moulsworth's poem is highlighted in other ways, too, when approached from Ezell's more recent vantage point. Ezell notes, for instance, that much modern feminist scholarship tends to "privilege the novel as a true female genre" (*WW*, 32).[12] Moulsworth assumes added importance, then, not simply as an early woman poet but as a woman poet who insisted on speaking obviously *as* a woman and as one who wrote not merely for private meditation but as one who seemed to anticipate a readership. In fact, her insistent emphasis on personal identity illustrates Ezell's recent claim that while "the use of pseudonyms and anonymous publication undoubtedly was a strategy to disguise gender in the later eighteenth and the nineteenth century, it was not necessarily so in the preprofessional literary periods of the Renaissance and seventeenth century" (*WW*, 36).

Yet Moulsworth's "Memorandum" interestingly (and typically) transgresses another generalization made by Ezell, namely that "Manuscript circulation is social and noncompetitive in nature; works circulate in manuscript inviting additions and corrections, with no need for the author to establish ownership or copyright" (*WW*, 38). As a piece of explicitly autobiographical verse, however, Moulsworth's poem strongly resists "additions and corrections" from any outside source, and its author insists on her own authority. This is a poem not easily tampered with; like some of Ben Jonson's poems, it explicitly names its own author. Indeed, Moulsworth's clear assertion of literary ownership seems especially important coming from an early modern *woman*.

All in all, then, "Memorandum" seems exceedingly complex—both as a work of art and as a piece of cultural evidence. It supports assertions made both by Ezell and by the writers Ezell challenges, and thus it provides fascinating

Stimpson, "Ad/d Feminam: Women, Literature, and Society," in *Literature and Society,* ed. Edward Said (Baltimore: Johns Hopkins University Press, 1980), 174–92, especially 175; and Gilbert and Gubar, eds., *The Norton Anthology of Literature by Women: The Tradition in English* (New York: W. W. Norton, 1985), especially 14.

12. As examples of proponents of this view, Ezell mentions (for instance) the following (*WW*, 32, 170): Rosalind Miles, *The Female Form: Women Writers and the Conquest of the Novel* (New York: Routledge and Kegan Paul, 1987), and Dale Spender, *Mothers of the Novel: 100 Good Writers before Jane Austen* (London: Pandora, 1986).

evidence for our attempts to come to grips with numerous currently debated issues. Moulsworth seems to have been both feminist and conservative, both angry and content, both defiant and deferential, both a woman of her time and a woman of our own. Perhaps she and her poem, then, perfectly exemplify the very complexity implied in the phrase "early modern," since in "Memorandum" and in its author, we can glimpse the future (which is our present) without ever losing sight of a richly distinguished, and distinguishable, past. Her poem survives as both a complex work of art and a complex historical document, and thus it helpfully resists the simplification to which all interpretation is liable. In both respects it speaks, finally, with a still-living voice.

Paul A. Parrish

Richard Crashaw, Mary Collet, and the "Arminian Nunnery" of Little Gidding

There are three conditions which often look alike
Yet differ completely, flourish in the same hedgerow:
Attachment to self and to things and to persons, detachment
From self and from things and from persons; and, growing between
    them, indifference
Which resembles the others as death resembles life,
Being between two lives—unflowering, between
The live and the dead nettle. This is the use of memory:
For liberation—not less of love but expanding
Of love beyond desire, and so liberation
From the future as well as the past.

—T. S. Eliot, "Little Gidding,"
from *Four Quartets*

I was permitted to salute the Mother and Daughters, as we use to salute other women: and after we were all sitten Circular, I had leave to speak ingenuously of what I had heard and did or might conceive of their *House.* I first told him what I had heard of the *Nunns* at *Gidding;* of *two watching and praying all night;* of their *Canonicall houres;* of their *Crosses* on the outside and inside of the *Chappell;* of an *Altar* richly decked with *Tapestry, Plate* and *Tapers;* of their *Adorations, genuflections,* and *geniculations,* which I told them plainly might strongly savour of Superstition and Popery.
    —from *The Arminian Nunnery: Or, A Briefe Description and Relation of the late erected Monasticall Place, called the Arminian Nunnery at little Gidding in Huntington-Shire*

"Crashaw's life," Leah Marcus has observed, "was clearly an attempt to escape from the world," and the majority of his religious verse is "completely cut from history, from all passage of time, from human society, from learning—dead to the world, in short." In a further observation that rather remarkably mirrors Eliot's comments on the condition of detachment, she notes that, "unlike most religious lyrics of seventeenth-century England, Crashaw's are also dead to himself."[1]

Consider these notions of detachment in the context of Crashaw's various treatments of women. On the one hand, the influence of the feminine on the life and writings of Richard Crashaw is beyond dispute. One thinks most obviously of the numerous women who populate the best known of his poetical works: Queen Henrietta Maria, his "supposed" mistress, the Countess of Denbigh, "Mrs. M. R.," the Virgin Mary, Mary Magdalene, and, most notably, Saint Teresa. In these and other instances the capacity of a feminine figure to excite Crashaw's imagination is evident. Almost always, however, the figure is distant from the poet or reader, a distance—or detachment—realized through a process of idealization or elevation above the passion and immediacy of living.

What is further suggestive about Crashaw's women is that they emerge from a life that is itself largely devoid of deep or prolonged associations with women. The absent lover or mother—indeed, the absent feminine—more aptly characterizes Crashaw's experiences than does the immediate presence of powerful feminine models. Losing not one but two mothers before he reached the age of eight, Crashaw lived with a stern father, attended the Charterhouse (boys') school in 1629, and entered the male environs of Cambridge in 1631. During his life at Charterhouse and Cambridge and after his exile from the university, we have evidence from the poetry (and elsewhere) of Crashaw's allegiances to men who influenced his life and thinking, but we know little of women in his life, save those whom he counseled in his poetry (such as "Mrs. M. R." and the Countess of Denbigh) and those we have already identified as the idealized subjects of his verse. The example of Crashaw, one might say, gives powerful testimony to the vitality of the feminine, but little evidence of real women. Feminine heroics arise out of, or lead to, the absent mother and the idealized saint.

I

The most significant challenge to this summary judgment about Crashaw and the women represented in his poetry is posed by the remarkable community established by Nicholas Ferrar and the Ferrar family at Little Gidding. Although isolated from the world at large, Little Gidding was widely known throughout England and was frequently visited by outsiders, including Crashaw. He participated even in some of the most intimate of ceremonies at Little Gidding— the night watches conducted by Nicholas himself—and there is substantial

---

1. *Childhood and Cultural Despair* (Pittsburgh: University of Pittsburgh Press, 1978), 140.

evidence that the devotional life that was the definitive quality of Little Gidding appealed to Crashaw enormously. The continuing associations between Crashaw and the Ferrar/Collet family—as seen, for example, in Crashaw's tutelage of Ferrar Collet at Cambridge and Crashaw's impassioned references to Mary Collet in his 1644 letter from exile at Leyden—confirm the impact of the Little Gidding community and spirit on Crashaw's life.[2] Among its other engaging features, Little Gidding was a community of men and women, boys and girls, in which women played decisive and transforming roles. To say it differently, women were prominent figures at Little Gidding and, further, were *represented*—or *represented* themselves—to each other and to a larger world through defined roles and attributes.

This is not to suggest that Little Gidding was a seventeenth-century feminist community. The religious boundaries of Little Gidding were strictly and approvingly observed, and there is ample evidence that the most significant spiritual and family leader was Nicholas Ferrar. Although he was not the elder son, all of the family recognized his role in establishing Little Gidding and continued to look to him for guidance. That said, it must also be noted that women and girls far outnumbered men and boys at Little Gidding and gave the affairs of the community a distinctly feminine cast. In this residence set apart from the patriarchy of government, society, and the church, women conducted much of the daily business of Little Gidding and directed the affairs of the community as equal, if not dominant, partners. Nicholas Ferrar wrote to his niece Mary as a brother to the "sister of my soule,"[3] and if we would argue that the preeminent position of Nicholas Ferrar casts Little Gidding itself into a patriarchal mold, the presence and authority of Mary Ferrar and Mary Collet suggest a measurable matriarchal counterweight. Much has been made of the accusation of detractors that the community of Little Gidding was Roman in ritual and ceremony, that it was, as the 1641 pamphlet puts it, an "Arminian nunnery." Such an accusation, whether just or not, also tells us that both the religious practices (Arminianism) and the prominence of women (a "nunnery") were, to some, cause for alarm.[4]

2. The first to emphasize the important relationship between Crashaw and Mary Collet was E. Cruwys Sharland, "Richard Crashaw and Mary Collet," *Church Quarterly Review* 73:146 (1912): 358–85.

3. From his letter of July 25, 1632, in which he urges her to continue to be diligent in her determination to remain a virgin. In B. Blackstone, ed., *The Ferrar Papers* (Cambridge: Cambridge University Press, 1938), 274.

4. A. L. Maycock offers substantial evidence that Little Gidding was decidedly not "Arminian" or "papist" in its practices or tendencies. See *Nicholas Ferrar of Little Gidding* (London: Society for Promoting Christian Knowledge, 1938), 133–35, 236–42. It remains the case, however, that, as Maycock also notes, Little Gidding was perceived by some radical Puritans as "no more than a nest of Papists, professing a hypocritical allegiance to the Established Church and secretly practising the degraded superstitions of Romanism" (239). Or, as the author of *The Arminian Nunnery* puts it, "*Arminianisme*

II

Before proceeding further, it is useful to remember that insistence on patriarchal authority was deeply ingrained in the society of the time and thought to be central to civil and family governance. In his monumental study *The Family, Sex and Marriage in England, 1500–1800,* Lawrence Stone discusses at length various developments in the late sixteenth and early seventeenth centuries that contributed to a "positive reinforcement of the despotic authority of husband and father—that is to say, of patriarchy." Changes in state governance, the church, law, and education merged to reinforce the primacy of male authority, the exercise of which, as Stone points out, was determined less by brute force or legal precedent than by "recognition by all concerned of its legitimacy, hallowed by ancient tradition, moral theology and political theory." This increase in the power of the father and husband can be attributed in part to specific transformations in the state, the household, the church, and the schools, but Stone also argues for a deeper cause: "The authoritarian family and the authoritarian nation state were the solutions to an intolerable sense of anxiety, and a deep yearning for order." He concludes, "Family patriarchy was no more than one aspect of a much wider and deeper phenomenon": the belief that only "the most drastic of measures" would be sufficient "to hold together the shaky framework of ordered society."[5]

Other examples of drastic measures advocated in response to instability and disorder can be seen in the various utopian schemes proposed in the sixteenth and seventeenth centuries. As a real-life community in the midst of but set apart from the larger society, Little Gidding partook of both the historical realities that Stone describes and the imaginative alternatives set forth by writers such as Sir Thomas More and Gerrard Winstanley. Situating Little Gidding in these contexts clarifies for us just how unusual Little Gidding was, especially in the willingness of the community to establish governing patterns that diverge from the assumed authority of the patriarchal elder.

Commenting on utopian schemes from More's *Utopia* through the end of the seventeenth century, J. C. Davis notes their frequent association with a monastic model:

---

is a bridge to *Popery* . . . but some have past over it," among them, he asserts, "this Familie in this Booke" (10).

5. Stone, *Family, Sex and Marriage* (London: Weidenfeld and Nicolson, 1977), 151, 217. The whole of Stone's analysis of "The Reinforcement of Patriarchy" makes up chapter 5 (151–218). He also points out different "attacks on patriarchy," but these, significantly, are not evident until the late seventeenth and early eighteenth centuries. Stone's massive study has received much praise as well as its share of criticism. Ralph A. Houlbrooke aptly summarizes the objections in his *The English Family, 1450–1700* (London and New York: Longman, 1984), 13–15; Houlbrooke also observes, however, that it "will be a long time before another work on the history of the family is attempted which matches Stone's in its scope and scale" (15).

> The utopian mode is distinguished by its pursuit of legal, institutional, bureaucratic and educational means of producing a harmonious society. . . . [Such means] must discipline man and nature to conform to them. . . . Essential to the exercise, therefore, was the setting up of such an apparatus of social control as would not be corrupted by the deficiencies inherent in men and nature. It is not surprising in this context to find so many of the early modern utopians drawn to the monastic model, for the monastery in its discipline, structures, rituals and rule of life had sought to subdue sinful nature in servitude to a perfect or holy commonwealth.[6]

Little Gidding may be similarly described. Although he wrote it in derision, the author of *The Arminian Nunnery* is not inaccurate in describing Little Gidding as the "late erected Monasticall Place," for in its isolation from the business of the world, its strict observance of routine and ritual, and its attentiveness to simpler virtues and values, Little Gidding exemplified the monastic model.

The monastic model, like the larger society from which it chooses to isolate itself, also promotes strict patriarchal authority, for such absolutism is thought to be grounded in biblical precedent and essential to the well-being of the ideal community. Writers from More to Winstanley and beyond, though remarking on this necessity with some differences of detail, never doubt that the authority of the father is the cornerstone of governance. In *Utopia* (published in 1516), More says, "wives wait on their husbands, children on their parents, and generally the younger on their elders"; in Winstanley's view (written in 1652), "a Father is a Commonwealths Officer, because the Necessity of the young children choose him by joynt consent, and not otherwise"; and in Samuel Gott's *Nova Solyma* (New Jerusalem, published in 1648), "patriarchal authority was the highest of all authorities and a major prop of social discipline." It is more than symbolic that the "Chief of the Senate" in Gott's government was also referred to as "the Father."[7]

In sum, in both the world of their experiences and the world of their imagination, a citizen of the sixteenth and seventeenth centuries in England viewed the authority of the patriarchal elder as right, proper, and inevitable. Such an observer might well have seen Little Gidding as troubling, if not dangerously revolutionary.

Those familiar with Little Gidding and the decisive role of Nicholas Ferrar often take his prominence for granted, but even his position involves some

---

6. *Utopia and the Ideal Society: A Study of English Utopian Writing, 1516–1700* (Cambridge: Cambridge University Press, 1981), 371.

7. More and Winstanley are cited and discussed in Timothy Kenyon, *Utopian Communism and Political Thought in Early Modern England* (London: Pinter Publishers, 1989), 88, 211; Gott's utopian scheme is outlined in Davis, *Utopia and the Ideal Society,* 162–63. Although the connection to Gott's titles is coincidental, it is nonetheless interesting that at Little Gidding the "Chief" of the Little Academy (Mary Collet), when elevated to a more authoritative position, becomes the "Mother."

challenge to convention. Under ordinary circumstances, Nicholas would have deferred to his older siblings, especially his brother John, and while most evidence suggests that residents of Little Gidding happily looked to Nicholas for guidance, perhaps not everyone did. At least one writer has speculated that the rebellious spirit of John's wife, Bathsheba, may be due in part to her expectation that John (and she as his wife) would have a more prominent place at Little Gidding, whereas in fact the authority rested with the younger brother, his elderly mother, and his young niece, Mary Collet.[8] Even if we assume that Bathsheba was alone in her discontent, this only means that we have the whole of the Ferrar-Collet family engaged in a kind of happy and willful conspiracy to endow with authority those whom they think deserving—regardless of age or gender. While various utopian schemes allow for the talented and mature youth to rise to a position of prominence above his years, virtually none admit of such a possibility for women. To do so would subvert what was thought to be the crucial and irrevocable relationship between the male and the female.[9] In fact, and in spite of its association with the otherwise patriarchal monastic model, Little Gidding openly and forcefully provided just such a subversion of roles and authority.

III

The actual number of inhabitants of Little Gidding was various, including some members of the family who moved in and out and other residents from the area, especially children, who would stay at Little Gidding only for a time. It is relatively easy, nonetheless, to identify the nucleus of the family who made Little Gidding their permanent residence beginning in 1626. In addition to the matriarch, Mary Ferrar, who was in her mid-seventies when Little Gidding was purchased, the family that Isaak Walton identified as "like a little college and about thirty in number" included Nicholas and his two older siblings, John and Susanna, and their extensive families.[10] John Ferrar and his second wife, Bathsheba, had four children (two sons and two daughters), three of whom survived infancy. Susanna and her husband, John Collet, had fourteen children, twelve of whom—eight daughters and four sons—survived infancy. The three oldest Collet sons had already embarked on careers in London at the time of the purchase of Little Gidding, and thus the younger Collets who joined their parents at the manor retreat included eight daughters and one son.

8. Margaret Cropper, *Flame Touches Flame* (London: Longmans, Green and Co., 1949), 42.

9. The studies of Davis, *Utopia and the Ideal Society,* and Kenyon, *Utopian Communism,* are replete with evidence of this essential patriarchalism. See especially Davis, *Utopia and the Ideal Society,* 50–53, 71–72, 101–2, 112–14, 162–63, 196–97, 290, and 296–97.

10. Walton is cited in Maycock, *Nicholas Ferrar of Little Gidding,* 158, whose observations on the family are reflected below.

The prominence of women does not, of course, ensure their preeminence. A review of some of the tasks assumed by the women of Little Gidding is unremarkable. They were given responsibility of "Household government," with each of the older daughters of John and Susanna rotating primary responsibility. They had charge of the household accounts and kept track of food ordered and received and food and other goods accepted as rental payments from tenants. To be sure that their own household skills did not become rusty, they also baked and sewed.

A little more out of the ordinary, but still firmly within the conventional emphasis on the household and on nurturing responsibilities assumed to be the particular duty and talent of women, the women of Little Gidding, with Mary Collet in the lead, gave themselves to "Surgery, the making & furnishing of Oyles, Salves, distilling of Waters &c and of furnishing a great Surgeons Chest they had, & a Roome for it wherein were cured all Such Persons as daily came for one thing or other to be helped of Some things that ayled them, in poynt of Salves, plasters, seare-cloaths &c." Among other "charitable Deeds," the elder Mrs. Ferrar and her female entourage saw to the building of an "Alms-house or Lodging-room for 4 poor Widows, in one part of the House, where they were competently provided for, & were looked upon as part of the Family, going daily to Church &c."[11]

While the women of Little Gidding had some say in the roles they assumed as household organizers and nurturers, it was apparently Nicholas who provided primary guidance. If we understand no more than this, we might wonder about the severity of the negative reaction to this "Arminian Nunnery," for it could hardly seem less threatening. In another and more influential activity, however, the central role of women in the affairs of Little Gidding is even more pronounced, and, significantly, it encompasses the intellectual and spiritual life of the community.

The initial years at Little Gidding, 1626–1630, required considerable attention to the facilities themselves. The manor house was found in considerable disrepair, and the church had been used as a hay barn. By 1630, with the buildings rehabilitated, there was opportunity to establish a more structured approach to intellectual and spiritual deliberations. The creation of organized "conversations" among the residents into a gathering that became known as the Little Academy was, in the main, an extension of existing mealtime discussions. Writing of these occasions in his biography of his brother, John Ferrar noted that because both silence and "common discourse" were judged unfit companions to eating, it was agreed "that there shall be always something read during mealtimes." The readings were performed by young girls or boys, and care was

---

11. From *A Life of Nicholas Ferrar*, in Blackstone, *The Ferrar Papers*, 30–32.

taken to see that both mothers and daughters were involved. Through these conversations, John observed, the apparent detachment of Little Gidding *from* the world was balanced by their knowledge *of* the world: "though they seemed to live privately and had not much commerce with people, yet they were well acquainted with the former and latter passages of the world, and what was done in it at home and abroad, and had gained knowledge of many actions of note and passages of consequence and the manners of other countries and nations and affairs of their own country."[12]

Mealtime readings and responses became, in time, the Little Academy. Much like a literary coterie, the participants in the Little Academy acquired special names or titles that they used in addressing one another that pointed to distinctive characteristics or roles. Seven of the initial ten are women, including Mrs. Ferrar, known as The Founder or Mother; Susanna Collet, wife of John, called The Moderator; and Mary Collet, eldest daughter of Susanna and John, called The Chief. The names and roles of the three men, even Nicholas, were comparatively less significant: John Ferrar was The Guardian; Nicholas, The Visitor; and John Collet, The Resolved.

There is no doubt that the duties and attributes signified by their titles put the women in a dominant role during the course of the conversations, though as with all things at Little Gidding the situation defies easy interpretation. Nicholas initially provided materials for the readings and discussions and was joined in the decisions about topics and organization by Mary Collet.[13] Any one of the participants might be the leader for a given day, and the group as a whole knew that they might be joined by other members of the family or even visitors to Little Gidding. Thus, although organized as a private and family gathering, the Little Academy could, and did, reach out beyond the immediate community of Little Gidding.

Of all the family members, the one most remarkable for her pronounced independence and, at the same time, her allegiance to the aims of the community was Mary Collet. As the oldest daughter of John and Susanna, she was in a position to act as a mediator between parents and elders and children and youth. In her mid-twenties when the Ferrars went to Little Gidding, she was only eleven years younger than John Ferrar and nine years younger than Nicholas. She was thus much closer in age to her uncles than she was to her own brother Ferrar (who was nineteen years younger) and her niece and nephews, the children of John and Bathsheba Ferrar.

Beyond her important role as a link between generations, Mary was notable for her character, devotion, and resolute commitment to her faith and her

---

12. In A. M. Williams, ed., *Conversations at Little Gidding* (Cambridge: Cambridge University Press, 1970), xviii.

13. Ibid., xxi.

family. She soon became, succeeding the senior Mrs. Ferrar, the intellectual and spiritual "mother" of Little Gidding. She was possessed of both practical skills and nurturing instincts, the latter, we should note, in spite (or because?) of her resolution to remain a virgin. A. L. Maycock remarks on other of her attributes:

> It was she who had principal charge in the dispensing of prescriptions, the preparation of dressings and all the manifold work of the surgery. She acquired a great skill in bookbinding, and herself bound the first Concordance which the family presented to the King—a superb volume in crimson velvet covers, tooled and adorned in gilt. She was widely read, and her erudition is well displayed in a learned little treatise, preserved amongst the Magdalene papers, in which she is concerned to show that St. Athanasius was in fact the author of the Creed that bears his name. It was she who took charge of [smaller children at Little Gidding] . . . and brought them up as though they had been her own.[14]

It is equally clear that Mary Collet—in the flesh and in the spirit, as she was and as he responded to and re-created her—had a particularly compelling influence on Crashaw.

IV

We do not know when Crashaw began his regular visits to Little Gidding; if, as Maycock has suggested, Crashaw had met Nicholas Ferrar in London, the visits may have coincided with Crashaw's admission to Pembroke College in 1631.[15] At Little Gidding, there was much to satisfy and excite someone of Crashaw's emotional and religious temperament, and there was, even more than acquaintance with Nicholas himself, the commanding presence of Mary Collet. Crashaw saw in this very real woman the strong and determined yet nurturing figure who populates so much of his verse. When in 1632 the elder Mrs. Ferrar resigned her position as "The Mother" of the Little Academy, it was Mary—not her mother or her aunt—who was elected by the others to assume the role of "Mother." And it is as his "mother" that Crashaw explicitly praises Mary and reveals his passionate regard for her.

Crashaw left Cambridge, probably in early 1643, to escape the increasingly hostile response of Parliament toward the university, a hostility that culminated, late in that year, with the physical destruction of many religious icons and artifacts at the university through the actions of parliamentary forces led by William Dowsing. Writing from his exile in Leyden in February 1644, Crashaw

14. Maycock, *Nicholas Ferrar of Little Gidding,* 178.
15. Ibid., 231.

addressed a letter to an unnamed friend from his Cambridge days, requesting assistance in obtaining some part of the income from the fellowship from which he was about to be expelled.[16] Taking precedence over that request, however, was a more wrenching concern about the severing of his relationship with his "mother," Mary Collet, who was in Leyden as well and who, for reasons that Crashaw professed not to understand (and that we do not know), was kept from him. She was residing with an uncle who denied Crashaw access to her, and no small portion of the letter is aimed at informing his Cambridge friend of what has happened. The anguish Crashaw feels in what we may well see as a third instance in which he loses his mother is evident in the words, the cadences, and the spaces of the text. "There has hapned in my condition of residence," Crashaw says,

> a chang so little expected by you I know and to mee so litle pleasant as puts me to't eu'en for expression. It was you say a word welcome to your embraces that which told you I was still the same. And how shall I do to obtrude the same to a beleife with you when I shall haue told you I that I am now not onely not with my mother but a stranger to her and haue been these 2 months. But I must make hast to correct and heal if I can these ill sauouring phrases. Let me resume that word and I will see if I can qualify it. Did I say I am become a stranger to her? I should haue sayd to her house. Did I say to *her* house. I should haue sayd to her Uncles. Some mystery there is you'l think in the matter, and tis best suffer it to be so till further oportunity may be of better satisfaction by freer discourse then at this distan[ce]. I say no more but that you beware the least suspition of ought upon my noble mothers part unworthy of he[r] self or wherefore she too may not plead still the same. And what is that to say but the gentlest kindes[t] most tender-hearted and liberall handed soul I think this day aliue? And I would she had no more of the affliction then the faut of this busines falling to her share. In sum (and that I may make my transition to the more pertinent part of my letter and leaue bemoaning whats past to looke forward to what lyes yet perhaps under our providence) she hath in all this matter so demeaned her self, that I find my self still foulded in and round wrapped about with a still encreasing ty of inextricable engagements.[17]

16. The usual view is that the intended recipient of the letter is either John Ferrar or John Collet (see, for example, L. C. Martin, ed., *The Poems, English, Latin, and Greek, of Richard Crashaw* [Oxford: Clarendon Press, 1957], xxvi). More recently, Elsie Elizabeth Duncan-Jones has argued that the recipient was Crashaw's friend Joseph Beaumont ("Who Was the Recipient of Crashaw's Leyden Letter?" in *New Perspectives on the Life and Art of Richard Crashaw,* ed. John R. Roberts [Columbia: University of Missouri Press, 1990], 174–79). Although the question remains not fully resolved, if Beaumont is in fact his addressee, Crashaw's willingness to reveal so fully and so intimately his feelings about Mary Collet to a friend not part of the Ferrar-Collet family testifies even more to the powerful effect she had on him.

17. The letter is reproduced and edited in Martin, *The Poems, English, Latin, and Greek, of Richard Crashaw,* xxvii–xxxi. I have retained original spelling in the letter but have silently modernized certain other features such as "the" and "that."

Crashaw's attachment to and adoption of a third "mother," followed by her apparently forced separation from him, resulted in an extraordinary response that merges feelings of disappointment and extreme adulation with worries about disloyalty and neglect. The letter arose out of a deeply complex set of emotions, not unlike those Hamlet feels for his mother, when strong attachment and love are threatened by the interference of others and, possibly, by misconduct on the part of the beloved. While confirming the worth of his "mother," Crashaw reveals his awareness of an interpretation of her actions that would make her responsible, at least in part, for the separation. Linking in one sentence "my mother" and "a stranger," Crashaw hastens to "correct and heal" the "ill sauouring phrases" that might suggest her complicity. Acknowledging a "mystery" in the matter, he hopes that "the least suspition of ought" will not fall upon "my noble mothers part," and he reiterates his view of her as the "gentlest kindes[t] most tender-hearted and liberall handed soul I think this day aliue." Still, his very language betrays his own uneasiness and his concern about her involvement when he wishes for her "no more of the affliction then the faut of this busines falling to her share." As he moves to what he says is the "more pertinent part" of his letter, Crashaw's words reveal again the pain and puzzlement the affair has brought him and the ambiguity of the language with which he writes about it. When he says that Mary has "in all this matter so demeaned her self," he is saying, at a primary (and neutral) level of meaning, that she has "conducted" or "employed" herself in a certain way, but the word *demeaned* may betray a secondary and more troubling possibility: that in her conduct Mary risks being lowered in Crashaw's eyes.[18] While the precise force of the word is left uncertain, it is clear that Mary's present situation, whether innocent or leaving her mysteriously culpable, has put Crashaw thoroughly in a quandary: "foulded in and round wrapped about with a still encreasing ty of inextricable engagements."

Crashaw's response to Mary Collet as a person is best captured in the string of superlatives with which he describes her; indeed, the very pain and frustration evident in the letter only confirm the extraordinary attachment he feels toward her. But the letter also advances what are for Crashaw deeper and much more far-reaching implications and consequences in his *representation* of a living virgin woman as his "mother," implications discussed in the "more pertinent part" to come.

As I have indicated above, the designation of Mary Collet as the "mother," not only within the immediate religious community in which she dwelled but

18. See the *OED* "demean," v.1,1 and v.2,1. It should be noted that the *OED* records only two uses of "demean" to mean "lower" in the seventeenth century, and both of these are uncertain. The word *demean* does not appear in Crashaw's verse.

also among close outsiders, is noteworthy and unusual. That it is testimony to her spiritual and intellectual gifts seems irrefutable. In age and position, other women were more immediately in line for the title, but to be the "mother" of Little Gidding and to be "elected" as such by her companions clearly resulted from achievement, not a family circumstance. It is equally certain that Mary's assumption of the role of "mother" did, in spite of John Ferrar's angry denial of the "abominable falshoods" in *The Arminian Nunnery*,[19] confirm the community's association with a convent, with Mary, the committed virgin, enacting the role of mother superior to her brood of (mainly female) aspirants.

For Crashaw, the emotional commitment was even deeper and the implications of a severing of the relationship even more profound. It is the virgin, Mary, who is for Crashaw the "gentlest kindes[t] most tender-hearted and liberall handed soul," and it is "excomunicacion" from the virgin, Mary, that puts him into "the greatest exigence both spirituall and temporall I was euer cast into." Writing about his "mother," a woman in fact no more than eleven years his senior, Crashaw sees in this flesh and blood Mary the virtues represented by saints and saintly women and, certainly, by the Virgin Mary herself in many of his most memorable poems.[20] But he is, after his exile from Cambridge and from Little Gidding, forced to confront the further reality of separation from Mary and with it the challenge to his faith in and devotion to someone who is, even if aptly characterized in superlatives, finally only flesh and blood.

When he makes the transition to the "more pertinent part" of his letter, Crashaw does not in fact leave his "mother" behind, referring to his former pupil Ferrar Collet as his "mothers Brother" and again taking up the injustice he is suffering at the hands of those who deny him access to Mary. Indeed, the imminent removal of his fellowship serves to remind him of his more painful removal from Mary. He writes,

> Between that Remoueuall and this Resignation, or rather between these two Resignations myn of my fellowship and my mothers of mee, (but Hers I dare say as unwilling as mine is willing) what is likely think my friends to be the result. Why Ile tell you. Nothing but a third resignation of all to God. . . . I confess this last peece of my persecution the very sorest

19. From *A Life of Nicholas Ferrar*, in Blackstone, *The Ferrar Papers*, 62. Given the complicated history of the transmission of accounts of Nicholas Ferrar's life, one cannot always be certain of the authorship of specific words and phrases. But as Blackstone's account makes clear (xvii-xxi), the ultimate source is John Ferrar's *Life*, and the angry disclaimers about *The Arminian Nunnery* read very much as coming from someone close to Nicholas's life and circumstances.

20. Maureen Sabine's recent study, *Feminine Engendered Faith: The Poetry of John Donne and Richard Crashaw* (London: Macmillan, 1992), is the fullest discussion to date of the influence on Crashaw of devotions to the Virgin Mary.

> I yet haue suffered, in my exclusion and compleat excomunicacion from
> my gratious mother to whome I had so holy and happy adherence, & in
> whome I tresured up to my self as much as you could wish (I need say no
> more of sacred satisfaction and Catholick contentation, my extrusion and
> exhaereditation hence, I say has been such a concussion of mee such a
> dislocation of my whole condition, as puts mee into the greatest exigence
> both spirituall and temporall I was euer cast into.

Leah Marcus rightly points to Crashaw's "complete disorientation" as revealed in the final lines just quoted, but she too quickly attributes it to his
expulsion from Peterhouse and his exile from Cambridge and England.[21]
Surely, the passage confirms that his separation from Mary, the "exclusion
and compleat excomunicacion from my gratious mother," is the immediate
cause of Crashaw's anguish and the precipitating factor behind his "greatest
exigence both spirituall and temporall." But Marcus is also right in recognizing
that Crashaw is responding to more than his immediate difficulties with Mary
Collet's uncle. This "last peece of my persecution" is by no means the only
separation that Crashaw felt, and in the loss of his mother he is experiencing
as well the loss of the nurturing environs of Little Gidding and Cambridge.
Furthermore, the "dislocation of [his] whole condition" anticipates the crucial
decision lying in Crashaw's near future—the loss (or rejection) of the religion
to which he has devoted his life and the affirmation of a religion where (to draw
from Herbert's "To All Angels and Saints") worship of all angels and saints and
the "Blessed Maid, / And Mother of my God" will bring a fuller measure of
"sacred satisfaction and Catholick contentation."[22] In a very real and powerful
sense, the separation and dislocation from the virgin Mary Collet, the very best
of the women Crashaw knew during his life, led him ultimately to devotion to
the Virgin Mary, the "gratious mother" from whom "exclusion and compleat
excomunicacion" will not be possible.

I said earlier that we cannot call Little Gidding a feminist community, but it
was surely a very feminine one. Represented most compellingly by its "mother"
and maintained by its various women, Little Gidding was precisely the kind of
community to which Crashaw would have had a "holy and happy adherence."
There is no doubt that the women of his reading, devotions, and imagination
excited and comforted him, and there is no doubt that his faith ultimately led
him to worship of the "Blessed Maid, / And Mother of my God," but it is equally

---

21. *Childhood and Cultural Despair,* 140.
22. I am citing the Oxford Authors edition, Louis L. Martz, ed., *George Herbert and Henry Vaughan*
(Oxford and New York: Oxford University Press, 1986).

certain that the living women of Little Gidding, especially Mary Collet—both as she was and as she was transformed into the object of his adherence and devotion—were examples who could spur his imagination and confirm his highest aspirations for faith of the feminine gender.[23]

23. See Crashaw's Latin epigram on Matthew 15:28 (Martin, *The Poems, English, Latin, and Greek, of Richard Crashaw,* 55).

Roger B. Rollin

Robert Herrick's Housekeeper

Representing Ordinary Women in Renaissance Poetry

In the nearly three centuries since Robert Herrick's rediscovery, the fourteen fictional "mistresses" who pose so prettily in 158 amatory poems of his *Hesperides* have received considerable attention, negative as well as positive. There is, for example, Gordon Braden's dour view—that Herrick's poetic paramours "have the same characteristics as 'Anacreon's' loves: passive, unreal, and evanescent, as absurdly numerous as shadows." But considerably more numerous and by no means evanescent or shadowy are the twenty-nine historically identifiable women to whom or about whom Herrick wrote a total of forty-six works. *Hesperides*'s mistress-poems have sealed Herrick's considerable reputation as a love poet but have also tended to reinforce the erroneous impression that the world of his book is mainly romantic, fanciful, or even trifling. That these amatory verses are partly counterbalanced by his poems to actual women—who also appear throughout *Hesperides*—has not been pointed out. Nor has it been observed that these representations of women—who, for the most part, lived in the everyday world of the seventeenth century—make Herrick's collection unique among those of his important contemporaries and ground *Hesperides* as firmly in the social history of his age as his political verses ground his book in the turbulent times of the first half of the seventeenth century.[1]

1. See Ann Baynes Coiro, "Herrick's 'Julia' Poems," *John Donne Journal* 6 (1987): 67. Other recent studies include: John T. Shawcross, "The Names of Herrick's Mistresses in *Hesperides*," in *"Trust to Good Verses": Herrick Tercentenary Essays,* ed. Roger B. Rollin and J. Max Patrick (Pittsburgh: University of Pittsburgh Press, 1978), 89–102, and Heather Asals, "King Solomon in the Land of *Hesperides*," *Texas Studies in Language and Literature* 17 (1976): 362–80. Gordon Braden, *The Classics and English Renaissance Poetry* (New Haven: Yale University Press, 1978), 219. Among the most recent studies of the ways in which Herrick's poetry reflects the real political world of the seventeenth century are: Leah S. Marcus, *The Politics of Mirth: Jonson, Herrick, Milton, Marvell, and the Defense of Old Holiday Pastimes* (Chicago: University of Chicago Press, 1986); Claude J. Summers, "Tears for Herrick's Church," *George Herbert Journal* 14 (fall 1990/spring 1991): 51–71, and "Herrick, Vaughan, and the Poetry of Anglican

It is impossible to enumerate the mistresses of Donne's *Songs and Sonnets* because—unlike most of Herrick's—none of them has a name. The only contemporary females actually named in the rest of Donne's canon are all—with the possible exception of Cecilia Bulstrode—titled personages. Only seven of Herrick's twenty-nine are. Herrick, in fact, wrote more poems to or about female commoners than the rest of his important contemporaries combined. Whether Metaphysical or Cavalier, Vaughan, Crashaw, Traherne, Carew, Suckling, Lovelace, and Marvell compose only a few poems to or about identifiable untitled women. Even Herrick's "father," Ben Jonson, from whom we might expect otherwise, eternizes only four female commoners—but seventeen titled women. The Milton of the Minor Poems wrote to or about five positively identifiable female commoners, although only to Catharine Thomason of Sonnet 14 did he give a full name.[2]

As might be expected, Herbert's *The Temple* refers to only a few women, and all of them are biblical figures. Herrick's *Noble Numbers* mentions six such archetypal females in ten poems. Because these women stand somewhere between history and myth they will not be considered here.

The most extraordinary real woman of *Hesperides* is Prudence Baldwin. What makes her so extraordinary is her very ordinariness. She was, of course, Reverend Herrick's housekeeper, undoubtedly a local, a woman of "dull Devonshire" (H-51), and probably illiterate.[3] However, it is quite possible that she appreciated her master's verses, for he wrote four of them about her (twice as many as he wrote for Queen Henrietta Maria), and he would have had less motivation to do so had Pru been unable to take some pleasure in them.

Prudence Baldwin apparently was the successor to the poet's sister-in-law, Elizabeth Herrick, who kept house for him at Dean Prior[4] and whom we initially meet early in *Hesperides* in the epigram "No Spouse but a Sister" (H-31). Herrick's first poem to "Prue" appears in the third "century" of his collection, immediately following a highly commendatory piece to a far grander personage, " . . . the most accomplisht Gentleman, Master Edward Norgate, Clark of the

---

Survivalism," in *New Perspectives on the Seventeenth-Century English Religious Lyric,* ed. John R. Roberts (Columbia: University of Missouri Press, 1994), 46–74.

2. Milton does not actually identify his sister, Anne Phillips, and her daughter, Anne, as such in "On the Death of a Fair Infant Dying of a Cough." A beautiful lady is only identified by her first name (Aemilia) in "Sonnet 2," as is a Neapolitan singer (Leonora) in "Ad Leonoram Romae Canentem," "Ad Eandem [I]," and "Ad Eandem [II]." Mary Powell or Katherine Woodcock may be alluded to in "Sonnet 23."

3. In the England of Herrick's time, female illiteracy varied from nearly 100 to 80 percent according to Antonia Fraser, *The Weaker Vessel* (New York: Knopf, 1984), 129.

4. J. Max Patrick, ed., *The Complete Poetry of Robert Herrick* (New York: New York University Press, 1963), 22 n. All quotations from Herrick's poetry are from this edition and are identified by its poem numbers.

Signet to His Majesty . . ." (H-301). The latter is routine poetry of praise, by no means one of Herrick's more memorable verses. But "Upon Prudence Baldwin her sicknesse" (H-302) sounds quite a different note as, in seriocomic fashion, it establishes the importance of this humble countrywoman to the poet:

> Prue, my dearest Maid, is sick,
> Almost to be Lunatick:
> *Æsculapius!* come and bring
> Means for her recovering;
> And a gallant Cock shall be
> Offer'd up by Her, to Thee.

The combination of possessive and superlative—"my dearest Maid"—expresses a concern that is at once intensified and rendered half humorous by the adjective "Lunatick." Invoking the god of medicine rather than the more current deity resolves the ambiguity of tone—and may lessen concern as to the seriousness of Pru's malady. So too does the allusion to the sacrifice of the traditional offering to Æsculapius (Patrick 167n), the "gallant Cock," particularly in light of the fact that Prudence would be quite accustomed to decapitating fowl in preparation for her master's suppers. Nevertheless, the poem's humor in no way is at Pru's expense and does not diminish the fact that she has been immortalized, by name, by a poet who entirely believes in the eternizing power of poetry. Moreover, Mistress Baldwin becomes the first real-life female servant in English literature—and possibly the last—to be mentioned by name by a poet of note. That allusion, like Herrick's several (but neglected) poems on everyday life, helps anchor his collection in the quotidian—here an affectionate master-servant relationship. It also transforms one of ordinary life's familiar vicissitudes, the illness of a member of one's household, into a kind of comic-mythic event by "classicizing" it.

That Herrick's relationship with Prudence Baldwin was indeed an affectionate one and that, like so many of his familial and social relationships, he intentionally immortalized it, are confirmed in a poetic tribute titled "To his maid Prew" (H-387):

> These *Summer-Birds* did with thy Master stay
> The times of warmth; but then they flew away;
> Leaving their Poet (being now grown old)
> Expos'd to all the comming Winters cold.
> But thou *kind Prew* did'st with my Fates abide,
> As well the Winters, as the Summers Tide:
> For which thy Love, live with thy Master here,
> Not two, but all the seasons of the yeare.

The "here" of line 7 is the vicarage at Dean Prior, but also Herrick's Hesperidean world, where Pru, unlike most of her betters, transcends *"Times trans-shifting"* (H-1)—the reward of loyalty to a master who is also a poet. The birds of summer (and possibly fair-weather friends) depart with the arrival of autumn, depriving Herrick of their heartwarming presence, but Pru's "Love" persists despite changing seasons and changing fortunes. In the seventeenth century we would expect *masters* to be characterized as "kind," and the imputed "kindness" of patrons actual or potential is a cliché of Renaissance poetry. But the kindness of a servant *to* a master locates this tribute in everyday reality, in the complex socioeconomic and psychological relationship that Americans have lately come to appreciate thanks to the television series *Upstairs, Downstairs* and the film *The Remains of the Day.*

The everyday reality of seventeenth-century rural life is the subject of a remarkable poem of Herrick's titled "His content in the Country" (H-552). In form it is a "catalog of contentments," a list of the modest pleasures available to a country parson. Here Prudence Baldwin is only mentioned, but she is mentioned prominently—in the poem's opening lines:

> Here, here, I live with what my Board,
> Can with the smallest cost afford.
> Though ne'r so mean the Viands be,
> They well content my *Prew* and me.

Several things are noteworthy about Herrick's reference to his maid. (1) He is assuming that his readers, at this midway point in *Hesperides,* know who *"Prew"* is on the strength of the two allusions to her earlier in his book—which means that he expects his poems to be read seriatim, in the order in which he arranged them.[5] (2) Were it not for those earlier poems, the possessive "my" might lead readers to assume that the lady alluded to is Herrick's wife, but now we understand that "my" is a term of endearment (as is the shortened form of Prudence's name) for the humble housekeeper of the poet's "poore Tenement" (l. 8). (3) "His content" is one of many examples of Herrick's tendency to "domesticate" the pastoral, to "English" that classical mode, and a good English name such as "Prudence" contributes to that process of transformation in a way that, say, "Amaryllis" can not. (4) That the poet and his housekeeper enjoy the same "Viands"—"Pea, or Bean, or Wort, or Beet" (l. 4)—implies that this graduate of Cambridge and Church of England divine and this countrywoman coexist, if not on an equal footing, at least in a relationship where class

---

5. This crucial point about reading Herrick is made in Ann Baynes Coiro's *Robert Herrick's "Hesperides" and the Epigram Book Tradition* (Baltimore: Johns Hopkins University Press, 1988), 2; and in my *Robert Herrick* (New York: Twayne Publishers, 1992), 11–12.

distinctions seem not to make a great deal of difference. (The pronoun "I" appears only in the poem's first line; elsewhere the operative nominative is "we.") All of this does not, as I have observed elsewhere,

> make the old Royalist a democrat, but [it does] say something about his sensibility, which it would be presumptuous to call "modern." [And it does show Herrick recognizing] that ordinary people and ordinary life can be as much the stuff of poetry as great ones and glamour.[6]

"His content in the Country" does not seem like a radical poem, but its subtle elevation of Prudence Baldwin across class lines is something that we might more likely expect in the writings of Herrick's nemeses, the Puritans.

Prudence Baldwin's farewell appearance in *Hesperides* is literally that, in an epitaph "Upon Prew his Maid" (H-782):

> In this little Urne is laid
> *Prewdence Baldwin* (once my maid)
> From whose happy spark here let
> Spring the purple Violet.

Herrick's habit of composing epitaphs for himself finds its parallel here, for Prudence Baldwin would not be laid to rest for some thirty years after the publication of *Hesperides*. Mortuary verse like this poem, then, is, at its most basic, an exercise, an *imitatio* of the poetic practice of Herrick's mentor, Ben Jonson. On a pragmatic level, epitaphs for the living can serve as insurance against the possibility that one's stone will bear an inscription composed by another less talented versifier. In Pru's case Herrick's epitaph may be an attempt not only to commemorate her appropriately (as he himself would hope to be commemorated) but also to hedge against the possibility that if this poor countrywoman were to outlive her employer (as she did, by four years) she might not have a gravestone erected for her at all. Finally, even though marble and gilded monuments would not be Pru's destiny, this poem becomes a means of shoring up a friend's name against the oblivion that Herrick himself dreads.

This epitaph has brought the reader full circle, from the poem on Pru's sickness to one on her death, from a "classicized" prayer for her recovery to a classicized inscription for urn burial. "Upon Prew his Maid" is the second of the four poems in which she figures to give her the dignity of her full name, and it perpetuates the tone of affection that unites them. Pru's "happy spark" is

---

6. Roger B. Rollin, "Robert Herrick," in *Dictionary of Literary Biography*, 126, Seventeenth-Century Non-Dramatic Poets; Second Series, ed. M. Thomas Hester (Detroit: Gale Research, 1993), 178.

her "vital or animating principle" (OED.3) that will issue forth in the fragrant purple flower that "bring[s] / In the Spring" (H-205, ll. 2–3). The small miracle Herrick predicts (it should not escape notice) in effect serves to beatify his housekeeper. This poem, moreover, in historical context is another example of life imitating art: while Pru's epitaph endures within the pages of Herrick's book, her actual tombstone—like that of her poet master—has not survived the ravages of time.

The generosity of Herrick's tributes to Prudence Baldwin is all the more remarkable considering the fact that it is possible that she was in his service only a few years before the 1648 publication of *Hesperides*—unless she served an apprenticeship in the parsonage under the supervision of the poet's sister-in-law, Elizabeth Herrick. Robert Herrick was installed as the vicar of Dean Prior in 1630, but it is not known when Elizabeth arrived to take charge of his household. All we are certain of is that she died in 1643, at which time Prudence Baldwin likely took charge of the domestic side of the vicarage. We are not even sure whether Elizabeth was the widow of the poet's brother William or of his brother Thomas. What is certain is that, like Pru Baldwin, Elizabeth receives the tribute of a Herrickean epitaph, in "Upon his Sister-in-Law, Mistresse Elizabeth Herrick" (H-72):

> First, for Effusions due unto the dead,
> My solemne Vowes have here accomplished;
> Next, how I love thee, that my griefe must tell,
> Wherein thou liv'st for ever. Deare farewell.

Conventional Renaissance funerary poems can be like modern sympathy cards: it is difficult to gauge the depth of feeling behind them. This brief "effusion" or outpouring of emotions, however, seems more than merely perfunctory. The poet has vowed—more than once, he suggests—to commemorate his sister-in-law, and this epitaph is the fulfillment of those promises. His love for her, he affirms, is without measure, as endless as his grief will be. No bathos or parading of wit here: only the simple valedictory, "Deare farewell," befitting a relationship based on kinship and a shared domesticity, a personal history together.

The emotional life out of which such an epitaph proceeds is hinted at in an earlier poem that almost certainly alludes to Elizabeth Herrick, "No Spouse but a Sister" (H-31). This comic epigram in trimeter couplets shows the poet mocking himself as a confirmed bachelor as well as wives who "crucify" men's lives, but its characterization of the compromise relationship into which he and (we assume) Elizabeth have evolved is at once affectionate and bemused:

> A Sister (in the stead
> Of Wife) about I'le lead;
> Which I will keep embrac'd
> And kisse, but yet be chaste.

Even in remotest Devonshire it must have been both politic and convenient for a vicar who was also a bachelor to have a respectable kinswoman on his arm on certain occasions. Such a woman can with propriety receive and bestow the common affectional gestures that typically enhance the marital bond. But the poet who ends his book with *"Jocond his Muse was; but his Life was chast"* here, in similarly public fashion, insists upon the chastity of a relationship that would quite naturally pique the interest of the curious and titillate the prurient. Of such possibilities Elizabeth Herrick would had to have been obtuse not to be aware. Her handling of her delicate role then might have been one of the reasons that the poet-priest was motivated to immortalize her in an epitaph.

An epitaph for yet another Elizabeth Herrick, this time the daughter of the poet's brother William, is believed to be the first poem by Herrick to have been printed. Its provenance is unusual. According to J. Max Patrick, "It appeared in Stow's *Survey of London* (1633), p. 812, as taken from a memorial tablet in St. Margaret's, Westminster. . . ."[7] Thus, "Upon his kinswoman Mistris Elizabeth Herrick" (H-376) may be one of the few epitaphs by an important seventeenth-century poet actually to be inscribed upon a churchyard stone. Herrick begins the poem conventionally enough, apologizing to the "Sweet virgin" for not commemorating her with "pillars of weeping *Jet*, / Or mournfull *Marble*" (ll. 1, 2–3), but he assures her that this poem will be her "living Epitaph" (l. 8). Elizabeth was only eleven when she died, and Herrick captures the poignancy of that fact in his concluding couplet: "Sleep, while we hide thee from the light, / Drawing thy curtains round: *Good night*" (ll. 13–14). Here the conventional bed/grave metaphor is transformed into a seventeenth-century domestic moment, with the image of a doting uncle tucking his niece into a curtain-enclosed bed of that period.

Robert Herrick names himself in his poetry more than anyone in English literature up to his era—and perhaps since. Naming oneself is, of course, a form of self-eternization, but it also is a way of asserting one's historical identity—"I am a poet and a man and once I lived." The effects are the same for the actual women he names: unlike his Julias and Corinnas and Perennas, we need not wonder whether there actually was or was not a real "Mary Stone," for example. In his epitaph for her Mary is identified in Herrick's title as his "Kinswoman" (H-764), and kinship is reiterated and thus emphasized in the epitaph's final

---

7. Patrick, *Complete Poetry*, 198 n.

couplet, where the poet instructs "fragrant Virgins" to "strew some Roses on her" and thus "do my *Neice* abundant honor" (ll. 9–10). She died, we are told earlier, in her "blooming years," and "This Stone, for names sake, melts to teares" (ll. 5–6). Here Herrick's wit is as complex as it is serious: the personified tombstone weeps because Mary died young and because she is, like it, a "Stone," and now further "related" to it by the inscription, "Mary Stone," engraved upon its face. Donne himself would have been proud of such ingenuity, but Mary Stone is no Elizabeth Drury: she is a commoner, a young girl whose only claim to poetic immortality is that her uncle is Robert Herrick.

Hesperides is many things, but it is in part a family album—or a kind of family Bible—commemorating the births, weddings, and deaths of the sizable Herrick clan, a public record of a personal middle-class history. As Ann Coiro has observed, it is "one of the most intimately familial books in the seventeenth century."[8] The seventeen poems scattered throughout *Hesperides* that are dedicated to or refer to female members of the Herrick family constitute a significant part of that history. Ordinary women, none of them particularly wealthy or powerful, they have been immortalized because they are kin—and most likely because Herrick was fond of them. For, it should be noted, the poet's most famous, wealthiest, and most powerful relative, Sir William Herrick, who reduced his nephew to begging for money during Robert's Cambridge days, never appears in *Hesperides*. Less understandably, the book that contains a powerful poem to his suicide-father, "To the reverend shade of his religious Father" (H-82), offers only a passing reference—not a poem—to the widowed mother who raised Herrick. In "His tears to Thamasis" (H-1028) the poet bids good-bye to *"Golden-cheap-side,* where the earth / Of *Julia Herrick* gave to me my Birth" (ll. 15–16). Coiro has noted that Herrick's mother here is assigned the same name as the subject or addressee of seventy-seven of his mistress poems, "Julia," even though she is typically referred to as "Julian or Julianna in extant records."[9] The kind of psychoanalytic speculations these facts invite are beyond the scope of this essay, as is the fact that two women who kept house for him are more directly and fully immortalized by the poet than the woman who bore and raised him. However, it is also the case that even Herrick's poem to his father (H-82) is, despite its reverential title, a curiously ambivalent sort of tribute.[10] There is no reason to suppose that Herrick was a more thankless child than other poets of his age—most of whom did not honor their fathers and mothers in verse either—but the very complexity of the parent-child relationship may render panegyrics to perfect strangers considerably easier to compose.

---

8. Coiro, *Epigram Book Tradition,* 83.
9. Ibid.
10. Roger B. Rollin, "Robert Herrick's Fathers," *Studies in English Literature* 34:1 (winter 1994): 41–47.

The custom of honoring titled personages obviously posed few problems for the poets of the seventeenth century, including Robert Herrick, but only about a quarter of his poems treating identifiable females deal with royals and gentlewomen—a small percentage for the time. (Herrick could flatter with the best of them, but his output of versified flattery of the high and mighty is, for the Caroline era, relatively modest.) Three of these works, the most on one titled woman, have to do with Lady Jane Crewe, presumably because she was the wife of a Cambridge friend of Herrick's and subsequent patron, Sir Clipseby Crewe.[11] In these three poems—an epithalamium (one of the most spectacular of the genre [H-283]), a consolation on the death of one of Lady Crewe's children (H-514), and an epitaph for the lady herself (H-978)—the ages of the seventeenth-century woman are succinctly and affectingly represented.

For all his monarchism, Herrick treats Henrietta Maria in only two works, although one of them, "To the Queene" (H-265), is truly a tour de force. In this compliment-poem, Charles's consort, hailed as the *"Goddesse of Youth, and Lady of the Spring"* (ll. 1–2), is invited to enter *"This Sacred Grove"* (l. 3), the pastoral world of *Hesperides,* and become "both its *Princesse* . . . and *Poetresse"* (l. 10). (Given the real world's bad political season, this may well have been the best offer Henrietta Maria had had in some time.) Of the remaining poems to titled women, two are nuptial verses (H-149A, H-618), and three are compliment-poems (H-169, H-341), including one "To the most fair and lovely Mistris, Anne Soame, now Lady Abdie" (H-375), who was also Herrick's cousin on his mother's side—kin again.[12]

In the Renaissance it is by no means unusual to direct love poems and pastorals—amatory or otherwise—to women unnamed (the practice of Donne) or women mythical (often the practice of Herrick). It is, however, far less common for poets to address love poems and pastorals to historically iden- tifiable women, especially women who happen to be commoners, as Herrick does. Although versions of realism are possible even in seventeenth-century love poetry (such as Donne's "The Good-Morrow") and pastoral poetry (like Herrick's "His Grange, or private wealth" [H-724]), the primary modes of both genres are, of course, enhancement and elevation—toward the romantic, toward the ideal. What, then, is a reader to make of poems that simultaneously insist upon the real and the ideal?

Dorothy Keneday has not been specifically identified,[13] and thus one can only guess at her relationship to Herrick. The poet does something unusual, however, with his two amatory verses to her, for he immediately follows "His

---

11. *Complete Poetry,* 198 n.
12. Ibid., 197 n.
13. Ibid., 60 n.

parting from Mistresse Dorothy Keneday" (H-122) with "The Teare sent to her from Stanes" (H-123), creating thereby a kind of romantic minidrama. It is, however, a minidrama that has the ring, at least, of docudrama, given the specificity of the lady's name and of the place-name, Stanes (about seven miles from Windsor). "His parting" is a valediction commending weeping in which the speaker suffers mightily but the lady apparently does not. In contrast to more conventional valedictories, the relationship is not mutual: there is a parting kiss, but no sigh from Dorothy, "t'acompany [Herrick's] teare" (l. 5). He is bewildered: "Me thought 'twas strange, that thou so hard shoud'st prove, / Whose heart, whose hand, whose eve'ry part spake love" (ll. 6–7). With a lover's paradoxical wit he begs her at least to *say* that she has shed one solitary tear— even though he knows she has not.

The ambiguity of this poem parallels the ambiguities surrounding the true history behind it. Is this one of Herrick's autobiographical efforts or only a romantic fiction? Seventeenth-century readers would likely be no more certain than we. The poet had to have recognized, however, that it would be quite natural for readers to suspect that a real relationship might go with a real name, especially when such a poem is put in the context of all of those amatory lyrics featuring Herrick's archetypal mistresses: willful English Dorothy is no pliant Anthea.

With the next poem, "The Teare sent to her from Stanes" (H-123), the sense of romantic reality increases. Herrick and Dorothy are now separated, and he sheds a tear into the Thames to be conveyed

> To that coy Girle;
> Who smiles, yet slayes
> Me with delayes;
> And strings my tears as Pearle.
>   (ll. 3–6)

The rest is a metrically unusual but otherwise conventional love complaint, implicitly affirming the moral superiority of the lovesick male to the alternately demanding and indifferent female. Nevertheless, "The Teare sent to her from Stanes" and its predecessor constitute the first love poems in *Hesperides* that seem to invite the reader to link Herrick's art and his romantic life—as opposed to those more familiar amatory verses that invite an appreciation of the poet's art in service of his wish-fulfillment fantasies. One function of these paired poems and later amatory lyrics to real women then may be to serve as occasional reality checks to the majority of *Hesperides*'s love poems: Herrick using the relative facticity of the former to hint at the fictiveness of the latter. If that was indeed the case, the device did not work, as evidenced by all the ink spilled on speculations regarding the "true identity" of Julia, Corinna, and so on.

Only one other verse to a female commoner in *Hesperides* qualifies as a love lyric, "To Mistresse Amie Potter" (H-837). Here again Herrick's self-referentiality invites an autobiographical reading: "AI me! I love, give him your hand to kisse / Who both your wooer, and your Poet is" (ll. 1–2); and again: "Deare, can you like, and liking love your Poet?" (l. 5). This sprightly invitation to like is markedly different in tone from the melancholy poems to Dorothy Keneday—perhaps because Amie Potter is a highly improbable love interest: she was the daughter of the Reverend Barnaby Potter, Herrick's predecessor at Dean Prior,[14] and that fact makes the poem an in-joke, for few contemporary readers could be expected to be aware of it. Thus, this witty address's inclusion in *Hesperides* serves several purposes: it titillates readers with the prospect of an actual romance, reinforces Herrick's persona as a poet-lover, and stands as a compliment to the charms of the otherwise unknown Amie.

Other Hesperidean poems to untitled women fall into the category of nonromantic verse compliments. For example, a poetic triptych on "Mistresse Susanna Southwell" is actually a catalog of beauties broken down into individual (and metrically distinctive) epigrams on Susanna's cheeks, eyes, and feet (H-523, H-524, H-525). Other poems, such as those to a Mary Willand (H-516), a Margaret Falconbridge (H-789), and the wife of the poet's brother Nicholas, Susanna Herrick (H-977), are variations upon a major theme of *Hesperides,* the eternizing power of poetry. They stand as testimonies to Herrick's serene self-confidence, his conviction that form takes precedence over content, that so long as one's "Numbers" were "sweet," then their poet and his subjects (however ordinary) "With endless life are crown'd" (H-201, l. 52). And, in point of fact, if Mary Willand, Margaret Falconbridge, and Susanna Herrick did indeed put their trust in good verses, that trust has been repaid.

Immortality is not one of the many alleged benefits of teaching, but what Ben Jonson did for the renowned master of Westminster School, William Camden, Herrick does for an otherwise unsung female educator in the rather pedantically titled "The School or Perl of Putney, the Mistress of all singular manners, Mistresse Portman" (H-1080). It is one of the poet's longer compliment-poems, and those compliments are lavish. Miss Portman is called "the *Reverend Rectresse*" who is "(As with a *Magick*)" able both to inspire the young women in her charge and to offer them "precepts" (ll. 15, 19, 18). The college at

14. Ibid., 61 n.

Putney is, like Herrick's book, a world unto itself, *"(A happy Realme! When no compulsive Law, / Or fear of it, but Love keeps all in awe)"* (ll. 19–20). Few personages in Herrick's book are so amply praised as this schoolmistress whose Christian name even is uncertain.[15] "Live you," he charges, *"great Mistresse* of your Arts, and be / A nursing Mother so to Majesty" (ll. 21–22). With Herrick's final compliment, in loco parentis acquires a new dimension: speaking of Miss Portman's students, he exclaims: "One Birth their Parents gave them; but their new, / And better Being, they receive from You" (ll. 25–26). The deification of aristocrats and royals is, of course, a commonplace of versified flattery in the Renaissance. Herrick's poem, however, may be the only one of this period to represent a "mere" schoolmistress, one of the age's few career women, in terms normally reserved for mere titled celebrities, the blue-blooded rout of countesses and queens.

Both queens and shepherdesses have always figured importantly in the pastoral tradition. In the hands of the likes of Spenser, Jonson, Herrick, Marvell, and even Milton (specifically in "L'Allegro/Il Penseroso"), pastoral, which is always in danger of becoming clichéd, was revivified and "Englished," transformed into a vehicle for a wide range of literary functions and into a literary mode in which the mythic landscape of Arcadia and the authentic scenes of the English countryside met and melded. "Corinna's going a-Maying" (H-178) is the most famous instance of Herrick's tendency to synthesize ancient and modern bucolics.

Less well known is a pair of pastorals where the classical tradition is domesticated in the person of a young woman of rural Devonshire.[16] "The meddow verse or Aniversary to Mistris Bridget Lowman" (H-354) and the poem that immediately follows it, "The parting verse, the feast there ended" (H-355), record the celebration of a particular May Day in England's West Country and celebrate Bridget Lowman as queen of the festivities. Bridget is a Corinna who has gotten out of bed: "COme with the Spring-time, forth Fair Maid, and be / This year again, the *medows Deity*" (H-354, ll. 1–2). She is "the Prime, and Princesse of the Feast," with an entourage of "sweet-breath Nimphs," and the "Lady of this Fairie land" (H-354, ll. 6, 8)—rude Devon raised to the mythic.

In the space between these two pastorals, May Day has wound down, and the mood of celebration turns, in Herrick's sequel, to one of fatalistic melancholy,

> LOath to depart, but yet at last, each one
> Back must now go to's habitation:

15. Ibid., 360 n.
16. Ibid., 431 n.

> Not knowing thus much, when we once do sever,
> Whether or no, that we shall meet here ever.
>
> (ll. 1–4)

And self-pity:

> As for my self, since time a thousand cares
> And griefs hath fil'de upon my silver hairs;
> 'Tis to be doubted whether I next yeer,
> Or no, shall give ye a re-meeting here.
>
> (ll. 5–8)

But where there's poetry, there's hope:

> If die I must, then my last vows shall be,
> You'l with a tear or two, remember me,
> Your sometime Poet; but if fates do give
> Me longer date, and more fresh springs to live:
> Oft as your field, shall her old age renew,
> *Herrick* shall make the meddow-verse for you.
>
> (ll. 9–14)

Bridget Lowman's name begins the sequence and Robert Herrick's concludes it: the ordinary English girl elevated to Queen of the May, the humble country parson aspiring to poet. As pastoral lyrist he is able to transform "loathed Devonshire" into "Fairie land," a rustic holiday into an occasion at once subject to "Times trans-shifting" and transcendent, and this niece of an obscure rural knight into a representation of the muse.[17] On the other hand, Bridget's historical actuality (like Herrick's) serves to locate these poems at an intersection of real time and real space—not as snapshots do, exactly, but as Seurat's pointillist masterpiece, *La Grande Jatte*, does—by permanently capturing the evanescence of a holiday moment.

Arcadia and England also merge in three poems in which Herrick transforms a relative of his into a pastoral nymph. That fusion is made explicit—again, by naming—in the title of "Upon Mistresse Elizabeth Wheeler, under the name of Amarillis" (H-130). Herrick's first name and his lyric craft are artfully concealed in this little fable about a *"Robin"* that "chirpt for joy" when he discovered that "Sweet *Amarillis*" is only sleeping and not dead.

More serious in tone is the second poem of this widely dispersed trio, the pastoral complaint, "Mistresse Elizabeth Wheeler, under the name of the lost

---

17. Ibid., 190 n.

Shepardesse" (H-263). Here "Love" tells the speaker that "all [his] hopes" of
the lady "must wither," like the flowers he has plucked to make a garland for
her. Most seventeenth-century readers would not know that Herrick's "love"
is doomed because Elizabeth is in fact his married cousin. They, then, could
appreciate the pastoral as a romantic enhancement of what might have been
an actual affair, whereas readers in the know could savor the poem as a bucolic
tour de force, a kinship compliment disguised as a love complaint.

Most traditional of the three pastorals to the same cousin is "A Dialogue
betwixt himselfe and Mistresse Elizabeth Wheeler, under the name of Amarillis"
(H-1068). Here again the deliberate confusion of fiction and fact conveyed by
the poem's highly explicit title is compounded by Herrick's arrangement of his
eclogue: Elizabeth's lines are indicated by the abbreviation *Amaril.*[lis], while
the poet speaks out in his own name—*Her.*[rick]—at once deconstructing
the eclogue's literary conventionality and its basis in Herrickean reality. Here
too readers of unannotated editions of *Hesperides* could be forgiven if they
imagined that real lovers' sweet sorrow has inspired this poem of parting.

What is certain, however, is that this trio of bucolic lyrics do for an otherwise
anonymous commoner what a pastoral court masque could do for a titled
lady—translate her individuality into archetype, her reality into myth. To their
subject these poems express the courtliness of one relative toward another,
but they exemplify as well the sincerest form of flattery, the kind intended as
courtesy that is not for sale.

Like Herrick's poems to Mrs. Wheeler and Miss Lowman, "To Mistresse
Katherine Bradshaw, the lovely, that crowned him with Laurel" (H-224) domes-
ticates the classical by focusing on a symbolic gesture by a female commoner.
It begins with Herrick again characterizing himself as a pastoral poet:

> MY Muse in Meads has spent her many houres,
> Sitting, and sorting severall sorts of flowers,
> To make for others garlands; and to set
> On many a head here, many a Coronet.
>
> (ll. 1–4)

"Crowning" others, the humble as well as the proud, with life immortal is
a cottage industry in Herrick's Hesperidean world. But how is eternity to be
guaranteed? Who can certify that a versifier is a true poet and thus capable
of granting "endless life?" Apparently the answer is an ordinary woman like
Katherine Bradshaw, but one who can appreciate Robert Herrick's muse:

> But, amongst All encircled here, not one
> Gave her a day of Coronation;
> 'Till you (sweet Mistresse) came and enterwove

> A *Laurel* for her, (ever young as love)
> You first of all crown'd her; she must of due,
> Render for that, a crowne of life to you.
>
> (ll. 5–10)

Whatever Herrick's reputation was in the earlier seventeenth century (the historical record is unclear here), it is certain that he was something less than one of that age's most eminent poets. It is understandable, then, how Katherine's formal and consciously classical valorization of his art, like Prudence Baldwin's more homely appreciation, would earn her the poet's grateful reciprocity.

Indeed, it is such gestures as this, or Prudence Baldwin's domestic kindnesses, or their virtue, that typically are responsible for the appearance of twenty-two untitled women as "saints" in Robert Herrick's "Poetick Liturgie" (H-510). (It is chiefly their youth and beauty that gain the admittance of all the Corrinas and Julias.) Kinship, as we have seen, can have something—but not everything—to do with it as well. But whatever the reasons for their presence in *Hesperides,* the representation in Herrick's collection of these actual women (along with the various identifiable male commoners who appear in other poems) brings us closer to the ordinary world of the seventeenth century than we get in the work of any other important poet. *Hesperides* is a mythic garden, an English Arcadia, but it is also a world of relatives and friends, female as well as male, and of an everyday life that, for Robert Herrick, turns out to be not so separate from the world of his art after all.[18]

18. My thanks to the Department of English, Clemson University, for support for this project, and especially to Mr. Brian Powell for his research assistance. This essay is dedicated to the memory of the distinguished seventeenth-century scholar and critic, editor of the poetry of Robert Herrick, and my longtime mentor, colleague, and friend, J. Max Patrick.

Sidney Gottlieb

An Collins and the Experience of Defeat

Let me be the first one to say it: the title of this volume—*Representing Women in Renaissance England*—is an optical illusion, like one of those images that you stare at that first seems to show a candlestick and then shows two profiles facing one another. As I stare at the title it first seems to urge that we consider how women represented themselves in the Renaissance and how we can represent them. Right before my eyes, though, the title then shifts and proposes that we address a somewhat broader theme and examine the newly emerging group of "representing women" in the Renaissance, women who represent not only themselves, their gender positions, their constructions, and their constructedness but also a variety of other topics in which gender is not the figure but the ground. I have not resolved or rejected this figure-ground oscillation. Instead, I have adopted it as a structuring principle in the essay that follows.

I focus on three increasingly expanding but consistently related areas. First, I briefly introduce An Collins, in part as an exercise in what Virginia Woolf was rightly so fascinated by, the genre—in fact, the highly gendered genre—that she called "the lives of the obscure."[1] Second, I attempt to summarize recurrent themes, images, attitudes, and dramas in Collins's poems, foregrounding as much as possible gender issues, such as her particular sensitivity to the vulnerability of her body; her struggle with contradictory imperatives, one urging patience, passivity, and silence, another urging active, even defiant testimony; and her ambivalent presentation of the human voice, which is the source of some of both her greatest pains—particularly in the form of the

1. Throughout this essay I draw from the introduction and commentary in my edition of An Collins, *Divine Songs and Meditacions* (Tempe, Ariz.: Medieval and Renaissance Texts and Studies, 1996). All quotations from Collins's poems are from this edition and are cited by line numbers in the body of my essay.

scolding, denying, and criticizing voices that surround and torment her—and her greatest pleasures, particularly as she affirms her own enduring, poetic, female, and godly voice.

Third, I turn to the topic indicated by my title, which alludes of course to Christopher Hill's study of "how some individuals coped with the experience of living through a revolution which they initially welcomed, and with the defeat of that revolution." In his introduction, Hill says that he "was disappointed not to be able to find any woman who left adequate evidence of her experience of defeat."[2] Collins, although no thoroughgoing radical, does provide adequate and compelling evidence. Her poetry is self-consciously situated in the often painful mid-seventeenth-century politics of reforming the reformation. She identifies herself as part of the godly, yet struggles with the many signs that the godly are afflicted and have lost direction and that the wicked have triumphed.

My turn to this broad topic illustrates that, for me, the study of gender is invariably the study of "gender and. . . ." I say this not to be dismissive or to relegate the female to the realm of the "supplemental," as some postmoderns might have it, but rather to emphasize the complex, overdetermined, and interconnected status of all human consciousness, all human activity. At the risk of making an easily misunderstood statement that may strike some readers as both memorable and—alas!—unforgivable, my operative assumption is that the category of gender is necessary but not sufficient for a comprehensive critique. Gender is not history, but is in history. Gender is not the social matrix, but is in the social matrix. Gender study is one key to a door with many locks. I hope that such premises appear to be truisms rather than fighting words—but truisms worth asserting. In any event, they lie behind my attempt in this essay to present one particularly intriguing "representing woman" of the seventeenth century via a critical method that uses the methodology of gender study as nontotalizing, oscillating between figure and ground, and invariably embedded, like the work it attempts to describe, in a larger analytic and interpretive project.

An Collins is in most respects a poet nearly anonymous. We know nothing about her apart from what we can glean from one book, *Divine Songs and Meditacions,* which survives in only one copy, held by the Huntington Library. Although the volume contains an autobiographical address to the reader and tantalizingly personal comments throughout the poems, this information is both skimpy and slippery. The book is dated 1653 and published in London by Richard Bishop, but this still does not help us place her exactly: we do not

2. Christopher Hill, *The Experience of Defeat: Milton and Some Contemporaries* (New York: Penguin, 1985), 17, 21.

know the circumstances of its publication, at what point in the author's life it was published (or indeed if it was published at or after her death, like the volumes of some other religious poets), when the poems in the volume were written, or where the author lived.

What, then, do we know—or imagine we know—about An Collins? From the evidence of her writings, she may have been sickly, even homebound or bedridden. Physical affliction is a common trope for devotional writers, a predictable metaphor that helps describe the uneasy but ultimately triumphant journey from this world to the next. But one senses that illness, weakness, and bodily pain were more than devotional or expressive devices for Collins, not only because of her specific references to having been "restrained from bodily employments," her "retired Course of Life" ("To the Reader"), and confinement to her house because of "weakness" ("The Preface"), but especially because the experience of pain and vulnerability is central in her poems, in all her attempts to understand her temporal and spiritual life.

Suffering does not, of course, necessarily generate great or even interesting writing, and some of her verses are commonplace discourses on topics such as how "sufferings are of speciall use" ("A Song exciting to spirituall alacrity," l. 60). But sometimes her complaints strike fire. The opening of "Another Song" ("Excessive worldly Greife"), for example, is a logically structured meditation on a familiar topic—that virtue is not rewarded and sometimes not even respected during one's lifetime—but it is also a haunting and emotionally exacting confession of how difficult it is to argue away the shame imposed by an unjust world:

> Excessive worldly Greife the Soule devouers
> And spoyles the activenesse of all the Powers,
> Through indisposing them to exercise
> What should demonstrate their abilities,
> By practicall improvment of the same
> Unto the Glory of the givers name.
> Though Envy wait to blast the Blossoms green
> Of any Vertu soon as they are seen,
> Yet none may therfore just occasion take
> To shun what Vertu manifest should make,
> For like the Sun shall Vertu be beheld
> When Clouds of Envy shall be quite dispeld;
> Though there be some of no disart at all
> Who no degree in worth can lower fall,
> Prefer'd before the Verteous whom they taunt
> Onely because of some apparent want,
> Which is as if a Weed without defect
> Before the Damask Rose should have respect,

> Because the Rose a leafe or two hath lost,
> And this the Weed of all his parts can boast;
> Or elce as if a monstrous Clout should be
> Prefer'd before the purest Lawn to see,
> Because the Lawn hath spots and this the Clout
> Is equally polluted thoroughout.
>
> (ll. 1–24)

We shall perhaps never know the details of what may well have been a physical disability, real or hypersensitively imagined, that lies behind the experience and figures described in these lines: do the "spots" on the "purest Lawn," for example, allude to the common scars of smallpox? does the "Rose" that "a leafe or two hath lost" call to mind a bodily part missing or paralyzed? Throughout the volume Collins is somewhat vague and indirect about her physical condition and what specifically caused her retirement and restraint from "bodily employments" ("To the Reader," ll. 1–2), but she is always precise about her sense of physical vulnerability, and she argues plaintively and forcefully that while the "want of comlinesse" ("A Song manifesting The Saints eternall Happinesse," l. 24) is often the humiliating taunt of the ungodly, it is not the measure of spiritual perfection. In "A Song declaring that a Christian may find tru Love only where tru Grace is," she affirms that

> . . . internall ornaments,
> Will ever lovely make him
> Though all things pleasing outward sence
> Should utterly forsake him.
>
> (ll. 93–96)

And in the lengthy passage from "Excessive worldly Greife" quoted above, Collins links and anatomizes both physical and spiritual pain, and what might easily have become an abstract protest about the wicked world mocking or rejecting the godly, a merely pathetic complaint about the strong taunting the weak, or a superficial contrast of secular and sacred beauty becomes a multileveled dramatic argument that is emotionally charged, brave, and broadly applicable as well as subtly gendered: it is no surprise, to Collins or to us, that in seventeenth-century England a woman would be particularly sensitive to such taunts about "comlinesse," feelings of bodily deformity and vulnerability, and worries about the relationship between physical and spiritual grace.[3]

---

3. See Diane Purkiss, "Producing the Voice, Consuming the Body: Women Prophets of the Seventeenth Century," in Isobel Grundy and Susan Wiseman, eds., *Women, Writing, History, 1640–1740* (Athens: University of Georgia Press, 1992), 139–58.

Her faith always assures her that pain has both a meaning and an end, and this makes her, like George Herbert, a poet of not only the vagaries of but also recovery from affliction. But her knowledge of the ultimate triumph of the holy through God's abundant grace never effaces her sense of vulnerability. As we see in her finest poem of affliction, "Another Song" ("The Winter of my infancy"), the struggle to "persevere / In Piety and Holynesse" (ll. 56–57) is often a delicate balance of patient and anxious waiting, characterized by both unexpected disappointments and unexpected rewards.

Helen Wilcox briefly describes Collins as a "poet who writes from an avowedly passive femininity,"[4] but Collins is no statue of Patience. On the contrary, her boldness is evident throughout the volume, and this quality will be of particular interest to those studying Collins not only as an individual devotional poet but also in the context of the development of women's writing and the expression of their "voices" in seventeenth-century England. Perhaps most obviously, her boldness is manifested in her repeated defense of her writing. Elaine Hobby notes how frequently in Collins's volume "Writing is described . . . as a delightful and empowering activity for the author."[5] Besides being an enjoyable task, one to which she was "called," writing serves several worthwhile purposes: returning praise to God and testifying to God's grace and glory ("the fruits of righteousnesse / We to the glory of God must expresse," she says in "A Song shewing the Mercies of God to his people," ll. 19–20); drawing "neare Kindred" or others who may happen across the book closer to the holy Scriptures, which figure prominently in the poems; and establishing her life as an exemplary model demonstrating that grace is given even to believers who are afflicted or of low status (see "The Discourse," ll. 29–56). It is interesting to note that each of these purposes has a socializing component: the act of writing is interactive, characteristically associated with the formation of extended families and communities of the godly.

Collins admits that others may be more capable and knowledgeable, "Directed by a greater Light," "Yet this cannot prevayl to hinder me / From publishing those Truths I do intend" (see "The Preface," ll. 85–98). Spiderlike readers, full of venom, may willfully misunderstand her, but more sympathetic readers, like bees making honey, will excuse her defects and profit from her holiness and sincerity (see "The Preface," ll. 113–26). Finally, she must write to show that she is not intimidated by the pressures of the ungodly or the

4. Helen Wilcox, "An Collins," in Elspeth Graham et al., eds., *Her Own Life: Autobiographical Writings by Seventeenth-Century Englishwomen* (New York: Routledge, 1989), 56.
5. Elaine Hobby, *Virtue of Necessity: English Women's Writing, 1649–88* (Ann Arbor: University of Michigan Press, 1989), 59. I disagree, though, with Hobby's subsequent description of Collins as habitually "calling for retreat from argument" and her retirement from public concerns (60).

recurrent frustrations in the rhythm of the holy life, as she does here in "A Song demonstrating The vanities of Earthly things":

> Shall Sadness perswade me never to sing
> But leave unto Syrens that excellent thing,
> No that may not be . . . .
>
> (ll. 1–3)

That simple but hard-earned "No that may not be" is a resounding anthem for a devotional poet, and especially so for one who is a woman.

Her boldness is evident not only in her decision to write but also in the particular topics she addresses. Her constant emphasis on knowledge, for example, both implicitly and explicitly contests the conventional pronouncements on women's limited intellectual capacity. In several places she issues a commonplace warning against "vain knowledge," part of her continuing argument against the misdirected energies of the ungodly (see, for example, "A Song demonstrating The Vanities of Earthly things," especially ll. 25–32), but one of her central premises is the statement in "The Discourse" that "holy Zeal . . . must with knowledg dwell" (l. 202). She is a deeply meditative poet, and her meditative method—which directs and structures her lyrics as well as her poems titled "Meditacions"—is based on finely developed skills of observation, rational analysis, and thoughtful judgment.[6] These skills are perfectly consistent with faith and help lead one to "right information" ("The Preface," l. 90) and "saving Knowledg" ("Another Song" ["Having restrained Discontent"], l. 37). Throughout the volume, Collins's precepts and especially her example affirm that knowledge is every bit as much the woman's as the man's part.

The final and in some ways most pervasive sign of her boldness that I will discuss is her attention to current controversies, both theological and political. Collins notes in several places how she was restricted, through illness, to her home, but she resists this particular counterpart to the more pervasive cultural relegation of women to the domestic sphere by commenting throughout her poems on public issues and events. She may have been a beneficiary of the general freeing-up of published discourse during the Civil War period, which helped account for what Hobby calls "the first great outpouring of women's

---

6. Several of Collins's poems (for example, "This Song sheweth that God is the strength of his People," and the first, second, and fifth "Meditacion") follow the tripartite meditative structure described by Louis L. Martz in *The Poetry of Meditation: A Study in English Religious Literature of the Seventeenth Century*, rev. ed. (New Haven: Yale University Press, 1962). But Collins's volume also shows the influence of the Reformation biblical poetics and models of meditation described in Barbara Kiefer Lewalski, *Protestant Poetics and the Seventeenth-Century Religious Lyric* (Princeton: Princeton University Press, 1979).

published writings in English," many of which address current affairs and issues.[7]

One such theological issue is mortalism. Collins seems particularly exercised by the claim, often associated with radicals of the time, that the soul dies with the body and is revived only later in a resurrection at the end of time. In the concluding poem of the volume, "Verses on the twelvth chapter of *Ecclesiastes*," she introduces a long digression (ll. 47–72) chastising those who with overly subtle human ingenuity and no scriptural warrant "vent their falacy" that the soul and body remain "Dead till judgment-generall" (l. 58). Throughout her poems Collins anchors herself on the power, stability, endurance, and godly connection of the human soul, so it is perfectly consistent that she would deny any claim that the vulnerable body might drag the soul with it, however temporarily, into a limbo of death. The chapter from Ecclesiastes that she is versifying does not specifically raise the question of what happens to the soul at death, but perhaps the grim images of death and decay in the biblical text alongside the repeated warnings against apparently irrepressible human vanity are easily associated in Collins's mind with contemporary mortalists, who strike her as dangerous and ungodly imposters (l. 53) and deceivers (l. 73). Unintimidated by controversy, she answers her adversaries directly, "Truth for to defend" (l. 74).

While Collins foregrounds the devotional realm in her poems, this overlaps rather than excludes what more modern ages would describe as the world of politics. For example, her descriptions of the spiritual and moral vanity and envy of the ungodly often shade into sketches of a "gracelesse crew" ("A Song declaring that a Christian may finde tru Love only where tru Grace is," l. 65) that confiscates property, breaks up familial and social harmony, and misinforms the common people ("Another Song" ["Time past we understood by story"], ll. 36–37) about what true reformation is.

Rather than taking a full inventory of such allusions, let me conclude by focusing briefly on one poem that is an interesting blend of the topical and the personal, that shows Collins reflecting on her predicament as a faithful woman writing under spiritual, political, and social duress. With the exception of technical and stylistic variety and experimentation, which one can find elsewhere in the volume,[8] much of what may interest us in Collins coalesces in "A Song composed in time of the Civill War, when the wicked did much insult over the godly."[9] This poem offers a commentary on a particularly troubling

7. Elaine Hobby, " 'Discourse So Unsavoury': Women's Published Writings of the 1650s," in Grundy and Wiseman, *Women, Writing, History,* 16.

8. See, for example, "A Song shewing the Mercies of God to his people," "Another Song exciting to spirituall Mirth," and "Another Song" ("The Winter of my infancy").

9. Stanley N. Stewart did not include this poem in his facsimile reprint of a selection of Collins's poems because "its subject matter was not thought representative of the work as a whole." See An

moment of civil war disruption; a vision of impending apocalypse that will take one beyond the pressing tensions and contradictions of history, both personal and political; and a close analysis of what a woman poet may and, indeed, must do in the sad time before the apocalypse.

The poem has a three-part structure, and begins with Collins carefully assessing different options available to her as a woman poet. She cannot see the specific details of the future, she says, like *"Sibells"* (l. 1): perhaps this is her way of distancing herself from the many, often-unruly women prophets and visionary petitioners of the 1640s and 1650s,[10] although by the end of the poem she has adopted a poetics of prophetic vision. Neither will she "with *Parnassus* Virgins Nine / Compose in Poëms neat" (ll. 2–3), presumably wasting her time with mere fantasies, "mental mocions" (l. 5) and "free / Concepcions of the mind" (ll. 5–6). Deborah, the biblical prophetess, warrior, ruler, and poet of Judges 4:5, presents a much more attractive poetic model for Collins, but she is concerned that if, like Deborah, one waits to sing until the contemporary troubles have ended, until "the Land hath Rest" (l. 10), one might spend an entire lifetime lingering in silent expectation. The obligation, then, is to "speak / Betimes in Truths defence" (ll. 17–18). There is no historical name or biblical analog given to identify this option: perhaps Collins recognizes that her proposal is in some respects unprecedented.

The second section of the poem (ll. 25–64) gives a quick picture of the malicious and energetic "Foes of Truth" (l. 25). Collins at first relies heavily on the conventional and predictable vocabulary of moral allegory and satire, broadly envisioning the wicked as ambitious followers of Satan, enemies of life who sow seeds of error (l. 35), tempt others to "false Worships" (l. 36), and support their "Errors" by false application of Scriptures (ll. 37–40). But she then moves to more precise contemporary references:

> And to bind Soul and Body both
> To Sathans service sure
> Therto they many ty by Oath,
> Or cause them to endure
> The Losse of lightsom Liberty
> And suffer Confiscacion,

Collins, *Divine Songs and Meditacions* (1653), Augustan Reprint Society, number 94 (Los Angeles: William Andrews Clark Memorial Library, 1961), iii. While "A Song composed in time of the Civill Warr" is indeed more directly topical than most of the other poems in the volume, we cannot take the full measure of Collins's intentions and achievement without closely examining this poem in particular and the historical density and allusiveness of her poems in general.

10. For important discussions of mid-seventeenth-century women prophets, see Hobby, *Virtue of Necessity*, 26–53, and Phyllis Mack, *Visionary Women: Ecstatic Prophecy in Seventeenth-Century England* (Berkeley and Los Angeles: University of California Press, 1992), especially 87–124.

> A multitude they force therby
> To hazard their Salvacion.
>   (ll. 41–48)

The parliamentary government tried to use various oaths as a way to impose obedience, culminating in the widely controversial Engagement Oath of January 1650. Such oaths were resisted as an affront to both political and religious freedom by many, not only by Royalists but also by radical sects such as the Quakers.[11] Royalists and radicals faced "The Losse of lightsom Liberty" by imprisonment during the early 1650s, and although it was the Royalists whose estates were sequestered and compounded by the 1649–1653 Rump Parliament eager to punish its enemies and meet its expenses, "Confiscacion" (l. 46) may also generally allude to the economic sanctions (such as tithes) that all were bound to pay for religious and governmental institutions and services that many did not support. Collins has been called a conservative and a Royalist,[12] but her broad theme is "insults" to all people of good conscience, by no means exclusively or specifically Royalists. It is thus far more accurate to describe her poem as a radical protest rather than a protest against the radicals.

Collins envisions a variety of "Enimies / To Lady Verity" (ll. 49–50), including those

> . . . who no Religion prise,
> But Carnall Liberty
> Is that for which they do contest
> And venture Life and State,
> Spurning at all good meanes exprest,
> The force of Vice to bate.
>   (ll. 51–56)

11. Hill emphasizes the amorphousness of Quakers in the early 1650s and suggests that "There must have been many early 'Quakerisms' " (*The Experience of Defeat*, 130). It is intriguing to note how much Collins shares with what we know of these "early 'Quakerisms' ": she is nonpredestinarian, critical of fixed forms of worship, occasionally "puritanical" and moralizing, attuned to what she frequently describes as a personal inner light, apocalyptic, committed to the "Good Old Cause" of reformation, ever ready to do combat in print with enemies of the godly (whether carnal or spiritual), more impressed by the need for continual trial rather than reliance on assured perseverance, deeply aware of being alienated from and even shunned by "respectable" secular society, and both consoled and cheered by the only earthly society that matters—the community of godly saints and friends. Modern scholars have emphasized the variety of ways in which seventeenth-century Quakerism enhanced the role of women in the godly community and contributed substantially to the development of women as prophets and writers. See Mack, *Visionary Women*, 127–261, on the midcentury period; and Mack, 265–402, and Margaret J. M. Ezell, *Writing Women's Literary History* (Baltimore: Johns Hopkins University Press, 1993), 132–60, on the later seventeenth century.

12. Hobby, for example, says that in general Collins promotes "a particular (and reactionary) political ideology" (*Virtue of Necessity*, 60); and both Stewart, in the introduction to his facsimile (iv n. 6), and Wilcox ("An Collins," 55) argue that "A Song composed in time of the Civill Warr" is critical of essentially disruptive and innovative radical parliamentarians.

Throughout her poems she criticizes the "carnall crew," whose concern for a freedom of desire and material possession sets them beyond the pale of any religion. Her description of the wicked here may very well allude to Independents, Diggers, Levellers, Ranters, or other such groups who were petitioning, agitating, and even fighting for freedom just then. She may also be glancing at displaced Royalists, the libertines of the Cavalier court in exile in France. Whoever these enemies are, the deepest irony and greatest danger is that they are in power or must be relied upon to restore order:

> Yet these are they, as some conceit,
>   Who must again reduce,
> And all things set in order strait
>   Disjoynted by abuse,
> And wakeing witts may think no lesse
>   If Fiends and Furies fell,
> May be suppos'd to have successe
>   Disorders to expell.
>
>   (ll. 57–64)

Between 1649 and 1654 there was a fluctuating ascendancy of Presbyterians, Levellers, Independents, generals, grandees, and self-styled saints, any of whom she might suspect and accuse. Even without knowing the particulars, the basic picture is clear: the government—and perhaps even more broadly speaking, the promised reformation—is now in the hands of the devils.

That this is only a temporary triumph of the wicked over the godly is confirmed in the final section of the poem (ll. 65–104). Truth may appear to fade, "Yet can shee never fall" (l. 66), and though the friends of truth will "seem wasted all" (l. 67), a holy remnant will persist and arise to "vindicate" "Truth," "Wronged Right," and "Order" (ll. 70–72). She herself is part of the truth-telling "holy Seed" (l. 69), and one of her tasks is to describe the foreseeable "perfect Day" (l. 76) of abundant light, blessings, and knowledge when "The *Cause* that's now derided so, / Shall then most just be found" (ll. 79–80). Hill shrewdly notes that in the 1650s "The rhetoric of God's Cause could not conceal that there was no longer agreement as to what the Cause was."[13] Collins powerfully evokes the apocalyptic realization of this cause without giving us the particulars we may long for. Still, we understand that her language is that of one who has had great hopes for the success of the godly, endured an assault on these hopes as "Reformacion" turned back to "Prophanacion,"[14] and finally

---

13. Hill, *The Experience of Defeat*, 189.

14. This process is described in more detail in the next poem in the volume, "Another Song" ("Time past we understood by story"), in many ways a necessary companion piece to "A Song composed in time of the Civill Warr."

achieved a sustaining vision that "Prophanesse" and its defenders "Must be ruind or overthrown" (ll. 81–83), a phrase that is both an imperative and a prophecy.

The traditional signs of the apocalypse are not yet visible, but they are imminent: the ascendance of the Son of Peace, the arrival of bright, "auspicious dayes," the conversion of the Jews, the fall of the "Man of Sin," and the destruction of "New Babell" (ll. 87–96). The poem ends, though, not with the cosmic and dramatic but with the local, personal, communal, and understated, and an intimation that the redemptive future penetrates the mundane present:

> Then Truth will spread and high appeare,
>   As grain when weeds are gon,
> Which may the Saints afflicted cheare
>   Oft thinking hereupon;
> Sith they have union with that sort
>   To whom all good is ty'd
> They can in no wise want support
>   Though most severely try'd.
>   (ll. 97–104)

If we ever have more information available, we may be able to identify Collins's political and religious affiliations with more confidence and come up with a more precise interpretation of this poem and its many teasing references. Until then, we may have to let it stand as a somewhat indeterminate but still evocative and multilayered rendering of personal and political affliction, of the strain and success of faith in an age of adversity, of the experience of defeat—a phrase that despite its somewhat dour, desperate sound, calls our attention to qualities of resiliency, creative accommodation, and artistic and expressive as well as physical and emotional courage. These are indeed some of the qualities that recommend not only this poem but the entire volume of An Collins's *Divine Songs and Meditacions* to us today.

Stella P. Revard

KATHERINE PHILIPS, APHRA BEHN, AND THE FEMALE PINDARIC

In 1683, *Triumphs of Female Wit* appeared on the London scene, a slender volume that contained three Pindaric odes and a "Preface to the Masculine Sex" defending the right of women to pursue learning and most especially to use their wit to compose poetry. The first ode, "The Emulation," purports to be "Written by a Young Lady" and argues the case for female poets, maintaining that "the *Muses* gladly will their aid bestow, / And to their Sex their charming Secrets show" (5).[1] The ode following, ascribed to a Mr. H, challenges not only the rights the Young Lady claims for her sex but also her temerity in claiming these rights in a poetic form reserved, he asserts, for masculine composition.

> What daring *Female* is 't who thus complains,
> In *Masculine* Pindarick Strains,
> Of great *Apollo's Salique* Laws,
> Both breaks it, and pretends that she
> Pleads only for her Native Liberty.
>
> (6)

It is not astonishing that a gentleman-poet of this era should argue against female rights, but it is rather astonishing that he should carry his argument even to the point of denying a specific verse form to females, claiming Pindaric ode and its poet (Pindar) for an all male preserve of pure poetry. We might ask

---

1. I am grateful to Warren Cherniak for his illuminating discussions on Aphra Behn and her place in the Restoration. See his book: *Sexual Freedom in Restoration England* (Cambridge: Cambridge University Press, 1995). My thanks also to Achsah Guibbory and Robert Hinman, who read an early version of this paper and offered helpful commentary. *Triumphs of Female Wit, In Some Pindarick Odes, or The Emulation. Together with an Answer to an OBJECTOR against Female Ingenuity, and Capacity of Learning. Also, A Preface to the Masculine Sex, by a Young Lady* (London: T. Malthus, 1683). I am indebted to Warren Cherniak for pointing out this collection to me.

indeed whether Mr. H's words are only an address to the presumptuous Young Lady of the Pindaric or whether in truth he was aiming his objections at one of the most celebrated women poets of the 1680s, a poet who was in fact employing Pindarics for a wide range of her verses, which were on many occasions as diverse as saluting fellow poets on their work to addressing compliments to the king himself. The woman poet was, of course, Aphra Behn, not only the leading poet-playwright of her time but also, following in the footsteps of Abraham Cowley, its leading Pindarist.

With the publication of his *Pindarique Odes* in 1656, Cowley largely invented the genre as it came to be practiced in the seventeenth century. His odes in irregular metrical patterns and irregularly numbered stanzas or sections were free imitations of the ancient Greek poet, and in the posthumous *Works* published in 1668 became his favorite form of address to a poetic subject. Two of his 1668 Pindarics were directed, in fact, to Katherine Philips, the first in commendation of her poems, the second commemorating her death. That both poems use the Pindaric genre to celebrate a woman poet is not without interest to us, for both Pindarics raise many of the same questions about women and poetry that the 1683 volume, *Triumphs of Female Wit,* raises—that is, the acceptability of a woman pursuing learning and contesting in the domain of poetry that had been almost exclusively male.

Katherine Philips's success as a poet is one of the arguments that Mr. F, the writer of the third Pindaric in the collection, uses to assert that women should be permitted access, along with males, to learning since they could be, like Philips—that is, Orinda—successful as poets. Mr. F, adopting a female persona in this Pindaric, pleads: "Did good Apollo e're deny / Charms to *Orinda's* Poetry?" (13). In both his Pindarics Cowley ostensibly takes the same position on Philips and her poetry. He has come, after all, to praise and to use the Pindaric medium to render that praise.[2] But the very questions that he raises about Philips and her poetry illustrate the difficulty that a male poet has in praising a woman who is neither a mistress nor a patron nor a sovereign, but is, rather, a so-called peer in the poetic profession. In assessing the acceptability of a woman as a poetic equal, Cowley faces some of the same stumbling blocks that the three Pindaric poets grapple with in *Triumphs of Female Wit.* A man's view of a "learned" woman almost always involves a man's view of women in general, and assessment of her literary achievement cannot take place without considering the acceptability of her competing "equally" in the domain of

2. Robert Hinman describes Cowley's pindarics on Philips as unqualified praise: "his lofty eulogy of the matchless Orinda's verse celebrates the emergence of woman as man's intellectual peer, and his elegy for her includes his view (also held by Milton) of the necessary relationship beween successful poetry and virtue." See *Abraham Cowley's World of Order* (Cambridge: Harvard University Press, 1960), 83–84.

poetic performance. At stake is more than the man's monopoly of wit. For if a man and a woman compete in a literary contest and he "loses," as a man he also loses the right to dominate in other areas. This is precisely what the Young Lady of the *Female Wit* volume argues.

> For should we understand as much as they,
>   They fear their Empire might decay.
>   For they know Women heretofore
> Gain'd Victories, and envied Laurels wore:
>   And now they fear we'll once again
>   Ambitious be to reign
> And to invade the Dominions of the Brain.
>
>   (2)

I do not doubt Cowley's real admiration for Katherine Philips nor the cordial relations between the two poets. Katherine Philips, after all, visited Cowley in his retirement at Chertsey and addressed a commendatory Pindaric to him, "Upon Mr. Abraham Cowley's Retirement" (*Poems* [London, 1667], 122–24). She not only expressed admiration for him as a man and poet but also conferred the additional compliment by addressing her words in a medium—the Pindaric—that Cowley had made his own.[3] In a way Cowley's Pindarics to Philips merely return the compliment in kind. I also recognize that the effusiveness of Cowley's address to Philips is part and parcel of the genre of commendatory poetry in the seventeenth century. In a genre marked by extravagance—a genre practiced by both male and female poets—it is difficult to sift out the sincere from the overweening compliment. But at issue here is not whether Cowley liked Katherine Philips and admired her poetry. Jean Loiseau contends convincingly that Cowley appreciated her virtue, her hatred of vice and ugliness, and her cultivation of pure and disinterested friendship.[4] But did he truly regard her, as both his poems say, as his equal as a poet? For this is the question: How was the female poet accepted vis-à-vis the male poet as a fellow practitioner of poetry? Was there a real equality in the arts? Not only Cowley but also the other poets who address poems to Philips maintain there was. Should we believe them?

Cowley's first Pindaric to Philips was one of two commendatory poems printed in the 1664 edition of Philips's *Poems;* it was reprinted together with the funeral ode in the 1667 edition of *Poems* along with a preface on her works and with other commendations of Philips by the earl of Orrery, the

---

3. For a description of the circumstances of Philips's visit, see Philip Webster Souers, *The Matchless Orinda* (Cambridge: Harvard University Press, 1931), 242. See "An ode upon retirement, made upon occasion of Mr. Cowley's on that subject," *The Collected Works of Katherine Philips, The Matchless Orinda,* ed. Patrick Thomas (Stump Cross, Eng.: Stump Cross Books, 1990), 1:193–95.

4. Jean Loiseau, *Abraham Cowley: sa vie, son oeuvre* (Paris: Henri Didier, 1931), 166.

earl of Roscommon, Philo-Philippa, James Tyrrell, and Thomas Flatman—
Tyrrell's and Flatman's odes were also in Pindarics.[5] All of the commendatory
poems, even that of Philo-Philippa—allegedly the only female voice—remark
on Philips's sex as well as her status as a poet. It seems an unavoidable issue. None
praise her simply as a poet. Like these other commendatory poems, Cowley's
Pindarics begin by looking at the woman first. The issue of sex becomes so
important a motif that the assessment of Philips as a poet takes second place. But
in this he is representative of most of Philips's male admirers; it was apparently
almost impossible in this era to be gender blind. Further, both of Cowley's
Pindarics emphasize the rivalry between men and women poets as well as the
rivalry between men and women. Beauty and wit are the themes, and they are
interconnected.

Almost inevitably involved in any consideration of a literary contest between
men poets and women poets is that of the amatory contest between men and
women, a contest in which men traditionally award the victory to women. As
Cowley noted in his anacreontic "Beauty," when women contest with men in
affairs of love, their advantage of beauty allows them to carry the day. No need
for them to put on arms in the contest of love; they win without them:

> Who can, alas, their strength express,
> Arm'd, when they themselves undress,
> *Cap-a-pe* with *Nakedness?*
> (ll. 21–23)[6]

What happens, however, when women seek to dominate in that other contest
too? In his first ode, "On *Orinda's* Poems," Cowley simply extends the amatory
to the literary contest, protesting that men who have been constrained to submit
to Woman's beauty must now—in the case of Orinda—submit to her wit:

> We allow'd You Beauty, and we did submit
>   To all the Tyrannies of it;
> Ah! Cruel Sex, will you depose us too in Wit?
>   *Orinda* does in that too raign,
> Does Man behind her in Proud Triumph draw,
> And Cancel great *Apollo's* Salick Law.
> (1:1–6)[7]

While connecting these two "supposed" contests appears at first to confer
a gracious compliment, it actually limits the woman that it seems to praise,

---

5. A facsimile of Philips's 1667 volume is now available. See *Poems (1667)* (New York: Scholars'
Facsimiles and Reprints, 1992).

6. "Anacreontiques," in *Miscellanies, The Works of Mr. Abraham Cowley* (London, 1668), 33.

7. Verses written on several occasions," *Works,* 2–4.

linking her wit to her beauty and confining her to a sphere where she is judged as a woman first and a poet second. Throughout this poem and its sequel, "On the Death of Mrs. *Katherine Philips*," Cowley never passes beyond the easy compliment to Philips's beauty and the virtues of her sex to evaluate the quality and substance of her poetry. The funeral Pindaric opens, like the ode "On *Orinda's* Poems," with a reference to Philips's beauty, deploring (as Dryden later deplored in his Pindaric for Anne Killigrew) that the smallpox that killed her assaulted first "The Throne of Empress Beauty, ev'n the Face" (1:8) before it overthrew "th' inward Holiest Holy of her Wit" (1:19). The funeral Pindaric is a lament for Philips's death; the first Pindaric, written when Philips was alive, purports, however, to be on Orinda's poetry, not on Orinda. Some of the other commendatory poems of the 1667 volumes at least mention one or another of Philips's works (often the ambitious translations of Corneille); Cowley makes no direct reference to either Philips's poetry or her translations.

Whereas it is not rare for commendatory poems to focus on the person, rather than on the work, Cowley in his complimentary poems to male writers and artists pays attention to the work also. When he addresses an ode to Thomas Hobbes, it is not Hobbes's virtue and wit that he praises, but Hobbes's accomplishment in having brought philosophy beyond the age of Aristotle into the modern era. Similarly, his Pindaric to Dr. Harvey may begin with an elaborate and showy amatory myth. But Cowley in comparing Harvey to Apollo pursuing Daphne is alluding to Harvey's scientific work, not to his amorous adventures. Like Apollo, Harvey pursued a Daphne-Nature until she revealed "her" secrets to him. The comparison leads us not to the man but to the scientist. In his poem "On the Death of Sir *Anthony Vandike, the famous Painter*" (*Miscellanies,* 9), Cowley is quite specific in applauding Van Dyke's excellence in drawing, considering the artist first, before he comments on the virtue of the man:

> His All-resembling *Pencil* did out-pass
> The mimick *Imag'ry* of *Looking-glass,*
> Nor was his *Life* less perfect than his *Art,*
> Nor was his *Hand* less *erring* than his *Heart*
> (ll. 15–18)

All these complimentary poems to men are extravagant; but all look at the artist, the writer, the scientist first, then at the man. But in his odes to Katherine Philips, he never lets us forget that we are looking at best at a most curious phenomenon—a woman who writes. Both odes dwell therefore on the qualities that most properly characterize woman: above all, beauty and virtue first and then wit—female wit.

In the first Pindaric, Cowley launches a witty protest that women possess an unfair advantage over men merely because they are women; their sex alone confers beauty, virtue, and fecundity—all female qualities. Now, in aspiring to wit, women conspire to take away the weapon that amorous male poets have used in the battlefield of love to secure themselves against women's natural advantages. The contest of the sexes is an antique one—going back at least to Ovid and his taking arms against the all conquering mistress and her artillery of beauty. Cowley tells us that Orinda has turned this contest topsy-turvy, now taking arms against men in the contest of wit too and, winning that, "she / Turn'd upon Love himself his own Artillery" (1:17). How seriously should we take this poetic sparring? These witty protests are little different from those the beaux of Restoration comedy use against the supposedly triumphant belles; Cowley has only removed the amatory combat to the realm of poetry. The compliments Cowley confers on Philips resemble those that Congreve's Mirabell resigns to Millamant. When Fainall comments, for example, that Millamant has wit, Mirabell retorts, "She has Beauty enough to make any Man think so; and Complaisance enough not to contradict him who shall tell her so" (*The Way of the World*, 1:i).[8] Apropos of this question of beauty and wit (but now on the subject of male and female poets), another quotation of Congreve springs to mind. In his "Notes on Ovid's Art of Love" Congreve once more resorts to an allusion to women's beauty as a measure for her wit, commenting on the rivalry between Pindar and the ancient Greek poetess Corinna, "who as we are told won the Prize of Poetry four or five Times from *Pindar;* however those that say so, own her Beauty contributed much to that Advantage."[9] We must be suspicious, therefore, of any reference to women's wit that couples it with an aside on her beauty. Cowley has done this consistently in the first two sections of the Pindaric. In section 3, when he appears at last to be discussing Philips's poetry—"thy well knit sense, / Thy numbers gentle, and thy Fancies high" (3:4–5)—he gives all away by once more linking Philips's poetic skills to her beauty, as he completes the rhyme: "Those as thy forehead smooth, these sparking as thine eye" (6).[10] This courtly game confers apparent victory

---

8. *The Way of the World* in *The Complete Works of William Congreve,* ed. Montague Summers (Soho: The Nonesuch Press, 1922), 3:18.

9. Congreve, "Notes to Ovid's Art of Love," *Works,* 4:130.

10. Also see the Earl of Orrery's poem to Philips that links poetry and love:

> In me it does not the least trouble breed,
> That your fair Sex does Ours in Verse exceed,
> Since every Poet this great Truth does prove,
> Nothing so much inspires a Muse as Love.
> (*Poems* [London, 1667], sig. b)

on women but reserves real power for men. By the very wit of his own verse, Cowley has demonstrated that neither Orinda nor any other female poet can carry away the laurels in a real contest of wit. Cowley retains supremacy, even as he "says" he gives it away.

Another issue in this contest between men and women is the question of women's "natural" creativity. Should you not be content, Cowley asks Philips, that Mother Cybele has made you fecund of womb (the sex's natural prerogative), but must you aspire to exceed men in being fecund of brain— men's (he would imply) natural prerogative. Again Cowley appears to award Philips supremacy in creative intellect, as in wit, as he comments how easily she brings forth the children of her brain. She has as many literary offspring as the prolific "*Holland* Countess" has children. But is it praise of a poet's prolific production to link it to another female's fecundity in the proper female sphere of reproduction? The comparison of these two kinds of "production" reminds us of one of the basic issues this age and those that follow often pondered: should women exercise creativity beyond the domestic sphere? Nature gave woman creative energy for the procreation of children, which, when employed elsewhere, may threaten that natural creativity. Mr. H in *Triumphs of Female Wit* reminds the Young Lady of Nature's true design for women's creative impulses: "But sure she ne're designed it / To make your Brains prolifick, or your wit" (7). Cowley never directly criticizes Philips's prolific production of poetry; he doesn't have to. Merely raising the question is enough to remind us that a woman's prolificacy can be misplaced.

Cowley reserves, however, as men traditionally do, his greatest praises for Philips's virtue. So preeminent is she in virtue that she wins through it victory not only over male poets but also over all previous female competitors:

> *Orinda's* inward virtue is so bright,
> That like a Lanthorn's fair inclosd Light,
> It through the Paper shines where she do's write.
> (4:7–9)

At this point Cowley comes as close as he ever does to commenting on Philips's poetry. He praises her mastery of the themes of "Honour and Friendship"; these are the "instructive Subjects of her pen" (4:14). But even here he is qualifying his praise, for he is suggesting that it is Philips's preeminence in virtue—woman's proper sphere—that makes her acceptable as a poet. In a poetical as well as a societal context, a woman may excel in virtue. In teaching "Arts, and Civility," she may be so successful that "she overcomes, enslaves, and betters Men" (4:16–17). Virtue is the highest thing that any woman poet—indeed any woman—can aspire to. In commending Philips's virtue as her supreme achievement, Cowley is not alone. Thomas Flatman sums Philips up in the last line of his Pindaric: "all that can be said of vertuous Woman was her due" (*Poems,* sig. f).[11] The best way for a man to deal with a woman competitor in poetry as in life is to deify her—and so remove her from the competition. Effectively, this is what Cowley does in the final section of "On *Orinda's* Poems." He places Philips in the special category of "virtuous" women. Comparing her to Boadicia—the warlike British queen who fought against, but failed to conquer, the Romans—he awards Philips the "Roman" victory in poetic arms that Boadicia coveted in battle. By deferring to yet another kind of contest, Cowley successfully evades the real question of women's place in poetry's and learning's sphere.

Cowley's funeral Pindaric takes up the same issue of Philips's poetic status, without arriving at any more satisfactory conclusion. It substitutes for the contest in arms of the first ode the famous beauty contest of the three goddesses for the apple. Here Apollo takes Paris's place as judge, presiding over a contest of literary merit and awarding Orinda the prize that Sappho and the Muses stand by and covet. Beauty is not ostensibly the issue here, but it can hardly be dismissed from the reader's mind, as Orinda wins the poetic apple, thereby becoming the "goddess of beauty" for the literary world. Cowley has also deftly confined the competition to woman against woman. Just as he had in the final sections of the previous ode when he alludes to Boadicia as the exemplar of the military "female," he allows Philips to excel in competition with other women.

> *Orinda* on the Female coasts of Fame,
> Ingrosses all the Goods of a Poetique Name.
> She does no Partner with her see,
> Does all the business there alone, which we

---

11. The Earl of Roscommon links Philips's supremacy in virtue to her supremacy in a virtuous game of love:

> Vertue (dear Friend) needs no defence,
> No arms, but its own innocence;
> Quivers and Bows, and poison'd darts,
> Are only us'd by guilty hearts.
>   (sig. b2)

James Tyrell links virtue and wit:

> Whether her Vertue, or her Wit
> We chuse for our eternal Theme,
> What hand can draw the perfect Scheme?
>   (sig. e)

When Milton published *Paradise Lost* in 1667, how many admirers linked his wit to his virtue and his beauty?

> Are forc'd to carry on by a whole Company.
> (3:16–20)

Any question of comparative talent or achievement or of admitting women poets into a competition with men Cowley simply bypasses. When he allows men into the competition, he couples wit with virtue. Virtue once more serves to assure Orinda the prize in this poem as in the last: "*Orinda* does our boasting Sex out-do, / Not in Wit only, but in Virtue too" (4:8–9). Cowley has so manipulated the terms of the contest that while seeming to award the highest poetic laurels to Philips, he has done no more than concede that she is the best of the *female* poets. By employing the language of courtly compliment for his address to Philips, he announces to his audience that he is engaging in the game of sexual diplomacy. The issue of Philips's status as a poet is never really entertained. Cowley confers only such supremacy in beauty and wit and virtue as men have always conferred on women whom they court poetically, reserving (tacitly) real intellectual superiority for males and male poets.

It is certainly no accident that many of the arguments that Cowley uses when he appears to compliment female wit reappear in *Triumphs of Female Wit*. There, however, Mr. H argues the countercase—women's inferiority in the intellectual sphere. Like Cowley, he is lavish with courtly compliment, graciously granting women supremacy in "captivating hearts." But in return for such supremacy women should be content to remain the object of wit and wisdom and must not dig and delve in "Apollo's mines." The last part of Mr. H's Pindaric takes up an issue that Cowley does not touch on, but one that both the Young Lady in "The Emulation" and Aphra Behn raise: the right of women to the education of the schools. The Young Lady protests:

> But they [men] refuse to let us know
> What sacred Sciences doth impart
> Or the mysteriousness of Art,
> In Learning's pleasing Paths deny'ed to go
> From Knowledge banish'ed, and their Schools;
> We seem design'd alone for useful Fools . . .
> (2:4–9)

She takes the view—in fact a Miltonic one—that knowledge is necessary to the confirmation of virtue and the progress of the soul. Women, after all, have souls just as worthy and noble as men. Mr. H counters her arguments fiercely, using in fact another Miltonic argument—Christ's from *Paradise Regained*—that knowledge does not in itself bestow virtue: " 'Tis not a studeous life that brings / Knowledge of revealed things" (6:9–10). In fact, he continues, women may be seeking at their soul's peril "that full view of intellectual Light" (7:4–5).

We are never far in the seventeenth century from the fatal tree of knowledge and the trespass of mother Eve against it. By seeking to gain the *"Tree of Knowledge,"* he cautions, women will surely lose the *"Tree of Life."* With biting sarcasm he commends their would-be quest:

> May you walk safe in Learnings milky way,
> Know all that Men and Angels say,
> Expand your Souls to Truth as wide as day.
>   (7:8–10)

But at the same time he warns the lady against ambitious pride—Eve's and Satan's sin. The learned Young Lady is firmly put in her place.

This lively debate over women's education is one in which Aphra Behn— the era's leading female poet after the death of Katherine Philips—also had a stake. In a Pindaric ode that she sent to Thomas Creech, commending the translation of Lucretius that he published in 1682, Behn raises the issue of women's exclusion from the universities. Behn's poem, however, is not per se a feminist protest. The ode is framed as a compliment to the learned Creech, a scholar at Wadham College, Oxford, and Creech published it with other commendatory poems in the reissue of his translation in 1683.[12] Whatever other issues Behn takes up, she is generous in looking first and foremost at Creech as a learned and accomplished translator of Lucretius. Both Behn's poem and the Young Lady's Pindaric appeared in the same year—the protest for women's education was something very much on the tongues of women in this decade. After Behn offers Creech the usual opening compliments on his work, she points out how his translation has brought the classical author, Lucretius, to a new set of readers—women. While she warmly thanks Creech for enlightening women such as herself, she ironically criticizes the system that has withheld classical authors from women by denying them education in Latin and Greek that would have enabled them to read him themselves.

That she chooses Pindaric ode as a verse form both for her compliments to the learned Creech and for her protest against the exclusion of women from the classics is yet another irony. For Behn could not have come to Pindar or the Pindaric ode—just as she could not have read Lucretius—on her own. To do so she needed the help of a learned man—in this case, Abraham Cowley, whom she

---

12. "To the Unknown DAPHNIS in his Excellent Translation of Lucretius," in *T. Lucretius Carus, The Epicurean Philosopher, His Six books. De Natura Rerum, Done into English VERSE with NOTES.* The Second Edition, Corrected and Enlarged. (Oxford: L. Lichfield, 1683). Behn's poem is signed and dated London, January 25, 1682. Behn published her own version of the ode in 1684; it was reprinted after her death in the 1697 edition: Mrs. A. Behn, *Poems upon Several Occasions; with a Voyage to the Island of Love* (London, 1697). Also see *The Works of Aphra Behn*, ed. Janet Todd (London: William Pickering, 1992). Todd cites a different version of the Creech ode.

openly acknowledges as her mentor in this mode.[13] The form of Pindaric ode that she wrote is, of course, the Cowleian Pindaric, whose metrical irregularities differ markedly from the absolute regularities of true Pindaric ode. It is a verse form that Cowley invented to approximate Pindaric ode and that poets of the seventeenth century, who, like Behn, lacked knowledge of Greek, followed, perhaps thinking that they were writing true Pindaric odes.

Behn's ode to Creech is couched in the courtliest of language. She learned not only her Pindarics from Cowley but also the art of playing at the game of courtly compliment. She addresses Creech as Daphnis and in speaking to and of him assumes the attitude of a shepherdess to an admired shepherd. Much of Behn's own verse was pastoral and courtly. Both in her plays and in her commendatory verse, Behn often plays the game of sexual politics, adopting the language of Ovidian love combat for her address to men and poets alike. In not relinquishing that artillery of love poetry in her poem to Creech, she imitates the tactics of male writers such as Cowley and their use of a smoke screen of overblown compliments. Behn poses in her address to Creech-Daphnis the kind of courtly rivalry that we saw in Cowley's own address to Philips.

Behn is the mistress of this coy game. She knows how to use the so-called advantages of her sex. Sometimes, however, she can be perfectly straightforward— even gender blind, as she addresses a fellow playwright, such as Edward Howard, warmly encouraging him not to forsake playwriting despite the failure of his play. On the other hand, when she addresses Rochester, whom she idolizes, she is all melting female before the superior master. She can be ambiguous also, as she is in her Pindaric ode to Dr. Burnet, and use courtly language not to compliment the man but to maintain a discreet distance from him and his importuning "Pen." Dr. Burnet was trying to persuade Behn to write an ode to welcome William III to the throne. Behn, who was a Jacobite loyal to the overthrown James II, plays the courtly game to refuse Burnet's request. She does this by assuming the part of the love-struck maid resisting the wit of a persuasive seducer. So she overpraises Burnet and underpraises herself as a poor weak female, thus neatly sidestepping Burnet's request and exposing his less than honorable purpose. This is exactly what we would expect from the author of *The Rover* and the love songs to Lysander, a lover whose insincerity and faithlessness she exposes in her own courtly fashion.

Thus, when we look at Behn's fulsome compliments in the Creech poem to the learned Daphnis, we may be just a little suspicious of her ultimate design. Is she criticizing the learned world of Oxford University that excludes women

---

13. In her pindaric to Dr. Burnet, Behn notes that she is following Cowley in the Pindaric mode, but has never ventured as high as he in the mode. *A PINDARIC POEM to the Reverend Doctor Burnet, on the Honour he did me of Enquiring after me and my MUSE* by A. Behn (London: R. Bentley, 1689).

from its portals even as she appears to compliment one of its shining lights? First of all, I do not doubt Behn's basic admiration for Creech and his translation of Lucretius. Her Pindaric goes beyond the easy courtly compliment: throughout she commends Creech's achievements in Englishing Lucretius in a correct and effective manner. However much she may flatter Creech in his persona as the young Daphnis, she pays him the ultimate tribute of dealing with his scholarship first, his pleasing person second. Although we need not suspect the sincerity of her praise, we cannot ignore gender considerations. Can a woman poet set aside the attitudes of the male establishment toward women when she addresses a man on the subject that necessarily involves the male exclusion of women? On the surface Behn deftly plays the part of a woman content to sit at Creech's feet and bask in the afterglow of his brilliance, accepting, as men like Mr. H in his rejoinder to the Young Lady advised, to humbly sup at the table of man's knowledge. "Thou great Young Man!" she begins,

> Permit amongst the Crowd
> Of those that sing thy mighty Praises lowd,
> My humble *Muse* to bring its Tribute too.
> (ll. 1–3)[14]

In an almost coquettish way she apologizes for her "Womannish Tenderness" (l. 14); she had intended to write a strong manly verse, but she is overcome by her emotion. Daphnis kindles a fire in admiring souls. Shepherds and nymphs alike "strow Garlands" at Daphnis's feet, for he conquers, not only in the art of verse but also in the arts of love.

> Advance young *Daphnis* then, and mayst thou prove
> Still Sacred in thy Poetry and Love.
> May all the Groves with *Daphnis* Songs be blest,
> Whilst every Bark is with thy Distichs drest.
> May Timerous Maids learn how to Love from thence
> And the Glad Shepherd *Arts of Eloquence.*
> (ll. 127–32)

Is it the man or the translator that Behn is praising as she crosses the boundary from the language of compliment to the language of courtship?

Amid her hyperbolic praise of Creech and his translations, Behn includes some comments on classical learning that can hardly reflect favorably on Creech and his Oxford peers. While in context her comments appear laudatory, she adds a personal history that tells us something different.

---

14. I quote from A. Behn, "To Mr. Creech," *Poems upon Several Occasions: With a Voyage to the Island of Love* (London, 1684), 50–57.

> Let them admire thee on—Whilst I this newer way
>   Pay thee yet more than they:
> For more I owe, since thou hast taught me more,
> Then all the mighty Bards that went before.
> Others long since have Pal'd the vast delight;
> In duller *Greek* and *Latin* satisfy'd the Appetite:
> But I unlearn'd in Schools, disdain that mine
> Should treated be at any Feast but thine.
>
> (ll. 17–24)

This looks on the surface like a straightforward thank-you from someone ignorant of classical tongues to the translator who has provided her with access to a text in Latin that she could not have read before. But Behn does not stop here. Instead she goes on to criticize a nation and an educational system that denies knowledge to those like her solely on the basis of sex.[15]

> Till now, I curst my Birth, my Education,
> And more the scanted Customes of the Nation:
> Permitting not the Female Sex to tread,
> The Mighty Paths of Learned Heroes dead.
> The God-like *Vergil*, and great *Homers* Verse,
> Like Divine Mysteries are conceal'd from us.
>   We are forbid all grateful Theams,
>   No ravishing thoughts approach our Ear,
>   The Fulsom Gingle of the times,
> Is all we are allow'd to understand or hear.
>
> (ll. 25–34)

Behn is too clever a writer, however, to allow this digressive passage to become the prelude to a peroration on the male-dominated educational system. No, instead she passes on to more praise of the translator who has so benefited the "ignorant" sex. Yet if we read the parable that follows ironically—as, I believe, Behn intended it to be read—we see that she has not at all changed her tune, only her tactics.

15. Behn was fluent in French, if not in Greek and Latin, and two French translations of Pindar from the early seventeenth century would have been available to her, one by Marin in prose published in Paris in 1617, another in prose and verse by Sieur de Lagausie, published in Paris in 1626. On Behn's lack of Latin see Angeline Goreau, *Reconstructing Aphra, a Social Biography of Aphra Behn* (New York: Dial Press, 1980). Although Behn published paraphrases of Ovid and a translation of Cowley's *Plantarum*, she made a point of saying that she did not know Latin. In his preface to Ovid, Dryden compliments Behn on the facility of her translation (despite her lack of direct knowledge of the original), but in his "A Satyr on the Modern Translator," he rebukes her and others for attempting to translate a language they do not know (54).

In olden times, she begins, the poet was the means by which knowledge of the gods and their laws was brought to men. He not only educated but also civilized men, bringing them from the savage woods to social order.[16] Now, proposes Behn slyly, the poet-translator has conferred a similar benefit on women, not only alleviating their ignorance and civilizing them but granting them "equality" with men as well.

> So thou by this Translation dost advance
> Our Knowledg from the State of Ignorance,
> And equals us to man.
>
>   (ll. 41–43)

With her gracious compliment to the divine powers of poet-translator, Behn ironically enlists Creech in the cause of female rights, making him the bene-factor of women and the one who will bring them closer to equality with men. Yet not for a moment has she quit her stance as earnest admirer: "Ah how can we, / Enough Adore, or Sacrifice enough to thee!" (ll. 43–44). Reassuming the posture of adoring female before wise instructor male, she lauds Creech for making all this terribly difficult philosophy comprehensible to the inferior sex, decking, as she says, the "Mystick terms of Rough Philosophy" in "so soft and gay a Dress" that "they at once Instruct and Charm the Sense" (ll. 45–49). Behn has learned a tactic from Milton's Eve on how to soothe the ego of an Adamic don explaining "angelic texts." Why, she seems to say, he has explained everything so clearly that even a woman can understand it.

Behn's poem to Creech was read by her time as gracious praise, not as a female's protest. J. W. in a Pindaric on Behn summed it up: "Well has she sung the learned *Daphnis* praise, / And crown'd his Temples with immortal Bays."[17] By imbedding her protest for women's rights in a poem that the male establishment would read as praise of one of their own, Behn has played a rather subtle double game. The Young Lady of "The Emulation" could be dismissed by a gentlemanly wit like Mr. H as merely hysterical and shrill—and her poem forgotten. Behn's more subtle attack could not so easily be shrugged off.

Behn did not, however, escape the fate of Katherine Philips or that of other women poets of her era, as being cited as a "female" poet, rather than as a

16. The ode to Creech is interesting not only as an example of commendatory poetry with a subversive aim, but also on its own merits as an example of late seventeenth-century Pindaric verse. Particularly impressive here is Behn's use of Pindaric techniques: her adaptation of the Pindaric myth and her extension of the Pindaric encomium to Creech to other figures connected with Wadham—notably Sprat, and her mentors Rochester and Cowley. The ode sets its criticism of women's exclusion from the classics in a poem that demonstrates an accomplished classical Pindaric technique.

17. "Upon these and other Excellent Works of the Incomparable Astyraea" in Aphra Behn, *Poems upon Several Occasions* (London, 1697), 3.

poet. As the commendatory verses to the 1684 and 1697 editions of her verse attest, she received the same shallow compliments, being dismissed merely as the "wonder of [her] Sex." Often compared, as Philips had been, to the Muses, to Sappho, and even to Orinda, her female predecessor, she could reach no further than combining the "Beauties of both Sexes"—a female sweetness with a manly grace.[18] Cowley had said a similar thing about Philips (assuming that masculinity is a necessary juncture to femininity to produce poetry). She is lauded, also, as Philips was, in masculine Pindaric strains. But she does not rise so high as to be, as Cowley had been called, Pindar's equal. She is permitted to dwell, however, in the company of Virgil's Shade and Ovid's Ghost and with Cowley, the first of England's poets.[19] Having no Latin and no Greek, Behn rose as high as a woman might in her age—to be included in a literary Elysium as a companion to Pindar's translator, Cowley.

18. See especially "To the Lovely witty *Astraea,* on her Excellent Poems," "To the excellent *Madam Behn,* on her Poems," "To *ASTRAEA,* on her Poems," in Behn, *Poems* (London, 1684). Even in "The Life and Memoirs of Mrs. Behn," attached to a reprint of *The Histories and Novels of the Late Ingenious Mrs. Behn* (London, 1696), written purportedly by "a Gentlewoman of her Acquaintance," Beauty is not divorced from Wit and Intellect. The Gentlewoman remarks that Behn was "Mistress of uncommon Charms of Body, as well as Mind . . . Wit, Beauty, and Judgment, seldom met in one, especially in Woman, (you may allow this from a Woman) but in her they were Eminent" (n.p.).

19. F. N. W. "To Madam *A Behn* on the publication of her Poems" (8:13–15) in Behn, *Poems* (1684).

Notes on the Contributors

Ilona Bell is Professor of English at Williams College. She has written numerous essays on Renaissance poetry and Renaissance women.

Pamela Joseph Benson is Professor of English at Rhode Island College. Her publications include *The Invention of the Renaissance Woman: The Challenge of Female Independence in the Literature and Thought of Italy and England, Italian Tales from the Age of Shakespeare,* and numerous articles and reviews. She is currently at work on a cultural study of the Florentine legend of Countess Gualdrada.

Robert C. Evans, Professor of English at Auburn University in Montgomery, is the author of four books on Jonson *(Ben Jonson and the Politics of Patronage; Jonson, Lipsius, and the Politics of Renaissance Stoicism; Jonson and the Contexts of His Time;* and *Habits of Mind: Evidence and Effects of Ben Jonson's Reading).* He is also coeditor of *"My Name Was Martha": A Renaissance Woman's Autobiographical Poem,* the first printing of the "Memorandum" of Martha Moulsworth.

Sidney Gottlieb is Professor of English at Sacred Heart Univesity and editor of the *George Herbert Journal.* His recent book publications include an edition of An Collins's *Divine Songs and Meditacions* and collections of writings by Alfred Hitchcock and Orson Welles.

Judith Scherer Herz is Professor of English at Concordia University, Montreal. She has published widely on seventeenth- and twentieth-century subjects. She is author of *The Short Narratives of E. M. Forster* and *A Passage to India: Nation and Narration.*

Cecilia Infante completed her Ph.D. in English Renaissance literature at the University of Michigan in 1994. She is currently associate director of the Lloyd Scholars Program at the University of Michigan.

Barbara K. Lewalski is William R. Kenan Professor of English Literature and of History and Literature at Harvard University. Her recent books include *Protestant Poetics and the Seventeenth-Century Religious Lyric, "Paradise Lost" and the Rhetoric of Literary Form, Writing Women in Jacobean England, 1603– 1625,* as well as an edition of *Rachel Speght's Polemics and Prose* in the Oxford University Press series Women Writers in English, 1350–1850.

Janel Mueller is William Rainey Harper Professor in the Humanities at the University of Chicago and editor of *Modern Philology.* Her current scholarly projects include an edition of Queen Katherine Parr's complete writings, including prose works and correspondence, as well as a collaborative edition, with Leah Marcus and Mary Beth Rose, of selected writings of Queen Elizabeth I.

Lawrence Normand teaches in the School of English, Cultural, and Communication Studies at Middlesex University, London. He has published essays on Shakespeare, Marlowe, twentieth-century poetry and gender theory, and is coauthor with Gareth Roberts of *Witchcraft in Early Modern Scotland: King James' "Demonology."* He is currently writing a critical biography of the Welsh writer W. H. Davies.

Paul A. Parrish is Professor of English at Texas A&M University. He is the author of *Richard Crashaw* and the commentary editor of volume 6 *(The Anniversaries and the Epicedes and Obsequies)* of *The Variorum Edition of the Poetry of John Donne.* He is the commentary editor of the forthcoming volume 7 *(The Divine Poems)* of the Donne Variorum and serves as the chief editor of the commentary for the project as a whole. The author of essays on Crashaw, Donne, and Milton, among others, he is working on a study of the ways in which male poets of the seventeenth century conceive of and respond to female presences in their poetry. He is president of the South Central Modern Language Association (1997) and president of the John Donne Society (1997– 1998).

Ted-Larry Pebworth is William E. Stirton Professor in the Humanities and Professor of English at the University of Michigan–Dearborn. He is author of *Owen Felltham;* coauthor of *Ben Jonson,* coeditor of *The Poems of Owen Felltham* and *Selected Poems of Ben Jonson,* and coeditor of collections of essays on Herbert, on Jonson and the Sons of Ben, on Donne, on the seventeenth-century religious lyric, on poetry and politics in the seventeenth century, on Marvell, on Renaissance discourses of desire, and on the wit of seventeenth-century poetry. A senior textual editor and member of the advisory board of *The Variorum Edition of the Poetry of John Donne,* he has served as president of the John Donne Society.

Stella P. Revard is Professor of English at Southern Illinois University, Edwardsville. She holds degrees in English from Yale University and in Classics from Washington University, St. Louis. She is the author of *The War in Heaven: Paradise Lost and the Tradition of Satan's Rebellion* and *Milton and the Tangles of Neaera's Hair: The Making of the 1645 "Poems."*

Gareth Roberts lectures on Renaissance literature at the University of Exeter. He is the author of *The Open Guide to Spenser's Faerie Queene* and *The Mirror of Alchemy* and coeditor of *Witchcraft in Early Modern Europe: Studies in Culture and Belief.* With Lawrence Normand, he is coauthor of the forthcoming *Witch-Hunting in Early Modern Scotland.*

Josephine A. Roberts, who died in an automobile accident in 1996, was William A. Read Professor of English Literature at Louisiana State University. She edited *The Poems of Lady Mary Wroth* and *The First Part of the Countess of Montgomery's Urania* and an edition of the second volume of Wroth's *Urania,* based on the holograph manuscript at the Newberry Library, Chicago.

Roger B. Rollin is William James Lemon Professor of Literature Emeritus at Clemson University. He is the author of *Robert Herrick* and coeditor (with J. Max Patrick) of *"Trust to Good Verses": Herrick Tercentenary Essays.* He has also published essays on Donne, Jonson, Herbert, Marvell, and Milton, as well as on popular-culture theory and practice.

Claude J. Summers, William E. Stirton Professor in the Humanities and Professor of English at the University of Michigan–Dearborn, has published widely on both seventeenth- and twentieth-century literature. Coeditor of collections of essays on a wide variety of seventeenth-century topics and author of book-length studies of Marlowe, Jonson, Isherwood, Forster, and twentieth-century gay fiction, he has most recently published an edition of *The Selected Poems of Ben Jonson* (coedited with Ted-Larry Pebworth) and the Lambda Award–winning *The Gay and Lesbian Literary Heritage.* He is a past president of the John Donne Society.

Helen Wilcox is Professor of English Literature at the University of Groningen, the Netherlands. Her research interests include Renaissance devotional writing, Shakespeare, and the literary achievements of early modern Englishwomen. She is editor of *Women and Literature in Britain, 1500–1700* and coeditor of *Her Own Life: Autobiographical Writings by Seventeenth-Century English-women.*

Index

This index includes only primary works. Lengthy titles are abbreviated, and anonymous works are alphabetized by title.